* * * *Studies in*

HUMAN

TIME

* *by* GEORGES POULET

* *translated by* ELLIOTT COLEMAN

BALTIMORE * THE JOHNS HOPKINS PRESS

* *Acknowledgments*

First published as *Études sur le temps humain* by the University of Edinburgh Press. In 1950 it was again issued in Paris (Plon). The Introduction was first published in English by *The Hopkins Review,* Vol. VI, No. 3–4 (Spring-Summer, 1953), and later in *Cross Currents,* Vol. V, No. 1 (Winter, 1955). The "Proust" chapter first appeared in English in *Cross Currents,* Vol. V, No. 3 (Summer, 1955).

The Appendix, "Time and American Writers," was written especially for this translated edition and appears here for the first time.

Distributed in Great Britain by Geoffrey Cumberlege
Oxford University Press, London

Printed in the United States of America by
H. Wolff Book Manufacturing Co.

Library of Congress Catalog Card No. 56–7715

* *to*
ELSA

Too rarely in the history of critical literature a thinker of such force of mind emerges that his work seems bound to be translated. Georges Poulet is such a thinker. His books have won swift recognition in France. The first volume of his *Études sur le temps humain,* here translated, was awarded in 1950 the *Prix Sainte-Beuve;* the second volume, entitled *La distance intérieure,* was awarded in 1952 both the *Grand Prix de la Critique littéraire* and the French Academy's *Prix Durchon* in philosophy. But more than that, though partly because of it, his thought continues to win the earnest attention and the gratitude of a widening audience, quick to esteem critical powers of a high order.

For although it is hard to put Georges Poulet in a category, he is a critic, a philosophical literary critic whose approach to literary art is new in the history of criticism. He reads French literature for us, from Montaigne to Proust, in the light of man's changing concepts of mortal time. He has seen that one of man's main preoccupations in literature is the problem of time and the nontemporal: how to deal with it; and how to express it. The author conceives the essential effort of the critic to be that of discerning the total meaning of a writer's work by paying attention to his sense of man's temporality and place. Once this is understood, in relation to all other human activity, then the philosophic temper of the literature of a time is seen as vitally determining the way life will take. The work of an artist can be penetrated and can penetrate us, unhindered, only if we are led to a view of the center of it, where the generative power is imparted. Without this second sight, works of art can hardly be seen or known at all.

But Georges Poulet has first viewed the work as a whole, and he has urged that the individual parts of a writer's work cannot be deeply understood in isolation. Only a concern with the totality of the work can reveal its fixed or shifting center. A main motivation, at that center, is seen to be man's singular interest in the disposition of ideas in the spaces of his mind: in his dread of time; or his pleasure in duration. That is not to say that Poulet is not a close reader of individual texts. Few are as astute at examining a poem, a play, or a novel as he is. Inductive philosophic criticism cannot be based on anything else; when it draws generalities, it draws them out of particulars. Its job is to interpret what is perhaps already appreciated or enjoyed, but up to the point of the maximum enjoyment or profit. And a critic in the true sense must be a linguist and equipped, as Georges Poulet is, not only with analytical astuteness and a poetic responsiveness to what is beautiful, but with a knowledge of other languages and literatures beyond his own.

Ideas about time have changed. In his Introduction, the author traces the course of such ideas through the medium of the writers of France, from the Middle Ages to the present. The depth and concentration of this passage, with its underpinning of theology, philosophy, and scientific theory, should not discourage the reader who, despite his pleasure in the brilliant figures, finds some of the abstractness difficult. Whether or not he is at home in French literature, the work will soon become plainer to him as he goes along.

The method of centrality is the search for meaning and for the sources of spiritual strength. If pieces of literature are only the echoes of resolutions, nevertheless they are splendid echoes, and all we have. For Georges Poulet, nothing is more precious than what man has thought; in these pages, horror and joy over the varying modes of the concept of time are seen to confer a timelessness that art can express, for it guarantees the future of an idea, from across the past, and thereby enlarges our present. If man's anguish over human time, as over human love, is today central to his present being and endeavor, then works of literature may furnish the illumination of its purpose. The uncommon illumination of this moving book consists in the reflection that strikes and the radiance that is seen finally to emanate from a core of darkness. To read it is to participate in a spiritual experience.

The author's suppression of his interesting chapter on Théophile Gautier has for one thing permitted the inclusion, at the end, of his commentary on several American writers seen, if only briefly, in their temporal and interior spatial dimensions.

The translator expresses thanks to the author for his faithful and indispensable collaboration. Any modifications of the original text had his approval. Without his corrections and suggestions, this translation would not have been possible.

BALTIMORE, JANUARY, 1956 *Elliott Coleman*

✳ *Contents*

I

✳ For the Christian of the Middle Ages the sense of his existence did not precede a sense of his continuance. He did not have first to discover himself existing in a present moment in order next to conceive himself as existing in time. For him, on the contrary, to feel that he existed was to feel himself *to be:* neither changing nor becoming nor in any way succeeding himself; it was simply to feel that he was and that he endured. There was no real distinction for him between existence and duration. And there was no essential difference between individual moments of duration. A human being as such, and as long as he was such, could never cease to be what he really was.

From this point of view nothing distinguished man from inferior or superior beings who below him and above him constituted creation. From top to bottom in the scale of existence everything was possessed of an intrinsic continuity; all being abided as it was. The world was a world of abiding things.

But it was a world of abiding things which did not abide of themselves. If from being nothing they came to be something, if from the possible they passed to the actual, if their existence remained contingent and dependent, that was because such existences were created existences. In one sense they were being created every moment; not that God was obliged each moment to create them anew, but rather that in all the range of their existence, by the same act of will, the Creator caused them to be and to endure.

> Creation and preservation are an indivisible action; thence the absolute unity of this action and the fact that its maintenance proceeds not by a succession nor by a continuation, strictly speaking, but rather by the permanency of a single indivisible action.[1]

Nor was it in terms of independent and successive instants that the relation between creatures and Creator was conceived.[2] It was not because God kept adding moments to their existence that this existence was lengthened. It was because an aptitude for being preserved corresponded in all the moments of created existence to the preserving act itself.

> The preservation of a thing is not produced by God as by a total cause; it requires on the part of the creature an aptitude for preservation, a preservative capacity, so to speak.[3]

The being of the creature, it is true, tended always toward nothingness; but it tended in that direction with only one part of itself. With another part it tended to continue being what it was by reason of the principles of its existence. Its tendency toward nothingness (*habitudo ad nihil*) was compensated for by an opposite tendency, the tendency toward the first cause (*habitudo ad causam primam*).[4] This habit, this mode of being was in the highest degree a mode of abiding. To tend Godward meant never to cease to possess one's aptitude for receiving one's existence from God.

The Christian of the Middle Ages felt essentially, then, that he was a man who endured. Nevertheless, within him and around him, he was unable to keep from seeing change. If he felt sure of his own permanence he was at the same time constrained to notice a profound lack of permanence. Paradoxically, he felt himself to be a permanent being and a transient being, a being who never changed and a being who always changed.

In order to understand what time meant to men of the Middle Ages, we must strip ourselves of our modern conceptions and of our knowledge of ancient conceptions. Time was for them neither a sort of substitute for space nor a formal condition of thought. If they accepted the famous definition of Aristotle—time is the number of motion—they gave it a very different meaning from that of its author. To change was to pass from potentiality to actuality. But this transition had nothing about it necessarily temporal. By virtue of the Christian doctrine of omnipotence, it could have a temporal quality only if there were some cause which did not allow the immediate transformation by divine action of the potentiality into the act. And this cause which required that time be involved in the change was a certain defect of matter:

> Succession in the formation of things is due to a defect in matter, which originally is not fitly disposed to receive form; but when it is so disposed, it receives form instantaneously.[5]

From this point of view, matter was nothing other than a resistance which, manifesting itself in the substance of a thing, hindered that thing from assuming instantly the fullness of being which its form would confer upon it; a resistance which introduced distance and tardiness, multiplicity and delay, where everything, it seemed, should have happened simultaneously and at once. *Tempus facit distare.*[6]

The remoteness and plurality, however, which thus insinuated themselves into being, and so established time in being, did not constitute a negation of being. On the contrary, this kind of duration was upheld by a double continuity: the permanent continuity of substantial form; and the successive continuity of change.

First of all, time was not a mode of duration absolutely different from permanence. It was only permanence incomplete, still in the process of achievement, and guided toward completion by the forms inherent in being. But if these forms existed and endured, it was through following the conditions of existence and duration appropriate to being. God, the preserver of being, was by the same token preserver of the principle of the actions of being.[7] Thus, far from resulting in occasionalism, continued creation confirmed the lasting efficacy of the second causes. Being was made capable of action. But this capacity was not in time; it was in permanency. It was the permanent form that established the possibility of existence and action.

But in order for this action to become act and for this existence to become time, it was necessary not merely that they should be possible. In order to wedge themselves into actual time, they still had need of fresh help from God. All *becoming* in the natural order, as in the spiritual order, required a determination direct from God.[8] Thus the divine operation founded time not only upon the permanence which made it possible but also upon the actuality which made it necessary and real—actuality which could be instantaneous, but which, when it was temporal, proceeded with the continuity of an uninterrupted movement toward an end.

Thus sustained by the permanent continuity of substantial form, the moving continuity of time unrolled itself, so mobile and so fluid that it was impossible to distinguish consecutive moments. No doubt, such fluidity implied a part of nonbeing. But what distinguished this time from Heraclitan time or even Platonic time—time of pure mobility—was that it was a movement toward an end. The finality of the movement gave it in return something that transcended its materiality. Even in his body the Christian of the Middle Ages felt a continuous orientation toward a spiritual perfection. Time had a direction. Time finally carried the Christian toward God.

On the other hand the temporality of the body implied as a consequence the temporality of the spirit. Incessantly the Christian felt time as a flood which, overflowing his flesh, penetrated his soul. For his soul was first of all the form and consciousness of his body. Each act of his sensitive, cognitive, or voluntary being appeared to him to be necessarily impregnated with time. Nothing rose up in his mind which had not previously been experienced as a corporeal image situated in space and moving in time. Long before Locke, the medieval thinker had discovered that the mere succession of his thoughts could give him the idea of time.[9] But for him this succession took place in a human soul in accordance with a continuity profoundly different from the pure volubility of Lockean time. Only angelic thought could pass from idea to idea and from instant to instant without a temporal medium to support the passage and join them. To this discontinuous angelic time (strangely similar to that which was to be the time of Descartes) there was opposed the continuity of human time. In mind as in body, in order to shift from one position to another, man was necessarily obliged to use the medium of continuous time.

All, therefore, that was naturally spontaneous and instantaneous in spiritual life—the act of comprehending, the act of feeling, the act of willing or of enjoying—all of this was being achieved in man only through time, only with the help of time, only as if borne by time toward its completion.[10] But in proportion as this act was brought close to its point of perfection, in proportion as it approached its own completion in time, it tended to release itself from time. At the very moment it attained its fullness, all its temporality disappeared. It was brought to perfection in an instant which transcended time and which, as long as it lasted, lasted within a duration that was permanent:

> This happens when all the operations of the soul resolve themselves into the pure contemplation of intelligible truth. In such an operation no error is possible, even as there is no error in the understanding of

first principles which we know by simple intuition. It is then only
. . . that the soul *attains a uniformity which is like that of the
angels;* having arrived at this stage, the soul lays all things aside that
it may continue in the contemplation of God alone.[11]

For the man of the Middle Ages, then, there was not one duration only. There were *durations,* ranked one above another,[12] and
not only in the universality of the exterior world but within himself, in his own nature, in his own human existence.

In his nature, but also in his supernature; in his *being,* but also in
his *well-being.* For the man of the Middle Ages did not feel that he
had a purely natural existence. He felt that beyond this he existed
supernaturally. To his existence as a fallen creature, grace super-
added an existence of regeneration. And in this regenerative order
of existence, which depended more intimately upon God than the
other did, there was repeated the same combination of continuities.
Perseverance in well-being, the permanence of supernatural duration in the human state, was assured by a supporting power which
could be called the preservation and continuous creation of
grace.[13] And just as on the natural plane there responded to the continual action of the Creator the continuous presence of forms and
natural virtues in the creature, so on the supernatural plane there
responded to the continuous action of sanctifying grace what Saint
Bonaventure calls the permanent *habitus* that dwells in the sanctified being.[14] This *habitus* made man capable of doing good. But for
such possible actions to become actual and to be performed in time,
it was necessary that divine aid operate anew. This was accomplished by actual grace, the efficacy of which exerted itself not upon
the permanent substance of the being but upon the vicissitudes of
its existence engaged in time.

Thus was completed the architecture of medieval duration. As
can be seen, everything rested upon two principles: the continuous
creation which established the permanence of the creature and of
his substantial activity; and the divine concourse which allowed
him to realize himself in time.

II

In short, the intuition by which the Scholastics came to apprehend
the action of God in his creatures presented this action to them as

one which created and incessantly sustained all coexisting orders
of duration; and at the same time it represented all creatures as disposed by their substantial form to receive the particular order
proper to them.

But by the end of the Middle Ages other conceptions had gained
ascendancy. Transforming in identity the analogical resemblance
between the generation of the Word and the creation of the world,
Eckhart had based all duration upon a moment eternally repeated
in which the genesis of God and that of the world were simultaneously effected by the interaction of the one upon the other. Abolishing in his turn all permanent forms whatsoever and depriving each
creature of any aptitude for a duration of its own, William of
Ockham could recognize divine preservation in nothing else but
the inscrutable act by which in each moment of time God made each
creature anew.

Thus by the time of the Renaissance the whole hierarchy of
forms which in the eyes of the Middle Ages constituted the permanent structure of the world had disappeared. In a universe which
now seemed entirely subject to vicissitude, there remained only
a double awareness of the vicissitude itself and the cosmic force
which produced it. From that moment the character of human duration changed profoundly. God no longer appeared to be the
transcendent cause which from without preserved his creatures and
their own individual and continuing existences; God seemed rather
the indwelling power that from within tirelessly sustained and prolonged the universal motion by which things and beings accomplished their temporal destiny. No longer creations of permanence,
no longer degrees of duration, but rather from top to bottom in the
universal scale a transforming and vivifying force which sustained
the universe but which sustained it only in its becoming:

> Thus the great universal mass
> Would see its discordant members die,
> Had it not within itself a spirit,
> Everywhere infused, which agitates and moves it . . .[15]

> Thou art the source and happy origin of all,
> The unity, sole principle of the machine,
> Of each of its effects the fertile cause,
> Fifth essence, chain divine

> Embracing, holding all, restorer of things
> Vicissitude would terminate in changing.[16]

> Who has not faith in new exchanges
> Of body for strange body
> In the womb of the great universe?
> Who does not recognize the work
> Contrived by Nature here below
> As beautiful only in ever-changing? [17]

So the world was no longer anything more than an immense organism, a gigantic network of interchanges and reciprocal influences which was animated, which was guided interiorly in its cyclical development by a force everywhere the same and perpetually diversified, that could be called indiscriminately God, or Nature, or the Soul of the World, or Love.

This being so, how would it still be possible to maintain in its pristine clarity the distinction Christianity had insisted upon making between the creative act and the created thing? "For God everywhere, in every thing, propagates himself," says Ronsard.[18] Creative causality had become immanent in the universe. Instead of imposing upon nothingness the reality of existence, it seemed now to emanate from all reality and to radiate from every creature: "Daemons, distributors of reborning lives . . ." [19] "for nothing abides in anything except it love and be loved." [20] Cause and effect coalesced in the same *fieri*. Essentially each being appeared to be no longer a created being which constantly received its existence from outside, but rather an autonomous activity which found in itself the inexhaustible resources to engender its continuance by a diversity of motion.

> For just as God in varying exerts
> His diverse power, Himself single and one,
> And is admirable in this great Universe
> For the variety of His diverse effects:
> So a single soul, image most small
> Of the image of God, imitates the Almighty
> With subtle artifice, and shows to us
> In the soul's diversity its deity.[21]

Therefore for the man of the Renaissance, time had come to have an entirely different meaning from that which it had for the

man of the Middle Ages. It was no longer the lowest kind of duration by which things that were in matter existed as well as they
could and by vicissitudes of which the engendered being unceasingly
discovered himself to be perishable and perishing. It is indeed true
that one felt then as always, and perhaps more keenly than ever before, the precarious and fugitive character of each lived moment:
"Every day, every hour, thus without ceasing/I must finish my life,
and recommence/In this death uselessly alive. . . ." [22]

But with this feeling which is the essential anguish of man—of
man in time—the poet or thinker of the Renaissance combined a
feeling exactly the inverse, one which can be described as the joy of
being in time: "For by time," says Rabelais, "there have been and
shall be brought to light all things which were hidden." Temporality
then no longer appeared solely as the indelible mark of mortality; it
appeared also as the theater and field of action where despite his
mortality man could reveal his authentic divinity and gain a personal immortality. There was no need of supplementary help from
the supernatural. Bound up with all epochs, possessor by thought
of the historical as well as the spatial universe, man felt himself to
be creator, if not of his being, at least of his destiny.[23] He affirmed
his cheerful confidence in the immanent efficacy of both cosmic and
human nature, a faith by the terms of which both natures could find
themselves capable of realizing in duration and by duration the
fullness of their existence. "I have made myself," said Pontano.[24]

But it is also in the same century and, one might also say, by the
same movement of the spirit that the absolute negation of this faith
expressed itself, and in a most energetic fashion. Not that the Reformers doubted for an instant the divine immanence in nature
and in man; in this they profoundly shared the belief of the Renaissance. For them, too, both man and nature were divinely animated.[25] For them also there had been a time when nature and man
had participated in the creative power, and when nature and man
had been, even as God himself, tirelessly employed in activities
which irradiated their energy. But that time existed for them no
longer. The time when nature was divine was now succeeded by the
time of fallen nature; fallen by its own fault, by the free act in consequence of which it had separated itself from its origin, cut itself off
from its source, denied God. And from that moment on, God had
withdrawn from nature and from man. The once-immanent crea-

tive activity had become transcendent. From being vice-creator of the universe man had fallen, fallen below the state of pure nature, fallen into a state of corrupted nature. So great was this corruption that it seemed as if the creative power could do no more than touch from a distance and maintain the creature in its existence; it could not quicken the creature nor save it from its monstrous state.

This absolute mistrust which the natural man inspired in the Reformers was, to be sure, not directly contrary to the no less absolute trust which the Humanists placed in man's virtues. They were not the same being at all. For the Humanists, the work of creation had hardly been grazed by the Fall; the exercise of the creative activity invariably followed its course as before, in nature and in the souls of men; it continued to communicate to them the same life; it continued to maintain the same duration. God the creator was always sufficient unto his creation. But for Luther and Calvin the reverse was true. Original sin had from the first robbed the creature of all right of participating in the creative act and of all power over his individual continuance; and further it had rendered the creative act itself insufficient to establish within the fallen being a true nature and a true duration. Man found himself at one and the same time cut off from God and incapable of receiving a real existence from any creative act of God.

Consequently the revolution produced by the Reformation in the conception of the relations between God and the creature revealed itself as of infinitely more importance than that produced by the Renaissance. For the first time in fifteen centuries of Christianity, the creation no longer appeared the cardinal event in the history of the world. For the first time it was no longer the ground upon which human existence was established. Human existence rested no longer in God-the-creator-and-preserver but in God-the-redeemer.[26]

Thence proceeded the Reformers' conception of two durations, from the one to the other of which the fallen being who became the regenerate being inevitably had to pass. The first was only the shadow of a duration. Devoured by anxiety, tortured by the view of his existence as suspended by a thread, perceiving the earth he inhabited as tottering "over a profound abyss into which it might topple at any moment of time," [27] the fallen being felt that he lived only from instant to instant and by a miracle. Each instant accorded

him was inevitably an instant of collapse. God seemed less to prolong human existence continually than to hold over man from moment to moment an act of vengeance and annihilation.

So frightening is the condition of the fallen being that nothing
less than the sacrifice of a God can change it. The redemption is the
mysterious sovereign act by which a new creation and a new preservation are made possible. But the supernatural existence which the
redemptive action confers upon the redeemed differs radically
from the natural existence conferred by the creative action. It can
be nothing other than a force that supports man's activities perpetually. It is a power from without which superadds itself to the being
and its depraved activities in order to transform them and set them
to rights. But the essence of the fallen being has become something
so inconsistent and so corrupt that any actual grace would only corrupt itself and vanish at the instant it was received; and any habitual and sanctifying grace would only lodge in a being incapable of
the least continuity, one in which no habit could reside. It was necessary, then, not only that the supernatural action operate in every
moment and redress each instant of temporal existence but also
that it have its foundation in the only precinct where there is complete stability and consistency: that is to say, in the predestining will
of God. The whole existence of the just becomes thereafter the continuing act by which a divine unalterable will is superimposed upon
a human duration incessantly failing. It is the permanence of eternity, constantly impressing itself upon the discontinuity of human
moments. On the one hand, the justified cannot help but feel that
his existence is that of a being which of itself can only fall into the
abyss, unless God renews for each new instant the operation of the
moment before. And on the other hand, because he has faith in the
validity of the divine promise, and because he knows that the foundation of this promise lies in past eternity and in future eternity
alike, man is convinced also that his destiny never has changed and
never can change; that the duration of the redeemed is eternal.

Thus by an act of absolute faith which he performs in the very
moment, the just man feels that this particular moment is joined to
an eternal moment. Something of the Cartesian *Cogito* already appears in the Calvinist *Credo:* I believe, therefore I am.

> Each moment of faith becomes the foundation of all existence:
> I see myself continually flowing away: no moment passes without

my seeing myself at the point of being engulfed. But since God sustains his elect in such a way that they never sink and drown, I firmly believe that I shall live despite innumerable storms.[28]

III

The seventeenth century is the epoch in which the individual discovers his isolation. The medieval edifice of the world, in which all forms of created being were ordered in a system of permanent relationships, no longer exists. With the end of the Renaissance the feeling of spontaneous intercommunication in all individual activity within the cosmic *becoming* has also disappeared. Human thought no longer feels itself a part of things. It distinguishes itself from them in order to reflect upon them, and thus is no longer upheld by their own power of enduring. From the motion of bodies which inexplicably and incessantly modifies it, human thought feels itself to be disengaged by the very act of thinking, for in this act it places itself outside the motion which is its object.

Isolated from exterior time, it feels also equally detached from the time of its mental life. The modifications which happen to affect it by turns can, indeed, in succeeding each other, give it the idea of an interior duration. But this duration, consisting in modes which replace one another, is by no means the duration of the thinking being; it is solely the duration of the successive ensemble of man's thoughts. Separated from the duration of things, and even from that of the modes of its existence, the human consciousness finds itself reduced to existence without duration. It is always of the present moment.

Such is the essential experience of modern man. The *Essays* of Montaigne first gives expression to it. But to Montaigne this disengaged consciousness still appears as irresolutely floating on the surface of the flux of phenomena; as an object which thrown into the middle of a river would not, however, be entirely submerged by the current. It is the greatness of Descartes, on the contrary, to have given consciousness its adequate basis. With Descartes, all the effort of thought is a struggle to withdraw from the current and go back to an initial moment which, preceding the duration of all things and the memory of all thoughts, is nothing but a moment of pure intuition.

Initial moment which in the domain of knowledge corresponds rigorously to the initial instant in the order of creation. In the naked moment when I discover that I think, I discover at the same time the immediate relation which unites the moment in which I think with the eternity that ensures my presence in that moment. The experience of the *Cogito* implies, then, the simultaneous affirmation of an eternal existence and of a created substance inserted into a moment of human thought. But far from implying at the same time the affirmation of a temporal continuity, the *Cogito* denies it categorically by asserting the independence of the moments of time. Related on the one hand to the supratemporal continuity of the divine activity, and on the other hand to the consciousness of the moment in which it senses that it thinks, human existence finds itself, thus, for the first time apprehended by the mind outside any specific duration. Existence and duration are no longer identical. To exist does not necessarily mean to endure. It is necessary to pass from one to the other, and this passage is no less difficult to conceive than the relationship of the spirit to the body or the transmission of motion in the universe.

Hence the extraordinary importance which the idea of continued creation assumes throughout the seventeenth century. Of all the innumerable medieval notions of duration, this is the only one which remains extant; and precisely because it is the only one, and because nothing either tempers or varies it, the role which it plays during the seventeenth century is infinitely more despotic than before. Instead of continually conferring upon man an existence which is a duration, it now confers upon him an existence which is confined to the instant, and which therefore needs perpetually to be prolonged from instant to instant. If, then, the seventeenth-century man feels with extraordinary intensity his need and his dependence in relation to the creative act, it is because in the perceiving of this act he is unable to perceive anything else. All his past life, all his future destiny are found to be erased or suspended. Nothing remains except the gift of actual existence; then, in a new instant, the same gift, and the same consciousness of that gift. Duration is a chaplet of instants. The creative activity alone permits passage from one bead to another.

An intimate awareness of an ever actual existence, an acute sense of the discontinuity of duration, and a total dependence upon a creation continually reiterated—these are indeed the essential traits of human time in the seventeenth century.

At first, on this island of the moment which isolates him but which he fills with his presence, man still keeps something of the joy he experienced in the Renaissance when he felt that he existed in all the reaches of space and duration. He is now given no more than a moment at a time, but each moment can be one of illumination and fullness. For example, whenever a clear and distinct idea appears in the field of consciousness, it is always with the same joyous alacrity that those who think bind their present assent to eternal truth: "Indeed," says Descartes, "it is by an act always distinct and always the same that they comprehend each truth once they have arrived at it." [29] Such is the Cartesian joy. Or again, whenever the human will affirms itself in an instantaneous act, it is always with the sense of triumph that, in the act of willing, the mind feels itself adhere to its present existence: "This is what I am and what I wish to be." Such is the Cornelian joy. Acts of knowledge and will which can be recommenced as endlessly as the very act of creation; acts which, however often they be recommenced, invariably bring back the thinking or willing creature to the prime and unique moment of his existence.

Later in the course of the seventeenth century this joyous feeling of the unity of the soul, forever original and indivisible, will take on a richer and more subtle character by contrast and intermixture with the multiple sensations which modify it in the very same moment: "How many sensations crowd my mind all at once," writes Père André. "The light and the colors that I see, the song of the birds that I hear, the perfume of the flowers that I breathe, the coolness of the shade that I enjoy, the sweetness of the fruit that I taste. I sense a thousand different objects which seem to me entirely separate, but while I thus separate them exteriorly, in diverse places, I feel them all re-united in myself, in a sole and unique self, where they differentiate themselves, one from another, without distinguishing themselves from me." [30]

But more and more frequently as the century advances, the feeling of joy that accompanies the gift of actual existence tends to give place to a contrary feeling. A fissure opens between what one is conscious of actually being and what one truly is. "We know nothing of our Souls," says Malebranche, "except what we know to

be happening inside us." Or another gulf yawns between the defi-
cient, impure being man knows he is and the divine character of
the gift of existence. Such is the Racinian anguish.

But of all the anxieties of the century the most frequent and the
most poignant is that born of a sense of the discontinuity of duration. Confined in the moment in which it exists, the consciousness
watches its successive modes of existence pass, one after another,
and escape it. To feel oneself live is to feel oneself leave behind, in
every instant, an instant which *was* the very self. So the famous
line of Boileau in *Épître III:* "The moment in which I speak is already far from me" is fully explained in *Épître V:* "Every hour we
are swept far away from ourselves."

Aware that the instant in which he thinks and wishes is slipping
from under him, man hurls himself into a new instant, an instant
of a new thought and a new wish: "But man without rest in his
mad course/Flutters incessantly from thought to thought. . . ." [31]

Mad headlong course, less like the flight of a projectile than the
ceaseless beating of wings by which a bird manages to support itself from moment to moment: "We are like birds in the air," says
Nicole, "unable to rest without motion; scarcely able one might
say, to hold their own, because they have no stable support and,
besides, no strength and vigor within themselves sufficient to resist
the force which thrusts them down." [32] Therefore, even for the
Epicureans of the day, there is no static pleasure within a completed moment. All that one can do, says La Mothe le Vayer, "is
adroitly to turn sail with every change of the wind of time." Both
spiritual and corporeal life alike are for the Gassendists a mere
generation of moments which replace and equate each other. For
La Rochefoucauld, the life of the heart is no more than a continuous begetting of passions.

Returning to the thought of Saint Augustine and Saint Bernard,
pulpit oratory expands in great commonplaces the double theme
of the disjointedness of duration and the successive multiplicity
of the passions. "Our heart escapes us every moment," says
Massillon.[33] "There is never more than an instant between us and
nothingness," says Bossuet. "Now we possess it, now it perishes;
and we would all perish with it if promptly and without any loss
of time we did not take hold of a similar one." [34]

Thus the same process of repeated creation and incessant dis-

solution, infinitely magnified and refined, is met with again in the
conception of supernatural order held in the seventeenth century.
Violent as religious quarrels are in this period, and deep as are the
differences of opinion, Molinists and Jansenists, Asceticists and
Quietists all agree on one thing: God's action and man's action,
grace and the knowledge of grace, are exclusively found within the
span of the present moment.

For the Molinist as well as for the Jansenist, there is no single
grace conferred once and for all; God's grace is always multiple
and successive, divine succor always momentary. The conflict is
fought solely over the *efficacy* of this actual grace. Habitual grace,
permanent and sanctifying, which for the Thomists of the Middle
Ages was the perfect analogue of continued creation, is relegated
to the background. Now, on the contrary, in exact similitude to
Cartesianism, the supernatural preservation of existence, no longer
lays any foundation for permanence. The opposite of Calvinism, it
sweeps away all assurance. It is no more than the renewed presence
of an ever instantaneous grace in an ever instantaneous being.
However righteous he may be, man can never be sure of anything
but his present need of present grace. The final orientation of his
life, the ultimate value of his being, the continuation or the non-
continuation of grace, remain a mystery to him. The nearer the
soul approaches perfection, the nearer it approaches, in the order
of grace, a state similar to the *Cogito* in the domain of natural
knowledge; each moment strikes the soul as the first in its supernatural existence: "The more the soul is imbued with love," says
the second Mère Angélique, "the more it feels reborn into that
youthfulness which, stripping it constantly of the virtues it practices
and even the good that God effects within it, thrills it with the
sense that each day of its life it is just *beginning* to serve Jesus
Christ." [35] Here we have a continual denudation of the soul, which,
like Descartes' continual denudation of the mind, brings man back
to an essential presence experienced in the naked moment. And
just as the Cartesian mind must, in each separate moment, recapture the evidence of truth, so the Jansenist soul must bend itself in
each separate moment to rekindle the ardor of its love: "One must
constantly make new efforts," the two Pascals write their sister,
"to acquire this newness of spirit, since one can preserve a former
grace only by acquiring a new one; otherwise one loses what he

thinks he retains; like those who wishing to wall in the light, manage only to shut in the darkness." [36] These words echo those of Saint-Cyran when he declares that for him the root of religion is "simply the interior piety which beholds God every moment with trembling and fear, yet with motions of love which are always new and which renew themselves day by day." [37]

By such a perpetual renewing of the heart, Jansenism concurs in those forms of devotion which in this century seem most opposed to it. The Jansenist moment is a moment of love, but of love in anguish; beyond its boundaries it casts fearful and hopeful glances into the past and into the future. Such is the Pascalian moment. The Quietist moment, on the contrary, is a moment without either past or future in which the human being in an act of self-renunciation renounces even his hope. Such is the moment of Fénelon: "Abandon yourself to the vicissitude that so deeply shakes your soul, for in accustoming itself to possessing neither permanence nor stability, the soul is rendered supple and flexible to any form God pleases." [38]

Yet, despite their profound differences, the religion of Fénelon and the religion of Pascal are both designed for a being which has "neither fixed state nor wholeness," a completely instantaneous being. And the same can be said of Bossuet's religion: "Thus the soul attached to God," he says, "constantly feels its dependence and knows that the righteousness which is given it never subsists by itself but is created within it by God from moment to moment." [39] The religions of the seventeenth century are all religions of *continued grace,* in the precise sense in which the thought of a Descartes and the thought of a Malebranche are philosophies of continued creation. The seventeenth century is the epoch in which nothing is interposed between divine eternity and each human moment.

IV

"If at certain moments," says Mably, "you feel devoid of any sense of pain or pleasure, or fear or hope, then your soul, emptied of thought and action, seems to be annihilated or disjoined from you." [40]

No passage shows more clearly the change effected in thought and feeling by the time of the eighteenth century. All the thought of the preceding century had been, as it were, one long meditation on the phrase of Saint Augustine: "If God should withdraw his creative power from the things he has created, they would fall back into their primal state of nothingness." [41] There is a curious similarity between these two passages: both conceive of a nothingness bordering existence everywhere; both affirm the conditional character of the act by which one exists. To the eighteenth century, as formerly to the seventeenth, existence seems constantly being saved from nonbeing. There is only one difference, but it is a radical one. This continued existence is no longer continued by an act of divine creation. The preservation of the universe and of the creature no longer is directly conceived as the immediate effect of the creative action. The latter is relegated to a remote past, to that far off, almost fabulous moment, the primal moment of created things. From the present moment God the creator and preserver is absent. The principal actor is no longer on the scene. For the supereminent role of the first cause we find substituted the play of second causes. In place of God there are feelings, sensations, and whatever causes sensations.

This retreat of God, this invasion of the actual by secondary causes is easy to discern in the new conception formed of the universe. For the Newtonian materialist of the eighteenth century, God is no longer even the ruler and still less the restorer of the world. He is no longer anything more than the initial author. The world is like the clock of Strasbourg: it is so ingeniously constructed that once it starts running it keeps going by sole virtue of the interaction of its works: "The idea of some philosophers," writes d'Alembert, "who pretend that all motion we observe in bodies is produced directly by the Creator, is not philosophical." [42] The universe can be described in the terms of d'Holbach as "an immense chain of causes and effects which proceed incessantly, one from another." [43] Such a universe being given, there is no longer any need of God to explain the continuity of things. "Divinity, superfluous wheel in the machine of the world," says Naigeon.[44]

But it is principally in the conception of the inner being that the disappearance of a divine preserver is most evident. For the eighteenth-century philosopher—disciple but unfaithful disciple of

Locke—the moment in which one feels he exists implies no longer the presence even of reflective thought: I am "odor of rose," and that is all. The moment of Condillac is indeed, like the moment of Descartes, an original moment which prior to any duration summons man back to being only what he *is* instantaneously. But no dialectical motion is involved in this initial moment; no relationship links momentary existence to eternal existence; no ontological necessity connects Creator and creature. The sole affirmation is the psychological necessity of the original sensation; if I feel, I am.

Then my existence is only a psychological existence. It appears and asserts itself, it resurges and is regained only by means of sensation. It is sensation alone, repeated, compared, analyzed, transformed—but in all states always sensation and always actual—which not only determines my existence but literally fashions and creates it. To be odor of rose is to be my own sensation of the rose; and to be my own sensation is psychologically to be created by my own sensation.

My feeling creates me. But if it creates me, it forms me out of nothingness. The *ex nihilo* is no less necessary a condition of Condillacian creation than of Augustinian or Cartesian creation. Nevertheless the nothingness out of which my feeling forms me is not the same as the nothingness out of which God formed Adam. It is simply a psychological nothingness. It is a state of absolute nonsensibility which has preceded the first sensation: "How many times," says Mably in the same passage, "have you not felt the need of some passion to propel you out of a kind of stupor." This stupor which one escapes is the sensationalist's nothingness. It is the root of human existence. Or rather it is that lower depth which always discloses itself as antecedent and subjacent to existence, that depth of which Madame du Deffand spoke when she said: "In myself I find only nothingness. . . . I am forced to try to extricate myself; I catch hold wherever I can. . . ." [45]

In a certain sense, therefore, human existence appears even to the eighteenth century as a kind of continuous creation, insofar as it is the perpetual recovery of existence by a being who is slipping every moment into nothingness. But since this nothingness is pure insensibility, to escape nothingness means to be aware of one's own sensations. The more intense they are the more one will feel his present existence; and the more numerous they are the more one will sense a duration in his existence.

There are, then, in the eighteenth century two distinct forms of interior temporality. Intensity of sensation ensures the instant; multiplicity of sensation ensures duration.

"We were made to think," says Crousaz; "and as thought is an act which is felt, it is quite clear that we are born to live by feeling. . . . The more alive our feelings, provided they are not painful ones, the more our condition is fitted and prepared to fulfill our intended purpose." [46] Occasionally, when his ability to feel incandesces into an emotion of highest intensity, man attains this fitness, this fulfillment: "There are moments of power," says Vauvenargues, "moments of elevation, of passion and enthusiasm, in which, self-sufficient, disdaining assistance, the soul is drunk with its own grandeur." [47]

Because of the grandeur and the intoxication of this human moment, man suddenly feels for the first time in the Christian era that the instant of his existence is an instant free of all dependence, liberated from all duration, equal to all its own potentialities, the very *causa sui*—moment which can be likened to the divine moment in which the Father begets the Son; moment in which the soul suffices itself, since it finds itself in the fullness it experiences. It loves itself. It knows itself to be faultless. The lived sensation *is* the consciousness of being. "Like God one is sufficient unto oneself," says Rousseau.[48]

But in contrast to this moment of fulfillment, or even within the moment itself, when a general diminution of sensible resonances insensibly succeeds to this fulfillment, man finds himself in a state very close to nonexistence: a condition of vague torpor, of indolent reveries but also of indefinable uneasiness which, before Diderot and Rousseau discover its charm, inspires with a mortal repulsion both men of feeling and men of wit: "The need of existing intensely," says Le Roy, "joined with the continual weakening of our sensations, throws us into an involuntary anxiety of vague desires stirred by the importunate memory of a prior state. Then in order to be happy we have either constantly to change our sensory environment or to carry to excess sensations of the same type. The result is an inconstancy which makes it impossible to check our wishes and an interspersion of desires which, always destroyed by

their very enjoyment but at the same time exacerbated by memory, diffuse themselves into the infinite." Admirable psychological portrait of the modern mind, in which there is repeated in secular fashion the classical descriptions of human anguish recorded by the great Christian thinkers and in which almost all the aspects of the romantic mind are already firmly delineated.[49]

And, in the first place, *excess*. For already the man of the eighteenth century wants to accentuate at any price the intensity of the moment of feeling: either by a sudden reversal of situation which transports the soul without transition from one pole of the affective life to the other—the pathetic instant dear to the Abbé Prévost; or by furnishing the mind with hitherto unknown and cruel sensations—the sadistic instant. But most frequently man succeeds in eluding the apathy which lies in wait for him only by varying continually his sensations and ideas.

Perhaps because he believed that continued creation implied the creation in each given moment of a radically different being, Bayle had provided at the beginning of the century the example of a way of thinking which continually changed its character and was unceasingly absorbed by the interest of the present moment: *diurnal* thought, he called it. He who says *diurnal* says also *journalistic:* anyone who, like Bayle, loves to "feel himself ready every hour to argue in a different way" [50] feels himself also ready every hour to conceive a passion for the event that hour brings. From Bayle (and Fontenelle) onward, philosophy becomes anecdotal, discontinuous; it becomes also versatile, picaresque, supple to the suggestions of ideas, just as the novel of the epoch becomes fertile in adventures and personal encounters. "The natural motion of our mind is to give itself to all that occupies it," says the Abbé du Bos. More precisely: "Our first task is to give ourselves to the impressions that outside objects make upon us." [51] All the literature of the century gives itself up to the variety of successive impressions. "We live, so to speak, from surprise to surprise," says La Motte Houdar.[52] "Let us forsake our delights in order to recapture them," urges Voltaire.[53] "One cures all by change," notes Montesquieu.[54]

If this variety of successive instants is so beguiling, it is doubtless, to begin with, by reason of the intensity with which in its turn each detached moment brings to man the delightful revelation of his actual existence. "We should like in every instant," says Helvétius, "by continually new impressions to be warned of our existence, for each of these warnings is a pleasure." [55] And, considered from this point of view, each new moment can be an absolute beginning, a coming to life: "Could I not say that my life does not last but is always beginning?" asks Marivaux.[56] But in another sense, as Locke has shown, it is this successiveness that makes us aware of duration. The promptness with which states of feeling succeed each other renders life richer, duration longer, existence larger. "Men of feeling have wider existence than others," says Duclos.[57] "To live is properly to enjoy," says Condillac, "and that man lives longest who is most proficient at multiplying the objects of his enjoyment." [58] Still more exactly Le Roy remarks: "He who has the greatest number of sensations and ideas has lived the most." [59]

But in order to live one's life and possess one's duration, it does not suffice to live and possess the successive moments which constitute life and duration. The atomic disconnectedness of continued existence appears infinitely more important to the eighteenth century than it did to the time of authentic continued creation since it is no longer corrected by the divine permanence, by the providential order, or by the supernatural action of grace. Disjoined, cut off from God, will not the human consciousness always find itself inexorably bound to the sole actual sensation? And will not the moment in which the animated statue imagined by Condillac becomes odor of rose be a moment ceaselessly begun over but never overpassed?

On the contrary, it is the greatness of the eighteenth century to have conceived the prime moment of consciousness as a generating moment and generative not only of other moments but also of a self which takes shape by and through the means of these very moments. The Condillacian being is not only a succession of instants of consciousness; it is a consciousness whose interior progress constitutes a life and a history. Each new moment of awareness reveals two distinct features: not only the new sensation which is the kernel of the moment, but also the ensemble of sensations already lived, whose resonances prolong themselves within it and surround it with their nebula. The great discovery of the eighteenth century is the phenomenon of memory. By remembering, man escapes the purely momentary; by remembering, he escapes the nothingness that lies in wait for him between moments of existence. "Without memory," says Quesnay, "the sentient being would have only sensation, or the idea of the actual instant. . . . All his ideas would be consumed by forgetfulness as fast as they were born; all the instants of his duration would be instants of birth and instants of death." [60] And Buffon: "In as much as the consciousness of our existence is composed not only of our actual sensations but also of the train of ideas which the comparison of our sensations and our past existences has brought to birth, it is evident that the more ideas one has the surer he is of his existence; the more wits one has the more he exists." [61]

To exist, then, is to be one's present, and also to be one's past and one's recollections. It is here that Diderot feels his present swell and echo with every vibration of a gigantic memory. "The vast, the total memory is a state of complete unity." [62] Here Rousseau ecstatically relives his most distant past: "Take away his memory, and his love will no longer exist." [63] The idea itself, the idea, this difficult conquest of mind over sensation, transforms itself and becomes something more than withered and desiccated sensation. It now appears possible not only to decompose it into its perceptible parts and retrospectively therein to rediscover its genesis, but also to revivify and restore to it each time its initial vigor. As Saint-Preux renews his passion at the sight of the crags which have preserved the freshness of tears long since shed, so the modern philosopher can reanimate his wisdom by contact with those first images which enabled him to acquire it. "Refresh thy reason," says Saint-Lambert; "often recall those deeds, those events upon which are founded the maxims of the Sages. Make thee vivid images of the good fortune which should reward the wise—and of the misfortune into which the foolish fall, and thou wilt interest thy heart in being virtuous. Separate not in thy memory the precept from the example; may virtue without cease be present to thine eyes, may it seem to thee so beautiful as to be impossible not to love; give it a body, lay hold of it with thy senses." [64]

Appropriating methods by which the devout thought of the preceding century sought to establish a Christian duration in the continual renewal of the heart, the secular thought of the eighteenth century conceives and tries to realize a *philosophical duration* which would be the continual renewal of a thought, sentient in its origin and continuously sentient, by regaining touch with its origin and the past.

. A duration based on affective memory.

V

Begotten by feeling, imbued more and more with feeling, the thought of the century which is ending becomes more and more apt to discover in the depths of its vibrant actuality the interflowing images of reminiscence and premonition. Always isolated in the moment which gives it form, it sees this moment incessantly invaded, overwhelmed, transfigured by states of mind from beyond. There comes to be superimposed upon actual existence the awareness of another existence, an existence which overlaps the frame of each moment and which is no less authentic an existence than the existence of the moment. It is as if to exist meant to live two lives at the same time: the life lived day by day; and the life lived before and beyond the day or the moment: a life which lengthens into duration.

Thus there appears again within the moment of consciousness precisely what for two centuries the moment of consciousness had suppressed: the feeling of duration. The essence of pre-romanticism consists perhaps in this: in the discovery, within the breadth of the instantaneous, of a self and of a reality which are not instantaneous and which consequently must always be experienced in the instant as if they were something never realized by the instant. On the one hand, I feel myself to be my life; and on the other hand, I feel myself to be only *this moment* of life. I feel myself a being who lives in the moment but whose life is just the opposite of the moment. My actual existence *is* and nevertheless *is not* my real existence: "Everything," says Tilly, "bears witness to my incapacity *to be*." [65]

It is this incapacity *to be* which the romantic is destined to observe endlessly in each new moment of existence, for each new emotion inevitably requires its portion of memory and desire, and then denounces in the instant the inadequacy of the instant to fill the void which they have made: "I was overwhelmed," says René, "with a superabundance of life. . . . Something was lacking to fill up the abyss of my existence."

To feel that one's existence is an abyss is to feel the infinite deficiency of the present moment. The moment begotten by man no longer suffices man. No matter how lively or manifold he renders his sensation or his thought, man discovers in each attempt how irremediably lacking he is in the power of creating himself by himself. Invariably he falls short of his own requirements. No matter what he feels, the vast and vague experience he has of himself warns him that he has left one essential part out of his self-creation. Or rather, this part is there, involved somehow, but unutilized: "a superabundance of life" which uselessly exists inside the present under the form of a void and a lack, and outside under the form of a desire and a regret. Man is revealed as the feckless creator of man. Having lost the sense of divine causality, having been reduced for a century to generating himself out of his sensation, man can now appraise the vast distance which separates this mere sensation-creature from that profound being of whom aspiration and remembrance give him a confused but gigantic conception. Capable of creating the moments of his life, man finds himself incapable of giving himself a being, of receiving from himself a life.

Romantic nostalgia appears thus as the forlorn desire of a life that the mind can never give itself fully in any moment and that, notwithstanding, it sees from afar, there, beyond both ends of the moment, in the elusive realm of duration: "I fly from the present by two routes," as Lamennais puts it; "that of the past and that of the future." [66] And George Sand: "I became aware that the present did not exist for me . . . and that the occupation of my life was to turn ceaselessly toward the lost joys or toward the joys still possible." [67]

Incarcerated in the instant, the romantic escapes into thought all the rest of his life. Or rather he tries to envelop his lifelong consciousness in the sphere of the present moment. It is no longer a question, as it was in the preceding century, of extracting from the moment all its sensuous substance; it is a question of giving the moment all the profundity, all the infinity of duration of which man feels capable. To possess his life in the moment is the pretension or the fundamental desire of the romantic.

Sometimes in a kind of lightning flash a moment seems to bring him what he looks for. In communing with nature, in merging himself in love with a being similar but nevertheless different, man can project and find reflected again from without the total image of his being. He possesses himself in others, and in this brief possession of himself he finds an unexpected joy which he calls an eternal moment: "Love is only a luminous point, and yet it seems to take possession of all time," says Benjamin Constant.[68] More often still, by one of those abrupt returns of which Rousseau was the first to discover the enchantment and value, all at once the mind is able to feel an entire past reborn within itself. This past, together with the whole train of its emotions, surges up in the moment and endows it with a life that is not momentary. One seems then to relive instantaneously, all at once, a long period of his existence. Such is the miracle of the affective memory of which, long before Proust, all the romantics at one point or another have had the dazzling and fleeting experience: "The smell of a violet," says Ramond, "brings back the felicities of many a spring." [69] And Musset: "Behold them, those bushes where all my youth/Sings like a swarm of birds at the sound of my footsteps." [70]

"If there only existed," muses Biran, "some means of making these happy sensations permanent, or some means of multiplying them!" [71] The history of romanticism is full of such wishful attempts. With Chateaubriand it is the art of displaying in a single moment reminiscences of different periods in order to reveal the whole extent of the retrospective depth. With Lamartine it is the constant pursuit, deep within himself, of a memory of the soul, perpetual dwelling-place of all the feelings once experienced, so that the poet may become the permanent subject of an immense and inexhaustible affective memory. Others, like Balzac or Gautier, endeavor to journey back to the past and there rebuild it by the almost magical operation of the evocative imagination. Then on the other hand, Nerval wants to find again in one moment which is always the *one alone* the ever actual incarnation of a love which always becomes, however, more and more mythical. "Poetry," says Madame de Staël, "is the *momentary possession* of all that the soul desires." [72] Possession, within the moment, of all that our soul desires to regain of itself.

But this momentary possession ends in becoming a dispossession;

it ends in the feeling of a loss renewed, in a consummate separation. An infinite distance separates afresh the present from the past. Between the two there reappears a sort of dead duration, a kind of negative time composed of destruction and absence, an existence finished. "I know my ruins," says Chateaubriand.[73] To remember, then, is no longer to suppress the interval, to unite time present to time regained; it is to realize all the distance that has to be crossed in order to discern "in the desolate depths of the gulf within" the dark, remote, and mysterious being of memory. Such is the sorrow of Olympio.

Sorrow all the more bitter in that all voluntary recollection is revealed ineffectual and sterile. Only the affective memory is of any avail; and once again, long before Proust, the romantics knew that it never obeys the orders of the mind. For as Bonstetten and Biran demonstrate,[74] it is in truth not a memory. "It is to re-feel, not to recall," says Madame de Staël.[75] Now if one cannot feel, what good is it to recollect? And how shall one resign oneself, on the other hand, to await the fortuitous awakenings of the heart? All of romanticism is full not only of triumphant but also of abortive memories.

Sadness of the past, to which is added the anguish of the future. In the depths of his soul, the romantic feels at once the presence and the absence of his future being. Presence, since to exist is to feel the bond which unites our present being to the time when it will achieve its destiny; and absence, since it is to feel also that in our present being our destiny is not yet accomplished: "True poetry," says Jouffroy, "expresses one thing only, the torments of the human mind as it confronts the question of its destiny." [76] Romantic poetry is then not solely the poetry of memory; it is also the poetry of prophecy. Such are the prose poems of Lamennais: poetry tortured by the torments of imminence and the dramas of presentiment: "A strange sickness torments us without respite today," writes Quinet. "What shall I call it? It is no longer like thine, René, a sickness of ruins; ours is more alive, more burning with pain. Each day it revives the heart the better to feed upon it. It is the *pain of the future,* sleepless, piercing pain which says to you every hour at your bedside: 'Art thou asleep? But I am awake.' Deep in our souls we already know what is going to happen. This nothing is already something; it beats within our breast. We see it, we touch it, though the world ignores it still. What kills us . . . is having to support the weight of the future in the void of the present." [77]

And so there opens, at the center of man's being, in the actual feeling of his existence, an insupportable void which real existence borders on every side; existence in time. It is as if duration had been broken in the middle and man felt his life torn from him, ahead and behind. The romantic effort to form itself a being out of presentiment and memory ends in the experience of a double tearing of the self.

But from the time of romanticism, throughout the length of the nineteenth century, man has also an entirely different experience of duration. Instead of centering oneself in the immobile moment of consciousness and trying to bring back to that center, across the temporal distances, both the past and the future, was it not possible to render mobile and migratory the actuality of one's thought, to travel through time in order to feel its continuity? Besides the romanticism of memory, and the romanticism of presentiment, there is the romanticism of *experienced continuity*. Continuity which becomes a living and a thinking experience solely because by an uninterrupted motion the mind unifies in a moving line the diverse temporal elements of a self-same existence.

This sense of continuous duration appears in several varied forms from the period of pre-romanticism to that of post-romanticism. For Senancour it is the haunting memory of a permanence acquired in high places, where "even to the variations of the mists, everything would seem to man to subsist in change itself," and where "each present moment would appear to be continuous." [78] For Joubert it is the patient and delicate weaving of affective moments into a musical composition whose continuity would consist of measures, rhythms and harmonies. For Sainte-Beuve it is rather a meticulous need to touch and "to keep always under his finger" the secret mainspring of things. For Vigny it is the inexorable training of the inward eye upon the maturation of thought. Amidst the deceptive discontinuity of the affective life, Biran discovers and isolates self-consciousness, conceived as the immediate voluntary act by the means of which "we are capable of recognizing the identity of our own being or of *perceiving our continued existence*." [79]

Hence, in the most intimate experience, that of personal continuity, an unexpected analogy is discovered between human time and cosmic time. For the first is now defined by Biran in the very terms in which the second has been defined since Newton: ". . . admitting only the power of the effort which is exerted upon different inert and mobile parts of the body proper, there will always be an identical and immediate feeling of personal existence, or of a duration which can be considered the line traced by the effort *uniformly flowing,* just as the mathematical line is the line traced by a flowing point." [80]

Human time and cosmic time are then both continuous. Instead of placing the discontinuity of inward duration in opposition to clock time, as the man of the preceding century did, the man of the nineteenth century tends to mingle the two durations in a sole continuity. The dream of Diderot is realized. The universe loses its "inhuman" character, the mind its isolation; time and space become the consorting place of thoughts as well as bodies. The human soul participates anew in the universal existence.

". . . I stood still," says Quinet, "to listen deep within me to the muted reverberations of the past centuries. . . . Scarcely has one made the law of humanity the law of one's being than one begins to live the universal life and to enjoy all the plenitude of the self." [81]

Plenitude which is no longer secured by the operation of a personal memory but by the operation of a general memory which, in one state of consciousness, takes in the life of all humanity. "Each being," writes Ballanche, "undergoes all the cosmogonic successions"; [82] and elsewhere: "All that has affected human destinies, in the future and in the past, echoed within him." [83] There exists then a magnetic chain of universal human destiny, a continuous chain which sometimes in certain privileged moments is "wholly reflected in the indivisible light of the present." [84] In a simultaneity analogous to that of the divine thought, this is the inverse experience of the infinite motion of duration.

Hence the assertion by the romantics, not only of an identity of nature in all men, but also of an identity of person. "Our predecessors and our successors are just as much *us* as ourselves," says George Sand, repeating Pierre Leroux. [85] The Saint-Simonians set about to preach a love of humanity which would be a love of oneself in humanity: so that through love man would have the feeling of his own profound existence in those who have lived and those who shall live. "I am desirous," says Enfantin, "of uniting myself to the past, of uniting myself to the future, and my life is a continuous effort of love directed toward this double goal." [86]

Historical self-awareness which is also a cosmic self-awareness. Not only do I find in myself the whole history of humanity and in the history of humanity my own entire history, but in addition I can discern this double history in the universe, deployed as it were in the reaches of interstellar space. Thanks to the transmission of light, the past life of worlds and beings is kept visible in space. Thanks to the magnetic fluid of which Mesmer discovered the existence, it seems possible to establish instantaneous communication between all points of the universe. Consequently it would no longer appear impossible to recover the sentient image of the past, and to stand in present witness of the occurrences of long ago. Such is the dream of Nerval and of Gautier. Each glance cast into the depths of space becomes a glance cast into the depths of time. To Hugo, extension is like a gulf, but a gulf that is both spatial and temporal, in which perceptions, presentiments and memories are entangled with each other. "The daguerreotypes of all things are preserved," notes Renan, ". . . the imprints of all that has existed live, spread out through the diverse zones of infinite space"; [87] and Balzac: "Just as bodies actually project themselves through the atmosphere, and leave extant there the spectrum caught by the daguerreotype which arrests it in its flight, so ideas, creations that are real and active, imprint themselves upon what must be called the atmosphere of the spiritual world, produce effects upon it, live there *spectrally* . . . and consequently certain creatures endowed with rare faculties can perceive perfectly these forms or signs of ideas." [88]

But this possession of time is not only the possession of images projected by time in space. It is also the intimate experience of the motion by which all beings endlessly achieve their becoming. Time thus lived is not completed time; it is a time which becomes and which never draws to a close. So the nineteenth century had in the highest degree what Renan calls the *intuition of becoming*. But for this intuition to be not simply that of a fragment of duration, but that indeed of a general becoming of the world and the being, it has, so to speak, to mold itself to this becoming from the primal moment which engenders and encloses it. The illuminism of the eighteenth century had already shown that human thought could of itself reascend to the origin of being, and that man could, as Saint-Martin says, "feel the divine source bubble up in him without cease." Motion of reimplication, to employ Amiel's expression, by which thoughts and things reabsorb themselves in their source. As a consequence, the true intuition of becoming consists in that motion by which, bringing itself back to an initial moment, the mind grasps in it the genesis of time and of things. Initial moment which is no longer, as with Condillac, one of psychic genesis but indeed one of cosmic genesis. "I see Being and Life and their unknown source," says Chénier. And Guérin: "Nature admits me to the most remote of its divine abodes, the starting point of universal life; there I detect the cause of motion, and I hear in all its freshness the first chant of souls." [89]

Thus nineteenth-century time seems essentially a continuous motion which can only be understood in its trend away from its original cause: it is a becoming which is always future. Reality is no longer, as in the Aristotelian becoming, the thing completed, but the very genetic process by which cause engenders effect. I exist and I participate in the existence of things only insofar as I experience their generation. Speaking of this inner experience which allowed him to understand the personality of the people, Michelet writes: "I understood it. Why? Because I was able to follow it in its historical origins and *watch it come out of the depths of time*." [90]

No one applied this genetic sense to the genre of the novel better than Balzac. In each event of the *Comédie humaine,* one can immediately distinguish the time of a force which precedes all the "times" of the novel and determines them. Whereas, on the contrary, with Flaubert each moment of life is perceived as the extremity of an infinite series of effects.

Never so much as in the nineteenth century had time appeared to be perceptible to the eyes of the spirit and assimilable by thought.

But this perceptible time is such only because it is conceived as an immense causal chain. Everything is manifested in it under the form of a continuous implication of causes and effects. Everything is developed in it as the necessary application of principles. Behind the concrete unfolding of things, behind the inner genesis of life, previous even to duration and its beginning, there is the non-temporal presence of the laws themselves. There is from the first, as Taine says, the original and unique deed from which laws are deduced and which engenders them.[91]

Back of genesis there is *generative law,* first principle of duration but lacking duration. In order to conceive it, the mind must exile itself from time to enter into a kind of negative eternity. From this point, it may again be possible for it to move onward once more into some sort of time, but this time is purely scientific, made of determinations and effects; it is not the time of the human being: "At one point in this vast world animated by a continual motion that is continually transformed, where from instant to instant nothing occurred except that which had its origin in a former state of things, I saw myself, beyond my memories, in my origin: me, this new-born me, this strange me which began by being, I saw deposited unbeknownst to itself at a point in the universe: mysterious germ destined to become with the years what its nature and its complex environment required." In these words of Lequier,[92] Guérin's intuition of origins appears hideously transformed; the lived experience of cosmic duration ends up in the thought of an existence in which everything is dealt out in advance: a dead duration; a diagram of time. Despite their efforts to give a formal or objective solidity to their representation of the world, such is the time of the Parnassians and the naturalists. A world of causes and effects becomes an illusory world, a world that vanishes like the mist in shreds of duration, some of which, the more hallucinatory, last a little longer than others. How frequently the naturalist novel describes the phenomenon of the dissolution of images in the consciousness! For example, in Zola's *Joie de vivre:* "Like those coffers which one empties of letters yellow with age, it seemed that before dying she was ridding her mind of the memories of her youth." [93] Or in Goncourt's *La fille Elisa:* "In this memory, day by day, whole chunks of her existence of long ago were sinking into dark holes of night, and her entire past, as if amputated and torn away from the prisoner, was removed and lost in empty space." [94]

A profound feeling of attrition characterizes the work of these postromantics. "I see only small fragments of my past existence," writes Maupassant. The past, he confesses, is for him no more than a "scattering of vanished events." [95] And so duration no longer seems the genesis of life, but the genesis of death: incompleted and

successive deaths which the brief blaze of affective memory interrupts from time to time, rekindling an ephemeral animation in an
existence which is burning out. Nerval had already had the anguished intuition of the exhaustion of the cosmic force, of the fatal
decline of beings from their genesis onward. Twilight of the gods
which is in truth the twilight of the god-universe and of the god-
man. As the romantics experienced the powerlessness of the creature to create itself in the moment, so the postromantics realize
the equal impotence of the creature to make of itself a being in
duration. No one experienced this double impotence more profoundly than Baudelaire; no one felt more grievously than he the
metamorphosis of human time into a time that was infernal.

And so the century ends by turning away with horror from duration, and the epoch which sees the first book of Bergson appear is
none the less that which sees everywhere only the failure of things
to endure and to be, and which claims to see in the vacancy left
by the failing world one inexpressible image: the formless image
of a timeless and being-less perfection. To create "the notion of
an object, escaping, that fails to be," is the longing of Mallarmé.[96]

A longing for non-creation.

VI

In its essence as in its historical role, the thought of Bergson is
transitional. Its function is to join the past and the future. On the
one hand it is deeply rooted in the nineteenth century. It revives, it
accentuates its themes, and resolves its difficulties. For Bergson, as
for the romantics, the human being discovers himself in the
depths of memory; and he no longer discovers himself there intermittently, fragmentarily, after a blind groping within the gulf of
the mind, but simply in allowing himself, in a moment of pure
relaxation, to be pervaded by an indelible and total memory that is
always on the very verge of consciousness. Again, on the other
hand, for Bergson as for the nineteenth century, all genuine thought
is thought of the continuous *becoming* of things; indeed, for Bergson, to intuit their becoming is to intuit their essence. Duration is
the only reality.

Nevertheless there is another aspect of Bergson's thought which
already belongs to the twentieth century, since for him *becoming*

no longer signifies *being changed* but *changing;* the act, that is to say, by which in transforming himself man incessantly reinvents his own being: "To exist is to change, to change is to mature, to mature is to create oneself endlessly." If the being endlessly draws its existence out of the past, it is not as one draws the consequences from a principle or as one copies the image of a pattern. It is a free adaptation of past resources to present life, in view of the future.

Philosopher of memory and philosopher of the continuous, appropriating the two characteristics of temporality of the preceding century, Bergson, however, with marvelous dexterity avoids their consequences: there is no longer any opposition between moment and duration; no longer any trace of deterministic fatalism; but in place of the hiatus between the actual feeling of existence and the profundity of existence, there is the possibility of a mutual communication, of a relationship between the moment and time; and in place of a determinism of cause and effect, the feeling that any moment can be realized as a new moment, and that time can always be freely created from the present moment forward.

It is, without doubt, in this that the originality of Bergson consists, and his share in establishing the thought of his century. Not in his conception of memory, nor in his philosophy of the continuous, but in his affirmation that duration is something other than history or a system of laws; that it is a free creation: "Instead of considering the present itself, the present present," writes Péguy, "what was in fact considered was a present that was past, a present congealed and stilled, a present arrested, set down; a determined present. An historic present. . . . Whereas the present is something that has not yet become past, and the cognizance of the present is of something that has not yet become history: it is freedom; the free is that which is not yet booked and jailed." [97]

Thus the twentieth century takes once more into account the notion of continuous creation: not necessarily in the sense of creation by God, but at any rate in the sense of creation by the mind. Each instant appears as the instant of a choice, that is to say of an act; and the root of this act is a creative decision. Every instant one acts one creates his action, and together with it one creates oneself and the world: "To make and in making to make oneself." "All philosophy of becoming," writes Maulnier, "ignores the act. For in

order to be known in its concrete reality, the act supposes apprehension on the part of the acting being . . . of a present
choice, the intuition of an instantaneous modification brought to
bear upon the world. The act is actual." [98]

To apprehend the present as the generative act of time in its
concrete reality is then, without doubt, the tendency of our epoch.
But as Jean Wahl has shown, nothing is more difficult, "since our
attention can be directed only to the past, and since whatever is
new eludes the grasp of consciousness, and when seized by it becomes transformed into a thing of the past." [99] By the same token
it is unavailing to go back, as Guérin tried to do, into the newness
of a moment of historical genesis which precedes time, since it is
—Bergson understood it so well—a sheer illusion the mind enter-
tains in placing itself in the "antecedent future." [100]

If then the mind wishes to apprehend itself as creator, it must
recognize in its act of creation an act of annihilation; it must create
its very nothingness in order to give itself a being. The "unheard of
work" of which Rimbaud speaks, the "marvelous body," the "first
time," [101] is possible and visible only if it immediately sets its "innocence" against a time abolished, assassinated, "the time of the
assassins." The creative act of time appears first then as a death
of time itself: "And do you not understand," writes Gide, "that
no instant would ever assume that admirable lustre unless standing,
so to speak, against a dark background of death?" [102] "Destroy,"
says Schwob, "for all creation comes of destruction." [103]

The being creates and finds itself only by setting its existence
against its own death, only by creating itself *ex nihilo*. Thus out of
the Mallarmean nothingness stands Gide's creation of the instant,
Valéry's creation of time; thus out of the Rimbaudian innocence
springs forth the surrealist creation of an over-instant and an over-
duration: "I am my mother and my child/At each point in the
eternal." [104] And if the true novel of the twentieth century appears
to be the Stendhalian novel, the novel in which at each instant the
hero *forgets* what he was in order to become as he wishes, it is
possible, however, despite appearances, to find the same attitude
in the Proustian novel, since it is built upon an experience which is
less an awakening of the remote past than the abolition of the
immediate past, and thus the creation of a vacant place where a
causeless being unexpectedly arises and displays itself.

Continuous creation becomes then a creation continually dis-
continued. On the one hand, self and the universe, forever chosen
anew, redivised, rediscovered; forever appearing to issue immediately from the creative act: "Striking out into new love and new
sound!" says Rimbaud. "With every breath we draw," says
Claudel, "the world is as fresh as the first breath of air the first
man ever breathed." But, on the other hand, this creation, even by
right of its constantly recovered freshness and newness, proceeds
somehow by fits and starts, or as Gabriel Marcel puts it, "by times
composed of heterogeneous series." The anachronism of duration
corresponds to and is superimposed upon an anachronism of
space. To endure is to be present, and to be present is to be present
to things distributed in a sort of time-space. Thus the human act
by which the mind becomes present to any group of images at once
local and temporal very often possesses the character of an incomplete, incongruous creation, as of things, says Supervielle, "which
are not made to go together." [105] It is a creation endlessly aborted,
travestied, corrected; a creation which, as Sartre has shown,[106]
continually demands the retouchings of the present and of nothingness.

A human creation. *Human, all too human.*

NOTES

[1] Suarez, *Métaphys. Disp.*
(Geneva, 1636), I, 385.

[2] Thomas, *Sum. Theol.*, i,
q. 104, art. 1; Scotus, *II
Sent.*, dist. 2, q. 1;
Suarez, *Métaphys. Disp.*,
I, 385.

[3] Bonaventure, *II Sent.*,
dist. 37, art. 1, q. 2.

[4] Albert, *Sum. Theol.*, tr.
5, q. 23, m. 2, art. 2.

[5] Thomas, *Contr. Gent.*, I.
II, chap. 19.

[6] Aristotle, *IV Physic.*,
text. 117.

[7] Thomas, *Contr. Gent.*, I.
III, chap. 67; *De Pot.*,
q. 3, art. 7.

[8] *Ibid.*

[9] Thomas, *In VIII Phys.*,
I. IV, lect. 17.

[10] Thomas, *De Verit.*, q. 8,
art. 14, ad. 12.

[11] Thomas, *Sum Theol.*, i–
ii, q. 180, art. 6.

[12] Scotus, *Quaest. Quodl.*,
q. 12.

[13] Thomas, *Sum. Theol.*, i–
ii, q. 104, art. 9.

[14] Bonaventure, *I Sent.*,
dist. 8, p. 1, art. 4, q. 2.

[15] Ronsard, *Oeuvres*, ed.
Blanchemain, III, 221.

[16] Jodelle, *Oeuvres*, ed.
Marty-Laveaux, II, 26.

[17] Belleau, *Oeuvres*, ed.
Gouverneur, III, 83.

[18] *Oeuvres*, ed. Blanchemain, VI, 72.

[19] D'Aubigné, *Oeuvres*, ed.
Lemerre, IV, 386.

[20] Jodelle, *Oeuvres*, ed.
Marty-Laveaux, II, 25.

[21] Ronsard, ed. Laumon-
nier, X, 101–102.

[22] Scève, *Délie*, ed. Partur-
ier, p. 184.

[23] Cf. Pic de la Mirandole,
De hominis dignitate,
Opera, p. 315.

[24] Cit. Ph. Monnier, *Le
Quattrocento* (Paris,
1912), I, 48.

[25] Cf. Zwingle, *Exposition
de la foi chrétienne*,
chap. 10.

[26] Cf. Harnack, *Luthers
Theologie* (1927), I, 84.

[27] Calvin, *Opera*, ed. Corp.
Reform., XXXI, 621.

[28] *Ibid.*, VIII, 321.

[29] Descartes, *Regulae*, ix,
Oeuvres, ed. Adam-Ten-
nery, X, 401.

[30] P. André, *Oeuvres philosophiques*, ed. Cousin
(1843), p. 266.

[31] Boileau, *Satire VIII.*

[32] Nicole, *Essais de morale*
(Paris, 1723), I, 54.

[33] Massillon, *Oeuvres* (Paris, 1754), II, 321.

[34] Bossuet, *Oeuvres* (1845),
III, 391.

85 *Conférences sur les Constitutions de Port-Royal* (Utrecht, 1760), I, 196.
86 Letter to Mme Périer, November 5, 1648.
87 *Lettres chrétiennes et spirituelles* (Rouen, 1645), I, 281.
88 *Oeuvres*, ed. Gaume, VIII, 663.
89 *Oeuvres* (1845), IV, 571.
40 Mably, *Oeuvres* (1794), XV, 175.
41 Augustine, *Civitas Dei*, I, xii, chap. 25.
42 Article "Mouvement," *l'Encyclopédie.*
43 *Système de la nature*, Part I, chap. 4.
44 Article "Ordre de l'univers," *l'Encyclopédie méthodique.*
45 *Lettres à Horace Walpole* (London, 1912), I, 449.
46 Crousaz, *Traité du beau* (Amsterdam, 1724), I, 178.
47 Vauvenargues, *Oeuvres*, ed. Gilbert, II, 224.
48 Rêveries, ed. Garnier, p. 50.
49 Charles-Georges Le Roy, *Lettres philosophiques sur l'intelligence et la perfectibilité des animaux . . .* (New ed.; Paris, 1802), p. 174. Cf. also article "Homme," *l'Encyclopédie.*
50 Article "Pyrrhon," E., *Dictionnaire philosophique.*
51 Du Bos, *Réflexions critiques sur la poésie et sur la peinture* (4th ed.; Paris, 1746), I, 9.
52 La Motte-Houdar, *Oeuvres* (1754), VII, 252.
53 Voltaire, *Oeuvres*, ed. de Kehl, X, 33.
54 Montesquieu, *Essai sur le goût.*

55 Helvétius, *Oeuvres* (Paris, 1795), I, 389.
56 Marivaux, *Spectateur français*, No. 17.
57 Duclos, *Considérations sur les moeurs*, chap. iv.
58 *Oeuvres*, ed. Théry, III, 308.
59 Le Roy, *op. cit.*, p. 227.
60 Quesnay, article "Evidence," *l'Encyclopédie.*
61 Buffon, *Histoire naturelle*, Impr. Royal, V, 306 sqq.
62 Diderot, *Oeuvres*, ed. Assézat, IX, 371.
63 *Nouvelle Héloïse*, Part IV, Book xiv.
64 Saint-Lambert, *Fables orientales, Les saisons* (Amsterdam, 1769), p. 344.
65 Tilly, *Mémoires*, ed. Jonquières (1929), II, 99.
66 Lamennais, *Correspondance*, II, 378.
67 Sand, *Lélia*, I, 214.
68 *Adolphe*, chap. iii.
69 *Observations faites dans les Pyrénées* (1789), p. 87.
70 Musset, *Le souvenir.*
71 *Influence de l'habitude*, ed. Tisserand, *Oeuvres*, II, 360.
72 *De l'Allemagne*, ed. Garnier, p. 152.
73 *Essai sur la littérature anglaise, Oeuvres*, XIII, 282.
74 Bonstetten, *Recherches sur la nature et les lois de l'imagination* (Geneva, 1807), I, 216; Biran, *Oeuvres*, VIII–IX, 499.
75 Mme de Staël, *Lettres sur les écrits de J.-J. Rousseau.*
76 Jouffroy, *Mélanges philosophiques* (2nd ed.; 1838), p. 417.

77 Quinet, *Ahasvérus, Oeuvres* (Paris, Pagnerre), VII, 3.
78 Senancour, *Obermann* (Paris, Droz), I, 47.
79 *Oeuvres*, ed. Tisserand, IV, 38.
80 *Ibid.*, VIII–IX, 322.
81 *Oeuvres*, II, 381 sqq.
82 *Ville des expiations.*
83 *Vision d'Hébal.*
84 *Ibid.*
85 *Comtesse de Rudolstadt*, p. 144.
86 *Lettre à Duveyrier.*
87 *Feuilles détachées*, p. 393.
88 *Cousin Pons.*
89 *Journal*, December 10, 1834.
90 Michelet, *Le Peuple* (2nd ed.; Hachette), p. 17.
91 Taine, *Les philosophes français du XIXe siècle*, p. 358.
92 *La feuille de charmille.*
93 *Joie de vivre*, ed. Charpentier, p. 232.
94 *La fille Elisa*, ed. Charpentier, p. 278.
95 Cf. Franck Harris, *Ma vie*, III, 48.
96 *La musique et les lettres.*
97 *Oeuvres*, N. R. F., IX, 242.
98 Maulnier, *Nietzsche* (Paris: Redier, 1933).
99 Wahl, *Vers le concret, Rech. Phil.*, I, 11.
100 Bergson, *Les deux sources . . .*, p. 71.
101 *Illuminations.*
102 *Nourritures terrestres.*
103 *Livre de Monelle.*
104 Eluard, *Poésie ininterrompue.*
105 Supervielle, *L'Enfant de la haute mer, N. R. F.*, p. 84.
106 Sartre, *Les chemins de la liberté, N. R. F.*, I, 212.

I

✳ Before Montaigne began to "keep the register" of his thought, how could it have had a history? Its history dates from the moment when he began to write. For writing, even when it is as desultory as his, gives a body to what is impalpable and a form to that which only flashes through the mind. Before he took his pen, then, to "register" his thought, where was Montaigne's thought? He himself said that it was not anywhere but every-where,[1] and that it wandered and "roved with the wind." [2] It had no history because it had no form. It bore "chimaeras and fantastic monsters" which issued forth "without order and design"; [3] or, left to itself, it "flagged and languished." [4]

Unformed and fluctuating, constantly passing from motion to inertia, the thought of Montaigne evaporated without leaving a trace. For, while it was thought without substance, it was also thought without duration. The "unbelievable lack of memory" which afflicted Montaigne[5] did not allow him to "retain three days the stores he committed into his own keeping." [6] Nothing remained to him of those states which his consciousness had swiftly traversed.[7] Originally this consciousness was simply a vague aware-ness of the general flux of things, carried away passively in infinite succession, or ready to founder in an indolence which is the neutral duration of zero and of nothingness.

But from the moment Montaigne begins to keep account of his thought, his thought begins to have a kind of history and conse-quently a kind of duration. Both the one and the other are re-stricted at first to being a mere agitation, an agitation which is "its life and its grace," which preserves the mind from not being and from returning of itself to non-being. It is an agitation still entirely external which is provoked in the field of consciousness by suc-cessive objects to which the mind clings like a drowning person:

"It seems that the soul, shaken and discomposed, gets lost in itself if not supplied with something it can grasp, and therefore always requires an object at which to aim, and to keep it in action." [8]

And what is this object? It is anything and nothing. It is nothing except what it is at the moment when it is. Carried by the winds of occasion in the void of consciousness, neither binding itself to anything in a past which is no longer anything, nor announcing or preparing for any consequence to come, the object appears against a background of nebulous duration, irrelevant to all that precedes and follows. It floats in the midst of time like a single cloud suspended in the air. It is not inserted into a causal chain. It is what is present to the mind, and that is all. Besides, it does not possess any significance of its own. All its significance is reduced to reflecting the thought. In the wavering transparency of the object, the being who is mirrored there distinguishes clearly only his own image; not his essential image, to be sure, but simply what he impresses upon an object, what he thinks of a certain object. It is simply occasion for thought, pure pretext for thinking and for watching oneself think.

For Montaigne, duration exists at first only under the form of the momentary consciousness which he has of himself, thanks to "occasions unexpected, actual and fortuitous." [9]

II

"I live from hand to mouth and, with reverence be it spoken, live only for myself; there my designs terminate." [10] But how can it be managed that they terminate there? Scarcely installed in the present, Montaigne's thought feels the immense difficulty of maintaining itself in the present. For it is the character of human nature to "pass over the present" [11] and "always to think somewhere else": [12]

. . . the frantic curiosity of our nature busying itself with anticipations of things of the future as if it had not enough to do to digest things of the present. . . .[13]

We are never present with, but always beyond, ourselves. Fear, desire, hope launch us forth toward the future and rob us of the sense and consideration of what is. . . .[14]

Between the motion of things and the motion of thought there is formed then, because of human disquietude, a sort of temporal hiatus. The movement of the perennial see-saw is so rapid that the mind grows weary of trying to keep up with it and ventures to outstrip it. But in doing so it creates a kind of gap in which there escapes not only the sense of *what* is but also the sense of what *it* is. In anticipating the future, it feels deprived of what composed its present. The faster it hurries along, the more keenly it perceives this flight toward the past which carries away with the object of its thought the feeling it has of it. So that to feel is at one and the same time to feel itself present and to feel itself becoming absent from itself, to feel one's own being gliding away toward the past and toward death: "Every moment it seems to me that I escape from myself. . . ." [15] "Every day I escape and steal away from myself. . . ." [16]

At its extremity this feeling becomes that of death. Life is an incapacity of being in the present, a failing of our will to last. To live is to feel oneself die.

The being who recognizes himself under this constant shadow of death looks for possible recourses: recourse to wisdom; recourse to religion. Montaigne tries his hand at the wisdom of Stoicism. To the spontaneous flight of the self Stoicism advises the opposing of a voluntary maintenance of the self; and that by an anticipated acceptance of the future, and especially of the future extremity, of death. Thus the permanence of being would be realized. The acceptance of death would at the same stroke imply the acceptance of the whole course of one's life. Such a position would put thought on a level with the ensemble of existence, and further, with the eternal cosmic order whose execution is entrusted to time. This would be a total adherence to destiny.

But in the same breath it would also be to deprive oneself forever of that position which is *the easiest and most natural:* that in which one puts oneself when one lives from hand to mouth, the central and unique position that the mind occupies at the core of the present moment:

> Transport yourself into the experience of the evils that may happen to you . . . prove yourself there, they say; affirm yourself there. But, on the contrary, the easiest and most natural way would be to dismiss them from one's thought.[17]

Thus Montaigne rejects the Stoical method, because it is against nature to transport oneself out of the present time into the "great course of the universe and into the chain-work of Stoic causes." [18]

The other recourse is the Christian one. If it is vain to try to give oneself a permanent being equal to the order of the universe, cannot one at least feel oneself participating in the existence, outside and above us, of a being whose very name signifies permanence? Born, like all the thought of his time, out of decadent scholasticism, does not the thought of Montaigne, like that of Raymond de Sebonde, recognize the scholastic dogma of the Being? The Being, the total actuality, whose reality infinitely transcends that of His creature that always of itself is under the dominion of nonbeing.[19] All Montaigne's experience confirms for him this negative definition of the created being: a being which hardly can be named being if compared to the being of the Divinity. In the *Apologie,* Montaigne repeats the words of Plutarch: "One must conclude that God alone is." But setting them in the vast tableau he composes of man's temporal misery, Montaigne declares at the same time: "We have no communication with Being because all human nature is always being born and dying." [20] This is at the same time to affirm the divine reality and to refuse to man the possibility of communicating with it; it is to leave the creature without being and without recourse to the Being.

"Being outside being," [21] how of itself could the creature rise to the level of the Being who is "perfection of being"? There is then no Christian permanence in this life, not anymore than Stoic permanence. No doubt, says Montaigne, man will lift himself up if God stretches out His hand to him.[22] Man is "a blank scroll prepared to receive from the finger of God whatever forms He pleases to write upon it." [23] But, in that, Christian wisdom only repeats natural wisdom. If the former teaches us to await the occasions of God, does not the latter teach us to welcome the "occasions unexpected, actual and fortuitous" which are like the graces of chance? On the one hand as on the other, there is no permanent recourse, but only an irregular and capricious recourse, valid only for the moment. Neither God nor nature gives being to thought; they give it only a momentary form. Only one thing remains: never to look for a phantom being outside the human condition, but to accept the situation for what it is, an existence which is not *being,* which is only "flux, shadow, and perpetual variation": "I do not depict being," says Montaigne; "I depict passage." [24]

III

I do not depict being. The astonishing novelty of this enterprise appears first in its negative aspect. Montaigne renounces the depiction of that which is; he even renounces the portrayal of who he is. What is discarded by this renunciation is the possibility not only of seizing and reproducing the unalterable being that each one carries within himself as the substantial principle of his thoughts, but also of seizing and expressing that immediate presence of thought that springs from each present moment. Living from day to day, Montaigne had proposed to himself, as the aim of all his existence, to record and portray that particular image of being, of his own being. And now he renounces it. He will no longer try to depict being; he is going to depict passage: passage, that is to say the very movement by which being quits being, by which it flies away from itself, and in which it feels itself dying. This decision is thus joined to the deepest feeling of indigence. It is an acceptance of the human condition in the radical imperfection of its essence, which implies in Montaigne the presence of the same feeling of spiritual nakedness as that of the great Christian thinkers.[25]

But to renounce the depiction of being for the depiction of passage is not only an enterprise of unprecedented denudation; it is a task of extreme difficulty. To depict passage is not simply to seize oneself in an object which fades away and by its own blurring lets the self appear more distinctly; it is not to paint a portrait of oneself which would be all the more faithful by the disappearance of all the traces of occasions which had led to its creation. It is to seize the self at the instant when the occasions remove from it its old form and impose upon it a new one. How can this double movement be described without at the same time describing the external action by which it operates? There is no painting of passage which is not simultaneously a painting of that which passes and that which makes it pass. What must be described then is a consciousness deeply engaged with the world. But what, in its turn, is this world except a world of occasions? The very spirit which quickens it cannot appear to Montaigne under the aspect of perma-

nent or continuous traits. An exterior life which manifests itself
in the winds of occasion can only be "an unequal motion, irregular
and multiform"; [26] or again, "a material and corporeal motion, an
action essentially imperfect and disordered." [27]

With the radical discontinuity of a world made of occasions there
is mingled the similar discontinuity of the successive selves which
are created by these occasions. "Our life is only motion," [28] and
this internal motion is no less irregular than the material motion of
things: "It is an irregular, perpetual motion, without pattern and
without aim." [29] And that, in the first place, by reason of the fact
that the irregularity of the one determines the irregularity of the
other:

> Our ordinary practice is to follow the inclinations of our appetite,
> to the left, to the right, upward, downward, just as we are wafted by
> the winds of occasion. We know what we want only at the moment
> we want it . . .[30]

but also by reason of a discontinuity which is at the root of the
mind:

> Not only do the winds of accident carry me about as they wish,
> but besides I am disturbed and troubled by the instability of my
> posture; and whoever pays close attention hardly finds himself twice
> in the same state. I give my soul now one face, now another. . . .[31]

Thus instead of one self there appears "an infinite diversity of
faces" [32] which one by one become me. Each time I am another:
"When fasting I feel myself to be another man than when
full. . . ." [33] "*I* now and *I* anon are indeed two persons." [34]

The self divides itself; it becomes infinitely multiplied in a series
of isolated appearances and disappearances; as if an interminable
procession of strangers walked the same corridor, separated each
from the other by an interval, passing one after the other in the dim
light of the present moment, finally to disappear leaving only a
confused memory of themselves: "I do not always recapture the air
of my first fancy. I don't know what I had wanted to say." [35]

The feelings of the past self become as enigmatic to the present
self as those of a stranger. "Thus *diversely* and *imperceptibly* our
soul darts out her passions." [36]

Imperceptibly indeed, as well as diversely; to anyone who wishes to depict passage, the soul is not discovered only in the incoherent diversity of duration; it finds itself in the same confusion in the interior of the instant. The instant is the kingdom of the impercepti-ble. It is the home of what Leibnitz was later to call the infinitely small entities. It is an instant which is an instant of passage, and which therefore is less an instant than the passage from instant to instant; there is, so to speak, an infinity of the microscopic changes in all the shades of being. It is a wager to attempt to "choose and lay hold of so many nimble little motions," [37] to hope to disentangle "a thing so mixed, so slender, and so fortuitous." [38] It is all the more so because the incommensurable volubility of tenuous ele-ments, which makes up the mind, is volubility of the thinking act as well as of its thoughts. Thus the self is dissolved, not only from instant to instant but even in the middle of the instant-passage, in a prismatic play like that of a spray of water.

Yet no one realizes more clearly the difficulties of his task than does Montaigne. To the multiplicity of the real he opposes the multiplicity of his activity; to the double discontinuity of the world and of the self he opposes the registering of the essays of his life,[39] short accounts, as disconnected as life itself,[40] but which, precisely as in life, overlap each other in a haphazard way and give thus to discontinuity a sort of continuity. This work now fills up all the instants of Montaigne's life; it absorbs all his energies. It is a world to which one dedicates himself for existence and by which one gives himself an existence. By its means "one engages oneself to keep a register of one's own duration, with all his faith, with all his strength." [41] On the other hand, there will be attached to the fluency of the states of the self an equal fluency in the thoughts of the self, in the expression of the self: "The finest minds are those which possess the greatest variety and flexibility." [42] As later Fénelon in the order of grace, Montaigne in the domain of occasion makes himself supple in the face of occasion. He becomes what he already is by nature, but what he perfects by usage, a consciousness wonderfully docile to the motion which animates and fills it; one apt to espouse the thought which the moment proposes to it.

Born of his renunciation of being and of the persistence with which he attempts to depict passage, little by little the wisdom of Montaigne extricates itself from confusion.

IV

The starting point of this wisdom is the idea of *"prise,"* that is to say, of taking something; not in the sense of taking it for oneself but *into* oneself, making it one's own. This taking does not belong to the category of *having,* but to the category of *being;* or rather it is the operation by which the object is made to pass from the category of having to that of being. Thus in an admonition which Montaigne addresses to the teacher: "Let him make the pupil put what he has learned into a hundred different forms and accommodate it to as many different subjects to see if he has really *taken it to himself* and *made it his own."* [43]

But if to take is to make one's own, what is it that must be made one's own? Only that, Montaigne replies, which it is possible to make one's own, that which is not out of reach: "We must learn how to grasp the present good, and rest there; we have no hold upon that which is to come. . . ." [44]

There is no hold except on the present. Nothing should be more prompt than the operation by which we seize it in order to make it a part of our nature. It is only thus that we are able to triumph over the flight of time: "I want to stop the rapidity of its flight by the suddenness of my seizing it." [45]

Not of its seizure but of my seizing. While time flies, I despoil it of what becomes me and what I detain within me. Instead of flying with time and letting it rob me of myself, instead of "incessantly succeeding myself and being captured by my inclinations," [46] I want by the promptness of my seizing to feel that what I seize becomes my own.

Each new occasion is a new source of richness which consists not at all in property but in the use and enjoyment of it, in a "possession of living," [47] which becomes in proportion "deeper and fuller." Each new occasion is an occasion of making a new use of oneself or of possessing oneself in another fashion. Finally the self becomes the locus of all the possibles: "Variety only, and the possession of diversity, can satisfy me." [48]

But his possession of all the possibles is in its turn only possible thanks to time and its flight. Without it nothing can be possessed.[49] Thus time now appears as the infinite possibility of all the moments out of which in its diversity life is procured and possessed. To live in time, to live conscious of time, is no longer as previously to live conscious of being carried far away from oneself by time; it is to live conscious of moving forward into a possession of oneself which is inexhaustible. The essential thing is to be ready all the time to receive the successive gifts of these possible selves: "I am at all hours ready to become anything I can be. . . ." [50]

But how then is it possible to realize in the instant this immediate transmutation of the instant which makes it become our being? For what operation of the mind ought the mind to be prepared every hour? The answer to this question is so important that it is taken up in a hundred different places in the *Essays*. The operation by which one makes hours and things one's own is none other than judgment.

Now in order to demonstrate what judgment is, Montaigne constantly contrasts it with memory, just as he contrasts wisdom with science. [51] Memory is of the past. It can be acquired but not possessed. It is like an object that one keeps somewhere without making any use of it and without being able to make it one's own. Judgment then is only possible when there is no science. Negatively it is an absence of science, [52] an ignorance. Ignorance is the "governing principle" [53] because it unceasingly brings back the mind to its proper function and summons it to confront each new occasion. Ignorance and judgment, therefore, are found to be inseparably bound together.

Positively, judgment is the act by which the mind makes something its own. It is a knowledge neither bookish nor theoretic. It is the act of thought by which the mind tries its skill on the object, tries the object, seizes it, uses it in such a way that the object becomes a kind of interior tool. But this act takes place only in the motion of the mind by which it envelops and unites the self and the object; and this act can happen only in the very moment in which the consciousness operates, and, in operating, possesses; and furthermore it can happen only upon the occasion of an object being present and capturable. Thus, in contrast to memory, judgment is accomplished entirely in a moment of actuality. It is "born of present occasions." [54]

But also, on the other hand, it appears as pure virtuality. It is not that which is possessed, but that which possesses, that which, in the final analysis, *can* possess. It is apt to be used in all matters and

involved in everything; but it is also distinguished from everything. "It plays an independent part." [55] It remains disengaged:
". . . Jealous of my freedom of judgment. . . ." [56] Letting the
appetites go their way without altering or corrupting, it keeps its
own identity: "My affection changes, my judgment never." [57]

Far from being an adhesion of the mind to things, judgment is an
integration of things within the mind by the mind. Thus its suppleness does not appear any more like the fluency of an internal life
reflecting the parallel fluency of external actions (a thing always
true of the affective life); but like the promptness and ease with
which the mind knows how to adjust itself to every moment in
order to draw out of it what it can. For this freedom of judgment
is of value only when it is transformed into a choice and into an
act. On the one hand there is pure virtuality, ceaselessly protected
by the absence of all preconceived knowledge, and on the other
hand there is, unceasingly strengthened by exercise, a spiritual activity which takes possession and cognizance of the present alone:
"I conceive that we have knowledge only of the present, and none
at all of what is past, no more than of what is to come." [58]

Thus, by a continual play, thought engages and disengages itself,[59] knots and unknots its ideas,[60] captures its prizes and returns
to the state of being free. The double repugnance of Montaigne to
see again the same places,[61] to repeat old ideas ("I hate to recognize myself"),[62] is simply the reverse side of the constant need to
find himself again, like Gide, fresh and free, when confronting the
object he has to seize and judge: "I do not know of any better
school to form life than constantly to propose the diversity of so
many other lives," [63] the diversity of other lives, but also the diversity of his very own. The mind is only faithful and identical to itself
when it preserves and augments its power of apprehension. But it
possesses that power only by virtue of seeing its object perpetually
renewed; only by virtue of perpetually renewing its action upon the
object; by keeping constantly in training. But thenceforth that training, insofar as it renews and extends the mind, provides a foundation for it. Out of the flux of duration into which the mind was
plunged, thanks to the exercise the mind performs, there emerges,
delineates, forms, and affirms itself in that mind an idea of it,
forever free and forever faithful, which, "finding itself always in
the right place," [64] no longer flitters between birth and dying, but

is and *endures*. By dint of portraying passage, Montaigne obtains communication with being; for real being is not at all a metaphysical entity, but the continuous action of a thought—on things and on duration: ". . . To be consists in movement and action; whereby everyone has a being in his work." [65]

NOTES

[1] *Essais*, Alcan, i, 37.
[2] ii, 453.
[3] i, 37.
[4] i, 47.
[5] i, 225; i, 38.
[6] ii, 105.
[7] iii, 123.
[8] i, 24.
[9] i, 47.
[10] iii, 60; i, 80; ii, 239.
[11] iii, 446.
[12] iii, 66.
[13] i, 48.
[14] i, 15.
[15] i, 109.
[16] ii, 422.
[17] iii, 359.
[18] iii, 40.
[19] Sebonde, *Theol. nat.*, chap. 23.
[20] *Essais*, ii, 367–70.
[21] i, 18.
[22] ii, 371.

[23] ii, 239.
[24] iii, 27.
[25] ii, 390.
[26] iii, 46.
[27] iii, 275.
[28] iii, 422.
[29] iii, 384.
[30] ii, 5.
[31] ii, 8.
[32] iii, 396.
[33] ii, 319.
[34] iii, 241.
[35] ii, 320.
[36] i, 303.
[37] ii, 65.
[38] iii, 396.
[39] iii, 398.
[40] iii, 417.
[41] ii, 453.
[42] iii, 46.
[43] i, 194; iii, 208.
[44] i, 15.
[45] iii, 445.

[46] iii, 46.
[47] iii, 445.
[48] iii, 274.
[49] iii, 305.
[50] i, 109.
[51] i, 38, 174, 193; ii, 104, 218, 445; iii, 190, 392.
[52] iii, 368.
[53] i, 384.
[54] iii, 240.
[55] iii, 393.
[56] ii, 445.
[57] *Ibid.*
[58] i, 175.
[59] i, 309.
[60] i, 109; iii, 69.
[61] *Journal de voyage*, 1774 ed., pp. 62 and 82.
[62] *Essais*, iii, 238.
[63] iii, 254.
[64] iii, 35.
[65] ii, 76.

✻ THE DREAM OF DESCARTES

I

✻ On the 10th of November, 1619, Descartes, aged 23, found
himself somewhere in Germany, returning from Frankfort,
where he had attended the festivities of the coronation of the Em-
peror Ferdinand III. Halted in a certain district by the onset of
winter, alone, without any care or passion to trouble him other than
his ardor in the pursuit of truth, he was very soon filled with an
extraordinary degree of enthusiasm.

It was not the first time he had felt, at the beginning of a discovery, a thrill of the spirit. "In the obscure chaos of this science
(geometry)," he had written Beeckman the preceding March 26th,
"I had become aware of a kind of light I could not describe, by
which the thickest shadows could be dispelled." This light that he
glimpses has an irresistible appeal for him; and not only is it the
light of one discovery in particular, but a light which makes possible
all discoveries. What he wants to do, what he must do, is "to penetrate to the very heart of the kingdom of knowledge." [1]

It was in this German quartering, in which all day long he was
shut in, that "the fire seized his brain," and he conceived what was
up to that time the greatest of his discoveries. It was no longer
the solution to one problem, nor even the discovery of the general
principles of a science; it was the discovery of the unity of all the
sciences:

> Quippe sunt concatenatae omnes scientiae, nec una perfecta haberi
> potest, quin aliae *sponte* sequantur, et *tota simul* encyclopedia ap-
> prehendatur.[2]

The possession of "everything at once" in a unique moment,
comparable to the divine eternity in the famous definition given by
Boethius, such is indeed the "heart of the kingdom of science."
Descartes feels that he has reached his goal, that he has arrived

at the supreme moment: "Cum plenus forem Enthusiasmo, et mirabilis scientiae fundamenta reperirem. . . ." [3]

Supreme moment at which one arrives in the full light of day, but a moment surrounded by a ring of darkness. For it is not without danger that one lifts oneself to the summits of the mind.

Complex and obscure dangers that are not easy to recognize, of which nevertheless we have evidence. In the crisis of enthusiasm which bursts upon Descartes, there may be perceived disturbing elements, physical and moral. The decisive moment has its bright face and its dark face. All day long on that 10th of November it is the bright face that is predominantly in evidence; during the night which follows the dark face is to be predominant. From the very enthusiasm there will spring forth an equal fervor of anguish. But to understand this other face of the crisis one must first discover its causes.

II

Physical causes first: the nervous fatigue due to extreme intellectual tension. "The search . . . threw his mind into violent agitation, augmented more and more by the prolonged contention he forced it to sustain, not allowing it to be interrupted by companionship or taking a walk which might have diverted it. He taxed it so thoroughly that the fire seized his brain. . . ." [4] Agitation, fatigue, agitation: a rhythm of excitement and exhaustion, not of one day only, but extending over several days, repeating and magnifying what he had already experienced over a period of several months. In the middle of a letter addressed to Beeckman, on the 23rd of April, he reveals almost simultaneously the opposite poles of the curve of this fever-chart: "My mind has already left on a voyage. I am still in uncertainty. Where will destiny take me? Where am I supposed to land?" and, several lines later: "I have done no work for a month. These discoveries have exhausted my mind." The mind which sometimes outstrips, upsets itself and then grows uncertain, astonished at being transported it knows not where, and sometimes also suddenly feels its fatigue: this is the rhythm of fever, the alternation of cyclothymia. The more violent the attack, the more closely exaltation and depression tend to follow each other, and finally the mind passes with disconcerting rapidity from an excess of joy to an excess of sadness or of anguish. By a foreshortening which perhaps reproduces the very terms in which Descartes has described his own state, Baillet expresses in striking fashion this double physical effect of the crisis: "He fell into a kind of enthusiasm. . . ." [5] *To fall,* as one falls into prostration, into a faint—and that is certainly what Baillet wishes to suggest, since he adds: "which left his mind *dejected.* . . ." Collapse, enthusiasm, dejection, the passage from low to high and from high to low is made so rapidly and so confusedly that in order to express it he has, in a way, to mingle the terms.

But to the physical instability, easy enough to comprehend, there corresponds a moral instability very much more difficult to lay hold of. Undoubtedly, in a sense, it is just to say that Descartes' mind was *fixed.* He had a goal. He devoted all his efforts to reaching it. But from the very fixation of the mind, from the concentration of energy which operates it, there emanate certain eddies of thought which travel more or less consciously in opposite directions. In the first place, single in its aim, his enquiry was double in its method: "to distinguish the true from the false" is, within oneself, to accept the true and reject the false, two distinct operations, the first of which, from the point of view of affection, is suffused with enthusiasm; but the second is marked with suffering. Now it is the former above all that preoccupied Descartes at first. "In the new ardor of his resolve he undertook the execution of the first phase of his design, *which consisted only in destroying.* This was surely the easier of the two. But he soon discovered that it was not so easy for a man *to get rid of* his prejudices as to burn down his house. . . . He had no less to suffer than if the issue in question had been to cast away his own being." [6] Indeed, the term "casting away" must be taken here in the most literal sense. The prejudices, the bonds of intellectual or sensible tradition are so much the very substance of what one has learned or experienced that *to get rid of them* is in some measure to separate ourselves, by an action at once heroic and tragic, from what has been our very existence. "The bare resolve *to rid oneself* of all the opinions one has held previously is not an example for everyone to follow. . . ." [7] Who can fail to hear in this phrase the sad echo of all that Descartes endured in his rash attempt to strip himself? The wound is still bleeding at the time of the *Discours.* His rash purpose implied a complete denudation of the mind. In this uprooting there is something similar to exile, an exile which would be not only an external exile in a foreign country but also an inner estrangement from all familiar mental landscapes in order to achieve a "stark naked state of mind."

Thus physical exile and material solitude are added to moral exile and solitude: an exile and solitude difficult to express except by comparing them to the extreme privations by which contemplatives prepare themselves for the positive experience of their ecstasies. The "naked mind" for which Descartes strove could not, and ought not to, recall anything that was recognizable. Unattached to any of the experiences of his youth, it did not reflect what he had once been; it was a mind outside of the past, outside of time, outside of human experience, a single spiritual flame burning with an abstract desire: "There remained for him only love of Truth." [8]

But it is impossible for the entire being to live in so rarefied a zone as to eliminate radically all lived experience. If the intelligence of Descartes, cut off from the past and from time, lived on these heights, another Descartes pursued its existence somewhere else. A precarious and obscure existence it was, but one in which doubtless there was preserved that infinity of images and associated feelings which are the texture of the past: faces of friends or strangers; boyish sensualities; memories of pleasure trips or of school days; and finally, most important of all, the practices of religious faith.

There is nothing to indicate that Descartes had ever dreamed of rejecting his faith; there is nothing to indicate even that in freeing himself from Scholastic doctrine he had ever felt any fear of undermining in this way the edifice of his beliefs. But everything indicates that in the unprecedented ardor of his intellectual "faith," and especially in those last hours of fever, of discovery, and of rapture, Descartes was so thoroughly absorbed by the search, by the conquest, by the presence of truth, that the presence of God was, so to speak, blurred and effaced in his mind. Let us not even say that he forgot God. Let us state simply that God is never named in any of the testimony which bears witness to the moment of discovery. But on the part of a serious Christian like Descartes that is a significant omission. It seems certain that during the decisive day of November 10th, and in any case during the extraordinary outburst of joy occasioned by the discovery, Descartes still did not turn toward God, and that his enthusiasm concentrates him entirely in the contemplation of the *mirabilis scientiae fundamenta.*

Foundation of an admirable science which his mind conceives as an ensemble of "concatenated" things: world of the *catena,* of pure determinism. Spontaneity, liberty, piety have no part in it.

III

The rapture of Descartes has then a dark side and a bright side. Let us try to imagine as clearly as possible the evening of that day during which the two sides were most tragically dissociated. For it is a veritable drama that then occurs in Descartes, a drama which began with the long, methodical disciplining of the mind to distinguish the true from the false, to set one in the full light of day and drive the other into the shadows, to affirm and to omit, to be exalted and to become depressed, to think and to suffer. The first act is over. It has ended with a complete triumph. It is the timeless side that has triumphed, the power capable of raising itself up to the world of law and harmony in which time has no part at all; where one is completely cut off from the past and from temporality; and it is the past that appears to be routed and destroyed, the concrete existence already lived, the sense of human duration.

Hence the cry of victory which is a cry of victory of Descartes over Descartes: *"Cum plenus forem Enthusiasmo . . . !"*

Cry of victory and joy. For a moment Descartes dwells wholly in joy and light. But already, by the inevitable pendulous movement we have described, the forces of reaction "so prevail upon his mind, already depressed, that they reduce it to a state receptive to the impressions of dreams and visions." [9]

And now there commences, with the first dream of Descartes, what we can call the second act of the drama. If the first act consisted of a series of interrupted and resumed strivings to reach a zone of joy and total light, the second will be enacted in shadow and under the sign of anguish. It is indeed the revenge of the routed and defeated elements. *"Transitus a passione in passionem per vicinas; saepe tamen a contrariis validior transitus,"* says Descartes in a fragment of the *Cogitationes,* which clearly refers to the experience of this dream. And he adds this astonishing phrase of sad truth, one of those sentences which suddenly seem to reveal something of such utter intimacy that we touch the very soul, the almost inapprehensible soul of Descartes: *"Ut si in convivio hilari tristis casus repente nuntietur."* [10]

But what is this *tristis casus,* what is this sorrow? No one up until now, apparently, has thought of connecting that phrase, which occurs in the *Olympica* among similar ones, with the crisis Descartes experiences, because Descartes had not received until then any intimation of great sorrow. But if his conscious being had not received any such news, another Descartes, precisely the one that returns to life and to a kind of awakeness in the sleep of its enemy brother, had for a long time understood: the great sorrow of the schism of the self; the great sorrow of the rupture of habit; the great sorrow of a time torn to pieces between the part of the mind which is situated in the timeless, and the rest of it which dwells in an obscure and confused duration. The first dream of Descartes is the dream of a discovery, the discovery that he is an unhappy being.

A short while before going to sleep, Descartes had already had a presentiment of what was going to happen.[11] Then, at the moment when the dream begins and the too-conscious self that forbade them to exist is obliterated in sleep, the undefined forms and the repressed feelings rise up out of the shadows. "His fancy was struck by the appearance of certain phantasms which frightened him." [12]

Then there is the symbolic image of the life divided-in-two which he leads, expressed from the point of view of the other Descartes, the one who is forced to proceed into the darkness without the support of thought. It is like a disjointed gait, in which all the weight of the body rests on the left foot (that of the unconscious), while the right foot (the conscious) refuses to lend any assistance: "Imagining himself walking in the streets, he felt himself constrained to lean on his left side in order to make progress toward the place he intended to go, since he felt a great weakness in his right side, which could not uphold him." [13]

Let us recall the text of the *Discours:* "Like a man *who walks alone in the darkness . . .";* and the sentence which precedes it: ". . . I found myself as if compelled to undertake *to find my way."* [14] What concrete value these lines take on when one applies them to the awkward and disjointed gait of Descartes' shade! All this second part of the *Discours,* without Descartes' making any formal mention of his dream, is filled with the experience the dream communicated. How, for example, is it possible not to contrast this difficulty of walking and supporting oneself which, in the dream, is the lived experience of Descartes, with that "intense desire of . . . walking through life with assurance" which, in the terms of the *Discours,* is the desire of the young geometer? It is certain that in 1637, in writing his book, Descartes chose the very words that, in a work in which only generalized experience ought to be expressed, would secretly bring to life before his eyes what had been most intensely personal in his history.

> Ashamed to walk in this fashion, he made an effort to right himself; but he felt an impetuous gale that, carrying him off in a kind of whirlwind, made him turn three or four times on his left foot.[15]

To the effort he made to right himself—to the desire manifested by the dark part of himself to return to a normal existence in which left and right would go together and act in harmony—there is opposed the resistance of the "conscious" in the form of an impetuous rising wind. For by "the wind is meant the mind" (*ventus spiritum significat*),[16] and its ardent, exclusive activity drives back the affective life of Descartes toward body and matter in a whirlwind motion which already is like a rapid, prospective evocation of what the Cartesian physics is to be. But what also makes itself clear here is the impression of a Descartes no longer in command, no longer fixed on his goal and intent upon his course and conscious of accomplishing his plan, but of a Descartes thrown off the track by a force which dominates and surpasses him. Here we are very far from the luminous domains of day, of enthusiasm and assurance. We enter that dark region of anguish to which our nightmares lead us, the primitive country of the soul, that first stage of human life which exists subterraneously within us, and whose action upon us never stops. But it is a country to which Descartes had remained a complete stranger until then: his conscious life had been an assured progression toward a certain goal, that rigid effort which never deviates from a straight line: "to proceed through life with assurance"; "to undertake to find my way." What he lacked was the sense of fear, and especially the fear of being lost. Later, when he writes the *Discours,* having known what it costs to pass by way of the subterranean regions and to become acquainted with the anguish of one who has lost his way, he will be able to write down that other sentence in which we still find the echo of the dream: ". . . resembling travelers who finding themselves lost in some forest ought never *to wander by turning about* to the one side or to the other, and still less to halt in a place, but to take as straight a line as they can, always in the same direction, and never in the slightest to change for insufficient reasons." [17]

> Yet this is not the reason why he was stricken with terror. The difficulty he had in dragging himself on gave him the impression that at every step he was falling down.[18]

From the zone of fear, Descartes passes to that of terror. For worse than the fear of being lost is the terror of being on the point of falling at every step. The former is of the domain of space, the latter of time. And the domain of time is veritably that of terror! In the conscious thought of Descartes, there was no place until then for anything except a mathematical *Totum Simul,* i.e. the concept of a timeless instant in which everything can be apprehended at once. By a greater and greater rapidity of a mind which surveys the concatenated parts, there is always the means of approximating or repeating this instant every time, but not of realizing a real continuity. Time does not exist in the consciousness of Descartes. And having excluded consciousness of time from his ideas, he finds himself all of a sudden in the presence of time in that part of ourselves where time cannot avoid being present: the affective part.

But if the affective part is neglected, the time that reigns there in some way intensifies its power and multiplies in us the changefulness which is its essence. The lightest touch can at once alter the whole system of sensibility: "violent transitions" that accentuate or precipitate once more the rhythm of cyclothymia. There is no longer only a dividing in two of the being, but an infinite multiplication of it into innumerable ephemeral personalities which are less and less in rapport among themselves. Then time itself is fragmented. There is no longer anything more than affective instants, each one experienced for itself alone and lived in isolation.

To the same degree, therefore, as ideal time, affective time must tend naturally with Descartes to reduce itself to an "independence of the parts of time";[19] "All the time of my life," he will later say, "can be divided into an infinity of parts, no one of which in any fashion depends upon the others." [20] This absence of "dependence," and the resulting difficulty of passing from one instant to another, is to dominate all of the thought of Descartes. From this moment it will dominate both his affective experience and his intellectual experience. But whereas earlier, ignoring his affective instincts as much as he could and transforming the others into timeless abstractions, it was possible for him not to sense the difficulty of the concrete problem implied, at this moment the sudden irruption of the affective into consciousness by means of dream forced him to declare the urgency and tragic character of the problem.

"From the fact that *I had been* a little while ago, it does not follow that I ought to be *now* . . .";[21] "From the fact that *I am now,* it does not follow that *I must be hereafter* . . ."; [22] "From the fact that *we* are now, it does not necessarily follow that we shall be hereafter, if there is not some cause. . . ." [23] Whether one is turned from the past toward the present, or from the present toward the future, whether one considers oneself in isolation, or all of reality together, the result is the same; nothing can assure us of one instant's being continued in another; nothing can guarantee to us that a bridge will be built between this instant and the following instant.

Thus at the end of this infinitesimal thing that each instant is, there is perhaps simply nothing, nothing more than an abyss into which one falls. This is the strongest anxiety of all; the "terror," as Descartes calls it; the terror of *failure in time* against which there is no recourse except by a veritable leap to God.

> Having noticed on his way the open door of a college, he went in to find shelter there and a remedy for his sickness. He tried to reach the college chapel; his first thought was to go and say his prayers there.[24]

A prey to the terror of time, Descartes is turned, as by a celestial inspiration ("he was entirely convinced that it was the Spirit of God which made him take the first steps toward that church"),[25] toward that alone which can save him from the chasms of time: "It does not follow that I must still exist afterward, if, so to speak, I am not created anew each moment *by some cause.*" [26] In the first cause is the only fixity; elsewhere there are only impetuous winds and stumbling steps; there it is possible to find a shelter and a remedy in the contemplation of the supra-temporal, in contrast to the temporal instability which consists of sickness and suffering. The God toward whom Descartes turns is not, however, the God of theology; it is not He whom one distinguishes by the operations of the reason, but He toward whom one is turned spontaneously by "a first thought." Act of freedom, act essentially voluntary, the only one which really can save the oppressed soul in this world of determining forces and ruptured duration: God is "the place where he planned to go voluntarily." [27]

In this manner the idea of God reappears to Descartes. Long neglected by the primary consciousness absorbed in the *"science admirable,"* it reappears in this spontaneous act of the secondary consciousness given to him by his dream. From this moment, so to speak, a change of atmosphere will occur in those dreamlike regions which seem to lead to some inevitable reality of despair. But in order for Descartes to arrive finally at the true "shelter" and to find the genuine "remedy," he must endure other trials. The spontaneous act by which he turns toward God does not possess at this moment the necessary efficacy: it is not *pure* spontaneity; it is not addressed directly to a God of the present, but to a God of the past. This view of a college—the courtyard of which he will enter and in which a chapel rises—this view is a memory. It appertains to his youth. And the first thought he has, which is to go there and say his prayers, is less an actual thought than the reawakening of a habit of mind formed in times that are now remote.

This return to God is basically, then, a return to the past, to the Descartes of the past: that is to say, to a being whose whole effort of conscious thought has divided him in two up till now, by an operation of systematic doubt and spiritual denudation; he is a being that has become half stranger, a sort of unknown, whose face, however, is somewhat familiar. And that is why Descartes passes by himself as one passes "a man of his acquaintance" without noticing him:

> Realizing that he had passed without greeting a man of his acquaintance, he wanted to retrace his steps in order to pay him his compliments, and he was violently driven back by the wind which was blowing against the chapel.[28]

The past is past. It is in vain that Descartes recognizes his mistake; it is impossible to turn back, to repair the wrong which had consisted in not recognizing at the right moment the tie that binds our actual being to our antecedent being, in having fashioned a time of beings detached, the ones from the others. For time is not made only of isolated "present moments" but also of a past situated at the back of consciousness; and this past has become inaccessible, since the mind is so made that continually—like the "wind"—it thrusts us toward the future. To the tragic discontinuity of the present, there is

added the tragic irrevocability of the past. If Descartes now knows
that his only recourse is God, it is not the God of his childhood. He
is violently driven forward.

He *is* driven. Singularly enough, the spirit that drives him in the
direction of God is an "evil genius" (*A malo spiritu ad Templum
propellebar*); [29] "the evil genius tries to hurl him into the place
where his own plan was to go voluntarily." [30] For if the spirit of man
becomes constrained instead of becoming pure light, if it sees only
"enchainments" in a world it reduces to laws and causes, doubtless
it can become capable of arriving at a sort of negative truth: indeed, in this sense it is driven in the right direction; error is eliminated; but "by this means," Descartes will say in speaking of absolute doubt (which occasions again the intervention of an "evil genius"), "it is not in my power to reach a knowledge of any truth." [31]
Truth is attained only by a pure, spontaneous act which excludes
any of the constraint of a driving wind; an act of which, an instant
earlier Descartes had had an idea, but one from which he had
turned aside in a vain effort to regain the past.

God is not to be found, then, by the mind's discursive advance
into the future any more than by an effort of retrospection. Like the
past, the future is closed. The present alone remains, this discontinuous present that continues to fill Descartes with dismay.

> In the meantime he saw in the center of the college courtyard an-
> other person who called him by his name in courteous and flatter-
> ing terms, and who told him that if he would go to M. N. . . . this
> gentleman had something to give him. M. Descartes fancied that it
> was a melon brought from some foreign country.[32]

This is the most bizarre episode of the dream, but by its very
bizarreness it should prove to us, if that were necessary, that the
dream is indeed authentic and not an allegory. If among all the
symbols one finds in it, the "melon" is the most difficult to interpret,
doubtless that is because it is the most "secret," the one which
Descartes' consciousness felt the greatest repugnance to explain and
translate. That fact alone should suffice to warn us that under this
symbol there is hidden a sensual and even sexual reality. Moreover,
in a veiled fashion, the explanation proposed by Descartes reveals
the truth: "The melon," he says, "signified the *charms of solitude,
but presented by purely human solicitations.*" [33] In the language of
the period, "charms of solitude" and "charms of nature" are equiv-

alent expressions. The charms of solitude are nothing other than those procured by the sensuous nature, the ensemble of which, fecund, succulent, compact and multiple at the same time, is indeed very well represented by this fruit. There is perhaps concealed within it another signification, that of sexual "solicitations," the melon often being a feminine symbol in erotic dreams.

This episode, in which the thought of Descartes approaches the instinctual life, is thus a counterpart of the one in which it reached the intuitive life: "For me," Descartes says later, "there are to be distinguished two kinds of instincts; one is characteristic of us as men and is purely intellectual; it is natural light or *intuitus mentis* . . . ; the other is characteristic of us as animals, and is a certain compulsion of nature to preserve our body in the enjoyment of sensual pleasures. . . ." [34] Descartes had never had so lively an awareness of the proximity of his body. He had been so far removed from it up until now that for him it is like something that comes "from a strange land."

> But what surprised him even more was that he saw that all the people assembled around this person and speaking with him were standing straight and firm on their feet, whereas he was bent and unsteady all the time, and whereas the wind, which had frequently nearly knocked him down, had considerably lessened. With this fancy he awoke, feeling at once an acute pain which made him afraid that it was the working of some evil genius who wanted to seduce him. [35]

The proximity of the body results in the estrangement or enfeeblement of the mind. In the midst of human society, which—a thing strange in his eyes—seems to be so well adapted to the tragic conditions of life, Descartes discovers himself to be "bent and unsteady" and intensely aware of this tragedy. And it is then that he awakens with a feeling of spiritual sorrow and associates with the sorrow the idea of a temptation.

IV

Between the first and second dream there is an interval of two hours: an interval filled with prayer, with the anguish the indignity of his state has brought him, with the presentiment of divine intervention, and with the meditation upon "diverse thoughts on the good and evil of this world." [36]

Baillet fails to tell us what these diverse thoughts were, but it is not impossible that they were directly suggested by the dream which preceded them, and even that already they formed a sort of commentary upon it. A passage in the *Olympica,* to which attention has not been drawn heretofore, doubtless because of its apparent banality, seems to refer to precisely this moment of meditation colored by religious awe: *"Ab amicis reprehendi tam utile quam ab inimicis laudari gloriosum, et ab extraneis laudem, ab amicis veritatem exoptamus."* [37]

Of all his "sins which he recognized as grievous enough to draw thunderbolts from Heaven," [38] none seemed more grievous to Descartes than the sin of pride. Had he not twice in the dream heard flattering words? Once from the "person who calls him by his name in civil and obliging terms" (*ab extraneis laudem*); finally by the "evil genius" itself, "who wished to seduce him" (*ab inimicis laudari gloriosum*). Intellectual seduction, the most insidious of all, to which Descartes had been on the point of surrendering with the more facility as the attitude it whispered to him to adopt seemed the utmost point of the rigor of his own method; to go *without aid* in search of truth. Without the aid of men, without the help of books, well enough; but had Descartes never been tempted to add secretly: without the help of God? This almost frenetic joy which had seized him in the clear light of day those hours ago, at the moment when he believed he had "penetrated to the heart of the kingdom of science," was there not something Promethean about it?

But this joy had been followed by the consciousness of unhappiness, of shame, of sin. He can already interpret the dream he has just had as "a menacing admonition concerning his past life." [39] He has merited the "reprimand" of God (*ab amicis reprehendi*) but has benefitted by it (*utile*) because he has repented and prayed, and he already confusedly anticipates the light of God (*veritatem exoptamus*).

But in his present state it is not so much repentance or hope which dominates; it is fear. He had wished to steal the thunderbolt; he fears the thunderbolt his "grievous sins" may draw down. And, as he falls asleep again, both thunderbolt and God are upon him:

> All at once there came to him another dream, in which he thought he heard a loud and piercing sound which he took for a peal of thunder. The fright he experienced awoke him then and there. [40]

A dream so brief that the very word brevity is inexact! Literally everything happens in a flash: thunder clap; fright; awakening; in one moment—in the same moment; not the whole life as in the preceding dream which, from a past marked irremediably by guilt, proceeds toward a forbidden future through a series of instants in which one thinks he is going to "fall at each step"; but the very moment, the naked instant, in which existence takes refuge and is condensed in one great crash, one great fright.

In the Inventory of Stockholm there is one line of Descartes' which, compared with this culminating and unique moment, takes on an exceptional significance: it is the title of a treatise, begun at this time and lost, which had been written down in the same note book as the *Olympica*. The terms are such that one seems compelled irresistibly to refer them to this precise moment of Descartes' dream: *"Praeambula: Initium Sapientiae Timor Domini."* [41]

The *Timor Domini,* the awe felt by Descartes, originated in the false science or the pride which could call down upon him the divine thunderbolt; but, by the thunderbolt, by the action of the Lord in the thunderbolt, this awe becomes the beginning of true science, of Wisdom.

Instantaneous transmutation in a naked "present" in which there is only the presence of God and of Descartes, in which the soul is face to face with light in a kind of eternity. A naked instant, but still not a pure one, for the grace which overflows it invades a soul still terrified of being guilty, and reveals the dazzling character of its present reality only over a depth of obscure past:

> The terror with which he was stricken in his second dream marked in his opinion his synderesis, that is to say his remorse of conscience concerning the sins he had up till then committed in the course of his life.[42]

But hardly at this instant, at the interior of this instant, has the consciousness of the sinner carried terror to its height, than God descends and possesses him: "The thunder whose peal he heard was the signal of the Spirit of Truth descending on him to possess him." [43]

But how could he be possessed, unworthy, filled with terror, accused by his past and his errors; how, except by grace? Grace, and supernatural action, does not act in human time, but in the present alone. Complete at one point without duration, it is what is veritably present: absolute instantaneousness! It is a thunderbolt. It acts like a thunderbolt. It creates: *"Activitas instantanea (significat) creationem."* [44] In this present of blinding clearness, neither the consciousness of the past nor that of the future has any place. Grace transcends the present; it makes of it a moment of infinitely simple illumination, of pure light, whose radiance lasts after it has disappeared: "And having opened his eyes, he perceived a multitude of sparks of fire about the room." [45]

"Perceptible things," says Descartes in the *Olympica,* "are well fitted to give us an acquaintance with Olympian things." [46] Inversely, the passage from the Olympian to the perceptible has something intensely disconcerting and vertiginous about it. One does not know whether it is the universe or the mind that reels. A great effort is necessary to re-establish connection with the norm. Let us not be astonished, then to see Descartes at the end of this divine experience set himself to observe and reason:

> He wanted to have recourse to reasons taken from Philosophy; and he inferred from them conclusions favorable to his mind, after having observed, by alternately opening and shutting his eyes, the qualities of the objects represented to him.[47]

Thus his fear is dissipated, and calm is restored to him; he finds himself once more in possession of his intelligence.

Much more! He finds himself in possession of an intelligence into which grace has shone. He knows now that "light signifies knowledge" and that "warmth signifies love." [48] It is first and foremost by the immediate possession in the thunderbolt instant of a light which is at the same time both natural and supernatural, and by the warmth of a grace which is love, that the intelligence *knows.* It knows by means of the "spirit of truth." And from there on, the human spirit in its turn, since it moves impelled toward the light by love, is no longer a *Spiritus malus:* it is good, of a positive goodness, the gift of God which returns to Him through reflection of His own brightness. What Descartes acquires in this moment that follows the gift of grace, is the certainty that his intelligence and all the discoveries it promises will not turn him away from God at all, but will bring him nearer to God, and even express Him: provided that the point of departure, the *Initium Sapientiae,* is always first a contact with light.

The calmness of Descartes, at the moment he goes to sleep again for the second time and in order to be the subject of a third dream, is the calmness of a soul that has emerged from division, terror, and anguish, and has gained "love, charity, harmony." [49]

V

The third dream will explain this harmony. "A moment afterward he had a third dream which was in no way frightening as the two previous ones were." [50]

This is the dream of deliverance, of reconciliation, and of assuagement. The reigning atmosphere has something about it that recalls *The Tempest* of Shakespeare. And indeed it is a dream that follows a tempest: in it the enchanter displays for himself the spectacle of his own power in a series of magical actions in which science is mingled with poetry, and wisdom with a delicious folly.

The two preceding dreams had been for Descartes "menacing admonitions *touching his past life.*" The first, almost entirely under the aegis of the past, of an irrevocable past, had seemed to exclude the future and to reduce the present to a tragic interval between two abysses. The second, issuing from the past, had transported Descartes into another present, as different as possible from the one into which he felt himself "falling at each step"; but which, like the other—and this time by reason of its miraculous character— seemed also to him to be detached from the rest of time and suspended only from a supra-temporal reality. In this direct impression of "divine splendor," [51] the instant and eternity reciprocally affirmed themselves; but by that very token the reality of the instant, as later in the *Cogito,* far from substantiating the reality of time, seemed to make it vanish. If the instant was real, it was not because it belonged to duration, but because it did not belong to it; because it belonged to eternity. In the third dream, on the contrary, we witness a genuine reintegration of the instant in time, and a sort of construction of duration.

A difficult problem it was for Descartes, but one which he had to face after having passed through the two preceding experiences: a problem the solution of which, moreover, is facilitated for him by this very fact. He is freed from his anguish and the past has lost its venom; the present, on the other hand, exists by virtue of the power of divine grace; the latter is more than a prop for the present; it is a kind of guarantee of the future. Who knows if it will not renew itself with each new step, provided this step is taken in the direction of the light?

So Descartes dares to turn toward the future: "This dream betokened the future; and it had regard solely to what was going to happen during the rest of his life." [52]

Hence the particular symbols which appear in this dream are those which have value for human duration rather than for the isolated moment. The dictionary, the collection of poems, the series of portraits, each of these symbols implies the same idea of something multiple and various, of a plurality and a diversity which are not of the plan of the instant but of that of duration; it is likewise with the idea of *order* and *economy* which applies only to number and for a calculable time, the idea of *choice* which involves succession, the entire succession of an *Iter vitae* indefinitely prolonged. There is finally not one of these features that does not tend toward the same goal: to give Descartes the acute consciousness of his future activity, of what his life will be.

"I thought that I could do no better . . . than to devote all my life to the cultivation of my reason, and to advance as far as I could into the knowledge of truth. . . ." [53] This sentence from the *Discours* sums up very succinctly the new "time" that Descartes is going to exploit. It will be an *occupation,* a *culture,* an *advance;* a progression of a curious kind, with, at each step, a start of surprise, then a sudden assurance; a rapid organization, and finally a volatilization of the instant to the gain of the one that follows; but, at the same time, a forward march, in which successive moments seem not only replaced but rectified, one by another.

First, there is the symbol of the dictionary. It represents "all the sciences assembled together." [54] It is the *"mirabilis scientiae fundamenta"* of the preceding day, the *"Tota simul encyclopedia apprehendatur."* It is with satisfaction that Descartes rediscovers his great idea: "He was transported in the hope that it could be greatly useful to him." [55] But hardly has it appeared than the image proves insufficient: complete possession of the sciences is only an accumulation of discursive elements, light without warmth, knowledge without love, a contradiction in terms, since light and love are simply the two faces of the same grace. Thus the outstripped symbol complacently fades away; and, miraculously leaping over an invisible interval of time, Descartes finds he has, "in the very moment," another book in his hand, another idea in his mind. This one is like a repetition of the first, but with a degree of supplementary perfection.

The *Corpus Poetarum* is, sure enough, no longer simply "all the sciences assembled together"; it denotes "in particular, and in a more distinct manner, philosophy and wisdom joined together." [56] Let us not be astonished to see symbolized thus by poetry the two pre-eminent "Olympian" sciences which contain all the others; for poetry is here the faculty of "enthusiasm," the "force of the imagination" which makes burst forth from our thought the light of unexpected truths: *"Sunt in nobis semina scientiae, ut in silice, quae per rationem a philosophis educuntur, per imaginationem a poetis excutiuntur magisque elucent."* [57]

Magisque elucent! The sort of Olympian science of which Descartes now dreams is a degree above the encyclopedic science of a moment before. It is a science which would preserve something of the divine luminosity and warmth. The seeds of science are the seeds of fire. The flint is dark and lusterless; but when, *in an instant,* one strikes it, by divine grace it spurts forth, it *creates* brilliant sparks. Such is the science of innate ideas, which are called innate only because every moment God permits them to be born in the soul so that natural light may shine there: a new assurance of the endless repetition of the creative act.

Meanwhile another instant has dislodged the old one with the same absence of transition characteristic of this dream. Having opened the book, Descartes has "fallen upon the verse: *Quod vitae sectabor Iter?"* [58] To the problem of innateness there succeeds that of freedom. If God is all activity and all truth, where is my choice, and what is my life going to be? I can do no other than choose God. Then my choice is necessary. And if it is necessary, where is my freedom?

To this question the moment after cannot fail to furnish a response. "At the same moment he perceived a man he did not know but who presented him with a piece of verse beginning *Est et Non."* [59] The passage of one instant to another is always so prompt in the thought of Descartes that it is as if a stranger brought him his idea. But this idea is indeed the answer sought. Between the *Est* and the *Non* no hesitation is possible. *Est* and *Non:* Truth and Falsity. *Necessarily* one must always choose Truth.

At once a side of Descartes rejoices in this reply: "The piece of verse is excellent"; it "conveys the good counsel of a wise man, or even of moral Theology." [60] This necessary choice has a power of attraction. Truth is what must be chosen. The experience of the preceding dream has given Descartes the intuitive knowledge of that light which trails golden sparks behind it; he "knows what it was";[61] this overwhelming necessity, in which one is irresistibly possessed by truth, does not frighten; it attracts. To be repossessed by it, Descartes begins at once "to peruse the book of which he boasts himself of knowing perfectly the order and economy"; for the "order" is indeed the effect of the light. When it shines, everything is perceived in its place, distinctly.

But by a sudden change all this beautiful order vanishes. One would say that this time the marvelous interval had not been so well cleared and that Descartes arrived in the following moment with one foot in the void. That is always what happens when the problem of free will arises. Now it is necessity, now liberty, which asserts itself, or both seem inconceivable. This leads to a grand confusion. One no longer knows where one is; one can no longer discover what one knew a moment before. Science indeed would incline us toward a rigorous determinism. The dictionary reappears. But science by itself now seems something "incomplete." And out of all this disorder there finally emerges an idea to which Descartes can entrust himself. If the *Est et Non* is a beautiful poem, the *Quod vitae sectabor Iter?* is "more beautiful still."

This is the last idea and the most exquisite that the dream has yet communicated to him, and he must hurry to express it before the enchantment is dispelled. The *Est et Non* is "the Truth and Falsity of human knowledge and profane science";[62] it is what exists and it is what does not exist; what necessarily is or is not. From this point of view truth appears not so much under its divine aspect of creative light as under that of governing law or governed order. "There is only one force active in the universe, love, charity, harmony";[63] but in the universe of sense divine love appears as if half-veiled by the character of necessity which it adopts. All comes of God; all is His active force, His determining force. But if one asks himself the question *Quod vitae sectabor Iter?* it is no longer the same. In contrast to the universe of sense, the universe of thought, of *my* thought which asks me this question, is based upon a mysterious reciprocity. God manifests His "active force" in me, but there is an active force manifested in me *toward Him*. To His love my own responds. I find myself, beyond necessity, even beyond freedom, in an act of love bursting forth from my own spontaneity, by which I decide for truth, by which I choose God. And this act, which is a present act involving my life, I can repeat without end. At every moment of my existence I can say to myself with delight: *Quod vitae sectabor Iter?* and choose "the roads I ought to follow."

For the act of love, like the act of thought, is also situated entirely in the instant; it is not a desire, "which is a passion apart and relates to the future"; it is the consent by which one sees "himself *henceforth* joined to what he loves . . . ." [64] If in the first dream Descartes could not reach the temple of truth, that was because then he was in the time of desire and regret, not in the "from this moment" of love. One can reach the truth only by an act of adherence which is pure spontaneity. Then one finds himself freed from the last anguish, from "uncertainty over the kind of life one ought to choose." [65] God is the surety that one will always choose Him.

There is therefore nothing astonishing in Descartes' finding this dream "exceedingly sweet and exceedingly pleasant." [66] From anguish he had passed to terror—then to a summit of unspeakable emotion—here he is led gently, pleasantly, to confidence. This choice of each instant is a choice for life: his lucid life, in broad daylight, to which he now returns with rapid stride. Here the book he leafed over is revealed to be full of "little portraits." It is the world of perceptible things with which little by little the sleeper takes up contact again. These images are the sign of his awakening —or at least of his passing to another sort of dream, lighter, closer to awakening, in which he sets out to reflect and interpret.

VI

This work of interpretation and elaboration continued in the weeks which followed. The notes of the *Cogitationes* allow us to catch a glimpse of what it was like.

We find a series of notes which little by little are transformed into the design and even into the outline of a work. This would have been an intensely personal labor, in which Descartes would have recounted his own history and at the same time set forth a method and a metaphysics.

The book itself would have been divided into two parts, each dealing in its own way with a central experience. In Part I, Descartes would have retraced his mental progress: the solitary effort;[67] the acquiring of fixed rules;[68] the discovery, through the reticences of science,[69] of a fundamental simplicity.[70] All this had been his life up until the 10th of November. But there would have been more: this simplicity is discovered only by an "estimation" which depends on self-consciousness.[71] It is first in the interior of itself that the mind experiences the truth and recognizes it as such.[72] But the human mind is dim.[73] And there is no criterion of truth in the rationality of things, for one can imagine a rational world contrived to present the illusion of it;[74] an hypothesis which—as later that of the "evil genius"—leaves the human mind in the impossibility of never knowing the truth, except thanks to some extraordinary means.

Later this means will be the *Cogito*. Now it is "the Spirit of truth which descended upon him to possess him." But, in substance, these two means are identical: that is to say, having plumbed the depths of ourselves, following an elimination of all knowledge, we perceive simultaneously, in an act of instantaneous thought, both our reality and that of God; the contact with absolute truth upon which there is finally erected a philosophy.

The philosophy outlined by Descartes is found in the five fragments of the *Cogitationes* which follow immediately after the *Olympica*.[75]

This philosophy is like a synthesis of the diurnal discovery and the nocturnal experience of the 10th of November. To the fundamental unity of nature there responds the unity of mind. And just as the spiritual unity is first manifested to Descartes in the central dream, under the form of *love*, of *charity*, of *harmony*, so the unity of nature is re-established by the *active force* which animates things.[76]

The first experience (*Initium Sapientiae*), then, is the consciousness of an active force (*Vis activa*), manifest at the same time in things and in thought, the simple act in which everything mingles and finds its harmony (*Una est in rebus activa vis, amor, charitas, harmonia*).

This simplicity of act renders nature inconceivable. But the symmetry which exists between perceptible and spiritual things permits one to perceive aspects (*Sensibilia apta concipiendis olympicis*). First this activity appears in a thought. This force, this influence, is and makes the consciousness (*Ventus spiritum significat*). It is manifested there under the double aspect of a spiritual light and a divine grace. It is knowledge and love (*Lumen cognitionem, calor amorem*). Immediate union of subject and object, a veritable creation which occurs in the very moment (*Activitas instantanea creationem*). But that again is inconceivable to the human mind, which knows that it acts not in the instant but in a duration (*motus cum tempore vitam*). Either its knowledge or its love had to be imperfect (*Plura frigida quam sicca, et humida quam calida*). Deficiency or privation of being that composes time and prevents the human mind from mingling itself with the instantaneous activity of the divine simplicity (*quia alioqui activa nimis cito victoriam reportassent, et mundus non diu durasset*). Life is nothing other than a perpetual failure of our love and our knowledge, which cannot maintain themselves in the creative instant.

This fall in time, this inexplicable deprivation of being, is bound, moreover, to the miracle of creation, in which God does not at all separate deprivation from pure activity, but creates, out of nothing, beings in which there is still a trace of nothingness.[77]

Beings who would be doomed to get further and further away from light and love and to return to nothingness, if by two other miracles in an inverse sense God had not left the mind the possibility of reunion with Himself.

First there is the singular faculty of freeing oneself, by an instantaneous act of will, from the temporal determination.

Finally there is the mysterious incarnation in life and in duration of a Redeemer who establishes a juncture between time and eternity.[78]

But for the mind alone. Nature, which, analogously, can represent the mind,[79] has in itself only an order of temporal perfection, that of a movement without end, of a continuous failure to exist in the instant.[80] Only spiritual beings have free will.[81]

Such is the philosophy at which Descartes would have arrived under the direct influence of his dreamed experience. All the elements are found in the dreams of the night of November 10th.

And all these elements are rediscovered in the philosophy of his mature age. They are:

1) The determinist mechanism of a nature which is perpetual movement.
2) The transcendental reality of the mind, guaranteed by natural light and free will.
3) The absolute reality of God, conceived as a simple and instantaneous activity.

These are the bases of Cartesianism.

VII

Such is the road traveled by Descartes during the decisive hours grouped about November 10, 1619; traveled with a speed so dizzy that only with difficulty can one embrace its extent at a glance. The discovery of the unity of the sciences, the enthusiasm, the moral anguish, the religious awe, the intuition of God, the metaphysical visions, the elaboration of a philosophy. All that is most subterranean and most exalted, most secret and most luminous in Descartes appears at one stroke in this episode of his youth. An episode of which the center is less perhaps a mystical experience than an experience that is simply but profoundly human. It is by contact with episodes like these that one can better grasp the affinities which exist between the anxieties of the soul and the speculations of the mind, and that there comes to be illuminated down to its very depths that out of which a philosophy is formed: a work not only of the purely intellectual part of one's being, but of the entire being.

NOTES

[1] Letter to Beeckman, May 6, 1618.
[2] *Oeuvres*, ed. Adam-Tennery (*A. T.*), X, 255.
[3] *Ibid.*, p. 179.
[4] Baillet, *Vie de Descartes* (1691), I, 81.
[5] *Ibid.*

[6] *Ibid.*, p. 80.
[7] *Discourse on Method*, Part II.
[8] Baillet, I, 80.
[9] *Ibid.*, p. 81.
[10] *A. T.*, X, 217.
[11] Baillet, I, 85.
[12] *Ibid.*, p. 81.

[13] *Ibid.*
[14] *Discourse on Method*, Part II.
[15] Baillet, I, 81.
[16] *A. T.*, X, 218, *Olympica.*
[17] *Discourse on Method*, Part III.
[18] Baillet, I, 81.

19 *A. T.*, VII, 369.
20 *Ibid.*, IX, 38.
21 *Ibid.*
22 *Ibid.*, p. 87.
23 *Ibid.*, VIII, 13.
24 Baillet, I, 81.
25 *Ibid.*, p. 85.
26 *A. T.*, IX, 87.
27 Baillet, I, 85.
28 *Ibid.*, p. 81.
29 *Ibid.*, p. 85.
30 *Ibid.*
31 End of the *Meditations on First Philosophy.*
32 Baillet, I, 81.
33 *Ibid.*, p. 85.
34 *A. T.*, II, 599.
35 Baillet, I, 82.
36 *Ibid.*
37 *A. T.*, X, 217.
38 Baillet, I, 82.
39 *Ibid.*, p. 84.
40 *Ibid.*, p. 82.
41 *A. T.*, X, 8. .
42 Baillet, I, 85.

43 *Ibid.*
44 *A. T.*, X, 218.
45 Baillet, I, 82.
46 *A. T.*, X, 218.
47 Baillet, I, 82.
48 *A. T.*, X, 218.
49 *Ibid.*
50 Baillet, I, 82.
51 *A. T.*, V, 136.
52 Baillet, I, 84.
53 *Discourse on Method,* Part III.
54 Baillet, I, 83.
55 *Ibid.*, p. 82.
56 *Ibid.*, p. 84.
57 *A. T.*, X, 217.
58 Baillet, I, 83.
59 *Ibid.*
60 *Ibid.*, p. 84.
61 *Ibid.*, p. 83.
62 *Ibid.*, p. 84.
63 *A. T.*, X, 218.
64 *Passions de l'âme,* art. 80.
65 Baillet, I, 84.

66 *Ibid.*
67 *A. T.*, X, 214, ll. 1–2.
68 *Ibid.*, l. 3.
69 *Ibid.*, p. 214, l. 4; p. 215, l. 1.
70 *Ibid.*, p. 215, ll. 2–4.
71 *Ibid.*, ll. 9–10.
72 *Ibid.*
73 *Ibid.*, ll. 11–17.
74 *Ibid.*, p. 216.
75 *Ibid.*, p. 218, l. 6; p. 219, l. 4.
76 *Ibid.*, p. 218, ll. 6–7.
77 *Ibid.*, ll. 15–18.
78 *Ibid.*, ll. 19–20: *Tria mirabilia fecit Dominus: res ex nihilo, liberum arbitrium, et Hominem Deum.*
79 *Ibid.*, p. 218, ll. 21–22; p. 219, ll. 1–2.
80 *Supra.*
81 *A. T.*, X, 219, ll. 2–3.

PASCAL

I

* Custom is our nature. . . . Who thus doubts that our soul
being accustomed to perceive number, space, motion, believes
in them, and in them only? [1]

Now time, like number, space, and motion, belongs to our customary experience. We believe in time because we are habituated to it.
It is part of our nature. It has become ourselves.

But the movement of Pascalian thought goes back to the source
of things: "In pushing our researches further and further, we arrive necessarily at primitive words . . . and principles. . . ." [2]

Time is one of these primitive words and one of these first principles. We do not come to know it by reason, but by the heart. It is
a truth of feeling: a thing which " is felt," the fruit of an immediate intuition, and not the conclusion of discursive reasoning.

But what does this intuition disclose? Nothing other than this
very feeling: the feeling that is reproduced in us often as we hear
or pronounce the primitive term; an intimate feeling which it is impossible to analyze, beyond which it is vain to hope to go; a feeling
which cannot be defined.

Time. . . . Who can define it? And why undertake it, since all men
conceive what is meant by speaking of time, without any further
definition? . . . At the expression *time,* all direct their thought towards the same object . . .[3]

toward the very object the term *designates.* It is useless to search for
a definition, since to designate objects is all a definition can do.
Thus our knowledge of time is entirely dependent upon the rapport
that exists between this first principle and the term which denotes
it. Hearing it pronounced, we are carried toward the object; we
have the feeling of it.

But we know no more of the nature of time than of other first principles: "It is not the nature of these things that I say is known to all; it is simply the relation between the name and the thing." [4]

Just as with space, motion, and number, when we wish to penetrate "the essence of time," our reason is engulfed in the infinities which enclose it on every side.

Nevertheless, if our thought is found incapable of conceiving temporal infinity, as it is of conceiving spatial infinity, this is because the idea of numeral infinity exceeds and comprehends that of time and space:

> Nature always begins things again: years, days, hours; just so space touches space, and number follows number without break. Thus is made a species of infinite and eternal. Not that there is in all this anything that is infinite and eternal, but these limited beings are infinitely multiplied; thus it seems to me there is nothing infinite but the number which multiplies them.[5]

Then the infinity of time is not time. It is only a multiplication of time by number. Infinity is in number.

Unless one can conceive a "point which fills everything," an "infinite motion," [6] a "point shifting everywhere with infinite rapidity";[7] no longer a perpetuity made up of the indefinite addition of "bounded entities," but an "infinity without quantity, indivisible." [8]

Then in the face of this true eternity which is inconceivable, the false eternity of time is dissolved. There remains no more than a time made of "bounded entities," and an unanalyzable feeling; that is to say, a series of concrete experiences on which the mind acts.

Let us look at these experiences.

II

The first is that of reason. There is a rational time, which is that of the sciences. Animals, unprovided with reason, possess only successive, unconnected moments:

> Nature instructs them in proportion as necessity impels them; but this fragile science is lost with the wants which give it birth; as they receive it without study, they have not the happiness of preserving it; and every time it is given them it is new to them.[9]

Fragile science, given to each instant for the instant only, and each time new. At the lowest level, in the world of the impulsive and instinctive life, there is discovered then an activity the essential character of which is of a being situated, not in a continuous duration, but in the radical novelty of the instant: a character which, with Pascal, as with Maine de Biran, will be found to be strangely identical, at the highest level, in the order of grace.

Between the world of animal nature and that of the supernatural extends the human world: a domain profoundly different, since it is the world in which beings "have the happiness of preserving science." Human time first appears, then, basically to be preservation. Knowledge depends upon reason, and reason depends on the preserving faculty, on memory.

> Memory is necessary for all the operations of reason.[10]
>
> . . . .
>
> Man is ignorant at the earliest age of his life; but he is instructed increasingly in his progress; for he derives advantages, not only from his own experience, but also from that of his predecessors; since he always retains in his memory the knowledge which he himself has once acquired, and since he has that of the ancients ever present in the books which they have bequeathed to him.[11]

There occurs in memory, then, a sort of continuous preservation of facts and ideas. And so it is not at all necessary each time to begin again the apprenticeship of knowledge. Experience, once accomplished, is acquired forever:

> The mind believes through reasons which it is enough to have perceived once in one's own life.[12]
>
> . . . .
>
> It is enough to have learned them once and to have kept them in mind, so as not to need to be taught them any more.[13]

To put it another way, thanks to memory it is unnecessary to begin anew each time the operations of the mind which have brought us to certain conclusions. They have been acquired. To the successiveness of the irrational world of animality there is opposed the permanence of the acquired rational and scientific knowledge of the human mind; a permanence which is an "effect of memory."

Thus human time is affirmed first of all as the contrary of successiveness. Time resides in the lastingness of acquired ideas.

But it resides also in the acquisition of ideas; in the fact that here a new idea does not exist as purely new, as isolated in the moment when it is born; but as adding itself to a long series of portions of knowledge already acquired all along a past preserved in the double memory of minds and of books, which is lengthened to result in this new idea and in this present moment.

Hence the particular significance of each of these moments seems to be to continue the line, to advance the past. The rational present is a "progress" of the prolonged past: "progress of reasoning of the geometric mind," [14] a progress which—if one regards it as it should be regarded, not setting out from the present, since the perspective of the future is hidden from us, but setting out from the most distant past and following the course of the centuries—appears like a temporal continuity which infinitely stretches beyond the individual being and embraces all the completed ages during which the human species has been developed:

> Thence it is that by an especial prerogative, not only does each man advance from day to day in the sciences, but all mankind together make continual progress in proportion as the world grows older, since the same thing happens in the succession of men as in the different ages of single individuals. So that the whole succession of men during the course of many ages should be considered as a single man who subsists forever and learns continually.[15]

Subsisting and apprehending; preserving and augmenting; in these two activities alone there consists for Pascal the progressive construction of time by human reason. It is a work of science; it is the whole work of science. Thus with sovereign clarity are posed the temporal bases upon which the two centuries to follow will establish their philosophy of progress.

But there are assembled here with the same clarity all reasons which deny any future to reason. "The geometric mind is slow, rigid, and inflexible in its views." [16]

Pascal's first reproach of reason is its slowness. A reproach which would be a light one if it were aimed only at the imperceptibility of the "progress of reasoning," and if time were only the insensible movement of the little hand of the clock. But it is graver, for in the activity of the mind there must, of necessity, be a synchronization of the rhythm by which ideas follow each other with the rhythm by which the mind takes knowledge of them. But to the quickness and multiplicity of views, there is opposed the slowness of reasoning:

> Reason acts slowly and with so many views upon so many principles which always must be present, that at any time it may fall asleep or get lost, for want of having all its principles present.[17]

Every hour, in discursive thought, there is this lagging, this *want;* every hour there is something at least within its present which has not yet had time to be present. Rational time is revealed not only as a slowing down of the pace of progress but also as the introduction into it of an anachronism and a deficiency.

A gap is made which is going to become a gulf. This applies not only to a difference in pace. Discursive thought, in its slow progress, proceeds by demonstrations toward conclusions. Every moment there is present to its memory all the long list of acquisitions which constitute its past. For this acquired knowledge is a thing of memory. But at each end of this chain of memory there is an element which is not at all a thing of memory. At the near end there is the assent; at the far end there are the principles. The assent to truth is given in that instant when the mind sees proofs. But utterly different from them, the assent is given only for the instant. As soon as the instant is past, the assent is no longer valid; it no longer is.

> The metaphysical proofs of God are so remote from the reasoning of men, and so complicated, that they make but little impression; and even were this to serve some persons, it would be only during the instant of their seeing the demonstration, and an hour afterwards they would fear that they had been deceived.[18]

On the other hand, the first element of the movement of thought, element that by itself alone reason never finds out, and which does not occupy any point on the progressive line of its search—this element does not belong to memory either, since it has never been acquired by the mind. "Principles are felt, propositions are inferred." [19]

That which is felt once is able to make itself felt again, but if it does not make itself felt in the instant, no matter what memory can bring, the feeling is not present; it is neither in the memory nor in the moment.

One understands then why it is necessary that "all the principles be present" so that reason shall not lose its way. Their presentness should not be the one of proofs or attainments; neither the one of data preserved and recalled by memory; but it should be an actual presence, always new, and, as it were, refound by the mind in each new moment. Thus the life of the spirit appears entirely other than the slow and continual augmentation of the past by the present. This past which is augmented and which one can remember, is composed only of ideas obtained by effort of reasoning. But the first course eternally escapes it. That which gives life is neither captured nor preserved. There is only preserved "the idea which remains with us in memory," a lifeless idea: "Our memory, as well as the instructions it contains, is nothing but an inanimate and Judaical body without the spirit that should vivify them." [20]

In brief, the construction of a human time by the reason ends only in forming an "inanimate and Judaical body." "That which always subsists" in knowledge, in memory, is a past without a soul, a time without life.

III

Time is not in science, it is in life. Human life appears at first like a spontaneous unity, made of an infinity of imponderable elements whose activity forms and fills the consciousness: "Everything is one, everything is diverse. How many natures in the nature of man!" [21] Incessant transformation, of which man is discovered to be at the same time the subject and the author: "I have learned that our nature is but a continual change." [22]

This movement, in which the essence of our being seems to consist, is manifested under the form of feeling, of love, of passion. It has its origin in the willpower of human nature. Therefore it is in the very act by which our mind wishes and desires that we have to seize the principle of duration. Far from being like rational time, a time composed of events experienced and gone, to which ceaselessly something is added, this time affirms itself a living and multiple entity, which from moment to moment advances, in metamorphosing itself, into the future. Its continuity is that of change, not permanence. Its substance is made of inventions, not of acquisitions. The existence it imposes is an existence "of stirrings and actions of which one feels in his heart those sources so alive and so profound." The very past, the source, takes there the gait of the future. It is like an original force, fecund and creative, which impels the being toward always new animations: "Souls fitted for love demand a life of action which becomes brilliant in new events." [23]

This affective duration, already so profoundly Bergsonian in its texture, converges also, as with Bergson, on the continual formation of a present filled up at once with the past which is projected into it, and with the future to which it aspires. But this present alone exists, in which the past is resolved and the future implied. There is neither recollection nor foresight, nor permanence of a time already fixed, but a passionate spontaneity, which, freed of all determination, seems to create itself and its own time as it goes along. "Love has no age; it is always born again." [24] And this quotation so Stendhalian:

> When we love ardently, it is always a novelty to see the person beloved.[25]

But this spontaneity, because of its very variety, overflows consciousness. The mind, in the instant, cannot encompass all the riches of the instant. "Principles so interwoven and so many in number that it is almost impossible that some of them should not escape." [26] Instantaneous profusion, of which the mind no doubt may take the elements one by one, in such a way as to go over all the space they fill. But the reality of these elements is not only due to their separate existences, but also to their simultaneous presence; as, for example, of two "opposed virtues" of which in order to seize the truth it would be necessary to have consciousness at the same moment: "One does not show his greatness by being at one extreme, but in touching both extremes at once, and filling all the intermediate space." [27]

To go from one to the other is to let escape an essential part of their reality, which is in their simultaneous implication; it is to introduce into reality an element which is not there; it is to put succession in the place of the instant.

Besides, by very reason of its radical novelty, each moment of time becomes something singular and unique—of a sort that the being we are, in the moment that we are, determined as we are by the passion of the moment, is found at bottom a stranger in the face of all the beings it has been:

> The principles of pleasure are not firm nor stable. They are different in all mankind, and variable in every particular with such a diversity

that there is no man more different from another than from himself at different times.[28]

Hence there is no longer continuity in our being, only "different times," through which we pass by turn. When we are in one of them, it is impossible for us to find and recognize ourselves in the others. We are always different from what we were:

> When we love, we appear to ourselves quite different from what we were before.[29]
>
> . . . .
>
> When we are well, we wonder how we should act if we were sick; when we are sick, we take medicine cheerfully. The disease brings us to this resolution. We have no longer the passions and desires for amusements and promenades which health gave. . . . Nature, then, gives passions and desires conformed to the present state.[30]
>
> . . . .
>
> Time cures pains and quarrels, because one has changed, one is no longer the same person.[31]

Thus it appears once again that memory is impossible, unless it be under the form of the "body inanimate and Judaical," for in order to remember the past truly it would be necessary to be able to reascend the stream of all that flood of will that sweeps us along, to re-experience its old passions, to want what one no longer wants, to remake the past of one's heart. But one has only the feelings of the very moment. "Past harms do not hurt any more, present ones smart." [32]

At the limit, there is the negation of all that is past: "I feel I might not have been: for the *me* consists in my thought." [33]

Finally, to the first dividing gap within the immediacy of consciousness, to the second gap created between the different moments of consciousness, there is added a third: the gap which appears in the very passage from one moment to another. For in the motion by which one "changes thoughts" there is a split of some sort between the inventive and reflective parts. The mind always feels itself outstripped by its own activity. Different from what it will be with Bergson, here the motion of thought is not an intuitive élan which faithfully accompanies—and yet erroneously—an intelligence which translates it in proportion; it is the asynchronous movement of two different clocks, of which the one registers what one feels and the other what one is conscious of having felt.

Thus there emerges an interval infinitely graver than the two others, for if the former ones ruined all possibility of establishing a continuity in time, the latter menaces the more intimate continuity which effects, so to speak, the changing of time at the interior of the very moment. An interval of duration appears in the instant one thinks. Through this cleft escapes, sometimes vanishes, what one thinks in the very act of thinking. "Thought escaped: I wanted to write it down; I write, instead, that it has escaped me." [34]

Disparition as prompt as was the apparition. Thus there is revealed that the movement ahead, by which thoughts surge up in the field of consciousness, implies a corresponding movement by which they withdraw from it. The one is at the stem, the other at the stern. The passage from the one to the other is so rapid that they seem to make only a single moment. And in a way they are one, yet the mind despite itself divides and decomposes them; more struck, moreover, in the bird's-eye view it has of their passage, by their "perishing and even already having perished," than by their "forever-borning" aspect which outstrips its attention.

From this there springs the impression that the object of our thought has passed, so to speak, through us, as if we were a phantom, and that at the very moment when we believe we see it rise up from the future into the present, it is already "down there," behind, flown away, and lost:

> The soul is afraid . . . in seeing that each moment snatches from her the enjoyment of her good, and that what is most dear to her glides away at every moment.[35]
>
> .   .   .   .
>
> It is a horrible thing to feel all one's possessions flowing away.[36]

IV

The thought of Pascal is like a series of windows which are opened and shut again one after the other; or like a subterranean labyrinth each winding of which one follows in search of egress. That of reason and science are already closed. It seems that the way of feeling leads to a dead end also. The anxiety of the mind increases proportionately, more and more oppressed by the urgency and struck by the tragedy of the problem. Time, at first an external and spacious construction of thought, has shrunk to no more than a narrow, dark room, but at the very center of one's being, where there passes from one grate to another an invisible stream which one tries in vain to arrest. Or again, it is like another sort of dream in which one tries to overtake someone who is withdrawing in the distance, and runs with all his strength without being able to advance a step.

The Pascalian mind, though, cannot be resigned. It never gives up the hope of overtaking, by means of new exercises, this movement out of the self which outstrips the self: tentative complex, in which are combined the patience of a premeditated design, the violence of the effort, and a kind of physical suppleness of mind.

For perhaps the narrowness and slowness of thought are due only to a lack of practice.

"Only thought can occupy us; we are unable to think of two things at the same time." [37] But perhaps there is a way of training ourselves little by little to think of two things at the same time. Doubtless the mind is slow; but it is not impossible, in the long run, to make it more prompt. Just as by dint of doing a certain thing one becomes abler and surer at it, so one can imagine a method by which the consciousness, instead of being only the tardy response of the reflective part to the inventive part of thought, would become the automatic echo of it, would wake up, would prepare itself, finally would fulfill immediately, and with a marvellous facility, its role of consciousness. Or rather it would be a matter of substitut· ing for the reflective consciousness—that deportment of thought still too close to reason and its heavy, successive steps—a light and sure adherence of all the spiritual muscles:

> One must acquire a more facile credence, which is one of habit, which, without violence, art, argument, makes us believe things, and bends all our powers to this credence, so that our soul falls into it naturally.[38]

"A more facile credence, which bends all our powers"; a credence aided by the simultaneous exercise of all the forces of the mind; as if, thanks to sustained application, the mind had learned to give its maximum of thought at the required moment; just as an athlete learns to produce at a precise moment his maximum swiftness, by systematic training, by repeated efforts in fortifying his muscles and in sharpening his vigilance, so well, that finally he acquires a per-

fect control of his movements, or rather that in finally being assured of their precision, he can dispense with all control, knowing that the particular motion which the race will demand of him will be as it were the motion of nature.

By dint of effort promptness of mind is accelerated; by dint of repetition speed is increased; by dint of deeds custom becomes nature. Little by little this fatal interval, triply denounced by Pascal, between the immediate presence of reality in the mind and the partial, successive, and tardy presence of the reality in the registering the mind makes of it—little by little this interval diminishes in proportion as the rapidity increases. It is like lips that meet, like an abyss that fills up to the brim. At the farthest limit, it is in an ineffable contact, the abolition of time, the instant seized in the instant.

Ineffable contact, for what is there found united can no longer be divided, distinguished. Reality and knowledge, first a movement of the heart and second a movement of the mind, love and the feeling that one loves, object and subject: all are made one. Between the immediate exercise of all the creative powers and the immediate exercise of all the cognitive and reflective powers, there is no longer any interval, no longer even any difference in nature. There is now only nature itself: one selfsame activity by which, in the instant we feel, we feel that we feel. Thus the instant attains its fullness.

Beyond the rational intelligence, beyond the reflective consciousness, beyond even custom, there is the feeling which "penetrates a view," [39] which "all at once sees the thing at a glance";[40] "the agility of the soul," [41] the "suppleness of thought," [42] "the spirit of acuteness," which is applied "at the same time to diverse parts," [43] which "acts in an instant and is always ready to act." [44] Here there is no longer any interval or hindrance; no longer anything except the free play of a thought which, with a beat of its wing, unites contraries: "sudden movement of the mind from the one to the other of these extremes . . . ." [45]

The human activity finds itself lifted almost to the level of a divine activity. Doubtless it is never more than "in one point like a firebrand." [46] But this point is carried with it upon a course that confounds duration; it is almost "the point moving everywhere with an infinite celerity";[47] it is almost the divine maximum and minimum of Nicholas of Cusa.

V

Those great efforts of the mind, which the soul occasionally reaches, are such as it cannot sustain. It reaches them only by a bound, not as on a throne, continuously, but for an instant only.[48]

For an instant! Shattering return to the misery of the human condition and to the tragedy of the experience of time: in the very instant man catches his prey, experience dupes him, and he knows he is duped. His prey is a shadow. In the instant he catches the instant, the instant passes, for it is instant.

Thus this continual changing, which, in the first moment of the dialectic had appeared a source of life, becomes a source of death. But is there not still the recourse of arresting the effort of mind at the precise point where it knew it had attained its goal? And since the mind had been strong enough to triumph over temporal successivity by the rapidity of its own motion, could it not triumph once more by the constancy of its attention, by its fidelity to the selfsame thought? Is there a sort of spiritual fixity, in which, in the continual contemplation of the *same thing,* one might, without succession, be maintained in an immutable time?

A "selfsame" thought; a "pure" thought; a motionless thought, or rather "the point which fills all," a thought whose motion, extending at one and the same time over the entire surface of temporal continuity, would cover it like a sheet of water: a "moment of repose," [49] as in God. The dream of the titan commences once again, only to vanish:

Pure thoughts which would render man happy, if he could always maintain them, weary and oppress him.[50]

. . . .
Attachment for one thought wearies and ruins the mind.[51]

To rest in the continuous repose of the selfsame thought is impossible:

All the misery of mankind comes from only one fact, namely their inability to keep still, in a room.[52]

. . . .
Complete rest is death.[53]

Thus there is discovered, to man's unhappiness, a new and fatal character of the moment. There is never a pure present. In the instant it exists, it already has abandoned itself; it calls, it anticipates the instant that follows it. Without repose, the present desires the future: "We never confine ourselves to the present time. We anticipate the future as too slow in coming, as it were to hasten its course." [54]

> The world is so restless that men scarcely ever think of the present life and of the moment in which they are living, but of that in which they will live. In this manner we are always living in the future, and never in the present. [55]

But where does this equivocal and heterogeneous character of the moment come from? How is it that we are in the state of living only in the future? Why "are we never directed toward things, but only toward the pursuit of things?" [56] Why "the chase" rather than "the catch"? [57]

It is because man "feels then his nothingness, his abandonment, his insufficiency, his dependence, his powerlessness, his emptiness";[58] it is because "always unhappy in all states, our desires picture to us a happy state, for they combine with the state in which we are, the pleasures of the state in which we are not." [59] Then the future appears to us, not as another "state in which we are," repeating its insufficiency and its dependence, but as the very place where there is to be found what is mysteriously lacking in our nature and what the present is destitute of. The future then becomes our *end:*

> The present is never our end, the past and the present are our means; the future alone is our end. Thus we never live, but we hope to live. [60]

Hope which comes of despair. If the future is our end, the past is not only our means, but our cause. If the sight of their "present weakness" leads men to imagine their future strength, it is by virtue of the "secret instinct that remains of the grandeur of our first nature." [61]

The present is always tragically inferior to the consciousness of a preternatural and grandiose past, whose disappearance opens an abyss from which "our nature takes its folds and its windings." It is this past that inspires in men the inexplicable horror they have of the present which wounds them. Finally, therefore, all the temporal motion of human existence is suspended from the "interior feeling of their past grandeur which remains in men" and from the "inconceivable mystery," without which our nature and temporal existence would be inconceivable, the mystery of original sin.

Thence the diversion, that is to say, in the etymological sense, the change of direction, the movement which departs from the fixed state or the direct line, the passage from one end to another end. Such was original sin—the sin by which the soul was "diverted" from its end, which is God, to search for another end—itself. But in every moment this new end proves insufficient. The soul can neither support nor find itself. It finds only "a violent and impetuous occupation which turns it aside from thinking of itself"; it cannot continue to live in the permanent consciousness of its identity; it is obliged each time to forget itself in order to reinvent itself, to reinvent itself in order to regain interest in itself, in short to effect a mocking simulacrum of continued creation, thanks to which it believes it will escape the authentication of its nothingness, and out of its nothingness refashion a reality.

From that moment on, there is in temporal motion a dual fatality that thought reproduces. We move to seize our being, we move to flee it. The agitation intensifies and at the same time confuses the consciousness of the *me*. Actually there are two *me's:* the imaginary *me* that we search for in the chase, in play, in diversion; and the real *me* that we flee from in horror. Nicole sees only the first. That is why he raises certain objections against the Pascalian conception. He sees only the "renewing" of the self by movement. But in the end Pascal sees this very renewal as a movement of flight. It is a kind of creative activity in reverse. One creates himself, finally, only to flee from himself; or rather, equally incapable of truly creating being and of "upholding the present," the perverted human thought presumes to reinvent and establish itself by an inverse movement, by a creation of nonbeing, by an indefinite multiplication of the objects of its interest, producing a perpetual stupefaction in which thought escapes from thought: then comes a successiveness more radical than that which comes from nature. Here we are no longer in the domain of a natural or ontological discontinuity; we are in the presence of a moral and truly anarchic discontinuity, in which, in opposition to providential order, there is on the part of the distracted and vitiated human will, a repeated creation of moments intrinsically different, one from another, and a continual invention of heterogeneous interests; interests the object of which is a shadow, but not so obscure as to be able totally to obliterate the preceding shadows, so that the human universe is like a chaos of heteroclite "times," of phantoms half annihilated and of phantoms which half emerge from the shadow.

It is worse than that. The blind movement by which thought is hurled forward is not only the will to flee from oneself, but the will to escape from another will than one's own. The continued creation of man hides from man the continued creation of God. Haunted by the desire to repair his deficiency of being, man is no longer astonished at *being*. In other words, the fallen being no longer wants to perceive itself as created by God, but as having to be created by itself. It rejects its true creation, it disavows the moment which God gives it. The present wounds it so deeply that it wants as quickly as possible to acquire another present as different as possible. From that instant its will is a will of discontinuation. Its time is radically discontinuous.

VI

There are three ways of believing: reason, custom, inspiration. . . . One must open his mind to proofs, confirm oneself in them through custom, yet also, offer oneself through humiliations, to the inspirations, which alone can have a true and salutary effect.[62]

The three ways are listed in a chronological and progressive order; the mind first opens itself, then confirms itself, and finally offers itself. But what Pascal says here of the experience of faith, he could say also of the experience of duration. He has constructed by proofs, by the series of acquired things, a rational time; he has experienced, by custom, by repeated movement, a natural time; finally, in the consciousness of the irremediably miserable character of the time of the fallen soul, there remains for him nothing else than humbly to offer this time, like the rest, to the divine action, to hope, by the operation of God, for the regeneration of duration.

Thus the movement of the Pascalian dialectic of duration has a perfect coherence. The works of the reason give place to an acquired spontaneity which recovers nature, and gives itself over finally, in sorrow, to the gratuitous spontaneity of the supernature in which a present God is made "palpable to the heart." In this drama everything seems to be arranged for the preparation of the moment in which suddenly grace *is*. It is the same thing as in the tragedies of Racine: a long past that a moment of supreme intensity follows and abolishes.

Instantaneous consciousness of the action of God: "The miracles point to Him and they are like a lightning-flash." [63] The time of grace, like that of the miracle, is the time of the lightning flash. It is instantaneous, "always new," and like the creative gesture which gives and re-gives us being, it incessantly gives and re-gives life to the soul: "Thou alone couldst create my soul; thou alone canst create it anew." [64]

Grace is then continued creation:

> It is a continual flow of graces that the Scripture compares to a river, and to the light which the sun continually emits from itself, and it is always new, so that if it ceased an instant to emit it, all that we have received would disappear, and we should remain in darkness.[65]

This flow renews itself in the soul

> as God continually renews their beatitude in the blessed . . . as likewise the Church holds that the Father perpetually produces the Son and maintains the eternity of this essence by an effusion of His substance, which is without interruption and without end.[66]

From then on, continuity is bound to instantaneousness: a successive duration, made up of a series of distinct graces, but continuous since its tide flows without interruption:

> Thus the continuation of the justice of the faithful is nothing else than the continuation of the infusion of grace, and not a single grace that subsists continually.[67]

Under this aspect of a heavenly effusion, grace is finally discovered to be always identical with itself: a substantial identity which, by the idea of the unity of the divine will, the human intelligence can indirectly conceive, but which the heart of man experiences directly as the unalterable freshness of grace:

> For this newness . . . is different from earthly novelties, inasmuch as worldly things, however new they may be, grow old as they endure; whilst the more this new spirit is renewed, the longer it endures.[68]

Continual flow, spirit renewed and enduring, perpetual youth, grace seems as if it were the time of God. Under the action of this divine "time," human time will change its nature profoundly.

First, like the time of grace, it will be instantaneous. No past, for that would mean to feel grace "grow old as it endures" in the same way as "earthly novelties"; no future, since that would be to suppose that present grace gives the soul the proximate power to act by itself alone in the following instant. Hence it is an error to believe that

> the just, considered in a single moment of his justification, has always the proximate power to accomplish God's commands in the next moment . . . (since such a belief) would imply that in order to act the just needs not in every moment a special succor.[69]

Grace is grace for only the single moment in which it acts. Thus, in the order of grace, "the present is the only time that is truly our own, and to be used according to the will of God." [70]

This human instantaneousness is going to entail, in its turn, a profound modification of continuity and identity. For human continuity is basically a thing of "memories." It is an "effect of memory." In this sense, there is no remembrance of grace; there is only the renewal of the interior movement it produces in us, and this renewal is not the preservation of an "idea" by memory; it is a new movement of the heart.

> Not that we may not remember and as easily retain an epistle of St. Paul as a book of Virgil; but the knowledge that we acquire in this manner, as well as its continuation, is only an effect of memory, while to understand this secret language, unknown to those who are not of Heaven, it is necessary that the same grace, which alone can give the first knowledge of it, shall continue and render it ever present by retracing it without ceasing in the hearts of the faithful. . . .[71]

In the plan of grace, as in the order of nature, there is preservation of feeling only by the renewal of feeling. But if the feeling of divine charity is, with regard to its existence just as with regard to its renewal, the product of grace, it is not less also the product of human activity. To continue, then, is to repeat the movements of the heart:

> you say that it is unnecessary to repeat these things to us, since we know them well already . . . (But) you should not fear to place again before our eyes the things which we have in our memory and which it is necessary to make enter into the heart again. . . .[72]

To make enter into the heart again, and, in order to do so, *to place again before the eyes, to repeat:* human activity, in the order of grace as in the order of nature, is basically revealed to be a matter of custom. It is an "assiduous renewal," a commencing again with the same gestures (as "in taking holy water, in having Masses said"), which brings to rebirth, which provides anew, which revivifies the freshness of the same feelings. It is to acquire a spontaneity which this time is supernatural: God is felt in the heart:

> It is necessary to make new efforts continually to acquire this continual newness of spirit, since we can only preserve the former grace by the acquisition of a new grace.[73]

Thus to the continued creation of the "interior movements of God," by grace, there corresponds the continued creation of the receptivity to grace by the creature's own movement: the repetition of words of prayer, of the signs of faith. It is by a continued creation that becomes natural and habitual, by an actuality which tends to become an aspect of his very nature, that man succeeds in spontaneously, ceaselessly willing what God wills.

Finally, to repeat a thing is to do it better and better. The Pascalian repetition, like that of Kierkegaard, is, contrary to reminiscence, turned not toward the past but toward the future. Let the movement of the heart be more and more purely of the heart! Instead of ending in a discontinuation, Pascalian repetition undertakes the continuation of the present; it constructs a true duration.

VII

This construction of duration in the order of charity is the last point of the Pascalian temporality.

> The order of charity consists of a digression at every point, which is referred to the end in order to make it always manifest.[74]

Like the diversion in the order of nature, the digression is first of all a changing of direction, not by a motion within the sphere of an order, but by the passage from one order to another. It is the entering, not into the instant of grace, but into the human time that grace gives us. Thus the time of the digression will be radically different both from the time of science and from the time of nature. First, digression is opposed to progression. In the rational order of the physical sciences, there was progress, that is to say, continuity and knowledge. Here there is neither the one nor the other. Each moment breaks away from a continuity conceived as a series of "principles and demonstrations," arranged in a line which travels from the past to the present. Each moment, in the order of charity, must be felt, not according to the knowledge of the historical development which causes it, but according to the consciousness of a "prophetic" movement, according to an *end* which is God and life eternal. But that can be accomplished only if one makes the present "diverge" in some way, only if one forces it to leave this continuity stretching backward, in order to confront the immensity ahead. The motion of the heart achieves a perpetual discontinuance of the duration-cause. And thereby a new continuity is obtained, that of an end which is "always made manifest."

But digression is nonetheless opposed to diversion. The latter was embodied in the final analysis in that movement ahead in which the soul fled its present in order to invent its future; a movement the tragic absurdity of which seemed to consist in the folly of the rejection of a certain good for a shadow.

Reversing the order of nature, digression will make appear foolish that which seemed wise, and wise that which seemed foolish. The tragedy and absurdity of the human condition is that man appears incapable of renouncing his present and choosing the future instead:

> And from all this I conclude that I ought to pass all the days of my life without thinking of what is to happen to me hereafter. . . . I want to go without forethought and without fear to try the great event, and will passively approach death, in the uncertainty of my future condition.[75]

This reversing of the human tragedy has for its origin the changing aspect of the future. For, in the order of charity, the future takes on a transcendent significance. It is no longer the future of time, it is the future of eternity. When the soul has lived the anguished experience of duration and is "frightened in seeing that each instant tears from it the enjoyment of its well-being, and that what is dearest to it slips away every moment," [76] then it becomes aware of an "unquestionable day" in which it will find itself "stripped of all things in which it had placed its hope." From this point of view, the temporal future suddenly disappears, as if crushed between the reality of the single present moment in which all time is reabsorbed, and that of the "unquestionable day" of eternity: "It is unquestionable that the time of this life is but a single moment and that the state of death is eternal, whatever may be its nature. . . ." [77]

Between the present instant and eternity, there is no longer anything. There is only *fear:*

> The first thing with which God inspires the soul that he deigns to touch truly, is a knowledge and most extraordinary insight by which the soul considers things and herself in a manner wholly new.
> This new light gives her fear. . . ." [78]

The instant, eternity: our destiny depends on the choice between these two *times.*

It is necessary to lay a wager.

Or rather, a God previously hidden, working upon us through this very fear, makes us stake our lives on eternity.

Then the soul discovers God, God present in its own fear, and its fear changes into joy.

VIII

At this extremity doubtless one should have halted, for where is there a stopping place unless it be the point where the search for God coincides with the discovery of God, where the present coincides with eternity? But Pascal wishes to follow the movement of grace over the extent of the whole field of human life:

> The least motion affects all nature. . . . Thus, in grace, by its consequences, the least action affects everything. Therefore all things are important. In each action one should consider, besides the action, our present, past and future states . . . and see the relations between all these things. [79]

Beyond grace, then, there is the reverberation of grace in the three dimensions of our duration. From the consciousness of the present, from the *fire,* from God acting in us like lightning, there bursts forth first an effusion in which are founded the immediate certainties of the mind and the feelings which express the state of a soul filled by its sole present: joy, peace. God is not the one who *has been found*. He *is* found.

But hardly have this certitude and this feeling in some way burst forth into a moment without duration, when this moment already belongs to the past. With the joy prolonged like the vibration of a string after the note has been struck, there is no longer the consciousness of the God who is *being found*, but of the God that *has been found* and known:

> Just Father, the world has not known Thee, but I have known Thee. Joy, joy, joy, joy, tears of joy.[80]

The joy continues to vibrate, but under the action of an idea which now looks backward. Beyond the past filled with God, there is discovered a past empty of God, a spectacle that changes joy into sadness: "I have separated myself from Him. *Dereliquerunt me fontem aquae vivae.*" [81]

". . . it is the joy," Pascal says elsewhere, "of having found God which is the source of the sorrow of having offended him." [82] Thence by a leap which carries it from the past into the future, the soul passes from sadness over its former sins to the dread of committing them anew and losing the succour of God: "My God, will you leave me? Let not me be eternally separated from Him." [83]

Thus the God palpable to the heart is not content with inspiring in his creature a delight which engulfs it in the sole consciousness of the divine moment. In its "double capacity of receiving and losing grace," [84] the human soul assumes a consciousness infinitely more affecting with regard to its past and especially its future. The whole future is suspended, between fear and hope, from the question of knowing whether the God who is *found* will be *preserved*. Hence the two almost identical sentences between which there is developed vertiginously the whole movement of the thought of the *Memorial*.

> He is not *found* except by the ways taught in the Gospel. . . . He is not *preserved* except by the ways taught in the Gospel. . . .[85]

From the present sanctified by grace, the just man lifts his eyes to the future, to the time when perhaps his justification *will be* preserved; to a time which is his but which does not depend upon him, wherein his already predestined lot is still to be accomplished.

Fear and hope, the two feelings which look to the future, never quit his present but create in him a consciousness intensely prospective, trembling at the time to come.

Temporal motions of an unprecedented agility unroll perpetually within him.

It is the apprehension of the divine future that surges up out of the memory of past downfalls: "The soul becomes confused for having preferred so many vanities to this divine master . . . it has recourse to His pity to arrest this anger";[86] or, by a return from the future to the present, it is the fear of the future which finds a motif of assurance in present joy, and darts anew toward the future, changed into hope: "Hope . . . is mixed with actual enjoyment as well as with fear"; [87] or farther back than the present, it is to the past—to a past whose merciful significance is revealed only to the present—that one goes to imbibe joy for the present and hope for the future: "Thou wouldst not seek Me, if thou *hadst* not found Me." [88]

Thus Pascalian joy, the Jansenist joy, is always blended; "a blending of sadness at having followed other pleasures, and of the fear of losing it"; blending of past and future, blending of times.

A time which has lost nothing of its first tragic and mysterious multiplicity, but which takes a direction, which is ordained toward an end; and which, on the other hand, finds its origin again in the double past, where God predestined the soul, where Christ thought of it in His agony. True time, lived time, is for Pascal (as it had been for Saint Augustine) the present of an immediate consciousness, in which appear, and combine themselves with it, retrospective and prospective movements which give to that present an amplitude and a boundless temporal density.

In this space-time the gaze of the heart shifts with the rapidity of a "firebrand." It sees God predestinating it in an eternal past to an eternal future; it sees Christ pouring out for it *in the past* a drop of blood which will *still be warm* at the "indubitable day" of the judgment. Finally it sees, ahead of it and behind it, in every event of its life, the secret work of grace. It reaches the center of a transcendent activity which, forming the duration of creatures, follows in them, through them, the temporal movement of their salvation.

Time is "the day of training on the earth." [89]

NOTES

1 *Pensées et Opuscules,* ed. Brunschvicg, p. 371.
2 *Ibid.,* p. 167.
3 *Ibid.,* p. 170.
4 *Ibid.*
5 *Ibid.,* p. 386.
6 *Ibid.,* p. 434.
7 *Ibid.*
8 *Ibid.*
9 *Ibid.,* p. 79.
10 *Ibid.,* p. 498.
11 *Ibid.,* p. 79.
12 *Ibid.,* p. 450.
13 *Ibid.,* p. 92.
14 *Ibid.,* p. 318.
15 *Ibid.,* p. 80.
16 *Ibid.,* p. 125.
17 *Ibid.,* p. 451.
18 *Ibid.,* p. 570.
19 *Ibid.,* p. 459.
20 *Ibid.,* p. 93.
21 *Ibid.,* p. 385.
22 *Ibid.,* p. 500.
23 *Ibid.,* p. 134.
24 *Ibid.,* p. 128.
25 *Ibid.,* p. 135.
26 *Ibid.,* p. 317.
27 *Ibid.,* p. 491.
28 *Ibid.,* p. 188.
29 *Ibid.,* p. 132.
30 *Ibid.,* p. 382.

31 *Ibid.,* p. 386.
32 *Ibid.,* p. 135.
33 *Ibid.,* p. 547.
34 *Ibid.,* p. 499.
35 *Ibid.,* p. 197.
36 *Ibid.,* p. 429.
37 *Ibid.,* p. 399.
38 *Ibid.,* p. 450.
39 *Ibid.,* p. 232.
40 *Ibid.,* p. 318.
41 *Ibid.,* p. 491.
42 *Ibid.,* p. 125.
43 *Ibid.*
44 *Ibid.,* p. 451.
45 *Ibid.,* p. 491.
46 *Ibid.*
47 *Ibid.,* p. 434.
48 *Ibid.,* p. 489.
49 *Ibid.,* p. 434.
50 *Ibid.,* p. 123.
51 *Ibid.,* p. 130.
52 *Ibid.,* p. 390.
53 *Ibid.,* p. 387.
54 *Ibid.,* p. 408.
55 *Ibid.,* p. 223.
56 *Ibid.,* p. 389.
57 *Ibid.,* p. 391.
58 *Ibid.,* p. 388.
59 *Ibid.,* p. 383.
60 *Ibid.,* p. 408.
61 *Ibid.,* p. 394.

62 *Ibid.,* p. 447.
63 *Recueil d'Utrecht.*
64 Brunschvicg, p. 59.
65 *Ibid.,* p. 219.
66 *Ibid.,* p. 92.
67 *Ibid.,* p. 93.
68 *Ibid.,* p. 216.
69 *Lettre sur la possibilité d'accomplir les commandements de Dieu.*
70 Brunschvicg, p. 223.
71 *Ibid.,* p. 92.
72 *Ibid.*
73 *Ibid.*
74 *Ibid.,* p. 461.
75 *Ibid.,* p. 419.
76 *Ibid.,* p. 197.
77 *Ibid.,* p. 424.
78 *Ibid.,* p. 196.
79 *Ibid.,* p. 560.
80 *Ibid.,* p. 142.
81 *Ibid.*
82 *Ibid.,* p. 221.
83 *Ibid.,* p. 142.
84 *Ibid.,* p. 566.
85 *Ibid.,* pp. 142–43.
86 *Ibid.,* p. 200.
87 *Ibid.,* p. 569.
88 *Ibid.,* p. 576.
89 *Ibid.,* p. 143.

MOLIERE

I

 "I find," says Molière, "that it is much easier to speak loftily of high feelings, to defy fate in verse, to reproach destiny
and abuse the gods, than it is to enter properly into the ridicule of
men. . . . It is a strange enterprise, that of making honest men
laugh." [1] An enterprise strangely difficult, in fact, for the precise
reason Molière gives us; for if, in tragedy, it is easier to speak
loftily of high feelings, that is because such feelings are at one and
the same time expressed and experienced. There is no separation
between the author and his character; not even between the character and the spectator. When the hero "defies fate," his mood and
his audacity are ours. There is established a kind of subjective
identity which makes of the author, the character, and the public
one single feeling being. The tragic moment is easy of achievement
because it is a moment lived by a unique person who expressly
manifests what everyone feels.

All else is the comic moment. The difficulty which that implies
is that it is not "given" to enter directly into the person of the
character. Far from entering into his being, it is a matter of "entering into ridicule of him." And to enter upon ridicule is precisely the
contrary of entering into a being; it is to withdraw from him: it is to
put the person in the position of an object one sees, and not a being
with whom one feels. It is to pose an object, instead of *being* a
subject.

The "strange enterprise" which permits the creation of a comic
moment is thus the very opposite of the unitive consciousness
which forms the tragic moment. It has for its province the consciousness of a disunion between the author and his public, on one
side, and the character in the play, on the other. On the one side,
us; on the other, *him.* And whatever the feelings of this *him,* they
succeed in touching only our external senses and presenting mani-

festations of a person with whom it is impossible for us to identify ourselves, but with whom it is necessary to confront ourselves. The comic character is the triple object of our attention, our judgment, and our feeling.

II

And first of all it is the object before our senses. As such, it is only what it appears to be. It is a face, a voice, some gestures. It is its actions and nothing more. That is what Molière himself declares:

> Let not anyone tell me that all the feelings which I attribute to men . . . are not felt as I describe them; for it is only in the occasion itself that it seems as if one has them or not; and not even then does anyone discover that he has them; it is just that one's actions make us suppose necessarily that one has them.[2]

These are words which can have been written only by someone who from instinct puts himself in the very situation in which the comic genius must put himself. It is not permissible in this situation to *feel oneself* experiencing the feelings of the character; one can only *attribute* them to him; and what is more, one can only attribute them to him on the *occasions* when he seems to have them; and their existence is perceived only because the character *acts* in such a way as to make one necessarily suppose that he has such feelings.

Thus the starting point of the comic art of Molière is situated in the *occasion,* in which a being is comprehended only through his actions.

And, in fact, did not the theater of Molière begin by being exactly that, and nothing more than that? A comedy of actions and gestures which did not "imply" anything else: the *Médecin volant;* the *Jalousie du Barbouillé?*

But this starting point is only a point without duration. A deed, a gesture, is still not a complete action, it is not a thing that endures, it is an instantaneous manifestation. In the comic art of Molière there is first of all the actual presence of a certain demeanor which is immediately clear to the spectator.

But in the instant in which the demeanor of the object is understood by the spectator, the latter grants to the object the particular being which the object's demeanor makes the spectator necessarily suppose it possesses. He no longer sees only the object under the sensible appearance of its deeds, but as a being distinct from himself, which consequently requires a judgment on the part of his reason, and which provokes a reaction on the part of his sensibility.

III

Every object, every being distinct from us, is judged by us. And this judgment, says Molière, is a judgment of conformity. Our "essential reason" decides whether, in the moment in which it performs its deed, the performer fails to conform himself to the rules and order connected with a truth, which has a permanent value. Thus the judgment of reason implies a curious transfiguration of the object; for if, on the one hand, its nonconformity is situated in the instant in which it arises, on the other hand it is a nonconformity only in connection with what transcends all instants. From the point of view of the eternal reason, the instantaneous manifestation of an eternal nonconformity is itself eternal. It is *sub specie aeternitatis*. What is unreasonable is eternally unreasonable.

But with the judgment of reason there is associated another judgment which is at bottom that of our sensibility. Because, says Molière:

> although Nature made us capable of knowing reason by following it, still, well aware that if there were not some visible mark attached to it which would render this knowledge easy, our frailty and our indolence would deprive us of the effect of so rare an advantage, she wished to give to reason some sort of exterior form recognizable from without. . . . Ridicule is the external and visible form which Providence has attached to all that is unreasonable. . . .[3]

This form is a "cause of joy," a "matter of pleasure." It is basically the immediate reaction of our being as we confront the deed which falls immediately under our senses. The instant it is perceived by our "essential reason" as incompatible with eternal principles, it is immediately felt by our "apparent reason" to be contrary to propriety. What is perceived as ridiculous is that which is perceived as an incongruous hiatus in the uninterrupted line of our customary experience. We say to ourselves: we are not accustomed to seeing gentlemen act like this.

This ridicule is the immediate perception of a sudden perturbation in the order of human duration. And, seen from this angle, it is no longer a permanent thing depending upon abstract reason alone. It presents itself in duration and appears there under the form of a moment which breaks up this duration. Ridicule is a moment of rupture.

IV

But rupture in the object, not in ourselves. It is because of this that the moment of rupture in Molière is so different from the moment of rupture in Corneille. Indeed, in Corneille the action by which the hero breaks with antecedent duration is a deed in which we adhere; it is an act of the will, a tragic act, to which we give consent. In Molière, on the contrary, the action by which the character is dissociated from the continuous duration of good usage is a deed by which he forces us simultaneously to dissociate ourselves from him. The instant he breaks with the order of things, we re-associate ourselves more closely with it. Thus the action of the character becomes absolutely isolated and, by consequence, inoffensive. It is a perturbation in the order which does not menace the order. The discontinuity it creates is localized in the single object which causes it. It is as if in following a well-defined path one saw someone stumble in it. Hence the simultaneous existence of two kinds of duration for the mind: the duration of the order in which one participates and which lasts; and the instant of disorder which is limited to the object and which interrupts time.

Thus the comic is the perception of an ephemeral and local fracture in the middle of a durable and normal world.

Let us imagine a seducer who one day is suddenly made to seem ridiculous: "These *first instants,*" says Molière, "are of important consideration in these matters; they produce almost the same effect as a long duration, because they always *break* the chain of passion and the course of the imagination, which ought to hold the soul attached, from beginning to end, to an amorous venture, in order for it to be successful. . . ." [4] But, in a certain sense, any relationship of a character to ourselves is a venture in seduction; any character, by the sole fact of his presence, tries to catch our sympathy. This is the case with the philosophy teacher when he praises moderation, or with Chrysale when he pretends to assert his authority. But when immediately afterward, in one of those "first instants which almost have the effect of a long duration," Chrysale yields before Philaminte, and the philosophy teacher to the impulse of anger, so in this precise moment the chain of our adherence finds itself broken. Our feeling is reversed. Suddenly we no longer feel *with* the character; we feel *against* him.

But we *feel* all the same. If ridicule is indeed, as Molière says, the coldest of all our feelings, it is none the less authentically a feeling. It is at once judgment and feeling. That is why Molière declares in the *Critique* that "the best way to judge is to abandon oneself to things." "Let us not consider in a comedy," he says, "what effect it is having on us. Let us abandon ourselves in good faith to the things that seize us by the entrails. . . ." And again: "When I see a comedy, I look only to see if things touch me."

But to abandon oneself to things, to let oneself be touched by them, is to react instantaneously in the order of sensibility. The comic genius operates, then, directly on the moment. Like the painter of frescoes, he knows his matter is "pressing" and wishes ". . . without compliance/That a painter come to terms with his impatience,/Treat it in his own way, and *with a sudden stroke/ Seize the moment* it gives into his hand."

The comic spirit is a seizure of the instantaneous.

But then the question arises, the same question as for the theater of Corneille: how shall we make a comedy out of the comic instant? How shall we prolong our laughter? How shall we give a temporal value to a character whom our rational judgment has assigned to a kind of negative eternity, and who "touches" our judgment of sensibility only in the lightning flash of the instant?

V

There are two Molierean universes: the one of customs; the other of passions. The first is a durable universe. It is the universe of persons of good sense, of spectators, of gentlemen. A sort of connivance unites them and situates them in a constant duration which is not at all on trial and which is not at all in peril.

But there is another universe, that of the passions, which in itself is not less tragic in Molière than in Racine. It is a universe in

which one is in incessant tension, in ceaseless agitation, in a perpetual renewing of the same desires. Such a mental universe inevitably recalls the conception of life held by the master of Molière,
Gassendi. For him, in reality, nothing is more radically temporal
than the life of the soul. Like the life of the body, to which it
clings up to the point of becoming indistinguishable from it, like
time itself, the life of the soul is "a flame which perpetually renews
its form." Our imagination, our sensibility, our organism, exist and
function only by virtue of a general effort of the whole being, an
incessant effort which above all is a labor of substitution and
equivalence. Compound perpetually changing, whose parts replace
themselves, the human being feels this same rhythm of reproduction repeat itself in the generation and regeneration of the passions: "There ensues afresh in the component parts a new imagination, then a new motion, and thus always more and more." [5]
And so passion can be described as "a hunger which returns, and
from moment to moment is resumed anew."

There is the same rhythm of passion in Molière. A perpetual
reincarnation of the hungry desire, the generation in a closed
cycle of passion triumphant and passion frustrated—such is the essentially repetitive process by which Molière's characters continually manifest themselves in duration. For him, too, the life of the
soul is a flame which perpetually renews its form. A precarious,
spasmodic duration, always under the menace of an instantaneous
explosion; a duration essentially tragic.

VI

But we do not experience this tragedy ourselves; we simply look at
it from the outside; and in so doing, we make it undergo a transformation so radical that it renders the character unrecognizable.
The continual generation of passion no longer seems to us like an
interior drama experienced by a subject who suffers, but more like
the comportment of an object which repeatedly strikes our attention and which, precisely by the force of this repetition, imprints
its essential characteristics more clearly upon our mind. Thus,
repetitive duration little by little takes on an exemplary value.
Each new manifestation of the same passion becomes a new example of the same passion. By the repetition, the character is little

by little dehumanized in our eyes; he becomes typical. For Molière does not take type as a starting point; he does not adopt the "realist" conception of an abstract being in more or less concrete finery. No, he comes to give his characters the value of types by the constant repetition of essential traits. The character becomes generalized as the play advances, by reason of the fact that, incessantly returning to strike our attention, the same traits are finally found to be retained at the expense of secondary traits; as if from an infinity of misers, one extracted little by little the idea of the exemplary miser, the paragon who represents them all.

An essentially nominalistic process, by which again Molière relates himself to Gassendi.

From this point of view there is no temporal movement in the plays of Molière. It is the same repetitive duration as in the drama of passion from which it eliminates the tragic. But in eliminating the tragic it eliminates movement also. It becomes a mere static repetition in which there is progress only in the pattern of the character and in the estimate we form of him. An historical progress, which has a place only in the order of knowledge, of abstraction even. In proportion as the character becomes more typical, he passes little by little from the actual to the absolute. He becomes the eternal example of an eternal unreasonableness.

Thus, if the resemblance, if the perceptible repetition were not there to reawaken within us in each instant the feeling of ridicule which those so decisive "first instants" had brought to birth there, the character would become completely detached from all temporality and all reality and would run the risk of falling into a schematic intemporality. There exists in this regard a veritably Proustian text of Molière's which marvelously lights up the subtle play of the "intermittences" of ridicule and of the "irregular progresses" of the comic. In the *Lettre de l'Imposteur,* speaking of Panulphe, that is to say of Tartuffe, he says this:

> The excessive ridicule of the manners of Panulphe makes it certain that every time they are presented to the spectator on some other occasion they will assuredly seem to him ridiculous. . . . The soul, naturally avid of joy, will necessarily be delighted at the first sight of things that it once conceived as extremely ridiculous, and *will renew in itself the idea of the very lively pleasure it tasted that first time.*

Thus each time we notice a new comic manifestation of character, "we shall be first of all struck by the memory of that first time," and this memory, mingling itself with the present occasion, will "fuse the two occasions into one."

Thus to the objective repetition of the course of passion there is joined the subjective repetition of the feeling it provokes in us. The character repeats himself, and we begin to laugh again, and in beginning to laugh again we accord to him once more the freshness of actuality. The comic art of Molière is eternal in two ways: first in the manifestation of a reason, which makes an eternally valid judgment upon human deportment; and then in that of the sensibility, which never ceases to make us feel this deportment eternally present and living.

NOTES

1 *Critique de l'Ecole des Femmes.*
2 In the *Lettre sur la comédie de l'Imposteur.* It is one of the most remarkable theoretical and critical essays of the seventeenth century; and if it was not written by Molière himself, it must have been written by someone of his circle, by dictation, or under his immediate inspiration. There is no document that better illuminates Molière's thought.
3 *Lettre sur l'Imposteur.*
4 *Ibid.*
5 Bernier, *Abrégé de la philosophie de Gassendi,* VI, 387.

✳

✳

✳ CORNEILLE

I

✳   "It is a great attraction," says Corneille in one of his first
     poems, "to be insusceptible to alarm, to neither hope nor
fear anything . . . to be master of one's thoughts." [1] Thus the
poet distinguishes between two states, the one in which one is
master of his thoughts, and the other in which thoughts are the
masters of the mind. The first is a state of freedom, the second of
constraint:

> With one glance the adorable constraint of her eyes
> Renews all my chains, tightens all my bonds
> And blinds my reason by so sweet a charm
> That I seek my sickness and flee my cure. [2]

Thus at the age of passion Corneille discovers in it an adorable
and mortal enemy. The experience of love is that of the loss of
mastery of himself. One feels constrained to hope, constrained to
fear, constrained to pass and repass back and forth between the
states of search and flight:

> Her eye acts upon me with a strength so great
> As suddenly to revive my dead hope,
> Combats the grief of my angry heart
> And sustains my love against her cruelty. [3]

The life of the lover is slavery. It is made up of confused moments in which dead hopes are revived, in which emotions of the
past begin once more to look toward the future. The human being
is at the mercy of the waves of duration, a troubled and imperious
duration which hurls him ahead and then backwards, in which
causes and effects succeed each other, creating every time a *re-
sultant me,* an *occasioned me.* It is produced out of the past; it is
driven toward the future; for it, the present is a battleground on
which opposing tendencies confront each other; a fragile balance

whose equilibrium is continually broken by the successive impulses of the life of the heart:

> Secret tyrants of my thought,
> Regard, love, whose laws
> By their just and troublesome counterpoise
> Hold my mind always balanced;
> How mighty at self-destruction
> Are your opposing motions,
> Your shafts, one shattered by the other! [4]

The time of love is a time of constraint and strife.

The revolt of Corneille against this love-slavery is indicated in *Clitandre:* "Love has died away and its smothered fires/Will impose no more their infamous constraints." But it is still indicated there only under the form of a love turned inside out, a love-hate.

"There is no longer anything in me that does not resent her life, Out, on, then . . . ." [5] In this flashing brevity, in which for the first time Corneille finds his true accent, the whole weight of the expression bears upon a present action. Doubtless it is still not at all a question here of a liberation from the reign of the affective life, since the hero gives himself up to his hate; but it is certainly a question of a being who suddenly escapes from the tyranny of successiveness in order to establish himself firmly within the circumference of the decisive moment. To passionate love, an insidious slavery in which the being finds himself swinging to and fro without respite from one pole of duration to the other, there succeeds a voluntary passion in which one musters one's will, ready for immediate action: "On, then!"

In the plays that are to follow, Corneille will only exploit and extend this discovery. Behind love there will appear more and more powerfully the role of the will. Love will become a lightning-flash love, a love without "dead hopes," and without "opposing motions," in which the human being gives himself over to the actual reality in one stroke:

> I had not taken counsel to give you my soul;
> Your very first aspect kindled my flame,
> And I felt my heart, by a secret power,
> As prompt to burn as my eyes to behold you. [6]

It is in the absence of, the obliviousness to, all "counsel"; it is in the present "gift" of all the being to the present object of its

will that Corneille's hero will find his own reality. The drama of
Corneille is to be that: a drama in which, upsetting a precarious
equilibrium of tendencies, the naked will will perform its action in a
precise instant.

II

What distinguishes Corneille's hero is the instantaneous identification of the being and the will: "Behold what I am and what I
wish to be. . . ." [7]

For whoever separates his being and his will separates himself
from reality, replaces his will with a desire, his *being* with an *appearance,* and is only a "liar":

> He wanted to appear
> Not as he was but as he wished to be.[8]

But whoever, on the contrary, situates his being and his will at the
same point and in the same moment, attains to an absolute reality
which is his own. He wills, and in willing what he wills he wills to
be what he is. Will posits being. Whatever the particular object of
this will, it is affirmed as the total expression of the being of him
who wills. I want to be he who wants this or that: and thus I possess
myself: "I am master of myself as of the universe,/I am it, I wish
to be it. . . ." [9]

Thus the very essence of the Cornelian being is implied in its
will, and so forcefully that it seems in the very act of its will to be
born into life finished and achieved. More than that, in this instantaneous act the Cornelian character is born also in its own eyes,
and is presented as a spectacle to itself and to the world. For the
act of will is not content simply to posit being; it is also knowledge
of being:

> I know what I am. . . .[10]
> I see what I am. . . .[11]

A knowledge of a special nature, more voluntary than intellectual, which manifests itself clearly under the form of an action
and a movement; as if the being drew his deed from the very
depths of himself in order to present it to the light of day; or as if it
were not enough for him to make the light fall on himself and he

had to take more positive action, such as the gesture by which one offers oneself to view: "Let us present ourselves to the eyes of men,/Brave the idolatry, and *show who we are.*" [12]

To show who one is: "Behold all my soul." [13] Voluntary knowledge is more than mere knowledge. It does not simply make it possible to know; it offers and it shows. Its significance resides in the perfect identity between the being who is shown and the being who shows; an identity to which it is impossible to attain, unless the two terms that comprise it be found enveloped in the same present by the act of will. That is why "he who follows his burning impatience and his vain desires," [14] and who, in following them, finds himself always tending toward the future is never able to attain to the whole will nor to the true knowledge of himself: "He neither knows what he wants, nor what he is." [15]

That is why, again, nothing is more different from this knowledge than the discursive steps which have preceded the instant which it fills; steps which, far from revealing the being, only revealed the alternatives through which his thoughts and feelings had to pass. And nothing could less resemble Cartesian knowledge, for it is not at all a question here of impersonal evidence, but the most personal that could be: "I know what I am and what I owe to myself. . . ." [16] It is simply that the act of will, whatever it be, posits both being and consciousness of being. A consciousness which, on the other hand, differs no less radically from the feeling of existence in Malebranche or Rousseau, for it is not at all the passive awareness of a being reduced to feeling itself to be alive, but the very active feeling of a being who, in willing to be what he is, takes himself and presents himself for what he wants to be and is. And so the act by which the will made its choice carries with it at the same time the vastest and the most precise choice: the choice of the entire being, as it is in the single instant of choice:

> Worthy efficacy of kings . . .
> Shine forth, it is time and this is your hour,
> Let us both show ourselves, no longer subjects
> But such as I am and such as you are.[17]

The instant in which one shows himself forth is thus the instant in which one accepts himself. In the instant in which one manifests himself, one recognizes as himself the being who is manifested. And the expression of this equivalence is contentment. Even in the most tragic instant, even in the midst of mortal dangers, the Cornelian character can find thus a mysterious happiness. Whatever he may have lost, he has lost nothing since he possesses himself; and that possession suffices him: "In so great a misfortune, what remains to you?—Myself,/Myself, I say, and it is enough." [18]

What does it matter then that this possession of oneself is limited in the instant, since this instant is one in which the human being attains his fullness and enjoys his sufficiency? The glory, essential object of the heroes of Corneille, is only subsidiarily the trumpet peal of their renown; before everything else it is an esteeming of the self by the self, the awareness of being glorious: "Everything about them is illustrious when they vouchsafe to believe in themselves." [19]

When the human being has realized the purpose of his life, when he no longer wants to be anything else than what he is, when he has become aware that his present existence and his whole self are the perfect expression of his will, then this very second in which he achieves faith in himself is the culminating point of his life; there is nothing beyond: "My glory cannot increase or be denied,/Today it exceeds that of the greatest man." [20]

There is nothing beyond this, and nothing to desire beyond it:

> Let us achieve this marriage, if it can be achieved;
> If it last only a day, its glory is matchless,
> To be for even a day the ruler of the world.[21]

Hence, such an instant can be the *final* instant, the instant of death:

> And since to enjoy so glorious a state
> I have only this moment before my death,
> I shall make it so lofty and enviable
> That it shall equal the most dazzling life.[22]

> And his last breath is a breath of glory
> Which, achieving the fate of a great soul,
> Reveals all of Pompey.[23]

III

Thus from *Le Cid* until his death Corneille will pursue in his plays a more and more superhuman goal. For it is no longer a matter for him now of demonstrating the will as a force that intervenes in the balance and conflict of tendencies only to superadd itself to them and impose a different equilibrium. This time it is a question of seizing the will in the instantaneous act by which, in the midst of mechanical causes, at the heart of the concatenation of events, it affirms itself under the unique aspect which, essential and unassimilable, is its very own, and causes a disrupting moment to burst forth in the course of time. On the one hand it is a refusal to adhere, by which the human being breaks, it may be, with himself and his former line of conduct, or with his background and the line it indicates he should follow; or again, with the destiny decreed for him from on high by the gods. But it is also, on the other hand, a moment of liberation. Man suddenly appears to be no longer united to a determining past, the antecedent cause of his being, but to a voluntary movement which is creator of being, *causa sui,* and from which there is no going back. The older he gets, the more Corneille accentuates this inclination. Whereas in his great tragedies he portrays characters for whom the voluntary act has, if not as its cause at least as its support, a permanent disposition toward virtue, already in *Rodogune* he has devised a monstrous character who draws her strength solely from a "greatness of soul which has something so lofty about it that, whereas we detest her actions, at the same time we admire the source from which they emanate." Or, instead of presenting us as in *Le Cid* with the continuator of a tradition and the defender of an ancestral honor, he gives us in *Don Sanche* a personage without any past, without ancestors and without race, whose greatness of soul is faithful solely to the present, acting self: "Let him boast who will of the name of his ancestors,/For myself, I wish to be only myself at all times." [24]

And if finally *Horace* was the play of local patriotism whose traditions laid down the hero's conduct and determined his constancy, *Sertorius* reduces patriotism to an abstract idea of inflexible liberty which is identified with the self who conceives it: "Rome is no longer in Rome, it is everywhere I am." [25]

Freed by his action, therefore, from the framework of habits which seemed to be the formal cause of his will, the Cornelian being finds himself more and more isolated in his actuality. The action by which he chooses to be what he is makes of him a new being who belies his former existence. What connection is there between the instant of the clemency of Auguste and the past of vengeance and defiance which his clemency abolishes? What connection is there between Pauline "disabused," and Pauline abused? What link is to be found between the constancy of the hate which had been Émilie's life ("I am always myself, and my heart has never changed") and that changed heart which she acquires in a moment so brief that it still holds within it the last beating of the heart it replaced: "I thought it immortal, but my hate is going to die:/It is dead. . . ." [26] By the very act of choice which introduces an essentially different duration into the midst of the causal duration, Corneille makes it burst. It vanishes at the touch of the voluntary moment. Corneille's hero becomes a being without a past.

But he is also without a future. He is without a future because he does not want a future. He could not desire a future without wanting himself to be something different from what he is, that is to say from what he wants. He has neither desire nor hope, for that would be to want to be what he is not, and not to will to be what he wishes: "I cease to hope and begin to live. . . ." [27] But, also, by ceasing to hope he *finishes* with living. Both the effect and the cause of his act are immediately present, and the ulterior consequences of that act exist neither for us who are spellbound before greatness nor for the hero who is conscious of it and satisfied with it.

Instantaneous cause of itself, and thereby freed of the past of efficient causes, the Cornelian character thus becomes in the same instant its own end, and frees itself of the future of final causes, and also, by the same token, it frees itself of having an object in existence:

> When two occasions press hard upon great courage,
> Honor avidly incites it to engage *the nearest one*
> Preferring to deal, without inconstancy,
> With *the immediate thing,* rather than what awaits it.[28]

The object of action becomes a simple pretext, an *occasion*. In a word, everything is reduced to a single act, the object of which is indifferent or absorbed by the self: "I take for sole object the satisfying of my glory." [29]

Indifferent to any other object than a glory that is instantaneously satisfied, realizing itself in a present without duration, Corneille's hero becomes a kind of God. For God is he

> Who never knows diversity of time
> Whose voice is one with its effect,
> In whom to speak and do are not two instants.[30]

God is a Cornelian hero: "God wills it, enough, the miracle is done." [31]

The hero enjoys the same "sufficiency." In the instant in which his will is asserted it obtains its end; by the same token and in the very same instant it satisfies itself and completes a cycle of energy which began in the self and is achieved in the self, without ever having left the self: a small eternity which exactly reproduces the essential traits of the divine eternity.

But unlike the divine eternity, the eternity of the human act exists on the edge of a void. For if the self depends for its existence on the act by which it *wills,* hardly has this act been consummated —and it is consummated as soon as begun—when the self no longer has a reason for being. In the very second in which it is created, the self has to return to nothingness. Then the question arises: How did Corneille save his characters from nothingness? How did he give them dramatic duration?

IV

The first kind of duration one distinguishes in the drama of Corneille is that objective duration which is common to all stories. It is made by the unfolding of an action which Corneille likes to render luxuriant and charged with events. What characterizes it is the speed with which it makes events succeed one another, and the impatience with which the hero views them, as if he wished to rush them along their course, in order the sooner to reach the decisive moment:

> And in order to progress more and more
> All place, all time is fitted to his *impatience.*[32]

> Let us lose no more time, the sacrifice is *ready,*
> We must hasten to keep the interest of the true God.[33]

> . . . There is no need to delay any longer,
> One is always *ready* when one has courage.[34]

Thus all this duration exists only as a continual *preparation* for those moments in which each time it finds completion: "Then keep thy soul *forever ready*/For every test, for every struggle . . . ." [35] The drama of Corneille is made up of moments and of the preparation for these moments. A preparation which includes first the exterior circumstances, then their complex effect upon the soul (a conflict of passions or of virtues), and finally the deliberation immediately preliminary to the moment in which the choice is made and which the act of will transcends; which forms, in short, a certain temporal substance, and however rapid its *tempo* (Corneille has a tendency to go faster and faster), it is nonetheless an authentic duration comprising successiveness, discursiveness, irreversibility, and even a sort of human continuity, since the characters live and participate in its flow. But what distinguishes this duration from all other durations and what robs it of almost all significance is the fact that it is never anything more than an antecedent duration. It paves the way for the present, but it does not produce or create it. Between its own nature and that of the moment of the exercise of the will, there is, as we have seen, nothing at all in common. The instant in which the will becomes act transcends everything that has preceded it; from that point on, the being made manifest in this moment seems separated by an abyss from everything it has been in all preceding moments.

To the difficulty of joining the instantaneous self to the "historical" self, there is added still another difficulty. How, actually, can the successive instantaneous selves be joined together? For unless one is to continue to recreate incessantly a play of the type of *Rodogune, Pertharite,* or *Oedipe,* in which the whole plot consists of a long historical preparation for the final act of will, one has to resign oneself to conceive a kind of action in which, throughout the length of the play and in the hiatuses of historical duration, there are distributed a greater or lesser number of nonhistorical moments in which the hero asserts and completes himself. But are this affirmation and completion an affirmation and completion of the same "self"? Historically speaking, one would have to say yes. But the difficulty resides precisely in the fact that the moment in which the self is transcended is not an historical moment but an antihistorical moment. The being transcends itself in it only because it transcends, with all its past, the very moments of the past which had been for it transcendent moments when they were present moments. Its past efficacy is not at all the gage of its actual efficacy: the latter is the *causa sui*. In the order of the life of the will there is no temporal causality. In every moment the being must begin over again and will itself anew.

In Corneille, unity of being does not constitute continuity of being; on the contrary, it seems to undo continuity and to make it unrealizable.

Nevertheless no one affirms his identity more strongly than the Cornelian character: "I am what I was . . . ." [36] "The same ardor consumes me . . . ." [37]

The reason is that the incessant tension in which the Cornelian character lives establishes a primary means of identity between his successive states. If he does not always exert his will, at least he is always impatient to exert it: "Is it not time to show who we are?" [38]

This continuity of ardor is doubtless not at all the continuity of self, nor does it make the latter any easier to establish. But at the very least it does constitute a continuity of tone, a continuity of style, which immerses in the same verbal flux both the historical being and the instantaneous selves.

Beyond this primary means of continuity there is a second one infinitely more significant. When the Cornelian character declares: "I am always the same," [39] he does not mean that he has simply stayed the same, and thus that his will is exerted upon a sort of permanent residue which it cannot modify. That would be to admit a distinction between being and will and would destroy at one stroke the all-powerfulness of the latter. No, if the Cornelian hero proclaims himself to be always the same, it is because he *accepts* and *chooses* not to be anything other than what he has been. His absolute will makes of his present being, in the present act not the *necessary* continuation of the past being, but the *free* continuation of this being, because he is free to decide whether he will recognize his past as a kind of anterior prolongation of his actual being.

Thus, with Corneille, the continuity of the self rests entirely upon a choice of the will. I am identical to myself only because I wish to be identical to myself. And I continue to be identical only because I continue to affirm my identity. This "possession of himself" which the Cornelian hero "preserves so perfectly among so many intrigues in which he seems confounded," [40] is due first to the fact that ". . . his heart is kept at the pitch he desires,/Always free . . ." [41] and finally to the fact that this liberty is manifested in a repeated act of ratification of self: "Thus, unshaken, he is always the same/In the great diversity of many events"; [42] continued creation of the self by the self, reiterated action by which the character at one and the same time invents and finds himself again. For, almost invariably, he chooses to find himself again in his past. And he does so because, when all the superfluity of being is eliminated, he finds nothing to choose except the essential, that is to say the voluntary substratum, the affirmation of self-possession. But through this affirmation and this repetition, which are the affirmation and repetition of the being in action, there is now discovered a reality which is their common ground. The continuity of my self depends upon a choice that I make by reason of the fact that I am free to make it. Behind my will in act is my potential will.

In his later pieces, more and more fatigued by perpetually maintaining the heroic continuity of being, Corneille, returning moreover to a theme he had touched lightly upon in his youth, [43] sought to express, beyond the instant and act of will, in an anteriority which is not of time but of nature, the Molinist notion of a liberty on the border of becoming will, on the point of being transformed into action. The being he wished to portray was no longer a man of action, but a being that was infinitely disengaged, infinitely ready for any action, "And always in a state of readiness." [44]

Empty of all individuality, even of all instantaneity, the Cornelian hero ends by becoming the symbol of free will or of the liberty of indifference: a nontemporal .being, existing only in the virtuality of his will and in the indefinite possibility of manifesting himself or not in as many moments as he wishes; free to consent or not to consent to being:

But I will that such a time should depend on me. [45]

NOTES

[1] *Oeuvres*, ed. Marty-Laveaux, X, 26.
[2] *Mélite*, Act I, scene 1.
[3] *Ibid.*
[4] *La Veuve*, Act II, scene 1.
[5] *Clitandre*, Act IV, scene 2.
[6] *La galerie du Palais*, Act II, scene 1.
[7] *Théodore*, Act II, scene 2; *Héraclius*, Act I, scene 2; *Pertharite*, Act I, scene 1; *Sophonisbe*, Act II, scene 4. Cf. also *Attila*, Act II, scene 6.
[8] *Le Menteur*, Act III, scene 3.

9 *Cinna*, Act. V, scene 3.

10 *Mort de Pompée*, Act IV, scene 3; *Don Sanche*, Act I, scene 1; *Sophonisbe*, Act III, scene 5.

11 *Imitation*, Book III, chap. 8.

12 *Polyeucte*, Act II, scene 6.

13 *Tite*, Act I, scene 2.

14 *Imitation*, Book II, chap. 3.

15 *Ibid*.

16 *Don Sanche*, Act I, scene 1.

17 *Rodogune*, Act II, scene 1.

18 *Médée*, Act I, scene 5.

19 *Mort de Pompée*, Act II, scene 1.

20 *Tite*, Act V, scene 5.

21 *Mort de Pompée*, Act II, scene 1.

22 *Héraclius*, Act III, scene 2.

23 *Mort de Pompée*, Act II, scene 2.

24 *Don Sanche*, Act I, scene 3.

25 *Sertorius*, Act III, scene 1.

26 *Cinna*, Act V, scene 3.

27 *La place Royale*, Act V, scene 8.

28 *Don Sanche*, Act II, scene 4.

29 *Sophonisbe*, Act III, scene 5.

30 *Imitation*, Book I, chap. 25.

31 *Oeuvres*, IX, 25.

32 *Imitation*, Book II, chap. 1.

33 *Polyeucte*, Act II, scene 6.

34 *Le Cid*, Act IV, scene 5.

35 *Imitation*, Book III, chap. 19.

36 *Cinna*, Act I, scene 2.

37 *Polyeucte*, Act I, scene 1.

38 *Héraclius*, Act II, scene 2.

39 As Emilie and Cinna do successively in the same scene (Act III, scene 4).

40 *La place Royale*, dedication.

41 *La Veuve*, Act I, scene 3.

42 *Imitation*, Book III, chap. 33.

43 Cf. *La place Royale*.

44 Cf. *La place Royale*, Act I, scene 4.

45 *Suréna*, Act V, scene 1.

I

＊ Racine's theater opens with *La Thébaide*. But in the very
first lines of it there is posed so urgent and so fundamental
a problem that the entire Racinian theater will do nothing more
than restate the question:

> O thou, Sun, thou that restorest light to the world,
> Why hast thou not abandoned it in the depths of night? [1]

It is the problem of existence, but posed with reference to the
continuation of being, and not directly to its origin. The double
reality which inbreathes and encloses these lines, the first in which
the authentic Racinian accent vibrates, is that of a sun which restores light to the world, and of a world that has not deserved that
light be returned to it. Why does the creative power consent to
begin over again a work which has been confirmed to be defective
and monstrous? Why does it consent to prolong for a single present day the series of past days which, of themselves, fell into "the
depths of night"? The more inexplicable a problem, for the creation of a new day does not simply imply, like that of the first day,
the creation of a being still pure and worthy of God; but this time
the invention of a being who has already had an existence and who,
by reason of this past existence, far from meriting a present existence, ought to be "abandoned to the night." Unless one can imagine
this absurdity: the perpetual creation of a world radically new
every time, and obliterated in each instant, in order to be "brought
back" in the following instant to its first virginity; once evil has
been acquired, and the worthlessness of the creature recognized,
there is nothing at all for God to do except stop creating or create
something that will be continuous, and which will continue precisely
a past into which evil has been introduced. Before the fault and

before the fall, God only continued to bring back to the light of day a being who was always the same, always equally worthy of the "light," and who therefore had no past. Now, on the contrary, the continued creation of the world implies the creation of a being which is prolonged backward, whose existence consists not only in living, but in having lived, and lived badly.

Such is the characteristic aspect which the problem of existence takes for Racine. Like Descartes and like the Jansenists, he poses in principle the *independence* of the parts of a duration in which God is obliged every day to bring back light to the world, instead of leaving the world to darkness; but on the other hand, he nonetheless feels the absolute *dependence* of each of the new moments upon a past out of which God is obliged to create them, to *co-create* them; so that in the Racinian, as in the Bergsonian universe, what one calls the present is not solely pure and ceaseless invention, but a preservation of the past and a continuation of the past into the present.

It is a continuation, however, which, for Racine, far from having as with Bergson the value of a progress and a promise, has on the contrary the most tragic significance; for it permits of no hope, except the hope that one day instead of being brought back to the light of day, we shall be abandoned to night and to nothingness. Even God is unable to make the past cease to exist and, therefore, also to make evil cease to continue and repeat itself; not even God can make hatreds cease to *persist* and prolong themselves from times elapsed to times not yet accomplished: "Sad and fatal effect of an incestuous blood," [2] the whole Racinian drama is presented as the intrusion of a fatal past, of a determining past, of a past of efficient cause, into a present that seeks desperately to become independent of it.

II

What is the subject of *La Thébaide?* It is the story of a man who believes that he can free himself from the past. All the other characters are supremely conscious of continuing in their present a past which is consummated in their hatreds or their present terrors. What they are is made clear only by what they themselves or their

fathers have been: "What, must I explain my thoughts any further?/One can discern them in the things of the past." [3] Creon alone
dreams of a state in which, in the absolute actuality conferred
by omnipotence, it would be possible to free oneself at one stroke
from this fatal fidelity; of a state in which "A soul possessed of
the pleasure of reigning,/Turns all his ideas away from time
past"; [4] royal state which would be that of a being capable of having no remorse, no memories, no past; capable also of doing without
a destiny; a state in which one could abandon himself to those
transports of joy which the feeling of living in a naked present
gives, cleansed of all blemish and so intensely real that past events
would leave no more trace than a dream:

> Then speak to me only of subjects of joy,
> Allow me to leave myself only a prey to my transports;
> And, without ever reminding me of the shadows of hells,
> Tell me all that I gain, and not what I lose . . .
> All that is past is only a dream to me now,
> I was father and subject, I am lover and king.[5]

Strange transport which expresses a feeling believed to be joy, but
which is unconscious despair; for the very motion by which the
man-living-in-the-present had wished, so to speak, to fabricate himself and to consecrate his independence, his radical actuality, entails and forthwith completes his frightful, direct dependence upon
the man he has been from his birth, the man he can never cease to
be until death: "I am the last blood of the unhappy Laius." [6]

The Racinian tragedy is the impossibility of limiting oneself to
the present moment. Fidelity to hatred, as in *La Thébaide;*
fidelity to love, as in *Andromaque;* fidelity to custom, as in
Bérénice; fidelity to blood, as in *Phèdre*—the subject of almost
every tragedy of Racine consists in the repetition and the ineluctable continuation of the past into the present:

> He disguises himself in vain; I read upon his face—
> The sad and savage humor of the proud Domitian race.[7]

> You belie not at all a deadly race,
> Truly you are the blood of Atreus and Thyeste.[8]

> Faithful to the blood of Achab. . . .[9]

III

Andromaque is, above all, the drama of beginning anew. Here passion is a "trail that one recognizes," [10] a "wound that one reopens"; [11] its objects are certain faces "which one remembers," [12] a vanished being which in a living being one begins again ceasely to love: "It is Hector. Behold his eyes, his mouth . . . ." [13]

Furthermore, *Andromaque* is a drama whose beings exist only insofar as they "represent" [14] certain beings who exist no longer but who, out of the depths of their past, must come "to be found again," [15] "to revive" [16] and be "recognized" [17] in living beings. And if, like Creon in *La Thébaide,* Pyrrhus is of all the characters in *Andromaque* the most significant, it is because he is the living proof that it is impossible to escape from this *representation* of the past in the present, and that it is no less vain to want to seize in passion an instant that is without faith and without memories. For one would not know how to resist the double weight of an opinion and a conscience that see in the being that one is, only the prisoner and the executor of the past:

> Ah! I recognize you . . .
> It is no longer the play of a servile flame.
> It is Pyrrhus, the son and the rival of Achilles
> Who triumphs a second time over Troy.[18]

Thus the whole drama is only an immense and infinitely complex repetition of a more ancient drama. It is a drama played for the second time—a gigantic phenomenon of memory, in which not only feelings but existences are resuscitated. No work has expressed more completely the repetitive power of duration.

IV

Lengthening backward of the Racinian tragedy; also prolongation forward; immense spaces of duration between which it finds itself pressed. For if Racine likes to set his characters in faraway times, and against a remote background, it is doubtless first because "the respect the audience has for heroes grows in proportion the farther away they are withdrawn from us"; [19] but it is also because this very withdrawal, and the respect it inspires, have the effect of placing events and personages in a *historical* perspective and of preventing us from seeing in the action the bare, brutal image of the immediate.

Andromaque and *Iphigénie* both evoke the historic totality of an epoch, all the durational length of a great epic subject, and in both plays the subject is the same; but in the one it is situated just before the historic action commences, while in the other just after it ends. *Andromaque* begins where the *Iliad* finishes: "Do you no longer remember, my lord, what Hector was?/Our enfeebled people remember him still." [20] *Iphigénie* takes place just before the *Iliad* begins: "And one day my death, the source of your glory,/Shall start the recital of so beautiful a story." [21]

Opening or closing a recital, the moment of action thus almost entirely loses its proper value, its quality of the single "present" moment, its privilege of being the sole real part of moment. Its "reality" is not rich enough in itself to triumph over a past and over a future, unreal doubtless, but arrayed in all the opulence of history and poetry. And so the Racinian moment becomes the slave of an anterior or posterior duration which inspires it and sets its extremity. Extreme point of a past that is ending, of a future, of a monster "being born," it is as though it were stifled between two walls of events which draw together, which already touch each other. It hasn't the time to be time.

The Racinian moment is a point, but in the sense in which one says: It is here, at this point, that the drama took place. Point of fatal encounter between the line drawn from the past and the line drawn from the future—point where efficient cause and final cause collide and are confounded.

v

Situated at a point without duration, possessed by actual action, Racine's characters nevertheless seem to be endowed with the power of looking at themselves, as it were, historically, as if they were not only themselves but also our contemporaries; they are the prey of the immediate, but also they contemplate at the same time both the causes and the remote conclusion of the drama in which they are engaged. They view themselves *in the future* as we view them *in the past:*

> Then I had traversed so many seas, so many States,
> And come so far only to prepare his death? [22]

> I foresee that thy blows shall fall upon even thy mother.[23]

> . . . I foresee already everything necessary to foresee.
> My only hope is my despair.[24]

The Racinian character is like Calchas: "He knows all that was and all that still must be." [25]

His foresight does not differ at all from his memory. It is of the same nature. It holds, in Racine, to a conception of life which, although profoundly different from that of the Greeks, is no less fatalistic: a fatality no longer external, but internal, which situates the determining forces in the interior of the soul. They are in the being, they are of the being, and if at the same time they are hostile and deadly to the being, they are nonetheless a source of vital energy from which there springs what the being is in each one of its moments. Prescience, as well as memory, consists only in referring to this source, the creative influx of which may vary in intensity but never in its nature. Monster coming to birth or monster being completed; Nero in the past or in the future confirms Nero.

It is foreknowledge which informs the being not only of his actions but of the particular nuance of emotion which the future reserves for him. Racinian characters are not content to suffer from their present ills; they experience suffering in the future: "In a month, in a year, how shall we suffer?" [26] Eternal future, "frightful, inexhaustible cup" [27] from which the damned in the Racinian world know they will continue to imbibe in the future the bitter knowledge of their past:

> Thus with a plaintive voice
> Will express its remorse
> The tardy penitence
> Of the inconsolable dead.[28]

The extremity of emotion to which they thus attain, has for its complement the most poignant intensity of poetry: as if, in uniting certain states of mind which the order of the times separates, in distributing their passions over the vastest space of duration, they invested them with an absolute significance, no longer that of a fault or an actual misfortune, but of a despair that gives its name to all existence:

One will know the roads by which I conducted him.[29]

I shall turn back, alone and desperate,
I shall see the roads all perfumed still
With the flowers they had sown beneath her footsteps.[30]

VI

The *feeling of self* in the Racinian being: it is that of a man who falls over a precipice, is terrified, and yet looks at himself in a detached and extraordinarily lucid fashion, as if his future death were already accomplished, and he saw himself *in the past*.

The Racinian tragedy is an action *in the past*. We see it less in its actuality, in its immediacy, in the palpable shock of it, than in the reflective thought and in the affective echo it produces afterward, mediately and almost indirectly, in its victims and spectators. At the moment in which we have become conscious of it, it has already taken place. It fulminates, like the lightning one recognizes only when it is gone and has become part of the past. In that respect, the tragedy of Racine differs from all other tragedy, which by its nature renders the action in a time that is progressive, that is in the course of being. Here, it is a time realized that engages us, and the action which confronts us, being in each of its consecutive parts an action which has just taken place and which in each instant is only just past, it seems that we are witnessing the process by which things in the last analysis become "fatal" in our eyes and force us to recognize that indeed they could not have happened otherwise. The Racinian fatality is characterized by this *retardation* of thought upon action, which paints the latter the color of unchangeable lead, and which brings it about that each past contingency, even if it be only one second past, becomes as necessary as the most general law. The Racinian fatality is the "What have I said!" of Phèdre. It is the fatality of irreversibility.

VII

I know my frenzies, I recall them all.[31]

There is no light more intense or more cruel than that projected by the self-awareness of Racinian characters. The reflective consciousness which leads them to the discovery of their own being, reveals to them not only the kind of being they are, but the kind of continuity or progression in time which has more and more made them become what they are. The particular lucidity they bring to this knowledge reaches as far as their past extends. It makes rise up in their course and development all the thoughts and actions which have issued from their very depths to bring them to the extreme situation into which they are thrown and of which they become aware. It even goes back further and seems to search the original shadows for a primary principle, a prenatal tendency, which, from before their existence, contained its germ and waited to enfold it in frenzies and passions. Thus the tragic consciousness is here found invested with the power of contemplating itself through the whole field of its duration: it everywhere recognizes itself as monstrously similar.

But it happens also, in Racinian humanity, that a human being finds himself provisionally saved from this fatal knowledge. He is then mysteriously allowed to remain ignorant of what he is and what he has been. He lives for a time in a present which has yet no past. And because of this fact, neither has it yet any destiny; for what is truly fatal for a human being is the clear-sightedness by which, in discovering what he has been, he finds out what he is going to be; ready to consummate his ruin and his doom:

> I ignore who I am; and to crown the horror,
> A dreadful oracle binds me to my error,
> And when I search for the blood that brought me to birth,
> I am told that without perishing I cannot know myself.[32]

Or again it may happen in the Racinian drama that sudden forgetfulness follows the recognition of self. There is occasionally a vivid moment in which, in the very shock of catastrophe, everything is effaced and collapses; a moment in which there no longer remains anything in thought except a sort of blind consciousness of the present instant. The past is swallowed up, and the being, face to face with the brutality of the actual, feels the sense of his identity vacillate:

"Is it Pyrrhus who is dying, or am I finally Orestes?" [33]
"Who am I? Is it Monima, and am I Mithridates?" [34]

Instantaneous testimonials of the being reduced to the instant, torn out of duration, which reveals how essentially the Racinian character differs from the Cornelian character. The latter exists only in and for the moment. It is realized there. The instantaneous makes rise from his lips, not a question, not a *Who am I?* but an affirmation: *I know what I am and what I ought to be.* With Corneille we are in a universe in which God has given a part to the human will. It thrills with the joy of feeling within it the perfect identity of the moment in which it wills and of the moment in which it feels itself will: I will, therefore I am. This unique moment encloses it, completes it, assures it, and gives it fullness of life. But the Racinian moment, as soon as it finds itself stripped of duration, is then no more than a shred of existence, a discontinuous being, a sort of fragment, as if in losing the feeling of being victim and prey, man lost at the same time the consciousness of the profound unity which, in binding together the different moments of his temporal life, creates the sense of his existence and his true self.

VIII

"Racine," says Thierry Maulnier, "goes straight to what is hardest and purest in life and death,—in destiny." How is it that one can speak of the *purity* of Racinian destiny, since nothing is less pure or more horrible than the successive visages it seems to present? "What wilt thou say, my father, of this horrible spectacle?" [35]

Let us be careful, however, not to confound with destiny the *horrible spectacle* which makes the consciousness of Phèdre, like the shade of Minos, shudder; for it is the spectacle offered to Phèdre by Phèdre, the light under which she sees herself in the horrible and incessant revolutions of the life of her senses: "I feel my whole body shiver and burn"; [36] experience of the self by the self, situated in the contact and contrast of the successive moments, but which immediately another presence replaces: "I recognized Venus and her terrible fires,/Inevitable torments of a blood she pursues." [37]

Upon the horrible, instantaneous spectacle of sensory experience there is superimposed the consciousness of an eternal, continuous, supersensible reality which Phèdre *recognizes:* a reality which, as much by its nature as by the extent of the field of duration upon which its action is performed, inspires no longer the horror that one has over impure things, but the awe engendered by the presence and perseverance of the divine. Immediately the tracked-down consciousness is lifted up to a zone more tragic still, but more serene, in which it even acquires a sort of grandeur; as if in the midst of feeling itself entangled in the miserable web of impassioned intermittences, of remorse and premonitions in which "each moment kills it," it saw itself endowed and arrayed, on the other hand—not indeed as in the romantic poets with the prestige of the rebel Titan, but rather with the dignity of a sacrificial victim, in the fulfillment of the rites by which his destiny is wrought. On the one hand it is a being stricken with the palpitation and rendings of a discontinuous time; on the other, it is a person whose destiny is inscribed above the eddies of duration, in the eternal zone of celestial wills—whose destiny is fulfilled in still another zone, in the order of providential temporality, unfolding regularly, inevitably, and serenely the arcanae of those wills. Hence the existence of three parallel durations in Racine as in the medieval thinkers: the discontinuous time of actual passions; the continuous time of the fulfillment of the divine will; and finally this will itself in its pure nontemporality.

IX

Close as Racine's superimposition of times comes to the medieval conception, there is a point of difference; and this point is so important that, despite everything, it forces us to place Racine at the very antipodes of the scholastic spirit. Racine's three times are indeed disposed in the stages of the scholastic order; but in the Racinian tragedy there is the constant impression that these stages brush against each other; that in some way these planes of existence are liable to unite or to be confused. The triple existence of things does not stand out with the clearness of design which, in a Saint

Thomas or a Dante, allows a distinction to be made, then and there, between eternity and time proper. In Racine, on the contrary, there is something indecisive and turbid which makes the human drama a long, anguished meditation and almost a religious mystery, in which it is no longer a question whether passion is passion, or evil is evil, but whether or not the gods themselves are malevolent, or infected by evil; whether, finally, the fatal discontinuity of human realities does not end by extending and even encroaching in some manner upon eternity; so that this eternal world whose image ideally transpires through the ferocity of human duration, far from having the serenity and the purity one fancied, far from assuring us, as we would wish to believe, of the continuity of a purpose and design in an existence which of itself is torn to pieces and perverted, this eternal world would seem in its turn contaminated and corrupted, becoming a mere reflection of our tragic condition, projected into the clouds: "Halt, barbarians:/It is the pure blood of the God that hurls the thunderbolt." [38]

This cry breathes forth the most authentic religious anguish. Suddenly it is no longer the question of a mother who fears for her daughter, but of a soul that fears for its God. We are in the presence here of one of the most undefinable and most profound of the fears which are at the base of all religions; the fear that in the contact between the divine and the human, which is religion itself, there may be something perilous, not only for the creature but for the divine itself; the fear lest the intangible become tangible, the light become dark, and the purity become corrupted. Let the thunderbolt split and destroy a sacrilegious creation; this is not the most terrible risk. The risk is that the thunder clap may be the signal for an annihilation of Heaven as well.

X

At the extreme opposite of this terror, and as if Racine had had to traverse the deepest shadows to emerge into the light, there is at the very end of that long tunnel which is the tragedy of *Phèdre*, the sudden restoration of day: "And death, robbing my eyes of their brightness,/Restores to the day all the purity they defiled."

The extraordinary beauty of these lines is owing to the double image of the dawn which they evoke: a dawn, on the one hand, so cruel to the dying; a dawn, on the other hand, so sweet to the eyes of those who will continue to live. For the former, the brightness of day is darkened; for the latter, its purity is restored. In the consciousness of Phèdre the reality of peace and of purity is perceived only at the moment when she must bid them good-bye forever. She is brought to the farthest limit of despair. She *is* that limit. The consciousness of the pure, of the bright, of the light of day, is achieved by her, as something *interior to her,* only at the moment it leaves her forever. Until then the world of daylight and purity had existed only by implication, as the reverse side of the world of shadows constituting her mind. And now at the moment of death she *sees* this purity and this brightness, she knows them to be true, but she has lost them.

Farthest limit of despair, but a despair that implies, though certainly not a hope, at least a discovery and a belief, let us even say a faith: faith in transcendence, in a being by which she has held on to being, in a brightness which makes her shadow be shadow, in a purity that, through an anguish from which she is delivered, she had come to fear that she had irremediably contaminated the nature. This is a purgation by which the consciousness of eternity is attained and which ends in an act of faith: I recognize the eternal; dying, and by my death, I pay homage.

From this eternity she is doubtless excluded. She knows that fact. She thinks of it only in passing. Her final lot, her eternal destiny is suddenly of very little concern compared with the immense reality in the face of which her humiliation overwhelms her. There is something here that is analogous to the pure love of François de Sales and of Fénelon: "O my God," said a mystic of that period, "I would choose not to be at all, rather than that you should cease to be." [39] "O my God," says Phèdre, "my being matters nothing, since you will not cease to be, and to be the one who washes away the stains of the world, but whom the stains of the world do not soil." An entire disinterestedness of self in the perception of the Being who is *light* and supreme purity. Perhaps one can see in this the action of a saving grace; perhaps, after all, Phèdre is a Christian in whom *grace has not failed;* perhaps she dies saved, without knowing it; because she has rejoined, in a transport of absolute humility, the same state of loving self-annihilation at which the great contemplatives arrive. Did not

Fénelon say that pure love consists in loving God in indifference to one's own salvation, even if one knows he is going to be damned? Phèdre dies, doubtless not in the divine love, not in *caritas,* but she dies *in renunciation,* in total resignation to the divine will. Her supreme, unique act is an act of perfect abandonment; she dies "a willing slave" of God and not "a slave of death." [40]

XI

In all the plays of Racine, up until the conclusion of *Phèdre,* the dominating idea is that of a world which reveals itself as radically evil, whose very survival seems for that reason to compromise or obscure the notion of a God of Light and a God of Purity. By dint of seeing the continuation of the world only as a repetition of the same crimes and the same passions, the mind ends by perceiving in the dark unfolding of things, only their interdependence. The entire duration of a being is no more in his own eyes than the ceaseless beginning again of what stains and destroys him—thus the more and more desperate tone of the earlier Racinian theater. But in *Phèdre* and after *Phèdre* a roundabout face is accomplished. Suddenly the accent is no longer on the ceaseless continuation of being, but on the ceaseless act by which it is continued, and on the dependence of the creature on the act by which it exists. Over and above the endless chain of causes and effects which seem to engender duration, there is distinguished the presence of a first cause that mercifully joins its eternity to the instant; and beyond the despair which indefinite perpetuity of evil engenders, the soul suddenly discovers in its infinite dependence upon God, a peace which lifts the instant to eternity: "The soul happily captive/Under thy yoke finds peace. . . ." [41] And in the same *Cantique* these lines, in which once more the creature is astonished to see the sun restore light to the world: "And who am I that thou deignest/ To condescend even to me?" Identical question to that of those lines of *La Thébaide* quoted at the beginning of this chapter; but here, without losing its urgency, it is robbed of the venom. The question is concluded in supplication, in prayer; for what shows through the most intense feeling of human indignity is the feeling, no less intense, of the prodigious dignity which in every instant the eternal act of creation confers upon and restores to this unworthy being. Thus the fatality of past cause and past evil is exorcised by the recognition of a cause which transcends all duration, and which is found immediately and almost miraculously, even in the moment of death—of the death of Phèdre, since this moment, like all moments, is the gift of God.

After that, no more remains than to set forth the divine acts of this Providence in human durations. That is what Racine will do in *Esther* and *Athalie*.

NOTES

1 Act I, scene 1.
2 Act IV, scene 1.
3 *Ibid.*, scene 3.
4 Act III, scene 6.
5 Act V, scene 4.
6 Act V, scene 6.
7 *Britannicus*, Act I, scene 1.
8 *Iphigénie*, Act IV, scene 4.
9 *Athalie*, Act V, scene 6.
10 Act I, scene 1.
11 Act II, scene 2.
12 Act I, scene 1; Act II, scene 1; Act III, scene 8.
13 Act II, scene 5.
14 *Ibid.*, scene 4.
15 Act III, scene 8.
16 Act II, scene 4.
17 Act V, scene 3.

18 Act II, scene 5.
19 *Bajazet*, preface.
20 *Andromaque*, Act I, scene 2.
21 *Iphigénie*, Act V, scene 2.
22 *Andromaque*, Act V, scene 1.
23 *Britannicus*, Act V, scene 6.
24 *Bajazet*, Act I, scene 4.
25 *Iphigénie*, Act II, scene 1.
26 *Bérénice*, Act IV, scene 5.
27 *Athalie*, Act II, scene 9.
28 *Cantiques spirituels*, 2.
29 *Britannicus*, Act III, scene 3.

30 *Iphigénie*, Act IV, scene 4.
31 *Phèdre*, Act III, scene 3.
32 *Iphigénie*, Act II, scene 1.
33 *Andromaque*, Act V, scene 4.
34 *Mithridate*, Act IV, scene 5.
35 *Phèdre*, Act IV, scene 6.
36 *Ibid.*, Act I, scene 3.
37 Ibid.
38 *Iphigénie*, Act V, scene 4.
39 Quoted by H. Bremond, *Histoire du sentiment religieux*, VIII, 418.
40 *Cantiques spirituels*, 3.
41 *Ibid.*, 4.

MADAME DE LA FAYETTE

I

The work of Madame de la Fayette has but one aim: to discover the relationships between passion and existence.

The point of departure is passion itself. When does it begin? As the story of the princess of Montpensier demonstrates, there are some passions which, at the moment they burst forth, already presuppose a certain existence behind them. It is an "inclination almost subdued"[1] which, by the help of chance, is rekindled: "and their hearts effortlessly took a road which was not unknown to them."[2]

But that only avoids the problem by pushing it back further and further. Certainly at some moment these "former impressions" were new. If one goes back to that first moment, what does one find?

Must love have had for its point of departure a choice determined by knowledge? That is the opinion of Rambouillet's circle. One loves only what one admires, and one admires only what one already knows. But this presupposes that the love has a definite past.

You will never persuade me that you can be in love with a person whose face you hardly know.[3]

. . . .

Allow me to love only a person whom I shall know well enough to esteem. . . .[4]

But the *Histoire de Consalve* shows how vain this pretention is. Love by choice, for a person known for a long time, is a dupery. True passion manifests itself in a lightning flash, for an unknown person thrown into our presence by a stroke of fate. This love has no past: "Passions which develop only over a period of time cannot be called true passions."[5] They are only "liaisons which we voluntarily entertain in our heart."[6] For the property of the will is

to resort to knowledge; and that is ordinarily obtained only after
certain trial steps are taken in a preliminary duration. But how
shall we characterize a state whose nature completely resides in
an emotion which up until that moment has not been experienced?

> . . . certain feelings which had been unknown to me before seeing
> you, and of which I had so little idea that at first they gave me a
> surprise which only increased the turmoil that always follows them.
> . . .[7]

Incomparable feelings, for which, at the time, it is impossible to
find any equivalent in past existence, and concerning which it is
even less possible to discover any bond connecting them with the
rest of existence: "There are no passions except those that strike
us at first sight and surprise us." [8]

This *first sight* is situated outside of time, in an instantaneousness which is an absolute beginning: a moment when something *is*
which before was not and which then would have been neither
intelligible nor foreseeable. Passion is truly an unknown with whose
presence the soul is suddenly confronted. And its mark of authenticity consists precisely in the very absence of any mark of
recognition. Passion is not recognized. It strikes at first sight; it
surprises: "If I am not surprised at first sight, I cannot be moved." [9]

There is then neither reflective nor voluntary passion. The soul
is in the presence of something that is absolutely new. But then this
poses another problem. Is knowledge, unrealizable in the first moments, to be acquired perhaps in those that follow? It is difficult to
grasp even the purport of this problem. For what does knowing
mean here? If passion consists only in the feeling which manifests
it, feeling exists only under the form of an actual emotion, actually
felt, for as long as it is felt; and its duration is then made up only of
successive present moments of which each one is sufficient unto itself. To know love would be simply to know, or rather to feel,
each one of these moments at the very moment.

But to the knowledge of love there is attached the knowledge of
the object loved. With the strangeness of feeling one experiences
there is mingled the feeling of curiosity one has about an unknown
being whom one has begun to love. And then there is rediscovered
in all its fullness the consciousness of the lived duration which the
first moments of passion had obliterated. Let us suppose conditions

at once the most rigorous and the most extreme: a being without illusion, full of experience, loves an absolutely sincere soul, one who assists him tirelessly in this knowledge of herself, to whom he is devoted. What happens to him? As he discovers such and such a detail of her life, he divines the existence of other such details that remain in the shadows; and the further he advances in the exploration of this heart, the more the heart of this heart seems to him uncertain and secret. All this becomes an inextinguishable desire in him, a retrospective torture of jealousy. This will be the torture of M. de Clèves: "You could not have told me the whole truth." Here it is the torture of one of the characters in *Zaïde,* the hero of the *Histoire d'Alphonse:*

> I gave her no more rest; I could no longer show her either passion or tenderness. . . . I always found that I had forgotten to make her explain some circumstance to me; and as soon as I had begun talking with her, I was in a labyrinth; I could not get out of it. . . .[10]

Thus in writing the *Histoire de Consalve* and the *Histoire d'Alphonse,* Madame de la Fayette brought together again in these two principle episodes of *Zaïde* the two complementary aspects which the experience of love in duration presents. On the one hand is the creative power of passion, its capacity for in some way inventing the moment in which it *is.* And on the other hand is its incapacity to give to the moment and to the being a past and a depth.

These early works already tend toward bitter conclusions. Indeed one finds here and there delightful phrases in which the freshness of a vanished ideal still lingers: "Love had for us all the grace of strangeness; and we found in it that secret charm one never finds except in those first passions"; [11] but clarity of glance has already dissipated most of the illusions and discerned the sternest realities. From there on, love appears as an explosive force that breaks the continuity of being.

All of this is clearly stated in *La princesse de Montpensier,* as in *Zaïde,* as, later, in *La comtesse de Tende.* For, first of all, if passion is involuntary, then the will has no hold over it: " 'You are right, madam,' he told her, 'we can do nothing about our passions; I am swept off my feet, without the power to resist; but mind you that at least you come to agree that it is not up to us to resist.' " [12]

It is in vain then for us to decide in one moment to take a particular action in another: "She saw the abyss into which she was falling, and she resolved to avoid it. She could not stick to her resolution." [13] "She believed she would continue in that resolution. When the hour of the assignation approached, she could resist no longer . . ." [14] a precise remark, for the powerlessness to resist is exactly a powerlessness to resist any longer; it is not a question of making resolutions, but of keeping them, of *holding out*. The central subject of *La princesse de Clèves* is already outlined: how to establish or re-establish a continuity in existence, amid the anarchic and destructive irruption, the radical discontinuity which is the very essence of passion.

II

A right and well ordered judgment, a heart possessed "neither of impatience, disquietude, nor vexation," [15] but one which holds fast in the deep-seated repose of innocence. And all of a sudden the rupture, the total disappearance of this perfect tranquillity, under the shock of passion. And not the slightest transition. From the moment love enters this soul, it is as if it possessed it completely.

And yet *La princesse de Clèves* is the recital of a progress, not of passion itself, but of the successive experiences it occasions in the heart; the successive discoveries it occasions in the mind. This double progression is accomplished in a double series of distinct stages, each one of which has its own character, but all of which have as a common trait the priority of the movement of the heart over that of the mind. Each time it comes as a new discovery, the discovery that this love is shared, the discovery of the torments of jealousy, of the joys of loving confidence; the discovery of the infinite unhappiness that the slightest infidelity involves. Each time the mind is, as it were, assailed by unexpected glimmers that light up its unsuspected depths: nearly instantaneous seizures of consciousness, under the immediate and extraordinarily urgent pressure of an emotion that seems nevertheless to produce it out of a very long subterranean labor.

In parallel fashion, another knowledge, another series of discoveries arises, following the same rhythm of immediate seizures of consciousness, isolated among lustreless intervals. Just as there is a consciousness of the power of passion, so there is a conciousness of the powerlessness of the human being in the face of passion: the knowledge that one cannot keep from loving; the knowledge that one is no longer master of his feelings, since one is no longer master of his gestures, nor of his facial expressions, nor of his words; then to know that one can no longer know, that the consciousness is embattled, that the center of the citadel is already, like the rest, in the hands of the enemy.

Thus Mme. de Clèves travels, stage by stage, a cruel road on which each momentary halt is a bitter surprise; on which passion is each time revealed as a new reality with which she becomes painfully acquainted; a road on which she finds herself reft, one after the other, of the traits which comprise her reality and her permanence; on which finally she is at every instant unfaithful to herself, so much so that in this multiplicity and this dispersion she discovers herself to be virtually unrecognizable.

> She regarded with astonishment the prodigious difference between the state she was in at night, and that in which she found herself then. . . . She no longer recognized herself.[16]

It is worse than the plight of "being abandoned to itself at a time when it is so little master of its feelings"; it means to lose sight of itself in every one of the dispersed moments of passion.

There remains a last resort: to place it in the hands of another, by a heroic admission, this possession and direction of thought which are now out of hand: "Regulate my conduct, make sure that I see no one; it is all that I ask of you." [17]

Ah, to be able thus to rediscover, whether by a blind obeisance, or at the price of some other form of slavery, that continuity of self, that fidelity to self which makes of life, not a chaos of instants, but a temporal unity!

After the failure of this attempt, nothing remains except the inevitable catastrophe and the denouement.

III

After the death of her husband, Mme. de Clèves is not free at all. She is less free than ever. The death of M. de Clèves, far from enlarging the narrow circle in which she moves, results only in making it still narrower. There is no longer any support; there is absolute isolation, invincible weakness. Nothing is left her but to achieve her defeat in the arms of Nemours.

Mme. de Clèves will not marry Nemours. Two reasons, she says, are against it: duty; repose. But beyond these two reasons, which are to support her in the struggle, there is one sovereign reason which accounts for both of them. Through her lived experience, Mme. de Clèves has reaped a judgment of condemnation which indicts not only her past love but any future love, and even passion itself. Passion is wicked not because it had had the precise effect of causing the death of M. de Clèves, but because the death of M. de Clèves is the symbol of all the disorders and sorrows it entails. The force of passion inevitably steers adventure toward some catastrophe: it is thus the cause of it even if this fatal effect might have been a different one. And passion, being the cause of this actual evil —even more, being the cause of an infinity of possible evils—is wicked by nature to a degree that is absolute.

To marry Nemours is to marry passion, to marry evil and unhappiness. But how shall one restrain oneself from it, since the very character of passion is to prevent one from being able to restrain oneself, and it is not a question of making resolutions but of keeping them?

Up to this point reason alone has been able to intervene. But it can go no further; it has made emerge from the interior disturbance one clear and distinct idea; it has offered what it could—rational evidence. It is evidence which, moreover, as Mme. de Clèves knows only too well, can in a moment—any moment—be destroyed, annihilated by the crushing return of passion:

> Mme. de Clèves saw him. . . . What an effect this momentary glimpse produced in the heart of Mme. de Clèves. What sleeping passion reawakened in her heart, and with what violence! [18]

There is left, then, only one possible means: to endow rational evidence with something of the violence or the urgency of the affective force: to meet fire with fire, and the irrational with the irrational; to devise passionate reasons. Mme. de Clèves furnishes herself with these reasons and hurls them at Nemours with a desperate energy: not to convince him; but to convince herself; *to gain time*.

It is striking that both these reasons are, by their very nature, in-

volved with time. All Mme. de Clèves' effort tends to reconstitute
things around this fatal, consuming moment, a hundred times repeated, which is the unique *time* of passion, in some sort of past
and future; that is to say, a veritable duration, an existence. To re-
establish in her present, cost what it will, the consciousness of a
double temporal depth, such is indeed the meaning of those two
reasons, "duty" and "repose."

For the *duty* of which she speaks springs from the "scruples of
the past," [19] that is to say, it is less a duty than a feeling of duty.
It is not at all necessary to look here for a universal moral rule, a
categorical imperative, discovered in the mind and applicable to
any moment of life. It is a particular duty, relating to a definite episode in the past and susceptible of recalling it to the heart, of making it live again. Mme. de Clèves finds an unexpected resource in
the very event which seemed to her to have razed her last defenses.
M. de Clèves living could represent only a duty of reason or of
esteem: an idea that was helpless against present passion. M. de
Clèves dead becomes a "phantom of duty," [20] a phantom that one
can summon up out of his past, completely armed with powerful
feelings which actually act on the soul; feelings so powerful that
they are almost unbearable: ". . . I would not have known how to
sustain the thought of it, it shames me so . . . ." [21]

And, by a heroic device, Mme. de Clèves succeeds in intensify-
ing still more the powerful conjuration of this present past. She accepts not only the shame, but also the blame: "I know that it is owing to you that he is dead, and that is because of me." [22]

Thus the past gathers all its force, the force of something irreparable.

But there is still another resource against passion; and it is cen-
tered in the passion itself. Mme. de Clèves had already had the
feeling twice, each time in the presence of a real or suspected infidelity of her lover. Then she had "her eyes opened to the possibility of being deceived"; she had thought "how little likely it was that
a man like M. de Nemours was capable of a sincere and durable
attachment." [23]

Durable! If Mme. de Clèves had then felt "how almost impossible it was that she could be happy in her passion," [24] how much
more vividly she felt now the impossibility in terms of duration!
The kind of suspension accomplished in the blind movement of

love, since the death of M. de Clèves (as formerly after the death
of her mother), allowed her to plumb the future and to foresee there
a "sure sorrow." [25] For it is of the essence of passion to endure only
by a sort of interior renewal, which grows by the resistance one offers it, and without which it is nothing.

> Can men preserve passion in these eternal engagements? Ought I
> to hope for a miracle in my favor? And can I put myself in the
> state of seeing the certain end of this passion which was my whole
> happiness? [26]

There is no real preservation possible except for what is beyond
passion. There is no durable existence except a passionless existence. And thus it is that her soul, fatigued by the immediate emotions, turns toward that state of *tranquillity* which her mother had
once recommended to her, toward that state which had been hers,
and of which M. de Clèves had complained when he told her that
she was *without impatience, or inquietude, or vexation.* The negative state whose sole activity consists in vigilance and mistrust. She
remembered her mother saying that she could *preserve her virtue
only by an extreme mistrust of herself:* [27] "I mistrust my own
strength in the midst of my reasonings." [28]

The negative state which is a kind of ascesis: *Accustoming oneself to detachment from everything;* [29] *taking the greatest and longest views;* [30] rendering *all other things of the world indifferent;* [31] to
sum it all up, attaining to a sort of fixity in which past, present and
future are alike; in which there is nothing besides existence and
duration—and, at the foundation of this sufficiency, perhaps the
action of God:

It is enough just to be. [32]

NOTES

[1] *Romans et nouvelles*, ed.
   Garnier, p. 434.
[2] *Ibid.*, p. 447.
[3] *Ibid.*, p. 20.
[4] *Ibid.*, p. 21.
[5] *Ibid.*, p. 22.
[6] *Ibid.*, p. 62.
[7] *Ibid.*, p. 418.
[8] *Ibid.*, p. 62.
[9] *Ibid.*, p. 22.
[10] *Ibid.*, p. 88.

[11] *Ibid.*, p. 26.
[12] *Ibid.*, p. 42.
[13] *Ibid.*, p. 468.
[14] *Ibid.*, p. 458.
[15] *Ibid.*, p. 259.
[16] *Ibid.*, p. 349.
[17] *Ibid.*, p. 362.
[18] *Ibid.*, p. 413.
[19] *Ibid.*, p. 426.
[20] *Ibid.*, p. 419.
[21] *Ibid.*

[22] *Ibid.*
[23] *Ibid.*, p. 350.
[24] *Ibid.*, p. 351.
[25] *Ibid.*, p. 427.
[26] *Ibid.*, p. 421.
[27] *Ibid.*, p. 247.
[28] *Ibid.*, p. 423.
[29] *Ibid.*, p. 429.
[30] *Ibid.*
[31] *Ibid.*, p. 430.
[32] *Segraisiana* (1723), I, 86.

FONTENELLE

I

 With Fontenelle a life commences that is to be a century
long, in a society whose great concern is in the interchange
of ideas and feelings. Within it the reasonable is so mingled with the
unreasonable that it seems that the purpose of existence is to introduce confusion among clear ideas. The world appears as an en-
chanted castle in which lovers search for each other, find each
other, and never recognize each other. Thus it is with man's happiness, Fontenelle muses: "It dwells in his thoughts, but he does not
know it is there." [1]

To eliminate the confusion and waste that life causes, to recognize happiness where it is, in one's thoughts, is what the young
Fontenelle proposes to do.

A very curious attitude, which consists in clearly imagining in
advance the happiness one will have and, that done, in denying
oneself the realization of it, because the idea is an ideal, and the fulfillment is bound to come short of perfection.

Two anecdotes recounted by Fontenelle quite clearly illustrate
this attitude. The Duke of Alençon goes to England to propose
marriage to Queen Elizabeth. He is accepted. Certain festivities
ensue. Then, on the eve of the marriage, Elizabeth informs him
that she is rejecting his suit:

> The true secret of my conduct is that I have found that there is
> nothing more enjoyable than *to conceive plans, to make prepara-
> tions, and then not to carry them out.* . . . Things must not pass
> from our imagination to reality, for then we lose them. You come
> to England to marry me; we have nothing but balls, fêtes, and rejoic-
> ings. . . . Up to that point there is nothing pleasanter in the world,
> *everything consists only in preparations and ideas;* and what is agree-
> able in marriage has already been *exhausted.* I hold to that and send
> you back. . . .[2]

The other anecdote tells about a company of people who are getting ready to leave for a masked ball:

> We promised ourselves enough pleasures to last the whole night through. At that point, Mlle. de N—— told us with an air of playfulness that I should like to describe to you, if you have never met with it: "I am going to appear mad to you, and perhaps I am. But if you believe me, we shall all undress, and instead of going to the ball, we shall all go to bed." I had already noticed at most parties of this sort that whenever one has expected to have a good time, one has not had it at all; and when the anticipation has been most pleasant, the realization has been disappointing.[3]

Let us not be deceived by this. Behind these paradoxes, as is always the case with Fontenelle, a problem is concealed whose terms are stated with precision. The present is only an instant. Its capacity for happiness is feeble. Its palpable substance is paltry. A certain indolence enervates it. So it is necessary to extend it, to enrich it, to revive it by exercising our minds. Happiness would seem then to consist in "taking possession in advance" of the future.[4] This future, lived anticipatively by means of thought, would give the moment the extension, the richness, and the life it lacks: "I count mostly on the pleasure of foresight, of hope, even of fear, and of experiencing the future beforehand."[5]

An intelligence which tries to increase the field of action and duration, of a sensibility which by itself feels ephemeral and tenuous: there you have Fontenelle, and the eighteenth century which begins with him, as well.

But it is as much the character of Fontenelle and of his epoch not to allow themselves to be duped by these prospects, or at least to know very exactly when they are duped. If one anticipates the future, it is inevitable that when the future becomes the present in its turn, it contains nothing more than what is already known and experienced. One is then doubly deceived; and the present, lived twice over, seems twice as poor:

> Men borrow so much on the future through their imaginations and their expectations, that when it is finally present, they find that it is entirely *exhausted,* and they can no longer reconcile themselves to it. Yet they never rid themselves of their impatience or their disquietude.[6]

There remains then a single issue: that of conceiving a future which one will not put into practice, and the expenditure of which one will decline to make; a future that remains in a projected state, or if one prefers, in a *hypothetical* state. There remains also the need of treating the present itself with prudence and parsimony. The whole attitude of Fontenelle, from the very beginning, may be summed up as the decision to spend time and life with economy.

II

Since the "great lure of men is always the future," [7] since "the future is a kind of charlatan that, dazzling our eyes, eases us of the present which we hold in our hands," [8] let us try at least to give this present all its worth and lose none of it. Now the present that matters is what we presently experience; and our present emotion is never so much alive as when we are passionate. But the more alive it is, the less duration it has: "Lively pleasures last only a few moments," a few moments "often fatal through an excess of vivacity which leaves nothing to enjoy afterward." [9] "For an instant I feel I know not what; but in the instant which follows the only certainty is that I feel nothing." [10] Indeed with Fontenelle one can enjoy only a limited amount of affection. He has a very clear feeling of limits, and especially of temporal limits. Living intensely matters less to him than prolonging as much as he can certain moments of mediocre intensity. Now it is characteristic of passion to intensify moments, and consequently to accelerate their succession or to hasten their exhaustion: "It is not the intention of love that attachments last a long time; it extracts from the heart all that is most alive in it . . . ." [11] What one gains by assiduousness, one loses in duration. One "gathers up into a day what could be spread over a whole week." [12]

Passion spent in a trice can be renewed only through diversity; it regains a certain vivacity by changing its object and its action. Different persons, to whom one is attached by turn, can thus make of our existence a series of intense but discontinuous moments. Such is not the policy Fontenelle recommends in matters of love. For him love is "so agreeable a commerce that one does well to give it as long a duration as possible." [13] One obtains this duration first by putting off the pleasure of the moment:

What would it be like if one were accepted as soon as he offered himself? What would become of all those attentions one takes pleasure in, all that disquietude one feels when he reproaches himself for not having pleased enough, all the alacrity with which one looks for a happy moment, finally all that agreeable mixture of pleasures and pains we call love? [14]

But one obtains this duration more surely still in persisting, even after one is accepted, in slackening pace and attenuating the naturally violent rhythm of passion. If love has little duration only because one intends to live through it in a "perpetual ecstasy," is it not much better, Fontenelle asks, not to force things to ecstasy, but to disengage one's soul from violent passions, to make sure they do not become more violent, to husband the "span of affection" one has? What then is essential is "to extend the duration of passions *with ingenuity,*" and in order to do so to intersperse moments of repose and intervals of variety and economy:

> Some movement, some agitation is necessary to men, but a movement and an agitation which adjusts itself, if it can, to the sort of indolence which possesses them, and this is found most happily in love, provided it be pursued in a certain way. It ought not to be suspicious, jealous, furious, desperate; but tender, simple, delicate, faithful, and, *to preserve itself in that state,* accompanied by hope.[15]

From the *Grand Cyrus,* therefore, one passes imperceptibly to the eclogues and the pastorals; from the fanciful one passes to an affectation of simplicity. The simple pleasures, Fontenelle tells us, unlike the passionate pleasures, *ordinarily last as long as one desires.* But this simplicity is only the height of artificiality. The succession of moments becomes a kind of existence, and the present prolongs itself in a fragile duration, only if the intelligence follows constantly toward the sensibility of an intricately balanced policy, moderating the sensual ardor, guarding passion from attrition, preventing it from falling on the one hand into ecstasy, and on the other into nullity.

Duration no longer consists in either a possession or a permanence, but in a quiet, continuous gliding of the mind over things and over pleasures: "Pleasures are not at all solid enough to be penetrable; one must only skim over their surface. They resemble marsh land over which one must run lightly, without ever setting foot down." [16]

III

But there are other marsh lands besides those of love. There are the lands of knowledge. And there is first that unknown region which extends in back of us, and which we call history or the past.

It is with the same light and cautious foot with which he skims over the lands of love that Fontenelle ventures into the domain of history. And, to be sure, are not these two domains identical?

> History has for its object the irregular effects of the passions, and a succession of events so bizarre that one formerly imagined a blind and insensate divinity directing it.[17]

· The study of history seems first to demonstrate uniquely the disconcerting facility with which human beings can change their goals and their actions. It appears at first sight the outline of an essentially discontinuous duration, a collection of small, particular durations, placed end to end by chance, "a strange assemblage having the appearance of an infinity of complicated chances . . . ." [18]

But if one inspects it more closely, one discerns that the assemblage of these chances implies "a kind of very subtle metaphysics" that presents to the mind's curiosity certain enigmas not less diverting than the course of love or the secrets of celestial mechanics. Behind the grandest events there is concealed a "succession of hidden springs," often ridiculous by reason of being microscopic, so that a thought shrewd enough to take notice of them would see the whole temporal perspective reduced to a kind of miniature universe, perceived through the wrong end of opera glasses, out of which bursts, from the extremity of a grotesque confusion of petty facts, the flower of the present moment:

> The magnificent and the ridiculous are so close that they touch each other. Everything resembles those works of perspective in which figures dispersed here and there form, let us say, an emperor if you look at them from a certain position; change this point of view and the same figures represent a beggar.[19]

Change the point of view, and it is the very meaning of history that changes. A see-saw motion in which one sees oscillate strangely, mingled with a ring of insects, the great historical perspectives and the great deeds of the past. The great and the small, the magnificent and the ridiculous, everything clings to or touches everything else, everything is mingled together, and the whole forms a moving continuity, a corpuscular universe that one agile thought embraces, passing rapidly over this unstable ground. This knowledge of the past is less knowledge than exercise. It barely touches events; it takes its facts, so to speak, on the wing, without stopping in its flight. Between certitude and ignorance it finds as many nuances as between the ridiculous and the sublime. It knows and does not know: the smallest fact can suddenly upset the aspect of things. Thus the past glides little by little from the real to the possible; it becomes, like the future, susceptible to the calculations of thought; it befits the ingenuity of the mind:

> Only witty minds feel the greater or lesser amount of certitude or of probability, and show, so to speak, each of these *minutes with their feeling*.[20]

IV

Besides historical knowledge, there is scientific knowledge: "Instead of this movement which agitates nations, which causes states to be born and overthrown, physics considers the great and universal movement which has ordered all nature . . . which, in always following invariable laws, infinitely diversifies its effects. . . . In a word, physics follows and unravels, in so far as possible, those traces of the intelligence and infinite wisdom which have produced everything." [21]

Notice that here the tone is different. We have gone back to the seventeenth century. But it is simply a matter of decorum. In history it is possible to look at men, but in nature it is necessary to begin by seeing God; one must first salute the master of the house. That being done, it is true that one can be dispensed of taking account of his presence. That is what Fontenelle gives us an inkling of in another passage in which he says that God has moved and disposed bodies "in such a way that the unaided natural communication of their movements brings about in every moment what God wishes to happen. It costs God no trouble except that of always preserving the same movement in the mass of matter." [22]

But also it costs man no more trouble than recognizing God as guarantor of the principle of the preservation of motion. After that he has no other role. Creation is no longer, as all the seventeenth century believed, dependent upon a divine energy which does not cease to create from moment to moment; rather it prolongs into a duration made of more and more diversified effects an initial impulse infinitely remote. Instead of finding the creative act in every moment, it would be necessary, in order to find it, to go back to the beginning of the temporal series. That would demand much trouble.

Now if God appears only very remotely here, Fontenelle nonetheless discerns invariable principles in the natural sciences. But at the same time Fontenelle has the conviction that these immutable laws are infinitely less known (and less knowable) than the innumerable variations of their effects. As God is confusedly discerned at the beginning of things, these laws are apperceived no less confusedly at the indefinitely postponed terminus of the researches of the scientist. They correspond, so to speak, in the domain of science, to what appears in the domain of history as "the very subtle metaphysics" which, tardily enough, is revealed as the mainspring of all. Thus for Fontenelle, scientific knowledge is somehow perpetually preceded by a characteristic mistrust of premature endeavors to gain possession of the truth. As with love, it is first a question of not letting ourselves be deceived by an anticipatory imagination and of not having been eased out of present realities. And Fontenelle congratulates the Academy of Sciences, which he directs and which he incarnates

> for taking nature in small portions only. No general system, for fear of falling into the danger of precipitate systems. . . . *Today one is assured of one fact, tomorrow of another that has no resemblance to it.* One cannot avoid hazarding conjectures as to causes, but they are conjectures. Thus the treatises with which the Academy presents the public year after year are composed only of detached fragments, independent of each other.[23]

To the first discontinuity of the affective life, and to that of historical thought, there is now joined a third discontinuity, that of the course of pure knowledge. But at the very moment when Fontenelle seems to resign himself to making of science only an assemblage of little facts, no less bizarre and no less uncertain than those which constitute the irregular course of human lives, he discovers in science—as in love, and as in history—a fragile principle of continuity. It is a question not only of collecting facts but of *hazarding conjectures.* Each physical event—like each historical event—being comprised of a throng of small components, it is necessary to take notice of as many minute details as possible, to make research last as one makes love last, finally to vary hypotheses cautiously as one varies the modalities of passion. It requires the same suppleness, the same patience, the same economy of effort, the same sense of proportion, the same ingenuity. It requires above all a capacity of thought capable of testing every idea in every way possible, and thus of prolonging indefinitely their immaterial existence in the mind. Who knows? Perhaps by virtue of lasting, an idea will end by becoming true:

> Such is our condition that it is never permitted us to arrive all of a sudden at something reasonable on any subject; first it is necessary that we should *go astray for a long time* and travel the road of diverse sorts of errors and divers degrees of irrelevancy. . . .[24]

But what were these irrelevancies and these errors in their time but conjectures? Now Fontenelle feels himself marvellously endowed for conjecture. A thought trained from the first for previsions of the future, habituated to live in a world where *everything consists of preparations and ideas,* on the other hand familiarized with an historical past in which things give way to *bizarre assemblages of an infinity of complicated hazards*—this thought is found superbly prepared to maneuver with ease in the newest regions of science, that is to say in the world of the *possible.* In order to move within it, the mind is aided by certain "ideas of supposition" made of the augmentation or combination of "express ideas." [25] Thanks to them, the structure of things seems made of an infinite diversity, framed on the one hand by immutable laws, and on the other by astonishing discoveries. Between the two poles, surveyed by the mind from a height, there stretch out all the minute variations of being, possible and real.

Variations which, from a certain point of view, placed in succession to one another—by virtue of their number, of the superposition of their actions, of the complexity of their machinery—form an authentic time, a time that the mind toils at imagining or traversing. It is thus that—before Buffon—the earth's past appears to Fontenelle:

Down to a certain depth, the Earth seems often enough to be only a heap of different materials, of ruins, of debris, of rubbish which has been assembled pell-mell by earthquakes, by volcanoes, by floods, by deluges. . . . *A long succession of centuries* has produced different mutations in this confused mass.[26]

But if a long succession of centuries has produced so many mutations, another succession of centuries might produce no less considerable changes. At the idea that one day the sun might be extinguished and the earth perish, the Marquise of the *Entretiens* cannot refrain from trembling. The infinity of a time to come implies an infinity of chances, and consequently the possibility of the immutable laws precisely realizing that possibility. The mere existence of time entails all the possibles. And because of that, duration takes on for Fontenelle a new significance, truly creative, a duration which already anticipates what time will be in the thought of Bergson, or even of Valéry:

Art, culture, and, still more, chance, that is to say certain unknown circumstances, every day bring to birth certain mutations in flowers. . . .[27]

in flowers, in things, in thoughts . . . Mind and time labor together in the same direction. Both invent or conceive of new possibilities of existence. Instead of a world in which celestial bodies by nature can never change, here we have outlined a universe in which nature is always changing.

Changes which, looked at in one way, are the slowest in the world, but which taken another way are just as fleeting. If the roses that last only a day wrote their memoirs, they would speak of their gardener as of an eternal being: "Should we decree that our duration, which is only of an instant, is the measure of any other?" Thus the relativity of time reveals to Fontenelle the possibility of different rhythms of duration, according to which the immense evolution of the universe and the fugitive variations of the briefest passion would be equal in value, and confused in the same impalpable whirlpool of corpuscles. Duration, then, is something equally retractible or expansible: "Without living for a longer time than we presently live, we could multiply the number of our years." Duration is reduced to being no more than a point of view, an attitude of mind.

Thus, far from being for Fontenelle the prime gift of conscious-ness, the first fact of reality, time is no more, in the final analysis, than an undulating texture that unites the thousands of forms of the real and the possible; a texture whose thread, which threatens every moment to break, the mind weaves and re-weaves with delicate art.

NOTES

[1] *Oeuvres* (1764), I, 119.
[2] *Ibid.,* p. 54.
[3] *Ibid.,* p. 246.
[4] *Ibid.,* p. 63.
[5] *Ibid.,* p. 65.
[6] *Ibid.,* p. 63.
[7] *Ibid.*
[8] *Ibid.,* III, 153.
[9] *Ibid.,* p. 155.
[10] *Ibid.,* I, 211.

[11] *Ibid.,* p. 233.
[12] *Ibid.,* p. 208.
[13] *Ibid.,* p. 30.
[14] *Ibid.,* p. 31.
[15] *Ibid.,* IV, 95.
[16] *Ibid.,* I, 55.
[17] *Ibid.,* V, 10.
[18] *Ibid.,* III, 225.
[19] *Ibid.,* I, 89.
[20] *Entretiens sur la plura-lité des mondes,* vi.

[21] *Oeuvres,* V, 9.
[22] *Ibid.,* IX, 65.
[23] *Ibid.,* V, 13.
[24] *Ibid.,* IV, 119.
[25] *Ibid.,* IX, 227.
[26] Quoted by Carré, *Philos-ophie de Fontenelle* (Al-can, 1932), p. 355.
[27] *Ibid.,* p. 357.

✱

✱

✱ L'ABBE PREVOST

I

✱ "The story that I am writing," says the Abbé Prévost, "is composed only of actions and feelings." [1] That is true of almost all his work. Each story seems to be a double series of actions and feelings juxtaposed, which have for exterior unity only the fact of following one another, and for their interior unity only their reference to the same person. Just as Lockean time consists in continually substituting one idea for another, in the same thought, so Prevostian time is constituted from the first by the perpetual substitution, in the same existence, of one adventure for another. This rhythm of pure successiveness is peculiar to the epoch, and Prévost accelerates it in two ways. On the one hand he multiplies episodes, precipitates the course of each, and hurries to finish one and begin another; as a consequence, hardly has the hero begun one adventure when he is seized and carried off to a denouement, from which he escapes only to be hurled into the following episode. But in still another fashion Prévost accentuates the essentially transitive character of duration. His dramatic method is of the simplest kind but also the most decisive; it consists in making of the particular denouement of each episode a totally unexpected catastrophe which leaves nothing remaining of the action that preceded. It is like a fracture in existence which from then on leaves no other alternative to hero and novel than to begin anew. Thus the Prevostian duration presents itself less as a true duration than as a collection of completely separated fragments of duration, with such incongruous edges that it seems impossible to reconstitute them into a continuous time.

But violent as it may be, this dramatic exterior is nothing in comparison with the accompanying dramatic interior which crowns it. On the one hand, feelings appear, in the novels of Prévost, as if entirely determined by events. Their intensity is equalled only by their passivity. They rise into view at the extreme point of each episode as if, carried along by the same current, they had invisibly participated in the motion which precipitated the action toward the catastrophe; but at the same time, they seem to have awaited this precise moment of catastrophe to become visible and to affirm themselves at one stroke as the very reality itself, for which the event was only an obscure preparation. As a result, for one thing, feeling seems to have the same sort of duration as event. The series of emotive facts corresponds to the series of episodic facts, to form as it were, a kind of Lockean time. The discontinuity of the emotions corresponds to the discontinuity of the actions. But on the other hand there is authentic existence of feeling only in the very moment when it bursts forth and attains simultaneously its maximum intensity. While each episode constitutes at the least a crude form of duration, feeling manifests itself in the precise instant when a schism occurs in the duration. It exists, not in time, not even in a fragment of time, but in the empty space which appears between the fragments of time, when time is broken apart.

Now this fracture of time is surely partially the result of a conjunction of events ending in a catastrophe; but violent as they may be, they could not all by themselves produce an end to their fluctuating time and, consequently, the existence of an instant which would be its final point: a point of interruption and suspension at the edge of a void; a point which would be the first of another series and would inaugurate a new duration. Such is not the Prévostian instant. Its positive significance is to be situated both at the extremity of one time and at the beginning of another, and to be, moreover, not that which binds these times together but that which separates them. It is exactly what prevents these times from joining each other and nevertheless allows one to follow another. Extraordinary and monstrous passage, truly against nature, the opposite of the impalpable flow by which one time passes into another. In this case one finds himself in the presence of an instant that is incomparable to all other instants and which erects between them the hiatus, both instantaneous and infinite, of its own reality, and which, despite the fact that because of it the future and the past cannot fuse and blend, exists only because they touch and create it in touching:

I do not know how the heart can pass so suddenly from one situation to its opposite; sometimes an instant produces this strange vicissitude.[2]

With Prévost, then, the instant-passage is a passage from one extreme to the other. It is the instant in which extremes meet. Indifferently, it is a passage from the greatest joy to the greatest sorrow, and from the greatest sorrow to the greatest joy:

> I have noticed all my life that Heaven has always chosen to strike me with its harshest punishments at the time when my fortune seemed to me most stable.[3]

. . . .

> By a change unbelievable to those who have never felt violent passions, I passed in a flash from the tranquillity I thought was mine, into a terrible transport of fury.[4]

. . . .

> Though my despair had mounted to the most terrible violence, it was coming to an end, and by utterly unhoped for revolutions; it was amidst the horrors of so dreadful a situation that Heaven was going to break the dawn of my loveliest days.[5]

. . . .

> Love which is successively capable of all the excesses can pass in a moment from the most shameful desires to the noblest feelings of virtue.[6]

The instant-passage consists, then, in the reversal of the emotive flow. It bears witness to an absolute instability of the being, which on the one hand fails:

> It is this very instability, this variety of motions and situations that I give here as witness and confession of my weakness . . .[7]

but on the other hand this weakness is a strength; for without the absolute instability of the soul, there could never spring forth from the instantaneous contrast of situations a double instantaneous response. Out of this simultaneity of the successive an instant is formed which belongs neither to what precedes nor to what follows, an instant of strange vicissitude.

II

What a passage it was from the tranquil situation I had been in, to the tumultuous motions I felt being reborn! I was staggered. I shuddered as when night falls upon one in isolated open country; one feels transported into a new order of things; one is seized with a secret horror.[8]

. . . .
I find myself at the gate of an unknown land. . . .[9]

This unknown land where one is transported into a new order of things, this country of the instant, which in the wreckage and splitting in duration rises up thus by means of contrast, resembles in no way the countries already traversed; and the consciousness, finding there no landmark at all, throws its astonished gaze about as if it had just been born. It is thus that Des Grieux describes the situation of his mind after having read the letter which Manon has left, breaking off their affair:

> I remained, after the reading of it, in a state which would be difficult for me to describe; for I still do not know today by what kind of feeling I was agitated then. It was one of those unique situations, unlike any that one has ever experienced; one would not know how to explain them to others, because they would have no idea of them, and one can hardly unravel them oneself, because being the only thing of their kind, they are unrelated to anything in the memory, and cannot even be compared to any known feeling.[10]

Thus in *Cleveland:* "I have difficulty choosing the terms to express to you what I had never before felt." [11]

The difficulty a man of feeling experiences in trying to express the movement which transports him is therefore similar to that of the mystic who wants to express what he has felt in the ecstatic union. A difficulty that is not caused only by what is utterly unspeakable in the experience but also by the confusion of mind of him who has been the subject of it. Like the mystic, he finds between what he experiences in that very moment and the life he has already lived neither any analogy nor any continuity. He lives in a present that is attached to nothing; in a time without relation to time past, the evidence of which, on the other hand, is so blinding that one cannot conceive that after it there may come a future. Such a one has neither past nor future. His existence is confined to an immediate reality, almost unbearable:

> What a moment! One dies of joy, it is said; one dies of the violence of a passion which disorders all the senses: Nay, one dies of nothing, since I was for an instant capable of supporting what took place in my soul.[12]

Not that this moment which transcends all others abolishes the consciousness of what one is. In contrast to the state of the mystic, the state to which the man of feeling is hereby brought is not at all a state of unity, but of the simultaneity of contraries, not a state of fusion but of confusion:

> The situation from which I emerge increases my amazement and my turmoil, by the extreme contrast between the state I am in now and the one from which Heaven has delivered me, but the memory of which is still present with me. Imagine, then, a man who, in the same instant that he finds himself relieved of a frighteningly oppressive burden, passes at one leap into a state so free that, feeling no further impediment, he is actually afraid, for want of being oppressed or weighed down, that every step he takes into the void will only expose him to some dangerous fall. He walks with a nimbleness that makes him tremble, and the movement that hurries him along is so rapid that he hardly recognizes what lies about him.[13]

The term *state* has here therefore an equivocal meaning. For it is not to any extent a question of a lasting condition of the heart, but only a state of passage, less a state than a movement by which, within the moment, one passes from one condition of mind to a condition or transport that is just the opposite:

> All my movements are transports. They carry me along with an inexpressible violence and confusion. I pass so rapidly from one to the other that they all seem to be simultaneously present in my mind, although it *can distinguish nothing* in the intoxication they induce.[14]

This is the essential point of the dialectic of the moment in Prévost. If the peculiarity of the moment-passage is to establish a confusion among extreme feelings, the result is that this confusion, born of the contrast between the feelings, ends, in the very instant in which this contrast creates it, in abolishing in its turn the contrast, and in replacing it by an identity. It matters little whether this passage be one of joy or sorrow. There is suddenly no longer either sorrow or joy; there only remains a feeling which is not properly speaking either of them but which holds the two together, or rather which transcends and expresses both, since this feeling through which one *distinguishes nothing* is pure feeling, feeling reduced to its elemental state, the undifferentiated feeling with which, according to the circumstances, life fashions out of sorrow or out of joy:

I do not know how the heart can pass so suddenly from one situation to the very opposite. . . . Is there so little difference then between those interior motions which constitute sorrow and joy? Or rather, is it not *the same motion,* which takes different names accordingly as it changes object and cause? Mark my words: true joy shows the same symptoms as deep sorrow. It makes the tears flow, it makes the voice break, it causes a delightful languor, it occupies the mind with the consideration of the cause of its emotions, and of two men transported one by joy and the other by sorrow, I do not know which of them would be the less willing to have the feeling he enjoys snatched away from him.[15]

The identity of contrasting feelings is thus something primal. Before there was cause or object, before the intervention of the cause or the object had launched the soul upon a fixed course, that movement existed, as it continues to exist. It existed in the human being, not in the sense that a pleasure or a pain exists, but in its basic form, that of "an active propensity which carries it, it knows not where":

The philosopher has only to reflect for a moment. What does he perceive? I am wrong, for he perceives nothing; but he feels in the depths of his being a secret inclination, an active propensity that carries him he knows not where. How will he be able to define this feeling? It is the exigence of some unknown need demanding to be fulfilled. If it is not actually a painful condition, it is at least the lack of a good, without which he cannot be tranquil; and he strains ceaselessly toward that good, impelled to search for it by an involuntary motion, as if swept along by an irresistible influence.[16]

A great many Christian writers before Prévost, before Locke, before Pascal, have made of this motion—joined to a feeling of deprivation—the starting point of the affective life. But what is peculiar to the thought of Prévost is that in his view this motion is not only at the origin of our emotions and our passions but that it *is* these very passions. Sorrow or joy, love or hate, all the opposing impulses in which, one by one, feeling invests itself, are only so many temporary designations or significations. They indicate the direction that is imposed, the provisory form inculcated upon feeling by the cause or the object. But they thereby conceal from us its authentic nature, and they almost continually prevent us from perceiving that our existence is expressed, from throughout the whole of our being, only by that unique, continuous note which is the basic sound vibrating in our depth.

In order to perceive it, if we want to hear again that note, we need the sudden encounter and simultaneous accord of what almost always appears in our life as contrary and successive. When both joy and sorrow are gathered up into the same moment, then there is no longer either sorrow or joy; there remains only one selfsame motion of the soul, and the soul takes sudden knowledge of that undifferentiated motion.

It is the same thing, moreover, in the instantaneous passage from peace of mind to profound passion. In love at first sight, in the instant when the soul is both shaken and undone, there occurs within it an immediate rediscovery of all the interior resources of its being. Thus it was that Des Grieux felt his mind was illumined by his great love in the lightning flash of a moment. Thus, in another novel of Prévost's the hero expresses, in the following terms, the feelings that the object of his first love inspires in him:

> The sight of her charms, the animated tone of her voice, the warmth of her regard, instantly made such an impression upon me as I had never experienced before; or rather a thousand feelings which *must already have been dwelling in my heart,* to blaze up in so vehement a flash, apprised me, then and there, of the nature of love.[17]

Thus at its extreme point the affective experience becomes the agent of knowledge. In an instant in which all discontinuous duration and all contrariety of being are abolished, man discovers in the depths of himself the permanence of a feeling upon which true duration is founded.

III

This unity of feeling gives the novels of Prévost their real significance: a primal unity which one discovers when one "takes things back to their origin"; a unity which one recognizes more clearly when one takes life to its terminal point, or like Cleveland, to the end of his existence, and "idolizing his melancholy," one meditates alone in the silence and the solitude, in order to revive, in picturing them to oneself, the emotional states of the past:

> The paper . . . becomes animated in receiving the impression of a sad and passionate heart; it preserves them faithfully in the hollow of memory; it is always ready to depict them; and this image serves

not only to nourish a dear and delicious sadness, but also to justify it.[18]

The affective revival requires for Prévost only a minimum of images. It seeks to summon up again its sorrows as divested as possible of all the too precise and too various memories which would come to spoil the regained harmony. It would like to eliminate all the sensations which ordinarily accompany it and conceal its existence, but which on the other hand bind it to the singularities of events. It tries to attain the pure emotional substratum of the past, and to express only that; for in this substratum the mind, nourished with its former emotions, feels no longer any distinction between them; it now experiences them only as a single feeling which is equally distributed over all the lived past. The mind no longer has to survey the episodes of its life, or to begin once more to live the successive successively; but it has to recollect itself once and for all in a condition that is *the same* in all the points of its duration:

> It is the state of mind that I consult, rather than the rules of narration and the duties of the historian. No matter how many misfortunes may have been mine, and in what diversity, they act upon my heart today, all at the same time; *the feeling that remains in me possesses no longer the variety of its cause;* it is now, if I may dare to say so, only a uniform mass of sorrow the weight of which presses upon me and overwhelms me constantly, and so I could wish, if it were possible for my pen, to assemble in one single stroke all my unhappy adventures, just as their effect is unified in the depths of my mind. One could judge very much better what happens. Order constrains me. . . .[19]

Despite Cleveland's wishes, he is unable to "depict all his misfortunes at once." For in contrast to sorrow, which is a feeling, and which, like all feeling, together with all feelings, can be made to vibrate at once, in every profound expression of being, unhappiness on the other hand is that complex thing in which, at a moment determined by history, feelings and events are joined together. The affective life can, in the final analysis, be reunited, thus allowing for the consciousness of a pure feeling that gives its color to all of existence; but it is not the same for the life of the senses, and consequently for that of the passions. The latter never gets entirely disengaged from its *history*. It remains involved in its own duration. For if all successive sorrows can finally be confounded into one uniform mass, how can one fashion a uniform mass out of the varied events that provoked these sorrows? One feels also in the Prevostian novel the presence of two opposing tendencies: the tendency toward multiplicity of exterior events; and the tendency toward the progressive simplification of their affective results. On the one hand, the story observes an order of succession; on the other, that order *constrains it,* because it is the one of discursive time, to the nature of which the uniform duration of unified feeling is profoundly opposed.

It is an opposition that is found again, to a higher degree, in the double conception which Prévost holds of human destiny. On the one hand man appears to be stricken by "distinct blows of destiny" that consecutively exert upon him their occasional but all-powerful force. In the manner of the Jansenists, he readily conceives the mind to be alternately subjugated by "irresistible leanings":

> A simple passion—I designate in this way all the spontaneous motions of the heart—whatever strength one might suppose it to have— will not hold its ground long against a stronger passion; victory is a matter of degree; and this ascendancy of strength, which renders the decision inevitable almost always arises out of *present circumstances,* the action of which fills the mind, discountenances the rival passion, and deprives it of the power to make itself felt.[20]

But, on the other hand, these alternate actions and these opposed destinies no longer appear contradictory when one considers them as incomprehensible but certain manifestations of a Providence that decides our whole destiny. Thus the history of our passions, assuming a semireligious character, acquires the unity of a providential fulfillment—so much so that, above as below the discontinuity of the life of the senses, one finds two continuities encircling it: the divine action; and the action of the heart.

NOTES

1 *Oeuvres choisies* (Amsterdam, 1783), I, 330.
2 *Ibid.,* V, 73.
3 *Ibid.,* III, 382.
4 *Ibid.,* p. 397.
5 *Ibid.,* VI, 343.
6 *Ibid.,* XXXV, 150.
7 *Ibid.,* VII, 23.
8 *Ibid.,* III, 279.
9 *Ibid.,* VII, 5.
10 *Ibid.,* III, 309.
11 *Ibid.,* VII, 5.
12 *Ibid.,* XIII, 168.
13 *Ibid.,* VII, 5.
14 *Ibid.*
15 *Ibid.,* V, 73.
16 *Ibid.,* p. 413.
17 *Ibid.,* XII, 39.
18 *Ibid.,* IV, 3.
19 *Ibid.,* V, 266.
20 *Ibid.,* XXIX, 154.

ROUSSEAU

The condition of man in infancy, says Rousseau, is "the life of an animal limited at first to *pure sensations.*" [1] It is the same for the infant as for primitive man: "all their knowledge resides in sensation." [2] Considered in its infancy or taken in its state of nature, the human being seems to be all sensation. He is subject to *pure sensation,* that is to say to actual sensation, "purely organic and local," [3] comparable neither to what precedes nor to what follows. He is without past and without future, without foresight and without memory. "His imagination depicts nothing for him; his heart demands nothing of him." [4] Sensation, for him, is not related to, is not constructed of, anything; it does not become idea: it remains image.

To be *limited to pure sensations* is thus to *be* the very sensation itself; it is, like the statue of Condillac, to be odor of rose. "Suppose," says Rousseau, "that a child had in its infancy the stature and strength of a grown man, that it sprang, so to speak, fully armed from the womb of its mother as Pallas sprang from the brow of Jupiter; this man-child would be a perfect imbecile, an automaton, an immobile and almost insensate statue. . . . Not only would it perceive no object outside itself, it would not even connect any one of them with the sense organ which allows it to be perceived." [5] This man-child is primitive man himself. "One cannot deny that this state is fairly close to the primitive state of ignorance and stupidity natural to man before he had learned anything from experience or from his fellow-creatures." [6] In this state, man could not perceive any object *outside himself:* "The very touch of his hands would be in his brain." Thus there is no opposition between object and subject; at the lower level of human life what is discovered is somehow analogous to what Fichte was later to establish on the plane of pure thought: the primal identity of subject and object.

But, for Rousseau, this identity being psychological, it manifests itself in a concrete fashion: not in the abstract, by a concept, but in the living soul through sensation. Mind and sensation then appear as originally identical. The mind appears to itself under the form of the sensation that fills it.

Being pure sensation, the primitive being is purely passive. The mind submits to what it is. But if this is so, the passive being will live a life that is irremediably stationary and discontinuous. It "will experience every object separately." [7] It must be, therefore (since man has emerged from this state), that there was within him, from the beginning, an active principle. Indeed the internal evidence reveals it irresistibly.

This active principle exists, to be sure. And just as the passivity in man is pure sensation—a simple, local, actual thing, always unique —his primitive activity will have the same character. The very simplicity of the sensation reveals even more clearly, outside of all action, in its pure virtuality, the activity of primitive man: "His mind, disturbed by nothing, gives itself over to the sole feeling of his actual existence." [8] "Man's first feeling was that of his existence." [9] At the moment of its birth, because the mind is still imprisoned in imperfect sense organs, "it does not have even the feeling of its own existence"; but suppose it were born with perfect organs; then even if it did not perceive any other object outside of itself, it would have a single idea, a sole awareness, "that of the *self,* to which it would refer all of its sensations." [10]

But is this active feeling of the self really single? Is it, like sensation, something given, which consequently becomes a part of the definition of man? Or, if it is only an effect, is it a compound of sensations, as the philosophers believe? Rousseau states the question at the beginning of the *Vicaire savoyard:*

Have I a real feeling of my existence, or do I feel it only through my sensations? That is my principal doubt, and up to the present it has been impossible for me to resolve it. For being affected by sensations, continually, or immediately, or through the memory, how can I know whether the feeling of myself exists outside of these sensations, and if it is independent of them? [11]

The answer to this main question is to be found throughout *Émile* and the *Discours sur l'inégalité:*

> To live is not to breathe, it is to act; it is to make use of our organs, of our senses, of our faculties, of every part of ourself that gives us the feeling of our existence.[12]

Thus it is not through sensations alone that the feeling of our existence is produced; it is by a use, even more, by an *action*. "No material being is active by itself, and I am active." [13] An inner certainty that is beyond all reasoning tells me so, and this is the very thing that I want to *demonstrate*.

> Let anyone try to argue me out of that; I feel it, and this feeling which speaks to me is stronger than the reason which contradicts it. . . . My will is independent of my senses. . . . I always possess will-power. . . .[14]

> Nature commands each animal, and every beast obeys. Man experiences the same compunction, but he recognizes himself as free to acquiesce or to resist.[15]

> The principle of all action is in the will of a free being; one can't get beyond that.[16]

But if to be active is to be free, and if to be free is to have the power of will, it is also, simultaneously, to have the power of thought:

> In my opinion, the distinctive faculty of the active or intelligent being is the power to give meaning to that word *is*.[17]

> In the power to will, or rather in the power to choose, and in the feeling of that power, one finds only certain purely spiritual acts which are utterly unexplainable by mechanical laws.[18]

There is no free will without consciousness of choice, without, beyond the sensations, a distinguishing of affinities; that is to say, without intelligence and without reason. But the primitive being, living in the instantaneous, identifying himself with the object of his actual sensation, without memory or foresight, cannot, it would seem, be free, any more than he can be passionate, reasonable, or moral.

Yes, he can! says Rousseau. Without memory, without foresight, without discrimination, without a distinct will, it is still possible to be free, and the primitive being is free before even having made a reflective act or a deliberate choice. Liberty and activity on the one hand, intelligence and will on the other, are mutually implied only in a world in which one has to join "the feeling of common existence to that of individual existence," [19] but not in a world in which common existence and individual existence being one in pure sensation, the feeling of this existence also has to be one. If the savage lives as if identified with nature, if the child exists only in a *common sensorium,* if the primitive man *seems* always to yield to the solicitations of instinct, if finally he accepts pure sensation without comparing it with anything else, that is because he is in the state of nature, that is to say in a state of harmony in which the being is what he wishes to be. "It is only in the primitive state," says Rousseau, "that there occurs a balance of power and desire." [20] Hence at that time and in that state all the faculties of man, memory, imagination, judgment, reason, remain virtual. I do not feel less free because I have not experienced freedom. I do not feel my own power any the less because I do not distinguish it from all the powers that bear upon or incite me. Primitive man is always passive, since he submits to all his sensations; but he is also always active, since continually and always he *wills* all of his sensations. He *is* his sensation, but he is also the feeling that he wills it, that he accepts it, let us even say, that he produces and creates it.

In other words, man, in this state of his existence is passive and active at the same time, in the totality of his being. Passivity and activity are confounded. It is only later that they become distinct. Finally, in this pure sensation which is also at the same time pure activity and feeling of existence, man possesses perfect happiness. There is no contrariety in him: his own being fills the universe, and the universe fills his own being. He lives in himself, but inversely nature lives in him. He suffices himself because nature, being what it is, suffices him. He lives completely in the present moment because there are no other moments, and if there are no other moments, it is because the fullness of each moment fills his mind at each moment, leaving no part of it empty, and thus leaving present no desire to return to a better past, or to invoke a more seductive future. "All its forces in action, the mind remains at peace." [21]

This peace, this accord with oneself, which is an accord with nature, constitutes the only true happiness, the only happiness that is not relative, an absolute happiness. Happiness is peace; peace is in the present moment, in the eternity of the actuality, the identity of *pure sensation* and of the *feeling of actual existence.*

II

From the state of nature, man passes or falls to the state of society. In this new state the subject is opposed by the object, the self discovers a non-self. Man no longer lives in a sort of absolute, no longer is limited to pure sensation, no longer is identified with nature, no longer confirms himself in the sole feeling of his actual existence. In addition to the present, the future and the past take form and invite comparisons and preferences. This is the kingdom of the relative, the kingdom of time.

This fall, if it is one, does not necessarily entail disastrous consequences. On the contrary, such a change of condition allows man first of all to develop his latent faculties. The primitive harmony is broken, but it can in each instant be re-established by an *effort*. The active no longer coincides with the passive. Man is no longer content with pure sensation; but his needs being simple and easily satisfied, his desires are not acute, his judgments are right, his choices are just, his actions prompt. "So all our faculties are developed: the imagination has come into play, self-love has awakened, and reason is made active." All the force of energy and thought which existed only virtually in the feeling of existence seems now to go to work, to get functioning. The soul becomes mind and will; that is to say, it establishes relationships according to which it freely chooses to act for its own good instead of simply accepting its satisfaction, as it did in the state of nature.

But this fall into time does not stop there. Man more and more comes to feel his limitations. The fundamental harmony which had formerly existed between nature and himself gives place to a growing disorder. His judgments become less simple, his choices less appropriate, his satisfactions more rare, his desires painful. The situation he finds himself in now is no longer the one in which his being blossomed, but one in which the non-self asserts its force, unyielding and opaque: the kingdom of matter. The present instant is no longer for him that which once made him happy and determined to gratify a simple need in the next moment. Now, when one invokes it, when one wants to see the unsatisfactory present replaced by it, the future is slow in coming. The past no longer serves simply as a point of view for comparison, but as a cause for regret: "We no longer exist where we are; we only exist where we are not." [22]

And so man begins really to live in time, and time is revealed to him in all its tragic reality:

> Everything upon earth is in continuous flux. Nothing in it retains a form that is constant and fixed, and our affections, attached to external things, necessarily pass and change like the things themselves. Always, ahead of or behind us, they recall the past which no longer exists, or they anticipate a future which often will never come to pass: there is nothing there solid enough for the heart to attach itself to.[23]

Time is the place of insufficiency and, as a consequence, the place of pain and unhappiness.

III

Up until now, as we have described it, Rousseau's thought has proceeded from the abstract to the concrete, from the ideal to the real. But that reality is still entirely general. It behooves him to present it in its most concrete form, to deal with the drama of time as it has been lived by an individual being whose sufferings and effort are a worthy example. In that, as in all the rest, Rousseau adduces himself and his existence as witness; he sets before us a drama which is both the most personal, and at the same time the most generally human.

For he has lived this drama of time to the point of distraction and anguish. There is discerned at the outset, in the temporality of Rousseau, the action of "an unruly imagination, ready to take umbrage at anything and to carry everything to an extreme." [24] The imagination, that is to say the power to live by the mind, both backward and ahead, the power perpetually to depart from the present: "My imagination, which in my youth always leapt forward, and now looks backward . . . ." [25] The anticipatory imagination dominates Rousseau's youth:

> In my youth . . . I was active because I was foolish; in proportion as I was disillusioned, I changed my tastes, attachments, and projects, and in all these changes I always lost time and energy, because I always looked for what did not exist.[26]

Thence that intense need of displacement, of change, those escapades, contradictions, and inconsistencies of his early life; thence the source of his aversion for whatever excites the imagination and sweeps the mind away from the present and deprives it of peace, his animosity for the sciences and the arts:

> Man is born to act and to think, and not to reflect. Reflection serves only to make him unhappy, without making him better or wiser: it causes him to lament the good things of the past, and prevents him from enjoying the present; it conjures up for him the happy future in order to seduce him by the imagination and torment him with desires—and the unhappy future, to make him suffer in advance.[27]

One knows to what point, in its unruliness, Rousseau's imagination carried the art of *suffering* the unhappy future *in advance;* and one can imagine the kind of tragic dilemma in which the anticipatory working of the mind places it every moment: Either what is anticipated is the evil future:

> My startled imagination, which allows me to foresee only futures that are cruel. . . .[28]
>
> . . . .
>
> My cruel imagination which is ceaselessly tormented with attempting to forestall evils which do not yet exist.[29]
>
> . . . .
>
> I drain, so to speak, my unhappiness in advance;[30]

or what is anticipated is a happy future and that means abandoning oneself with all the intensity of a passion actually lived to "chimeras" ("I fashioned a golden age which suited my fancy"), only to discover at once their inadequacy: "If all my dreams had been turned into realities, they would not have sufficed me . . . ," [31] and to feel tortured by "an inexplicable emptiness which nothing would have been able to fill":

> Thus one is exhausted before arriving at the end; and the closer we are to enjoyment, the remoter our happiness.[32]

Hence gradually Rousseau came to consider the future with dismay, then with terror, and he strove in vain to turn his mind away from it. The flight toward the future, the very direction of time, the normal direction in the lives of normal or passionate young men, became in his eyes a flight toward unhappiness. The anticipatory imagination appeared to him as the very symbol of what is most deadly in man; a need to invent needs, a longing to hurl oneself into a state of insufficiency and suffering:

> Forethought! The forethought that ceaselessly sweeps us beyond ourselves . . . that is the real cause of our miseries. What madness for

a being as transitory as man, always to look far into a future that
so rarely comes to pass, and to neglect the present of which he is
sure! [33]

If the future is the time of unhappiness, should the present be
that of delight? To live in the future, thought Rousseau, is to withdraw from happiness, which is made of sufficiency; to fix himself
in the present, in the actual, like primitive man, child or savage, that
is what he has to try to do.

IV

To be fixed in the present, but how is that to be accomplished? How
can one coerce into fixity a mind that escapes in every direction at
once and expands only in its very liberty? There is nothing more
pathetic than the spectacle offered by this being who wishes to de-
limit himself, and yet who always the more invincibly tends "to lay
hold of everything," "to range over the whole earth," "to spread his
sensibility over its great surface." [34] Yet it is undeniable that Rousseau wrote the following sentence: "The real world has its boundaries, the imaginary world is infinite; since we cannot enlarge the one
let us contract the other." [35] The contraction of the imaginary world
to the boundaries of the real world is what Rousseau proposes to
Sophie as a rule of conduct in the *Lettres morales,* for the education
of Émile in his pedagogical essay; that is what he maintains he has
accomplished in the *Lettres à Malesherbes,* in the *Confessions,* the
Rêveries, the *Dialogues.*

A constriction very evidently contrary to one side of his nature,
but which satisfies another. For this constriction is first of all a *withdrawal.* If one of the essential traits of the thought of Rousseau is a
centrifugal motion, of expansion outward and toward the future,
there also exists in him, and more and more pronounced with the
years, an inverse motion, centripetal, oriented inward:

> Feeling that I would never find among them a situation that could
> bring peace to my heart, I withdrew it little by little from the society
> of men. . . .[36]

A detachment, a withdrawal inward, to the center of the sphere,
into solitude, which perhaps implies an effort, but which seems,
however, less the effect of an heroic determination of wisdom than
the transference of the center of gravity of the spontaneous being.

Besides, withdrawal involves no essential sacrifice. On the contrary, the break with the exterior world furnishes—exquisite pleasure—the means of rediscovering the interior world. To contract is to recover the self:

> Let us measure the radius of our sphere and rest at the center, like the insect in the middle of its web. . . . O man! close up thy existence within thyself, and thou shalt no longer be miserable.[37]

> Let us begin by becoming ourselves again, by centering in ourselves, by circumscribing our soul within the very boundaries nature has given us; let us begin, in a word, by pulling ourselves together where we are. . . . As the first strokes of a drawing are formed of the contours that bound it, so the primary idea of man is to become separate from all that is not himself.[38]

In its temporal existence the human mind has only too great a tendency to disperse itself through imagination and passion beyond its own sphere. The fall into time has not only corrupted the pure sensation which was born of the actual. Multiplying the occasions of living in the future or the past, it has, so to speak, dismembered the different parts of our interior being, and by the same token, the feeling of our existence has grown faint. Through our desires we live in the future, through our passions in the past, through our sensations in the present. We are torn to pieces by the different points of duration. Therefore we must concentrate all the forces of our being on our being, on the seizure of our soul in the present instant:

> Let us begin by . . . reassembling ourselves where we are, so that in trying to know ourselves, all that we are may become altogether present within us.[39]

In this reassembling of the whole being in order to feel oneself be, what becomes apparent, at least provisionally, is the drawing of a distinct frontier between the self and the non-self and, as it were, an orientation of the soul toward the interior, toward what is *within.* Rousseau's mind again comes into possession of *the feeling of his actual existence,* which the savage enjoyed of old, which the child enjoys before he becomes a man. A return to the primitive state, but still it is an imperfect state. The feeling of the self now appears only as the sequel of a differentiation, of an exclusion of the non-self. On the other hand, in returning to the original attitude of the mind, nothing could be more absurd than to reject all the vast spiritual development that man owes to the play of his faculties. To feel oneself, then, takes on a more complex significance. Feeling has become consciousness.

But these differences ought not to hide the essential identity of that consciousness of self with primitive man's feeling of actual existence. Beyond the oppositions of self and non-self and the complexities and the acquisitions of the mind, what is reaffirmed here is the same operation, the most radically simple, that is: "I feel my mind," says Rousseau;[40] and in another passage: "The man who has lived the most is he who has felt life most." [41] Finally, in the *Lettres morales,* he sums up in a vigorous expression the act that is to be accomplished: "to wake up the inner feeling."

The spiritual activity in constricting oneself has not become the less intense for that nor, in the interior of his sphere, the less extensive:

> In what does human wisdom or the way to true happiness consist? It is not exactly to diminish our desires. . . . It is to diminish the excessive force of our desires upon our faculties, and to set poetry and will in perfect equality. It is only then that, with all its forces in action, the mind can remain at peace. . . .[42]

What is apparent in this attitude is the simultaneous and total concourse of all that makes up the self, in order to help it to be. Then, in that vibrant reassembling of all the energies, a harmony is established, a balance is struck and maintained: the mind, in feeling itself, feels its unity, its permanence, its fullness: "A happiness . . . which is not at all composed of fugitive instants, but is a simple and permanent state . . ." [43] and in another place: "My heart, uniquely occupied with the present, fills its whole capacity, all its space." [44]

Delimiting of the self, reassembling of the self, fullness and sufficiency, such are the characteristics of the feeling of existence regained.

I have a very loving heart, but who can be sufficient unto himself.[45]

V

In such a manner Rousseau means to escape the corruption of the ages and to regain—not in the chimera of a future ideal, but in the magic reality of a present that is felt and that is concrete—the feeling of actual existence, such as it was experienced by the man of nature: ". . . I tried to put myself completely in the state of a man who is just beginning to live." [46]

But as we have seen, man in a state of nature possessed this feeling of the self only in concurrence with another element, that of *pure sensation*. The feeling of the self does not rise up out of nothingness in the void, but in the seizure, by the mind, of the simplest sensory event. Doubtless by reason also of the fall into time and into society, that sensory and passive element also has lost part of its original purity. Our sensations are disguised by repetitions, desires, and habits. It is necessary to rid oneself of them like the rest in order to regain the power of feeling. To the rediscovery of the self made by Rousseau, there corresponds then a parallel rediscovery of pure sensation. There is no passage that allows us to observe more distinctly this double phenomenon of regeneration than the one at the beginning of the work that Rousseau consecrated to the union of interior feeling and pure sensation. On almost the very first page of the *Rêveries* one finds the episode of the fall of Ménilmontant. There Rousseau describes minutely what he experiences when he regains consciousness after a fainting spell:

> The state in which I found myself in that instant was too singular not to give a description of it here. Night was well advanced, I caught sight of the sky, some stars and a little greenery. This *first sensation* was a delightful moment. *I could feel myself, yet only through this.* I was born that instant to life, and it seemed to me that I filled with my featherlike existence every object I was perceiving. *Engulfed wholly in the present moment,* I could remember nothing; I had no distinct notion of my person, nor the least idea of what had just happened to me; I knew neither who I was nor where I was; I felt neither pain, nor fear, nor anxiety. . . . I felt through my whole being a *ravishing calm,* to which, every time I recall it, I find nothing comparable in all the activity of known pleasures.

It is therefore at the precise moment when the mind, detached from the world and from its own artificial personality, issues from annihilation in order to be reborn to life, that it suddenly, spontaneously regains in the depths of itself the twin elements which give the existences of primitive man and that of the child their particular perfection. The *coming to life* takes place in the flashing spontaneity of a *primal sensation* and with a perception of self completely confounded with the sensation, and simply forming a whole with it: *I could feel myself yet only through this.* Finally, from the identity between sensation and feeling in an indivisible moment there springs an impression of perfect fullness: *I filled with my tenuous existence all the objects I perceived.* All opposition between the self and the non-self is suppressed, and nothing remains but to enjoy a happiness without passion, due to the equilibrium of the active element and the passive element: *I felt through my whole being a ravishing calm.*

The *Rêveries* are full of these moments of grace. The most celebrated and the most detailed of all is the *moment* by the Lake of Bienne. Rousseau attains there a degree of ecstasy that is even more significant. The soul there regains not only the primitive human perfection, the "state of innocence" or of the "heir of the Sun," of which Rimbaud speaks; it is lifted up to a state almost divine: "As long as that state lasts, one is sufficient unto himself, like God." For, even in the actual, the liberation from time is still not absolute; beyond and above it is situated the zone of pure timelessness which is that of the divine eternity. For the first time in literature a text appears which sets out to recount—not as a didactic development or a mystical vision, but as an experience personally lived—the *totum simul* of the Alexandrians and the Scholastics.

The passage begins like the others with the statement of the contracting of the being to pure sensation and to the feeling of actual existence:

> When the evening was approaching I descended from the heights of the island and seated myself with pleasure at the shore of the lake, on the beach, in a secluded place. There, the sound of the waves and the agitation of the water, *fixing my senses* and *chasing from my mind all other agitation,* plunged it into a delightful revery in the midst of which the night often caught me by surprise before I knew it. The ebb and flow of that water . . . striking my ears and my eyes without intermission, were a substitute for the interior motions which the revery *extinguished* in me, and *sufficed to make me feel my existence with pleasure,* without taking the trouble to think.

This is still a purely psychological description of the return of the mind to the primitive state. Then follows a development that one cannot call other than metaphysical. Rousseau distinguishes the state in which he finds himself in these *reveries* from ecstasies that are purely actual, *brief moments of delirium and passion,* which are *too rare and too swift to constitute a state,* whereas here it is a question of a *simple and permanent state,* which radically escapes the power of duration:

> But if there is a state in which the mind finds a resting place solid enough to repose upon completely and *reassemble there its whole being,* without needing to recall the past or encroaching upon the future; where *time means nothing to it, where the present lasts forever,* but without indicating its duration, and without any trace of succession, without any feeling whatever of deprivation or of joy, of pleasure or of pain, of desire or of fear, beyond *the sole feeling of our existence, and that this feeling alone can fill it entirely:* as long as this state endures, the one who experiences it may be called happy, not of an imperfect happiness, poor and relative, such as one finds in the pleasures of life, but of a *sufficient happiness, perfect and full,* which leaves no empty place in the mind which it feels the need to fill up. Such is the state I often found myself in on the island of Saint-Pierre. . . .

The better to understand the purity of this *simple and permanent state,* one can compare it to that other non-temporal moment of which Saint-Preux gives Mme. d'Orbe a description:

> Days of pleasure and of glory, no, you could not be days lived by a mortal; you are too beautiful to be perishable. A sweet ecstasy *absorbed all your duration,* and *reassembled it in a single point like the one of eternity.* There was for me neither past nor future, and I tasted simultaneously the pleasures of a thousand centuries. Alas! You have disappeared like a flash of lightning. That eternity of happiness filled only an instant of my life. Time has resumed its slow course. . . .[47]

At first sight the two "states" appear identical: the reassembling of the being is found linked in both of them to the annihilation of time, but whereas in the first state this annihilation seems to be realized absolutely in the perfect serenity of *mind* of which Rousseau speaks in a letter to Malesherbes, in the second, on the contrary, it seems that we find ourselves in the presence of one of those *brief moments of delirium and passion* which, *animated as they may be, are, however, and by their very vivacity, only so many sparsely scattered points along life's path;* brief moments in which, in the terms of Mme. d'Orbe's reply to Saint-Preux, "one does not behold the *permanent state* of a sensitive mind, but rather the last delirium

of a heart that is burning with love and drunken with voluptuousness." Nothing describes better than this comparison the abyss
Rousseau sets between the false non-temporalness obtained by a
sort of multiplication of the motions of the mind under the sway of
passion, and, on the other hand, the authentic "eternal moment" attained, thanks to a kind of ascesis, by the conjunction of the feeling
of the self and pure sensation.

There is no doubt, however, that in both of these passages Rousseau had in mind, *in order to define his own state,* the definition of
the divine eternity such as had been formulated by the Neo-
Platonists and the Church Fathers, with which he was very familiar:

> All truths are, for it (the divine intelligence), only a single idea,
> just as all places are a single point, and all times a single moment.[48]

Still elsewhere he speaks of God as of one "for whom times
have no succession, neither places distance." [49] Thus ecstasy not
only identifies actual man with the primitive being. It lifts him up
toward God, up to a state similar to that enjoyed by the saints in the
beatific vision. Further still, since what matters here is a happiness intrinsic to the mind that experiences it: "One is sufficient unto
himself, like God." Let us not be surprised, therefore, that at a time
when he wished to state the kind of happiness he dreamed of enjoying after his death in the bosom of God, Rousseau declared in the
clearest fashion the self-sufficiency of the soul liberated from the
successive and living in a completely personal eternity:

> I aspire to the moment when, delivered from the fetters of the body,
> I shall be myself without contradiction, without division, and shall
> have need only of myself in order to be happy.[50]

Isolation of mind, but in the totality of the universe! By a disconcerting motion, but typical of Rousseau, the effort of contraction
finally ends in its opposite, in a movement of expansion. As soon as
the feeling of the self is regained by the identification with pure sensation, nothing prevents the extending of this feeling to the vastest
possible sensation; nothing prevents one from repossessing *oneself*
in the sensation of the entire universe. The absence of all succession
and of all consciousness of time inordinately reinforces this movement of spatial expansion. All the *Rêveries* are full of these diffu-
sions of the self over the felt expanse:

I feel ecstasies, inexpressible ravishments when coalescing, so to speak, in the system of beings, and identifying myself with all nature.[51]

The contemplator . . . loses himself with a delicious intoxication in the immensity of that beautiful system with which he feels himself identified. Then all particular objects escape him; he sees and feels nothing except in the whole of things.[52]

But it is in the *Lettres à Malesherbes* that one can apprehend this pantheistic motion of thought at, so to speak, its starting point and in its original confusion:

But what did I finally enjoy when I was alone? *Myself, the whole universe,* all that is, all that I can be, everything beautiful in the sensory world, everything imaginable in the intellectual world: I gathered about me all that could soothe my heart.

And this still more striking passage:

Soon from the surface of the earth I lifted my ideas to all the beings of nature, to the universal system of things, to the incomprehensible Being who embraces all. Then, the mind lost in this immensity, I did not think, I did not reason, I did not philosophize: *I felt myself* with a sort of voluptuousness, overwhelmed with the weight of that universe, I gave myself up with rapture to the confusion of these lofty ideas; I took delight in losing myself imaginatively in space. . . .

The identifying ecstasy ends then, simultaneously with the abolition of duration, and the spiritualization of space. The universe, infinite in extent and gathered together into a durationless instant, is the common sensorium in which the feeling being perceives himself in an act by which he emulates God.

VI

"I loved to lose myself *imaginatively* in space." Rousseau's thought has come a complete circle. It is in order to escape the distracting and painful action of his imagination, "ready to carry everything to an extreme," that he had turned away from the boundless future and restricted himself to the limited present. And now this straitened present, limited to pure sensation, becomes boundless in its turn, becomes all space, and even tries to expand beyond space:

"Space is not thy measure, the whole universe is not big enough for thee." [53] Thus the imagination, banished from the future, sets itself to build in the present a measureless abode: "I suffocated in the universe; I wanted to soar into the infinite." [54]

So the pantheistic ecstasy of Rousseau is not a state of pure passivity. There is an active participation of the mind in contemplation. Feeling is accompanied by transport:

> Have you never experienced those involuntary transports which sometimes seize hold of a mind sensitive to the contemplation of moral beauty and the intellectual order of things, that consuming ardor that suddenly sets the heart on fire with the love of heavenly virtues, those sublime frenzies which lift us out of our being, and carry us up into the empyrean, where we are at the side of God himself? [55]

Such a passage permits us to see how with Rousseau the contemplative state can be simultaneously the *simple and permanent* state, which we have observed, and a state of crisis which cannot endure. If, on the other hand, the self finds in pure sensation the feeling of existence, the very perfection of this feeling engenders within it something more than what comprises it: joy; the consciousness of beauty; a transport of love which rises toward a higher order, of which nature is the symbol. The moment of equilibrium—to which the perfect conjunction of sensation and self gave an eternal value —is surpassed by the very excess of happiness it engenders, by the very quality of the thought it awakens. Surpassed, it is then no longer present. It is left behind: "Ah, that its sacred fire might endure and its high ecstasy might animate our whole life . . . ." [56] But a *fire* cannot "endure," precisely because it is "fire," that is to say activity and motion, the perpetual generation of its own duration:

> There is scarcely an instant amidst our most ardent delights when the heart can in truth tell us: I wish that this instant might last forever.[57]

But, when that moment arrives, the desire alone—the Faustian or Lamartinian desire that time suspend its flight—already indicates that that moment no longer exists, that one has passed beyond it, that it has become part of the past.

To live in the present, in those present moments of isolated ecstasy, which are the time of the *Rêveries,* is thus to live only by detached instants between which extend great neutral zones. It is not the resolving of the problem of time, but solely of a splendid but minute part of that time which constitutes existence. Thus, if the future is excluded, if the present *is* only of an intermittent and fortuitous sort, where shall the mind establish its dwelling place, where shall it be at home, except in the past?

The older Rousseau grows, the more and more natural it is for him to live in the past:

> My imagination, which in my youth always leapt ahead and now looks backward, compensates with those charming memories for the hope I have lost forever; I no longer see anything in the future to tempt me; returning to the past is the only thing that pleases me.[58]

Here the past asserts its supremacy over the future. Its supremacy over the present is asserted in another passage:

> My imagination, already less animated, is no longer kindled as it once was by the contemplation of that which quickens it; I am less intoxicated by the delirium of revery; there is more of reminiscence than of creation in what it henceforth produces.[59]

The thought of the aging Rousseau is thus turned more and more toward the past. The future, the place of unhappiness and bad dreams, no longer has the power it once had of arousing the anticipatory imagination; the present, the place of happiness and of good dreams, kindles the creative imagination less and less frequently. There remains the past, the place of memory, where the "retrogressive" imagination will rekindle time regained.

VII

> When my griefs make me count sadly the hours of the night, and a feverish agitation prevents me from enjoying a single moment of sleep, I often distract myself from my present state by thinking about the different events of my life, and the feelings of contrition, tenderness, sweet memories, and regrets, help to make me forget my suffering for a few moments.[60]

Thus, in the year 1762, Rousseau strives to escape the dismal present by cherishing the memories of the past. They loom across the varied and complex feelings which most often accompany them in human thought: contrition; tenderness; yearning. It should be noted, however, that at this period Rousseau has scarcely experienced yet that nostalgia for his childhood which is later to become so pronounced in him:

> What times, Sir, do you think I recall oftenest and most willingly in my dreams? Not the pleasures of my youth at all; they were too rare, too much mingled with bitterness, and are already too far removed from me.[61]

At this period of his life when the creative imagination is still intense, what he seeks after is the more immediate past. It is full of ecstasies or raptures. How easy it is to prolong them by dreams! The times which are most gladly recalled are

> those of my retirement into solitude, my lonely walks, those swift but delightful days which I passed entirely by myself, with my good, simple housekeeper, with my beloved dog, with the birds of the fields and the deer of the forest, with all nature and its inconceivable maker.[62]

No doubt those dreams are memories in which he pursues, at night, the joys of the day; but above all they are the efforts of the imagination to prolong or reawaken emotions that have never stopped being actual. It is still only of his present, affective being that the Rousseau of Montmorency takes any cognizance. However, from that time, and already for some years, perhaps because of the brief visit he made in 1754 to his native land, he occasionally encountered within himself the child he had once been: it is in this vein that he writes to Vernes, in 1759:

> Having almost become a child again, I am moved in recalling the songs of my childhood in Geneva; I sing them with a faint voice, and I end by weeping over my country, thinking that I have outlived it.[63]

Very likely these old songs were the ones his aunt sang to him, when he was a little boy, of which he speaks in almost the same terms in the *Confessions:* ". . . I sometimes catch myself weeping like a child when I mumble those little airs in a voice already broken and quavering."

Among those airs there is one that especially affects him, and he asks himself what the cause is of the pleasure he experiences: "I seek to understand the tender charm my heart finds in this song." [64]

One can suppose, then, that Rousseau, having discovered the "tender charm" of the deep past, accustomed himself to return to it more and more often in spirit and to seek there a source of more abundant delights than those offered by the present or the immediate future. Because what he was always looking for was an interior ravishment; and the one produced by reviviscence is no less intense than the pleasure of the "moment eternal." He very soon came to feel, however, that all affective memories are not indistinguishably pleasant. Certain of them are related to painful events: "To recall them is to renew their bitterness." [65] If he dreams of an injustice of which he has formerly been the victim, "his pulse races once more," his former feeling of indignation is "revived in him." [66] If he recalls an evil deed he has committed, he feels the torments of remorse, "I cannot forget my mistakes," says Rousseau, though he hastens to add: "and still less my good feelings." [67]

Thus Rousseau discovers the resources and the inconveniences of the affective memory; for the latter is "a state which is reestablished by recollection of it," [68] and it can be a state of happiness, but it can also very well be a state of suffering or of passion. Luckily Rousseau's memory is such as permits him to re-establish the former more often than the latter: "My memory . . . recalls to my mind only pleasant objects . . ." [69] and, in the *Dialogues,* speaking of himself:

> He can recall only the image of times that he would see reborn with pleasure. . . . A nature loving and tender, a languidness of spirit that brings him to the sweetest pleasures, making him reject all painful emotion, dispels from his memory every unpleasant object.

Henceforth only "past pleasures" are going to constitute "his unique delights." [70] This for him is a resource "so fecund that soon it suffices to compensate for everything else." [71] He makes an art of it, he multiplies the occasions of it in order to "render the present bearable"; [72] for "the happy times of my life . . . have been rare and brief, but their memory multiplies them." [73] When he relives these instants of happiness, he wishes to lengthen their duration:

> Precious moments and so repined for! Ah! begin again for me your happy course, flow more slowly in my memory, if that is possible, than you really did in your fugitive succession. How can I prolong

to my heart's content this story, that is so touching and so
simple . . . ? [74]

And another perplexity seizes him in this delicious turmoil of relived pleasure, the same thing that Stendhal will experience later in
reviving the joys of the young Beyle: "How can one say what was
neither said, nor done, nor even thought, but relished, but
felt . . . ?" [75] A difficulty which is the very proof that what he experiences is indeed an authentic phenomenon of affective memory;
for the latter is the only kind of recollection which cannot be visual-
ized, converted into concepts, or translated into words.

But then another question arises. Are these memories accurate?
Sensuous memory and intellectual memory not only translate themselves into words, but also portray themselves by images, and in
ideas; one can compare the image of the present with the image of
the past, and thus verify the latter. But how can one know the truth,
when one is dealing with an untranslatable and ineffable ensemble
of feelings? All the psychologists agree in saying that of all the kinds
of memory the affective memory is the least trustworthy. For Rousseau the contrary is true: "I cannot be mistaken about what I have
felt. . . ." [76]

The veracity of the memory of feelings seems to him to be absolute. And one understands why. The memory of a feeling is a different thing from the memory of a deed. The memory of a deed is
not the deed itself, but the memory of a feeling is still a feeling.
Feeling is never mistaken. One can be mistaken in his judgments,
but not as to the feelings he experiences: that is an essential point
of Rousseau's doctrine, one upon which he can admit no compromise. But one easily discovers that there is a confusion here between two things: on the one hand the truth of the feeling in itself,
the absolute value of which is not in question; and, on the other
hand, the exactitude of the localization of that feeling at a certain
point in the past, which is another thing entirely, a judgment made
upon the feeling and, as such, susceptible of error.

But this chronological exactitude is not at all what interests Rousseau. It matters little to him to know that it was on such and such a
date that he experienced the emotion which comes to life in him
again and agitates him so deliciously. It even matters very little to
him that the emotion of the past and the emotion of the present
overlap and mingle so intimately that one never knows whether the

Rousseau who is speaking to us is the one who is narrating the story or the one whose life is being narrated:

> . . . in surrendering myself at one and the same time to the memory of the impression received and to the present feeling, I shall doubly portray the state of my mind.[77]

No, what it comes to is that the awakened feeling reveals itself authentically, unquestionably, aside from any judgment, as the state of mind of Rousseau; that it reveals Rousseau's state of mind to Rousseau himself.

Thus, by means of the affective memory, Rousseau gains a deeper consciousness of a self which, properly speaking, belongs neither to the past, nor to the present, nor even to duration. Memory, then, is another way, easier and surer than that of the "moment eternal" and of ecstasy, of *awakening in us the interior feeling:*

> As one re-warms a benumbed part of the body by a light rubbing, so the mind deadened by long inaction is reanimated by the gentle warmth of a moderate motion: it must be roused by happy memories that are related only to itself; there must be recalled to it the affections that have soothed it, not by the mediation of the senses, but by a peculiar feeling of its own, and by intellectual pleasures.[78]

The happy memories are the memories of those acts which have been morally good:

> If there existed in the world a being so miserable as never to have done anything in all the course of its life *the memory of which could give it an interior contentment* and make it glad to have lived: that being, having only feelings and ideas which would separate it from itself, would be unable ever to know itself.[79]

In the same way Julie writes to Saint-Preux:

> As long as those pure and delightful moments return to the memory, it is not possible that thou shouldst cease to love what renders them sweet to thee, that the enchantment of moral beauty shouldst ever be effaced from thy mind.[80]

In effect, the feeling of the self and the moral consciousness are one and the same for Rousseau. In a certain way—which is perhaps the only true way—our good like our evil deeds do not vanish after having been committed; they endure unalterably in our affections, in the joy or the horror of them that we have preserved: "One remembers it (an evil deed) for a long while afterward; since the memory of it never becomes extinct": [81] "When one is doing the right thing, a feeling of pleasure remains which is never effaced . . . ." [82]

Our consciousness is comprised of the sum-total of the feelings that reflect the morality of all of the acts of our existence. The "interior contentment" of the just man is only a cluster of memories:

> "And I do not doubt at all," says the Vicar Savoyard, "that this memory becomes one day the bliss of the good, and the torment of the wicked. Here below,"—he adds, however,—"a thousand ardent passions absorb the interior feeling. . . ." [83]

Disencumbered by the affective memory of "the thousand ardent passions" of the present moment, Rousseau's mind enjoys an inner peace.

VIII

In order to "be aroused by the happy memories which are related only to the self," is it nevertheless possible, as Rousseau avers, to dispense with the "mediation of the senses"? No one knows better than the author of the *Confessions* that, in order to be produced, the phenomenon of the affective memory needs the concurrence of sensation. One recalls the episode of the periwinkle: the flower Rousseau sees reminds him of the same flower noticed in his youth when he was coming home to Charmettes, and "the impression of so small an object" suffices to place him once more in the state of mind of those former years. Thus a present object, by the association of resemblance, recalls the image of an object of the past, which, in its turn, by the association of contiguity, causes the awakening of feelings. Whatever the worth of this associationist psychology, in any case there is no doubt that the affective memory needs the assistance of the ordinary memory, or at least the help of a recollecting sign,[84] and that the two memories are always inextricably mixed.

The recollecting sign is by nature various: for example, the Genevan air sung by Rousseau's aunt, which made him weep; the periwinkle; or again, the room in the inn of the *Nouvelle Héloïse:*

In entering the room which was reserved for me, I recognized it as
the same one I had formerly occupied in travelling to Sion. On seeing it again I had a feeling which I would have difficulty in convey-
ing to you. I was so vividly struck by it that *I thought I had become
in an instant all that I was then:* ten years of my life were obliterated. . . .[85]

The evocative object appears again in a still more famous passage in the same book: the high crags from which Saint-Preux, accompanied by Julie, sees once more the places where formerly he
had dreamed of her:

In seeing them again myself after so long a time, I understood
how much the *presence of objects* can powerfully revive the violent
feelings with which one was agitated in their presence.[86]

More than that, the whole novel is, as it were, penetrated by the
affective memory. The period in which it was written was the one in
which Rousseau was reviving by means of memory his love affair
with Mme. d'Houdetot; the subject of the book is the revivification
of interrupted passion. This situation is delicately formulated by
Mme. d'Orbe:

"Your lover," she says to Saint-Preux, "was taken away from you
at the moment when there were no longer any new feelings for you
to enjoy with her, as if fate had wished to guarantee your heart
against an inevitable exhaustion, and to let you live in the memory
of past pleasures, a pleasure sweeter than any you might still have
enjoyed. . . . Happiness and love would have vanished together;
at least you have *preserved the feeling.*" [87]

So the feeling endures because it is cut off from the present. It
remains in the mind but, as it were, *in the past,* as a retrospective
love; and when Saint-Preux meets Julie again, what he will love
will be the lost mistress, not the present and living woman, although, to be sure, it is the present woman who recalls to him the
lost mistress:

It is not Julie de Wolmar with whom he is in love, it is Julie
d'Étange. . . . The wife of another is not his mistress; the mother
of two children is no longer his former pupil. It is true that she resembles her greatly, and that she often recalls to him the memory
of her. *He loves her in time past.*[88]

By the surprising play of the affective memory, the Julie of the
present thus becomes the *recollecting sign* of the Julie of the past.

That recollecting sign may be also of a very different kind. Thus Rousseau's herbarium is, so to speak, a collection of these signs:

> All my botanical excursions, the diverse impressions of the locality of the objects which struck me, the ideas it kindled in me, the incidents that were mingled with it, all of that had left impressions upon me which are renewed at the sight of plants herborized in those very places.[89]

At the time when he contemplated writing a journal in collaboration with Diderot, Rousseau already had an acute consciousness of that evocative force which resides in certain objects: "The reappearance of the same objects usually renews in me similar dispositions to those in which I found myself the first time I saw them." [90]

He will make the same remark later, with no less clarity, but with greater depth:

> There are certain states of mind which do not depend solely upon the events of my life, but upon the objects which have been the more familiar to me during the course of those events. So that I could not recall one of those states without feeling my imagination being modified in the same manner as my senses and my person were when I first experienced it.[91]

IX

Everywhere, at every instant, the encounter with a recollecting sign can bring about the rediscovery of a former state of mind. But still it is necessary that a state of mind had once corresponded to that sign. It is to the quality of the emotion that sensation originally owed its beauty and its richness; it is also to the quality of this emotion that the sensation will owe the chance of being relived. Rousseau knows this very well and he distinguishes carefully between two kinds of sensations:

> If Jean-Jacques is a slave of his senses, nevertheless it is not any kind of sensation that affects him; and for an object to make an impression upon him, to the *simple sensation* there must be joined a distinct *feeling* of pleasure or of pain which attracts or repulses him. It is the same thing with the ideas that strike his brain; if the im-

pression does not penetrate to his heart, it is nothing. Nothing to which he is indifferent can remain in his memory.[92]

And more briefly, in. a letter to the Marshal of Luxembourg:

> I am able to see only in so far as I am moved; indifferent objects are nothing in my eyes; I can pay attention only in proportion to the interest which prompts it.[93]

But if there is no longer such interest? Then it is in vain, it would seem, that the recollecting sign presents itself. Once indifferent, an object will remain indifferent, and there will be no affective memory.

However, if it is certain that there will be no affective memory, will there not perhaps be something else? Rousseau states it very positively in two different places in the *Confessions:*

> As, in general, objects make less impression on me than their memories, and all my ideas are expressed by images, the first lineaments graven upon my brain stay there, and those that are imprinted afterward have combined with them rather than effaced them.[94]
>
> .   .   .   .
>
> I am unable to see what I see; I see clearly only what I recall and have no wits except in my memories. Of all that is said, of all that is done, of all that happens in my presence, I feel nothing, I penetrate nothing. *The exterior sign is the only thing that strikes my attention.* But afterwards it all comes back to me. . . .[95]

These two texts make clear an important fact. Very often Rousseau is scarcely affected by sensation *at the moment when he experiences it.* His "affective reaction" is slight. And it is later, that is to say in memory, that the sensation reappears in his mind, no longer as a mere "nothing," something "indifferent," but as capable of attracting his attention and stirring him. Then, but only then, "the impression will penetrate to his heart." Then only will he experience "a feeling of pleasure or pain"; and, being affected for the first time, for the first time he will be able to *"see well":* to see with the power which is given to perception by a passionate interest: "I only see well what I recall . . . ."

So one must keep from indistinguishably taking for phenomena of the affective memory, all the affective phenomena experienced by Rousseau in the wake of a simple memory. For how can we speak of an affective reviviscence when Rousseau is moved at the sight of an object that left him cold the first time he saw it? With

Rousseau, then, emotion frequently arises *belatedly,* after sensation. That is undoubtedly the reason why, in his psychology, he ascribed to them natures so different, one being only the passive element, the other the life of the soul and the active principal of the self. And so he would not allow himself to admit, as Helvétius maintained, that feeling and recollecting are the same thing. "There is this difference," he insisted; "memory produces a similar sensation, *not the feeling."* [96] Thus sometimes Rousseau *relives* the past; sometimes he lives it for the first time and discovers it to be a virgin landscape which his present emotion animates; and sometimes again both kinds of emotion, the affective memory and the purely present affection, are mingled and combined with one another: "In simultaneously giving myself up to the impression received and the present feeling, I shall doubly portray the state of my mind." Hence he will always have the tendency to embellish the images of the past. He will transform them, doubtless not by retouching the perceptible contour, but by giving them a subjective, an affective, value which they did not originally have.

A neutral, indifferent past is proportionately more easily transformed into poetry. That is why Rousseau likes music so much, for it effaces the exterior signs of things in order to put a passionate resonance in their place:

> The art of the musician consists in substituting for the imperceptible image of the object, those motions which its presence excites in the heart of the contemplator. [97]

The art of the musician, and the art of the poet, too. The beauty of the pages of Rousseau is owing to the freshness of an emotion that makes his pen tremble when it evokes the image; and also to the abundance of intact images which the emotion, in its turn, permits him to recapture. It is then that the affective memory and the belated emotion are united once more, as they were for man in the beginning:

> Afterward, everything comes back to me again: I recall the place, the time, the intonation, the glance, the gesture, the circumstance; nothing escapes me. . . .[98]
>
> . . . .
> Among the diverse situations in which I have found myself, some have been marked by such a feeling of well-being that in recollecting them I have been affected just as if I were still in them. I not

only recall the times, the places, the people, but all the surrounding objects, the temperature of the air, its smell, its color, a certain local impression which could only be felt there, and the living memory of which transports me there again.[99]

Such is the astonishing activity of the past in Rousseau. It has two faces. One is the object, the image, the "simple sensation" which for having been once experienced has not ceased to be capable of producing a new emotion. The other is feeling, always ready to revive at the slightest summons of the image, or to unite with it at the last moment by a swift leap that cancels distances, that abolishes time. Through that action, as in the "moment eternal," we discover once more the union of the two primitive elements: inward feeling and pure sensation.

NOTES

[1] *De l'inégalité*, ed. Garnier, p. 67.
[2] *Emile*, ed. Garnier, p. 97.
[3] *Réfutation du livre de l'Esprit*.
[4] *De l'inégalité*, p. 49.
[5] *Emile*, p. 35.
[6] *Ibid.*
[7] *Ibid.*, p. 315.
[8] *De l'inégalité*, p. 49.
[9] *Ibid.*, p. 67.
[10] *Emile*, p. 35.
[11] *Ibid.*, p. 314.
[12] *Ibid.*, p. 9.
[13] *Ibid.*, p. 328.
[14] *Ibid.*
[15] *De l'inégalité*, p. 47.
[16] *Emile*, p. 329.
[17] *Ibid.*, p. 315.
[18] *De l'inégalité*, p. 47.
[19] *Emile*, p. 324.
[20] *Ibid.*, p. 59.
[21] *Ibid.*
[22] *Ibid.*, p. 63.
[23] *Rêveries*, p. 50.
[24] *Correspondance*, ed. Dufour, VII, 36.
[25] *Confessions*, ed. Garnier, p. 200.
[26] *Correspondance*, VII, 50.
[27] Preface of *Narcisse*.
[28] *Confessions*, p. 243.
[29] *Ibid.*, p. 520.
[30] *Ibid.*
[31] *Correspondance*, VII, 73.
[32] *Emile*, p. 59.
[33] *Ibid.*, p. 62.
[34] *Ibid.*
[35] *Ibid.*, p. 59.
[36] *Correspondance*, VII, 50.

[37] *Emile*, pp. 59–63.
[38] *Correspondance*, III, 369.
[39] *Ibid.*
[40] *Emile*, p. 332.
[41] *Ibid.*, p. 9.
[42] *Ibid.*, p. 58.
[43] *Rêveries*, p. 50.
[44] *Confessions*, p. 114.
[45] *Correspondance*, VII, 77.
[46] *Emile et Sophie*, letter I.
[47] *Nouvelle Héloïse*, Part III, Book 6.
[48] *Emile*, p. 335.
[49] *Nouvelle Héloïse*, Part VI, Book 6.
[50] *Emile*, p. 346.
[51] *Rêveries*, p. 68.
[52] *Ibid.*, p. 65.
[53] *Emile*, p. 327.
[54] *Correspondance*, VII, 73.
[55] *Ibid.*, III, 360.
[56] *Ibid.*
[57] *Rêveries*, p. 50.
[58] *Confessions*, p. 200.
[59] *Rêveries*, p. 8.
[60] *Correspondance*, VII, 71.
[61] *Ibid.*
[62] *Ibid.*
[63] *Ibid.*, IV, 337.
[64] *Confessions*, p. 7.
[65] *Ibid.*, p. 243.
[66] *Ibid.*, p. 15.
[67] *Ibid.*, p. 243.
[68] *Rêveries*, p. 9.
[69] *Confessions*, p. 243.
[70] *Ibid.*, p. 114.
[71] *Rêveries*, p. 8.
[72] *Correspondance*, XV, 221.

[73] *Ibid.*
[74] *Confessions*, p. 199.
[75] *Ibid.*
[76] *Ibid.*, p. 243.
[77] Introduction to the first version of the *Confessions*.
[78] *Correspondance*, III, 371.
[79] *Ibid.*
[80] *Nouvelle Héloïse*, Part II, Book 11.
[81] *Confessions*, p. 115.
[82] *Correspondance*, III, 372.
[83] *Emile*, p. 333.
[84] *Dictionnaire de Musique*, article "Musique."
[85] Part V, Book 9.
[86] Part IV, Book 17.
[87] Part III, Book 7.
[88] *Nouvelle Héloïse*, Part IV, Book 14.
[89] *Rêveries*, p. 75.
[90] *Le Persifleur*.
[91] *Mon portrait*, Ann. J.-J. R. (1908), p. 272; quoted by Monglond, *Préromantisme*.
[92] *Dialogues II*.
[93] *Correspondance*, IX, 6.
[94] *Confessions*, p. 153.
[95] *Ibid.*, p. 99.
[96] *Réfutation du livre de l'Esprit*.
[97] *Essai sur l'origine des langues*.
[98] *Confessions*, p. 99.
[99] *Ibid.*, p. 106.

✳

✳

✳ DIDEROT

_____

I

✳ From the very first, Diderot seems less like a single person
    than a succession of persons. "Clamoring, shouting, carry-
ing on like a madman," the nephew of Rameau "was split into
twenty different roles." Similarly Diderot says of himself: "I who
live the most dissevered, the most inadvertent, the most heedless
life . . .";[1] and in another place: "In one day I presented a
hundred different physiognomies." This diversity is possible only
by reason of "a surprising rapidity of movement," which allows
the mind neither cohesion nor stability. It is one incessant metamorphosis of the self into the series of elements which one by one
comprise it and turn it into something else: "We are ourselves, always ourselves, and not for one minute the same." [2] The self is the
self only because it unceasingly differs from itself. To be is to become another person.

What is true of Diderot—and of man, as Diderot represents him
to us—is at the same time true of the universe as he describes it:

> If one does not insist upon taking into consideration only the things
> in his head, but also the things in the universe, he will, by the diver-
> sity of phenomena, be convinced of the diversity of elementary
> matter, the diversity of forces, the diversity of actions and reac-
> tions. . . .[3]

Hence, "everything is in perpetual flux," [4] "everything changes
ceaselessly."

> How many crippled, abortive worlds vanish away, reappear and
> vanish, perhaps, in every moment in the distant spaces which I can
> never reach nor you see, but where motion continues and will con-
> tinue to combine masses of matter . . . ? [5]

The all is all, just as the self is the self, only because the motion
that carries it along and which *is* itself forces it to change into an-

other thing; only because it invents, discovers, cuts itself off, and destroys itself in every moment of its existence:

> What is this world, Mr. Holmes? A composite subject to revolutions which all indicate a continuous tendency toward destruction; a rapid succession of beings which follow and jostle each other, and then disappear.[6]

A rapid succession of beings in the world and beings in the self; the consciousness of man and the spectacle of the universe offer only "a fleeting symmetry, a momentary order." [7]

In the world, as in man, there is no other continuity than "time which never stops," "whereas beings in passing are gradually altered by the most imperceptible nuances." [8] In the midst of the "continuous tendency toward destruction," there is no other reality than that of a motion which follows its course until it arrives at "the greatest difference," and than that of a duration, which is the requisite place of its activity: "All is annihilated, all perishes, all passes. Only the world remains, only time endures." [9] And, in the *Rêve de d'Alembert,* in almost the same words: "All changes, all passes, there is only the all that remains." [10]

All, time; they are interchangeable terms:

> Is it not a very singular thing to hear Seneca . . . attach importance to knowing whether time exists by itself, whether there is something anterior to duration, whether it began before the world did; whether it existed before things, or things before it? I avow that, if there are any questions impervious and alien to wisdom, they are these.[11]

Alien to wisdom, because wisdom informs us that the world and duration are not conceived separately, but imply each other, even create each other. Nothing demonstrates better the distance which, despite similarities, separates Diderot from Rousseau. In the former, there is not the slightest trace of a starting point, of a first moment of existence. Whether we open his work at the first page, or at any other page, it seems that his thought is always in midstream. One never sees it except in the process of leaving one idea to look for another, breaking itself away from the old to throw itself upon the new:

> But what is the voice of the present? Nothing. The present is only a point, and the voice we hear is always that of the future or that of the past.[12]

"Indivisible point which cuts in two the length of the infinite line," the present is situated for Diderot *in* the infinite line. It is in contact with the infinity from which it issues, and the infinity which it engenders: "I move between two eternities"; I move, and I know that this movement is going to bring me to a point from which it will then convey me elsewhere; and I see horizons of time opening and closing before and behind me: "The present . . . indivisible and flowing point, on which man can no more stay fixed than on the point of a needle . . . ." [13] Perceived in the motion by which it is seized and lost and seized again, the present moment, as it is experienced by Diderot, appears as the very antipodes of the present of Rousseau imagining his savage transfixed by the feeling of his actual existence; an Edenic present that is really outside time, situated in the non-temporality of a yet unimpaired nature; not fluent but static; an absolute beginning, which seems to be less one of time, of the world and of man, than of eternity itself.

To this Diderot replies curtly: "The animal exists only in the moment, it sees nothing beyond it; man lives in the past, the present, and the future." [14] It is when he is already plunged, then, in the Heraclitan flux of things that man sees the universe appear before him and simultaneously elude him. There is no full possession of the object in pure sensation, but an equivocal perception which is more a perception of the "transference" of the object itself. The universal fluidity sees to it that in the moment in which one thinks he grasps them, things slip between his fingers, like the other droplets of the durational stream. "Time dissipates all illusions, and all the passions end." [15] The only chance of fixing them, at least of giving them a form, a consistency, would be to surround and impregnate them once more with a duration, to plunge them into a bath of infinite duration. Perhaps only the totality of time could give reality to the object; for all partial duration is relative, therefore illusory:

> You judge of the successive existence of the world as the day-fly judges yours. The world is eternal for you, as you are eternal for a being that lives only an instant: still the insect is more reasonable than you. What prodigious succession of generations of day-flies attests to your eternity? What immense tradition? Meanwhile we shall all pass away without anyone's being able to fix either the actual extent of space we inhabited, or the precise length of time we have endured. Time, matter, and space are perhaps only a point.[16]

Thus, except for that *all* which is the totality of things, of space and of time, everything is relative and ephemeral: "No matter from where they are seen, the objects which surround me inform me of the end of things, and make me resigned to my own death. What is my ephemeral existence in comparison with that of this rock which is wearing away, or this valley which is being hollowed out . . . ." [17]

Alone and alone true, indifferently similar to a point or to infinity, an eternity of life is maintained in the midst of manifestations of successive and multiple lives:

> Feeling and life are eternal. That which lives has always lived, and shall live endlessly. The only difference I recognize between death and life is that at the moment you live in the general mass, and that dissolved, dispersed into molecules, twenty years from now you will live in detail. [18]

But of what value is this eternity of life to the individual whose molecules are dispersed? Of what value even for the species? "An individual begins, so to speak, grows, endures for a time, decays, and passes away. Might it not be so for the entire species?" [19] Whether twenty years or several million years pass by, the individual and the species nevertheless come to the end of their development. The universe, never: "Time is nothing to nature." [20] Only the world endures. Thus the tremendous depths of duration which Buffon discovered in the universe serve only, in the case of Diderot, to reveal cruelly the precariousness, the relativity, the unreality of anything that is not the *all*. Only the *all* sees time work to its advantage:

> And if all is a general flux, as the spectacle of the universe demonstrates to me everywhere, what will not duration and the vicissitudes of some millions of centuries produce here or elsewhere? [21]

A prodigal multitude of relationships is surpassed by a still more prodigious multitude of "throws." And the world is sure to win. That is inevitable, since the infinity of time allows for all the combinations.

But the fatality of the law of duration leaves the individual no recourse, neither respite nor chance of escape: "My duration is only a succession of necessary effects," says Jacques le Fataliste. "It is hard," says Diderot, "to abandon oneself blindly to the uni-

versal torrent; yet it is impossible to resist it"; and again: "One is
irresistibly swept along by the general torrent . . . ." Irresistibly
swept along in an action that never stops until it has destroyed us,
after it has exploited us in the infinite series of its experiences: "It
seems to me," says Diderot, after meditating on the melancholy
wisdom of Seneca, "it seems to me that I see its existence more
clearly (man's personal existence is meant) as a rather insignificant point between a nothingness that preceded it and the end
which awaits it." [22]

II

But out of this pessimism there springs an equal optimism. It is true
that we do not possess an existence of our own, that we are
absorbed by the universe, that *being* is not the property of the
individual but of the *all:* "There is only a single great individual,
it is the all." [23] But the very rigors of our deprivation provide us
with strength. For if we are not ourselves, we are the very flesh
and blood, the mind, of this world which dispossess us of ourselves. To live is not, as Rousseau thought, to have the feeling of
one's own self; it is to feel that one makes up a part of a stream of
existence. Consequently, what would it profit the mind to isolate
itself from time and from space, to distinguish the self from the
non-self, to want to persevere in its particular organization? The
worst way of being oneself is the way that arrests, that limits. The
only good way is the way of submission, of participation. So the
thought of Diderot, insofar as it takes the cosmic life into clearer
account, espouses more and more its multiple rhythm. This rhythm
makes his style pulsate, and his ideas combine into an improvisa-
tion of more and more intoxicating "momentary orders."

> The world ceaselessly begins and ends; every moment it is at its
> beginning and at its end; there has never been any other world, and
> it will never be otherwise.[24]

The *momentary order,* then, is not only an order which is destroyed, it is simultaneously an order which begins again. The present is that unprecedented thing, more marvellous than Rousseau's
Edenic age, a reality which finds its renewal: "He who admits a
new phenomenon renews a past instant, recreates a new world." [25]

A new reality, more than that, a *total* reality. If the world, in each momentary order, is at both its beginning and its end, that is because, from its beginning to its end, it is entirely assembled at every moment, in every order: "Time, matter and space are perhaps only a point . . . ."

That point is always regained; it is the point of the actual moment:

> "Why, if all is adjoining, contiguous . . . do I not hear what happens in the vast space which surrounds me . . . ?"

> ". . . Who told you so? Is it not possible that you have more or less heard it already?" [26]

Thus, if our sensibility were sensitive enough, we should perceive the infinity of space and of time; our self, in the instant, would expand to a consciousness most vast by a kind of interior acceleration of *tempo* of thought or, more precisely, of its immediate activity. Does this not become evident when, through absorption in a work, an object, an idea, one sees simultaneously the field of life enlarge and time narrow and tend to disappear?

> Let us labor then: labor, among other advantages, has that of shortening the days and lengthening life.[27]

> There is neither place, nor time, nor space for one who meditates deeply. A hundred thousand years of meditation, like a hundred thousand years of sleep, would have lasted for us for no more than an instant, without the weariness which apprises us more or less of the length of our exertion.[28]

It is the same with the intoxication in reading or conversation:

> I had undergone more in the course of several hours than the longest life ordinarily offers in all its duration.[29]
> How the hours fly! How short time is! Night has fallen before one is half way through what he wanted to tell himself.[30]

Thus by turn, following the accelerated or slackening rhythm of the sensibility, time is contracted or lengthened. The greater the force of the imagination, the more the mind's activity is multiplied, the oftener time is brought back to a single vibrant moment. At its acme, this energy ends up in a strange confusion of all the different durations, a confusion which is joined to a nonetheless singular lucidity:

Woman carries within herself an organ susceptible to terrible spasms, mastering her and arousing within her fancy all kinds of phantoms. In this hysterical delirium she returns to the past, she darts into the future, and all times are present to her.[31]

When the sensibility is acute, everything indistinguishably excites it. But the greatest sensibility is that of the man of genius:

The man of genius is the man whose more expansive mind, struck by the sensations of all beings, interested in everything in nature, does not entertain an idea without its awakening a feeling; everything animates his mind and is preserved there.[32]

Everything stirs it, everything animates it. Thus, for Diderot, the unity of the mind is made up of a plurality of impressions, just as the unity of the body is made up of a plurality of molecules. It is a unity that is always flowing and always instantaneous. It is true that the work of the analytical intelligence and the exigences of language sunder into distinct and successive parts that which springs forth in the mind under the form of a spontaneous synthesis, and thus seems to distribute over many diverse points of time what exists at first in the mass of a present whose amplitude remains unsuspected:

The state of the mind in an indivisible instant was represented by a throng of terms that the precision of language required, and which distributed a *total impression* into parts; and because those terms were successively pronounced and were heard only as they were successively pronounced, one was led to believe that the affections of the mind which they represented were the very same succession. But it is not so. The state of our mind is one thing; the account we render of it, to ourselves or to others, is another thing; or again, the *total and instantaneous sensation* of that state is one thing; the successive and detailed attention which we are forced to give it in order to analyze it, to make it manifest, and to understand it, is quite another thing. Our mind is a moving picture which we copy bit by bit; we take a great deal of time to render it faithfully; but *it exists in its entirety all at once;* the mind does not proceed step by step, like the expression of it. The brush only executes slowly what the painter's eye *embraces in a trice.*[33]

This admirable passage anticipates Bergsonian thought, not only in its distinction between intuition and intelligence, but also in its affirmation of a total life of the mind which overflows the limitations of *"successive and detailed attention."* Here moreover, foreshadowing Bergson, Diderot continues the thought of Leibnitz. Thus, in the article entitled "Leibnizianisme" in the *Encyclopédie:*

> Given a monad, the entire universe would be given. A monad is therefore a kind of representative mirror of all beings and all phenomena. This idea, which petty minds will take for a visionary thing, is the sign of a man of genius.[34]

By his transposition of this idea, Diderot will arrive at the basis of his own doctrine. It is no longer a monad which imparts to the elements comprising the body an ideal influence, and communicates with the infinity of other monads only by a pre-established harmony; it is an organization of molecules and forces in a center of sensations. The mind is no longer a simple substance whose unique office is to perceive; but it is the same thing as the body, as matter, as the universe, something which is filled up by the whole global life.

To be sure, this consciousness of totality is very dim in man, if one compares it to the consciousness of God, who "sees the order of the whole universe in the tiniest molecule of matter." [35] But its being granted that "all is bound up together, contiguous," [36] that "all beings interflow into each other," [37] what happens with God happens in us, and there is between the highest cosmic consciousness and our own only a difference of degree, an intensity less great with us, and less unequally distributed:

> Man, thrown into the universe, receives, in addition to more or less intense sensations, the ideas of all beings. For the most part, men experience intense sensations only through the impression of objects which immediately answer to their needs, to their taste, etc. Anything alien to their passions, anything without analogy to their way of life, is either not perceived by them at all, or is seen for only an instant without being felt, and is forgotten forever.[38]

It is thus by his contraction of the field of his interest that man refuses to see the literally universal things that happen in the reaches of his sensory and even conscious life. "One relates everything to the little moment of his existence and duration," [39] without understanding that this little moment can be made vast, *is* really vast, provided precisely that one feels one's existence is not *his own,* but a participant in that of the great whole: "We are the whole universe." [40]

It is here that from being metaphysical and psychological, the teaching of Diderot becomes moral; and here again, it is opposed to the thought of Rousseau: "O man," said the latter, *"confine thine existence within thyself* and thou shalt no longer be miserable." "My friend," Diderot exclaims, *"let us not straiten our existence,* let us never circumscribe the sphere of our delights." [41] What must be done, on the contrary, is *"to* extend life": [42]

> To enlarge the mind is, to my way of thinking, one of the things of the greatest importance, most easy and least practised. [43]

> Let us forget for a moment the point which we occupy in space and duration, and let us extend our view over the centuries to come, over the remotest regions and peoples still to be born. [44]

All of Diderot's optimistic and centrifugal force impels him outward, beyond the place of the circumscribed moment:

> There is a circumscribed happiness which remains in me and is not extended beyond me. There is an *expansive happiness* which spreads abroad, which invades the present and embraces the future, and which feeds upon both moral and physical delights, upon realities and chimeras, heaping up a conglomeration of money, eulogies, pictures, statues, and kisses. [45]

It is this expansive happiness which Diderot experiences in the ecstasy into which the "spectacle of justice" throws him:

> Then it seems to me that my heart expands within me, that it floats away; I cannot describe the delicious and sudden feelings which course through me; I can hardly breathe; the whole surface of my body quivers with excitement. . . . [46]

III

Such is the manner in which Diderot's exaltation is diffused through his whole being and throughout all space, but in a certain sense it is not dissipated and lost there. The happiness to which it attains is both physical and moral: *his heart* which expands within him; *his body* whose whole surface quivers. Thus the dominant feature of this state of euphoria is a feeling of fullness which arises, first, from the perfect equivalence of what expands in the mind and what traverses the body—an equilibrium which has for its effect the *felt* unity of the whole being; and second, from a kind of quietism, both physical and moral, which results in the mind's abandoning itself to what it feels, the self fusing bodily with the motion which transports it. Hence the notion of the time that is made of a kind of opposition of the self to the general displacement of things often gives place in Diderot to a state of intoxication that is almost non-temporal, very close to that which one notices so frequently in the Rousseau of the *Rêveries:*

> I cannot tell you how long my enchantment lasted. The immobility of persons, the solitude of a place and its deep silence, suspend time; it is no more; man becomes, as it were, eternal.[47]
>
> Be at peace, take thy rest like all that surrounds thee . . . let the hours, the days, the years go by like all that surrounds thee, and pass away like all that surrounds thee; that is the continuous lesson of nature.[48]

Nothing could be more significant than what is revealed by a comparison of these two passages; in the first, the pantheistic euphoria is expressed under the form of the non-temporal; and in the second it is expressed under that of the flux of duration. There is no contradiction here, because it is precisely when one makes no effort whatever to remove oneself from the current of time and abandons oneself to its general motion that the very feeling of time disappears and gives place to a feeling of the universal suspension of its course: just as one no longer notices the gliding of the boat that sweeps him along with the current. To be one with the boat, the river, the world, to feel the moving identity of things and of the self, such for Diderot is the character of the perfect happiness he so often enjoys in his own "reveries":

> Pleasure of being myself . . . sweeter pleasure still of forgetting myself. Where am I in this moment? What is it that surrounds me? I do not know, I ignore it. What do I lack? Nothing. . . . If there is a God, he is like this. He takes pleasure in himself.[49]

But this God takes pleasure in himself only because that self is the world, and because through him the consciousness of the world enjoys the world. Thus it is for Diderot. In contrast to Rousseau, there is for him no contradistinction between the feeling of the self and pure sensation; but there is basically for him a feeling of the essential unity of the *self* and the *all*. For instance, there is the following passage, which was written well in advance of Rousseau's famous revery at the lake of Bienne, which perhaps served the latter as a model, but which expresses, despite similarities, something very different from the revery of Jean-Jacques:

> But what is a delightful repose? He alone whose bodily organs were sensitive and susceptible, has known its inexpressible charm; he who received from nature an affectionate mind and a voluptuous temperament; who enjoyed perfect health, who found himself at the flower of his age, whose mind was never troubled by a single cloud nor his soul agitated by any emotion that was too passionate; who emerged from a slight and gentle lassitude, and who experienced in every part of his body pleasures so *equally distributed* that it was impossible to distinguish any of them. There remained for him in this moment of enchantment and faintness neither memory of the past nor desire of the future, nor anxiety over the present. *Time had ceased to flow for him,* because he existed wholly in himself; the feeling of his happiness abated only with that of his existence. *He passed by an imperceptible motion* from waking to sleep; but in this imperceptible *passage,* amid the lapse of all his faculties, he was still awake enough, if not to think distinctly of things, at least to feel all the sweetness of his existence: but he enjoyed it with a wholly *passive* joy, without being attached to it, without reflecting upon it, without rejoicing in it, without congratulating himself upon it. If by taking thought one could make permanent this situation of pure feeling, in which all the faculties of the body and the mind are alive without being active, and attach to this delicious quietness the idea of immutability, one would form for oneself the notion of the greatest and purest happiness that man can imagine.[50]

Lest we should be deceived, it is not that state of mind in which Rousseau "finds a resting place solid enough to repose upon it completely and reassemble there its whole being." Nothing, on the contrary, is more fluid than Diderot's state of mind, gliding *by an imperceptible motion* from waking to sleep. If time has ceased to flow *for him,* one still feels that it has not entirely ceased to flow; one hears its murmur to the last.

Thus instead of attaining to a moment of pure non-temporality and perfect repose, Diderot seems only to approach it indefinitely by a progressive slackening of the activities of the mind and the perception of duration; *adagio,* which is exactly the reverse of the *presto* habitual to his sensibility and thought; but which is nonetheless, like the other, a movement rather than a state, and a movement by which the mobile—without ever ceasing to be mobile—tends to coincide with an extreme point. The following passage shows to what a degree these two "movements" are, for Diderot, in some way complementary:

> *Mademoiselle de Lespinasse:* . . . I exist as it were in a point; I almost cease to be matter, I feel only my thought; there is no longer either place, or movement, or body, or distance, or space for me: the universe is annihilated for me, and I am nothing to the universe.
> *Bordeu:* That is the limit of concentration of your existence; but its ideal expansion can be boundless. When the actual border of your sensibility is crossed, whether by your coming into harmony with yourself, or by your being compressed within yourself, or by your expanding beyond yourself, no one knows what may come of it.[51]

Diderot very well knows that what may come of it is a feeling of perfect unity. For him, as he pointed out in one of the passages cited, there are two kinds of happiness possible: one is *circumscribed happiness,* obtained by a movement of concentration; the other is *expansive happiness,* obtained by a movement of dilation. The one restores totality to a unity; the other, unity to the totality. The former tends to abolish the distinction between the self and the world by the suppression of the consciousness of time and of the perception of the scope of things; the latter, by means of an unlimited extension of space and duration in the present of the consciousness, tends to arrive at exactly the same result. Sometimes the sphere is reduced to a point, and sometimes the point is expanded throughout the whole sphere.

But if we know what that infinite sphere is—the totality of matter, space, and all existence—what is the nature of this point, this unity, this terminus of arrival or departure in the movement of thought? This place of extreme reduction, this "point indivisible" in the setting out from which man is diffused and spread abroad, in the "point indivisible of the present." Only the present *is,* together with the world. And the movement which Diderot prefers is the one by which, in indefinitely enlarging the point of actual reality, he will inflate it until, for him, it represents the world.

There is, as it were, in Diderot a continuous irradiation of the present into the reaches of duration. But it would not be fair to say that he ever *escapes* toward the past or toward the future. One never sees him, like Rousseau, or like the Romantics, transported ideally to a time which is either the one of memory or of expectation. He cuts himself off neither from his own epoch nor from the present moment. Indeed, on the contrary, what essentially matters to Diderot is to reach the past and the future without abandoning the present, and in some way to actualize them. For Diderot the present has that singular quality of being at one and the same time, as it were, one single, indivisible mathematical point, and also a psychological expanse that is limitlessly extensible, the field of the temporal horizon embraced by the mind:

> It is impossible to maintain oneself on this point and glide gently along with it, without turning one's eyes backward or looking ahead.[52]
> The nature of man is incessantly to oscillate upon this *fulcrum* of his existence. He balances himself on this tiny point of support, carried backward and forward in proportion to the energy of his mind. The limits of his oscillations are confined neither to the brief duration of his life, nor to the small arc of his sphere.[53]

Consequently, to extend one's existence is not to live elsewhere than in the present, but to extend one's present. It is thus that the poet's imagination "embraces everything at once," [54] that the poetic description "embraces the past, the present, and the future." [55] Even the most instantaneous of the arts, the one which is most strictly reduced to a single *point* of time, painting, can have something of that faculty of extension: "I said that the artist had only an instant; but that instant is able to subsist together with some traces of the instant which preceded it, and intimations of the one to follow." [56]

It remains to be seen how one can attain to this *actualization* of the dead zones of the past, the obscure zones of the future.

IV

> The more man travels backward into the past, and the more he darts forward into the future, the greater he is.[57]

How, first of all, does one travel backward into the past? By memory. Memory, for Diderot, is always passive.[58] It is not, properly speaking, a simple sensation, since sensation in purely sensuous beings ceases little by little to vibrate and ends by becoming extinct.[59] "It (memory) is a sensation that endures." [60] But this durability of sensation is not owing to its nature; it is produced only when in the sentient being made up of an aggregation of mole-

cules, there exists "a certain organization," [61] an original centralizing force[62] which, furthermore, can "increase, lessen, and sometimes altogether disappear." [63] As long as it remains in force, however, its character consists in holding together, as it were, in a
bundle the simultaneous and successive impressions which manifest themselves in the being: "It takes account and is the record of
everything; it preserves the memory or a continuous sensation of
it; and the animal is brought along from its early formation to relate
itself to it, to settle upon it, to exist in it." [64]

Thus memories, interconnected like a network of vibrant wires,
one calling up another, without allowing man to fix a limit to the
reawakened and linked ideas," [65] constitute by their very continuity the consciousness of the self.[66]

Beyond the ideas borrowed by Diderot from the psychology
and physiology of his time we can see in what the originality of this
theory consists. The self, in Diderot's eyes, has not at all the character of a laboriously constructed machine that it has for most of
the other sensualists. For him, the self and the feeling of the self
always remain closely dependent upon memory. Memory, in its
turn, multiple and resonant, proceeding by disconcerting leaps, depends, on the one hand, upon an original centralizing force and, on
the other hand, upon exterior or organic causes which "bring it
into play." Thence the fluidity of the feeling of existence, constantly carried along by the undulating wave of the "sensations
which endure."

The more lively these sensations have been, the greater will be
their undulations, and the further the resonant sphere of the self
will be extended. This vivacity is greatest in a child. And a child
has the best memory. "The time of childhood is the time of memory," Diderot declares in the *Lettre sur les aveugles*. But there are
also adults "who have remained children, and in whom the habitual dependence upon signs has not vitiated the facility for seeing
things." [67] Thus Diderot says of the man of genius:

> He does not remember; he sees; he is not confined to seeing; he is
> moved; in the silence and obscurity of the study he revels in that
> pleasant and fecund countryside; he is chilled by whistling winds; he
> is burned by the sun; he is frightened by storms. The mind often
> takes pleasure in such momentary affections.[68]

One can see that it is the affective memory that primarily interests Diderot, with that most passionate interest which for him is almost the only thing that counts. Or rather, let us say, to employ an expression of Dugas, it is the *raw memory*—that which neither selects, nor abstracts, nor idealizes, but which restores both the old image and the emotion to their initial vigor:

> The sound of a voice, the presence of an object, a certain place . . . and here is this object, nay, even more, a long interval of my life is recalled. Here am I, plunged into pleasure, regret, or affliction.[69]

Sometimes even the intensity of this memory is so great that for the writer who yields to it—the remark will later be repeated by Stendhal—emotion paralyzes creation: "The pen falls from the hand, one surrenders to his feelings and ceases to write." Hence the *paradox of the actor,* or the necessity of his going back to intellectual memory, "the lesson learned by heart," because, if he abandoned himself to sensibility, *feeling* would prevent him from *rendering;* and the paradox of the writer, which results in one's being able to write a poem on the death of a friend only "when extreme sensibility has been deadened."

But true memory, for Diderot, is not intellectual memory. The latter is made up only of abstract elements that are combined together; it is only "a series of former impressions, a calculation of additions and subtractions, a combinative art, the system of Barrême." [70] It is a dead memory, serving merely the designs of the present, but not constituting an integral part of its substance. Nothing is more remote from the phenomenon of total reviviscence, of which, in the *Lettre sur les aveugles,* Diderot gives this curious example:

> I had the experience . . . amid the agitations of a violent passion, of feeling a shiver run through my whole hand; of being aware that the sensations communicated by bodies that I had touched a long time ago, were reawakened within me as vividly as if they were still present to my touch, and of noticing very distinctly that the limits of the feeling coincided precisely with those of the absent bodies.

Thus, true enough, authentic memory is "sensation which endures." And as sensations endure only because they are found to be linked one to another, and because "a reawakened idea sometimes spreads and makes vibrate a harmonic which is at an incomprehensible interval from it," [71] is it surprising that thenceforth at certain moments, for some unknown reason, all the past seems once more to start vibrating perceptibly within us? For it never ceases to vibrate, and to vibrate wholly. It is always really present deep within us, under the form of obscure perception, as Leibnitz said. And again: "Since it is linked and contiguous, why does not one hear everything that happens in the immensity of space?" But one can hear it! and hear it as well in the vast stretches of time and unconscious memory, as in those of cosmic space. Then "your memory should apprise you of all that has happened." [72] Our conscious memory is only partial; but there exists another, the true one, which is *total:*

> I am led to believe that everything we have seen, known, perceived, heard—even the trees of a deep forest—nay, even the disposition of the branches, the form of the leaves and the variety of the colors, the green tints and the light; the look of grains of sand at the edge of the sea, the unevenness of the crests of waves, whether agitated by a light breeze, or churned to foam by a storm; the multitude of human voices, of animal cries, and physical sounds, the melody and harmony of all songs, of all pieces of music, of all the concerts we have listened to, *all of it, unknown to us, exists within us.*
>
> I actually see once more, wide awake, all the forests of Westphalia, Prussia, Saxony, and Poland.
>
> I see them again in dream, as brightly colored as they would be in a painting by Vernet.
>
> Sleep has taken me back to concerts as freshly performed as when I attended them.
>
> Dramatic productions, comic and tragic, come back to me after thirty years; the same actors, the same pit. . . .
>
> A picture by Van der Meulen could not have more clearly displayed before my eyes a review of the troops on the Sablons plain, on a fine summer day, with the throng of incidents and the great crowd of people assembled, than the dream of it recalls to me after so very many years. . . .[73]

Thus, *unknown to us,* there exists in us a boundless memory which is the memory of the totality of our past: "What I call *boundless memory,* is the linkage of all that one has been in one instant to all one has been in the moment following; states which, bound together by the act, will recall to a man everything he has felt all his life." [74] A perspective which, according to Diderot, would prodigiously enlarge the field of the possible *present;* and which would extend it not only into the past, all of the past, but even into the future. For besides the phenomena of pure reviviscence, Diderot knew also those of premonition. For him these are literally memories which remind us of the future:

> We all have presentiments, and these presentiments are proportionately the truer and more prompt, the more penetration and experience we have. They are sudden judgments to which we are brought by very subtle circumstances. There is not a single fact that was not preceded and accompanied by certain phenomena. Fugitive, momentary, and subtle as these phenomena may be, men endowed with a great sensibility that is impressed by everything, and which nothing escapes, are affected by them, though often in a moment in which they attach no importance to them. . . . The memory of the phenomenon passes; but the memory of its impression will on occasion be reawakened. Then they announce that such and such an event will take place; it seems to them that a secret voice whispers to their heart and informs them. They believe themselves inspired, and indeed they are, not by some supernatural and divine power, but by a particular and extraordinary prudence. For what is prudence unless it is a supposition by which we come to regard the diverse circumstances in which we find ourselves as causes of effects to be feared or to be hoped for in the future? But it often happens that this supposition is based on an infinity of flimsy things . . . which, for all that, are nonetheless necessarily or strongly linked with the object of our fear and our hope. *A multitude of atoms, each one imperceptible, which, united, constitute a considerable weight* disposes us, almost without our knowing why. God sees the order of the whole universe in the tiniest molecule of matter. The prudence of certain privileged men contains a little of this attribute of the Divinity.[75]

Thus by the *law of continuity* it happens that our unconscious mind is the crossroad where there meet and rejoin, from the depths of the future as from the depths of the past, all the diverse states of our existence; perhaps—who knows?—all the diverse states of all the existence that, in their perenniality, the molecules which today compose us have lived; finally, even all the states of all the universe. To bring them into consciousness there are necessary only "the scope of the mind, the force of the imagination, and the activity of the soul," the three attributes of *genius*.[76] The man who possessed them in the highest degree would himself also be capable of seeing "the order of the whole universe in the tiniest molecule of matter." He would be like "the big or little spider whose web extends itself to all things." His eye, "embracing everything at once," would see that "time, matter, and space are only a point," that point which is "the point indivisible of the present."

"The immense and total memory," says Diderot, "is a *state of complete unity.*"

NOTES

[1] *Lettres à Sophie Volland,* N.R.F., II, 44.
[2] *Oeuvres,* ed. Assézat, II, 373.
[3] *Ibid.,* p. 69.
[4] *Ibid.,* p. 138.
[5] *Ibid.,* I, 310.
[6] *Ibid.*
[7] *Ibid.*
[8] *Ibid.,* II, 55.
[9] *Ibid.,* XI, 229.
[10] *Ibid.,* II, 132.
[11] *Ibid.,* III, 257.
[12] *Ibid.,* XVIII, 97.
[13] *Ibid.,* p. 115.
[14] *Ibid.,* p. 179.
[15] *Lettres à Sophie Volland,* II, 57.
[16] *Oeuvres,* I, 311.
[17] *Ibid.,* XI, 230.
[18] *Lettres à Sophie Volland,* I, 70.
[19] *Oeuvres,* II, 57.
[20] *Ibid.,* p. 111.
[21] *Ibid.,* p. 137.
[22] *Ibid.,* III, 372.
[23] *Ibid.,* p. 139.
[24] *Ibid.,* p. 132.
[25] *Ibid.,* II, 111.
[26] *Ibid.,* p. 142.
[27] *Ibid.,* III, 332.
[28] *Lettres à Sophie Volland,* I, 269.
[29] *Oeuvres,* V, 213.
[30] *Lettres à Sophie Volland,* I, 255.
[31] *Oeuvres,* II, 255.
[32] *Ibid.,* XV, 35.
[33] *Ibid.,* I, 369.
[34] *Ibid.,* XV, 461.
[35] *Ibid.,* XVII, 243.
[36] *Ibid.,* II, 142.
[37] *Ibid.,* p. 138.
[38] *Ibid.,* XV, 35.
[39] *Ibid.,* XI, 451.
[40] *Ibid.,* XVIII, 224.
[41] *Ibid.*
[42] *Ibid.,* III, 333.
[43] *Ibid.,* p. 542.
[44] *Neveu de Rameau.*
[45] *Oeuvres,* II, 306.
[46] *Lettres à Sophie Volland,* I, 148.
[47] *Oeuvres,* XI, 106.
[48] *Lettres à Sophie Volland,* II, 275.
[49] *Oeuvres,* XI, 113.
[50] Article "Délicieux," *Encyclopédie, Oeuvres,* XIV, 277.
[51] *Oeuvres,* II, 154.
[52] *Ibid.,* XVIII, 112.
[53] *Ibid.,* p. 115.
[54] *Ibid.,* XI, 73.
[55] *Ibid.,* II, 339.
[56] *Ibid.,* XII, 90.
[57] *Ibid.,* XVIII, 112.
[58] *Ibid.,* IX, 368.
[59] *Ibid.,* II, 159.
[60] *Ibid.,* p. 114.
[61] *Ibid.,* p. 112.
[62] *Ibid.,* p. 160.
[63] *Ibid.,* p. 112.
[64] *Ibid.,* II, 168.
[65] *Ibid.,* p. 113.
[66] *Ibid.,* p. 112; IV, 92.
[67] *Ibid.,* XI, 134.
[68] *Ibid.,* XV, 35.
[69] *Ibid.,* IX, 369.
[70] *Ibid.,* XI, 133.
[71] *Ibid.,* II, 113.
[72] *Ibid.,* p. 142.
[73] *Ibid.,* IX, 366–67.
[74] *Ibid.,* p. 370.
[75] Article "Théosophes," *Encyclopédie; Oeuvres,* XVII, 243.
[76] *Oeuvres,* XV, 35.

BENMAMIN CONSTANT

Another night that will never return! Another throng of sensations experienced for the first and last time! The interest we take in our happiness is basically ridiculous: instead of being occupied for years with the pains of preparing ourselves for moments which are ordinarily much less agreeable than we hoped, we ought to be occupied with depicting the different parts of our life. It is the reaction of the past and the future on the present that makes for unhappiness. In this moment I am not suffering at all. What does it matter to me what I suffered two hours ago, or what I shall suffer tomorrow? What I have suffered exists no longer, what I shall suffer has not yet appeared, and I am alarmed, I am tormented, I am done in by these two nothingnesses! . . . What stupid reasoning . . . what stupid, metaphysical irrationality, would you not say? [1]

No other passage expresses more clearly than this the principal state of mind of Constant, the essential state of mind, the one from which he will never be able to free himself, but against which, nevertheless, the main effort of his life will be directed. The moment he leaves off thinking of the present and concerns himself with his destiny, the absurdity of that interest suddenly dawns on him. On the one hand, there is only one thing in the world that matters: the happiness or unhappiness of existence; and on the other, there is the immediate conviction that neither happiness nor unhappiness is possible, because existence is a notion that is empty of meaning, and a person lives only in the present instant. There are moments in which one suffers and others in which one suffers less. Any continuity between these moments is fictitious, any reaction of one moment upon another is an artificial operation of the mind. Time exists only under the form of an instant whose affective value varies constantly. There is no duration because there is no true existence, and there is no true existence because sensations are always experienced for the first and last time.

Of course, such an attitude of mind is not at all rare in his time. It is that of the eighteenth-century writers, "men of the moment, limiting their existence to this moment." [2] A philosophy of sensation, pushed to the extreme, becomes a philosophy of the time-atom, of the sensory-moment. But what appears from the first as unique with this young student of Helvétius, is on the one hand the promptness with which his mind assents to such an attitude, and on the other hand the equal promptness with which his heart refuses to submit to it. For its part, thought says, "What does it matter!" But at the same time feeling, on its part, cries out, *"I am alarmed, I am tormented, I am almost done in by these nothing-nesses."*

Nothingness of the past, and nothingness of the future. One easily understands why, in the thought of Constant, the past was unavoidably annihilated on the spot, before it could offer any resistance. Amazingly precocious, mature in reflective thought by the age of twelve, without a mother, without a home, incessantly transferred from one tutor to another and from country to country, separated from his father and from other men by a timidity which "drove back the deepest impressions within his heart," Benjamin Constant never had either a childhood, an upbringing, or a feeling of tradition. His earlier life, as he relates it in the *Cahier rouge,* had been nothing more than a disconnected series of pranks that were forgotten as soon as performed. "He had never been allowed to suffer the consequences of his mistakes." [3] He had therefore never himself felt the consequences. Remorse and regret, those two feelings, which make one aware of the persistence of the past, were unknown to him. Like Adolphe before he met Ellénore, Constant had no past.

In that respect he found himself in harmony with his epoch; at least with the more general part of his epoch, in which were combined, often in a very strange fashion, recklessness and cynicism, a taste for danger and frivolity. Constant has given us a description of it in this picture of Paris in his time:

. . . Paris where all is overlooked, because nobody believes anything; where all is smoothed over because no one cares for anything; where there is ill humor because there is vanity but no vengeance, since there is no memory, and, indeed, nothing worth remembering; where every manifestation of yesterday is contradicted on the morrow; [4]

an epoch in which "minds no longer have the strength to retain, nor, consequently, to compare, anything. Their impressions flow through them fugitive and unseizable. No one notices that yesterday's event is in contrast with that of today." [5]

Constant is indeed the son of a senile epoch, in which the present moment easily triumphs over a past that never has the strength to endure. Now for the philosophy then dominant, duration was only a sensation which is prolonged in memory, and thought was nothing else than the feeling of the difference between that prolonged sensation and the actual sensation. He who no longer has the strength to retain anything has consequently no longer the strength to compare or to judge. Where there were no live sensations, there can only be now fugitive and unseizable impressions. They cross the mind. They leave no trace.

But if there is no past, then there is no longer a future—at least no consciousness of a future. A thought which cannot be established backwards cannot be established, so to speak, forwards. A thought which cannot be rooted in the past cannot be rooted in the future. It can see nothing beyond what it feels; it cannot *foresee*. As a consequence, the future must seem to it less a prolongation than a termination of the present. What is, is, but only in the moment when it is, and then it becomes something else. It is impossible, therefore, to establish any sort of continuity between the present and the future. The mind cannot spread beyond the narrowest limits; it cannot venture beyond sensation. Only two things are certain: one, that there is a present moment; and two, that this moment is going to end, and the following moment will not be the same. As a result, the future is presented to the mind under the form of an absolute otherness. It is nothing else than the possibility for any present moment to be replaced by a radically different moment. Hence the perpetual anguish over what the future may have most imminently in store:

> An impression which life gives me and which will not leave me is a sort of dread of destiny. I never finish writing down the account of one day and inscribing the date of the morrow without a feeling of disquietude over what the unknown morrow may bring to me.[6]

"If I could have the assurance of duration," Constant observed on one occasion, "I would be perfectly content with my lot." [7] But he does not have the assurance. The more spontaneous movement of his mind is a movement of mistrust.

Moreover, this innate uncertainty is aggravated further by the character of the epoch and the instability which is its salient trait. The internal confusions of the Revolution are followed, on a vaster scale, by the external confusions of the Empire. For the spirit of faction and anarchy there is substituted the will to power and the desire for conquest and usurpation. But terror and dictatorship have the same effect: they deprive men of the faculty of foresight: "If it were the kind of century in which one could be assured of some years of untroubled retreat, I would not hesitate . . . but a future is no longer one of this world's blessings; and one has always the feeling that what one does not do today cannot be done tomorrow." [8]

It is vain, therefore, to begin anything whatever today, since it is uncertain that one can finish it tomorrow; it is vain to act as if one could carry on one's action. But it is just as vain to wonder how an action begun can be continued:

> My sheet of paper blots so much despite the pains I take that I don't know how I shall do another page. But I am not there yet; I go ahead without worrying about the future. In this century, when one has even a page before him, it is a century. While one fills it a kingdom collapses. [9]

So to act or not to act amounts to the same thing. All action, like all inaction, is characterized by the same powerlessness of mind to allow for the future:

> You chide me for not having plans or projects, as if there were anyone who could form them in the state the world is in; as for me, I must declare that I cannot *see* two days ahead. We are at the mercy of a blind power; for the men, or rather the man who gives us orders appears to me to be directed much more by his nature than directing it. It was impossible, indeed, in the latter days of the Roman Empire, to plan on a future. [10]

Equally incapable of planning a future or keeping intact a past, man must stake everything on the present, and "everyday risk all he possesses." That is what soldiers and gamblers do:

There is no secure future for them; they live and move under the rule of chance. . . . For him who lives from moment to moment, or from battle to battle, time does not exist. The compensations of the future become chimerical. The pleasure of the moment alone has some certitude: and to make use of an expression which here becomes doubly suitable, each delight is so much won from the enemy.[11]

II

If life is, at bottom, nothing but a bizarre apparition, without future as without past, and so brief that one can hardly believe it is real, what good is it to immolate oneself before principles whose application is remote, to say the least? Better to profit by each hour, uncertain as one is of the hour to follow. . . .[12]

To profit by each hour. In another version Constant says: *"To profit by each moment, in order to shut one's eyes before the abyss which waits to engulf us."* [13] This variant brands with a still stronger indictment the troubled character of the metamorphosis that Constant makes the Epicurean *Carpe diem* undergo. It is not at all a question of installing oneself at the center of the present, as in the midst of a fruitful garden—that of existence—but of seizing the moment on the wing, so to speak, as the only tangible object one can catch hold of in the midst of a strange world, half unreal, which will shortly give place to an abyss. If at the slightest symptom of resistance passion bursts forth in Constant with the fury with which we are familiar, that is not solely because the obstacle delays and makes one risk losing the hour of delight; it is also because amidst a universe that is always on the point of vanishing like a mirage, the obstacle implies the existence of something authentically real, about which can be crystallized certain desires that always maintain an invincible repugnance toward being lost in the illusory. "The obstacle is a sort of galvanism which grants death *a moment of life."* [14] That is why the object and the moment of desire take on a wholly dramatic aspect. Like Esau's mess of pottage, they become priceless; and so, without hesitation, in order to gain possession of them, one sacrifices all the rest; even one's birthright, even one's right to exist: "I marched straight to my doom, with my eyes open." [15] There is no longer any possibility of life beyond the *moment of life;* there remains only that single moment in which everything is concentrated, the moment of *all or nothing:*

> . . . this torment can become so great that a man will succumb to it. When an accident or a malady that is foreign to the temperament of a sick person puts his life in danger, the doctors look for a way of averting the imminent peril, without calculating whether the remedies they employ in this *moment of crisis* will not be harmful to the patient's future health. The true concern of the passionate man is to emerge from the violent state into which his unsatisfied passion has plunged him: *if the present destroys him, what does a future matter which he will never attain?* [16]

Moment of life or death, "state violent and against nature," extreme state, from which a person emerges only to leap to the other extreme: "Extremes not only meet, they follow each other." The extreme of agitation is followed, in the same instant, by the extreme of indifference: "It is not the only time in my life that after a brilliant feat I was suddenly weary of the solemnity which would have been necessary to sustain it and that, out of boredom, I undid my own work." [17]

Boredom, sudden detachment, abrupt drying up of the vital source: without any transition whatever, Constant's indifference replaces "the state of the most painful excitement that could be imagined." But this astonishing metamorphosis ought not to have the effect of making us suspect either the authenticity or the intensity of the crisis that precedes it. Indeed it is at the precise moment—the one moment in which the being has concentrated all his concern with the momentary object—that the object and the moment must be dissolved. The moment invested, among all moments, with the privilege of becoming a *moment of life* cannot sustain this crushing role which consists in representing by itself alone all ardor and all life. It cannot continue to differ radically from all other moments. It gives way beneath the weight. It sinks back to the level of existence. It avows itself *mortal,* like all the rest. "In my most lively affections, the idea of death has always sufficed to calm me forthwith";[18] a calm which so quickly replaces and cancels the liveliest affection, simply because it has already reigned, with its reign of death, over all that surrounded the moment, over the whole periphery of existence. Now it penetrates the center. The present, also, is placed under the sign of a death which is the end of all, and which has the effect of at once reducing everything and every instant to *insignificance*. What good is it to cling to some portion of life or other, since in the last analysis it all comes to the same end?

> I have, as you know, the misfortune never to be free of the idea of death. It weighs on my life, it ruins all my projects, so that all events which confirm, or rather, recall this idea, have a very strong effect upon me: it is not the fear of death that I experience, but a *detachment from life* against which reason avails nothing, because, when all is said and done, reason corroborates this feeling instead of combatting it.[19]

> This conviction and the profound and constant feeling of the brevity of life makes the book or pen fall from my hands every time I engage in study . . . so that I pass my life in a painful and restless idleness, with the feeling that I ought to employ my time better, the vague regret of seeing it glide away and doing nothing about it, and the conviction that everything I do will come to nothing, and that at the end of fifty years it will all amount to the same thing. . . . Perhaps I have the misfortune to feel too strongly . . . that all our pursuits, all our efforts, all that we try, make, change, are only the pastimes of a few moments . . . that time, *independent of us,* goes along at a steady indifferent pace, and carries us along indifferently, whether we sleep or wake, whether we act or remain totally inactive. This trivial and always forgotten truth is always present to my mind, and renders me almost insensible to everything.[20]

These are lines of an unrivalled profundity, since within them Constant has succeeded in enclosing the double feeling of the independence of time and of our dependence with regard to time, in which is summed up the consciousness of all destiny. On the one hand, there is the conviction that to be concerned with ourselves is to be concerned with a being that exists through its sensations and thoughts, that is to say through activities which can take form only in time itself. I can exist and feel myself exist only if I feel at the same time that this feeling and this existence are supported and determined by a duration. But, by the same stroke, I become aware of this duration, and become aware of it as of an independent inhuman entity, which gives human things their existence, only to withdraw it, and consequently does not give it to them at all, but gives them rather only an illusion of life. As a result, by reason of this independence of time, all that is apparently and deceptively given by time becomes, like time, something independent and moving uniformly. Everything is made anonymous, impersonal, down to the least important incident of our past life, the least eventuality of our future life, the least modification of our present life, even to the very being we know ourselves to be. We are detached from ourselves; we can no longer bear that human visage which is nevertheless ours. We can no longer either love or regard ourselves:

> It is a great misfortune not to love oneself enough, not to take enough interest in oneself.[21]
> If you examine the men of this epoch carefully, you will see that they hardly ever fear pain any more. . . . They no longer love life. One might say that they hardly ever love themselves any more. They still love pleasure because that is attached to nothing, has neither a past nor a future, nor necessitates anything to follow, no enchainment of ideas, nothing durable, nothing that obliges or engages them beyond the moment.[22]

But if this moment and that pleasure are of themselves attached to nothing, how shall one attach oneself to them?

> The present alone remains to me, and the present is so close to being nothing, it is so disconnected, so isolated, so unseizable, that it is impossible to find anything in it which would further our happiness.[23]

If the moment is emptied of all passion and all sequence, it can only participate in the general debility. "The only means of happiness given to man on this earth is the abnegation of his will." [24] Now and then, by reversing one's skepticism, it may be possible to connect our own abnegation with the probable existence of some intelligent divinity whose creatures we should be. Then "one is freed of his own weight; one is no longer in charge of his egoism, no longer bears the burden of his individuality." [25] But most of the time this abnegation occurs of itself, without object and without faith. "One parcels out life hour by hour, day by day . . . ." [26]

> . . . a result that is similar, in its outside appearance, to religious resignation. Inside it is very different; for true resignation is life, but this disposition is nothingness.[27]

At this point, like a wave breaking over the whole surface of existence, the feeling of the shortness of life seems to flood and efface everything. Or rather, if life is still perceptible, it is as though seen through the transparence of some frozen substance. With singular detachment the mind watches itself rolled along by the waves. It watches itself live and discovers itself to be dead. Life and death are equivalent. It is as if one were a corpse that continued automatically to make live gestures:

> . . . we are dead ones who, as in Ariosto, have preserved of our live habits only that of fighting, which gives us an air of courage, because we bravely risk a life we no longer possess.[28]

Constant employs this image again and again, applying it to his epoch and to himself alike. The world and the self appear to the mind's eye as the same nothingness. Nothing any longer subsists. Nothing any longer *lives* except a consciousness that is infinitely detached, infinitely resigned, in whose view existence takes on a far away and unreal aspect:

> . . . See how the summer has passed; it has gone as quickly as if there were some happiness or peace in the future. I have never felt so keenly the rapidity of life. . . . Each day resembles itself, each hour is today what the same hour was yesterday. . . . All the restless agitation I see about me for position and positive advantage is so foreign to me that I am beginning not even to understand it. The din of empires in collision is only an annoying sound. The future no longer exists. The present is imperceptible. It is thus, I suppose, that the shades of Homer would have lived, had his Elysium existed . . . I neither suffer nor enjoy anything, and sometimes I have to pinch myself to know whether I am still alive.[29]

Such a life is withdrawn from the universe, from existence, from even the sensibility; it now exists only in reflective thought: "I let the days glide by without other desire than the absence of all emotion . . . ."[30]

> ". . . Let us enjoy the sight of time's passing away, of my days hurling themselves one on the other; let us stay a motionless, indifferent spectator to an existence half gone. . . ."[31]

Confronting the "time independent of us, that goes at a steady pace and carries us along with it," there remains only a passing thought, an impersonal consciousness, which feels as independent of time as time is of it.

III

Man, victor of the fights he has engaged in, looks at a world depopu-
lated of protective powers, and is astonished at his victory. . . . His
imagination, idle now and solitary, turns upon itself. He finds himself
alone on an earth which may swallow him up. On this earth the
generations follow each other, transitory, fortuitous, isolated; they
appear, they suffer, they die. . . . No voice of the races that are
no more is prolonged into the life of the races still living, and the
voice of the living races must soon be engulfed by the same eternal
silence. What shall man do, *without memory, without hope, between
the past which abandons him and the future which is closed before
him?* His invocations are no longer heard, his prayers receive no
answer. He has spurned all the supports with which his predecessors
had surrounded him; he is reduced to his own forces.[32]

In this incomparable passage which Constant believed so essential
to the elucidation of his own thought that he continually reproduced it, almost as it is, throughout his works, the main idea is that
the drama of time is the drama of isolation. The powerlessness of
man to preserve a past for himself, and to form a future for himself, the annihilation of the actual moment in indifference, finally,
the impossibility for the mind to have faith in duration, all this is
summed up, in the final analysis, in that interior suffering which,
under the name of *timidity,* Adolphe placed at the origin of the
movement of his thought: "I found myself at ease only when
alone." All the spiritual experience of Adolphe up until his meeting with Ellénore, all that of Constant up until his meeting with
Madame de Staël, is recapitulated in an inhuman isolation
scarcely interrupted meanwhile by the brief sensual episode of his
intimacy with Madame Johannot, and his purely intellectual relationship with Madame de Charrière. Everything in that existence
had been transitory, fortuitous, isolated. No voice yet heard had
been prolonged in his memory; no present voice had whispered in
his ear words that he wanted never to forget. The temporal isolation
of a thought which found a resting place in no single point of time,
was deeply grounded in a spatial isolation which hindered the
heart from finding *outside of itself* the true source of life. Detached thus from essential contact with other beings, individual
existence dried up, immobilized like a province cut off from its
capital:

In the capital all concerns conglomerate. . . . The rest is immobile. Individuals, lost in an isolation that is against nature, having
become strangers to their birthplace, without contact with the past,
living only in a swift present, and hurled like atoms onto a vast, level
plain, become estranged from a fatherland which they cannot recognize in any place, and the entire area of which becomes indifferent
to them, because their affection cannot rest upon any of its parts.[33]

The liaison of Constant with Germaine de Staël has, therefore, a
unique significance that distinguishes it from all the others. Not that
in itself this love was greater, more violent, or more durable; but
simply because, at last, thanks to it, contact was finally established;
established as it had to be, under the form of a reciprocal relationship between two persons who mutually recognized in each other
the quality of being human. The story of the love affair of Benjamin Constant and Madame de Staël is an extraordinary one. But
as to Constant's part in it, what matters is precisely the inverse
aspect, the normal aspect of it. From that point of view, the particular merit of this love is that it constitutes, made as it was by a human creature up until now deprived of all intimacy, the experience
of contact with his fellow-creature, and consequently the discovery
of the absolute worth of that relation. In the relation of oneself
with oneself, which is the only kind of relation for an isolated
being, there is nothing firm, nothing that *fixes* the mind. Nothing
seems real, not even pleasure, not even pain. There is only a fluid
movement of thought which extends to the most glacial regions of
life, and which finally returns, in a cross-surging of eccentric and
concentric waves, toward the always changing center of the actual
self. But in the relation of *self* to *another,* everything is changed.
From the instant man leaves his isolation to acknowledge the reality of an existence different from his own, he finds himself constrained by this different being to recognize the authenticity of
feelings and tendencies that by himself he would consider only as
an element of a play of wit. And looking then upon himself, he
finds himself forced at one and the same moment to recognize as
authentic in himself precisely what he recognizes as authentic in
his lover. The exceptional noetic value of love is that it rests upon
a feeling that is *shared:*

This story of a few weeks seemed to us to be the story of a whole
life. By a sort of magic, love makes up for the longest of memories.

> All the other affections have need of the past: love *creates,* as if
> by enchantment, a past with which it *surrounds* us. It gives us, so to
> speak, the consciousness of having lived, for years, with a person
> who but lately was almost a stranger.[34]

How long this duration lengthening backwards is, matters very
little here. What does matter is that it exists: that the loved person
by her sole presence calls to our mind and attests for us a past lived
with her. Will not Adolphe later write to Ellénore: "Have we not
all the past in common? Can we look back over the three years
which are now ending without recalling to mind the impressions
we have shared?" How can one doubt there was a past, and that
this past constitutes a part of what one calls existence? How can
one doubt any more the reality of existence? And so it is true that
having lived constitutes something that has an actual significance
and a permanent value. Thanks to love the past appears in its true
light. It is not only what has been and is no longer. It is still what
surrounds the present.

With these few lines of *Adolphe* the modern novel begins. In the
novel of the eighteenth century, duration had always been purely
successive. It cancelled itself out, as it went. Even in Prévost or
Rousseau the past appeared in the story only under the form of
reminiscences, and they, like all the elements of the action, took
their momentary place in the march of things. Here, for the first
time, the past appears to be a veritable past. It is affirmed as that
part of our experience which is already accomplished, but which
none the less remains the foundation of our being.

But in these few lines we must read something else also: the
expression of the spiritual conquest of Constant's thought. He who
was without a past, watches forming within him, as if by enchantment, what he was empty of. Love, by a kind of magic, makes up
for the memories of which he had been destitute. Constant's
thought becomes aware of this *creation.*

Love creates the past. It also creates the future. He who was
without a future, in the consciousness of whom the future, purely
negative, was only "the presentiment of the end of what one experiences," [35] discovers the future within himself as a positive faith
in the indefinite continuation of the present moment.

Any experience of the future had formerly been for him an experience of death, of death anticipated: "If sometimes a spark of

that tender and better nature I was pleased to ignore urged me to form ties beforehand, through a detestable foresight, I knew the moment when I would break them." [36]

> Woe to the man who, in the first moments of a love affair does not believe that this liaison will be eternal! Woe to him who, in the arms of the mistress he has just won, preserves a deadly prescience, and foresees that he will be able to detach himself from her.[37]

But in true love the experience is reversed; the thought of the future becomes an experience of life; the present is enriched by the belief in its immortality: "Love is ennobled, love is purified simply because, as long as it lasts, it believes it must never end." [38]

Thus in ceasing to exist in isolation man "saves a portion of his being from the ravages of time." The instant in which he lives, far from still appearing isolated or fortuitous, rests upon the two spans of duration; it lights up ahead, as well as behind, all the vast reach of *existence:*

> Love is only a luminous point, and nevertheless it seems to lay hold of all time. A few days ago it did not exist, very soon it will exist no longer; but as long as it does exist, it sheds its splendor over the time that preceded it and the time that must follow.[39]

IV

Love lays hold of time. He who loves, for as long as he loves, is not engaged solely for the moment when he loves. He is engaged for all his existence. He discovers and endows it by the same motion. The moment when one loves is therefore a moment of exceptional significance, a moment *surrounded by time,* a moment which adheres to the whole of life:

> Charm of love, who could paint you! This persuasion that we have found the being nature had destined for us, *this sudden light diffused over all of life,* that seems to us to explain its mystery, this unsuspected value that is attached to the slightest circumstance, those swift hours, every detail of which escapes the memory by their very sweetness, and leaves in our mind only a long trail of happiness. . . . Charm of love, he who experiences you will never know how to describe you! [40]

As long as love exists . . . But when it exists no longer? One knows how prompt with Benjamin Constant is the passage from passion to indifference: "It was no longer a goal; it had become a fetter." The moment one loves is followed by the moment one realizes he has ceased to love. On the one hand then, the novel of Constant is finished the instant it begins. But on the other hand, it is prolonged; one could almost say that it is just starting. The death of love introduces a new novel which is still a love novel, and not solely of love's dissolution.

That is true in the first place because Ellénore continues to love. Every love novel is a double novel. It comprises two different human durations that are seen to be joined to one another, confounded, and broken off. But that is still true for the essential novel, that of Adolphe. In one sense it is right to say that Adolphe never ceases to love. More precisely, he never ceases *to have loved.* His love, in the present, is dead. *In the past,* it continues and cannot die. The past love becomes the true past of Adolphe. He can renounce it only by renouncing life. Love no longer forms a part of his present, but it still forms a part of his existence.

Thus at the center is found death. Life resides on the periphery. Such is the kind of life that animates this novel so utterly penetrated by the past: a stunted life resembling the only landscape described in the book, a winter landscape, grayish, impregnated with cold and frost, but warmed from far away by a sun that "looks in pity on the earth."

> The distractions of travel, the novelty of objects, the efforts we made with each other, from time to time restored some vestiges of intimacy. Long habituation to one another, the varied circumstances we had gone through together, had attached to every word, almost to every gesture, memories that suddenly took us back to the past and filled us with involuntary compassion, as flashes of lightning flicker across the night without dispelling it. We lived, so to speak, by a sort of *memory of heart,* strong enough for the idea of our separation to make us sad, too weak for us to find happiness in being united.[41]

A memory too weak to dispel the night of the present, but strong enough to illuminate, and by its light reveal the sadness of it. For the sadness one finds expressed here is that of *knowing* that the present is not the past. In this particular sadness, it is not, it would seem, the sensibility alone that suffers: it is the intelligence. Whereas with Madame de Staël grief is a cry that directly bursts

forth from the heart, an emptiness of being immediately filled by
the resonance of the word; the pain, on the contrary with Constant,
is like the prolongation and complement of a thought. The mind
holds in its gaze not only the present and the past, but the difference
between them. He recognizes himself as no longer what he was,
but as a man who, in what he was, is now still more alive than in
what he is. He is like the shades of Homer who feebly revive in the
warmth of their former existence.

It is essentially a sad state, but one which is neither a state of
despair nor a state of indifference. Whereas the feeling of the
brevity of life strikes a mortal blow at life by dispelling all that was
on both sides of the present moment, here what one finds to be
mortally affected is the feeling of the present itself; and what
subsists in spite of everything is the feeling of existence. It seems to
have retreated into a region that is inaccessible to the present, but
which is nonetheless situated within the sphere of existence.

Hence this double return of Adolphe and Constant toward a
past that is anterior even to love, toward the past of youth and
childhood:

> I saw once more the old castle where I had lived with my father,
> the woods that surrounded it, the stream that washed against the
> foot of its walls, the mountains that bordered its horizon; all those
> things seemed to me to be so very much present, full of so much life,
> that they caused a trembling in me which I could hardly endure; and
> my imagination placed beside them a young and innocent creature
> who adorned them, who animated them by hope.[42]

> The past is actually the only thing that speaks to my heart, and it
> moves and interests me by the sole fact of its being past. I re-read
> the letters of men I loved twenty years ago, most of whom are no
> longer living. I recall to mind my hopes, the feeling of strength that
> I had, and all that rekindled my life, and it is only from the past that
> I can extract some vestige of ardor.[43]

Thus, a being who had begun by having neither a past nor a future finds a future in his past, and hopes in his memories. One
who had never been intimate with anyone, discovers retrospectively
in thinking of those from whom that person is separated now
by the distance of places or years, an intimacy he did not have,
but with which he enriches his memory:

I had often noticed that intimacy grew with distance. . . .[44]

> There is a degree of intimacy to which life is opposed; and it
> always seems to me that if I could see once more for a quarter of an
> hour friends I have lost, I would speak to them from greater depths
> of the heart than I did in the moments of greatest abandon.[45]

We see effect, as it were, of a mirage that makes the poetry of
regret rise up into view over dead sands in the distance: "My
heart is tired of all that it has, and regrets all it has not." [46] So
Constant's *memory of the heart* is not the affective memory. It is
not the total reviviscence which out of the present moment makes a
pure reproduction of the bygone moment. On the contrary, it opposes two profoundly dissimilar moments. It does not suppress the
interval of duration which separates them, but accentuates it. In
perceiving this difference between what is and what was, the human being understands the true meaning of time. His existence
does not appear to him as the permanence of an unalterable entity, but as a perishable substance upon which a continuous action
is exerted. He feels himself to be a creature "wrought by time."
The *Journal intime* is the monotonous verification of this difference and this deficiency:

> Nothing is sadder than to revisit precisely the same places one
> traveled to a short while before, with thoughts very different.[47]

> A month ago I was writing this same book, on the way to Geneva
> with projects and thoughts very different! [48]

> This time seventeen years ago I was roving the English shires all
> alone. It was on that journey that I first discovered the immense
> happiness of solitude. Today I am very far away from it.[49]

> Read my novel. How quickly impressions pass away when situ-
> ations change! I should no longer know how to write it today.[50]

A declaration that ends every time, that can only end, in record-
ing the powerlessness of the present to equal the past. That is how
there arises the deliberate tendency not to want to live any longer
in the present, to consider it a "stranger": "I am at my ease only
when I return again to a series of ideas that are not at all involved with anything in the present." [51]

What I like today, and have for a short time, lacks the support of
memories. . . . I believe that if I met Mme. Trevor again, I should
fall in love with her, considering the time. Something entirely new
would seem never to have the power of allying itself to my being, so
wrought upon by time.[52]

In marrying Charlotte, Constant marries the far off image of his
youth.

V

I do not know how it happens that what has become impossible becomes once more an object of desire.[53]

Temporal depth is relative. A distance appears between ourselves
and ourselves, and this distance is the past. As soon as there is
distance, as soon as the interior of the present breaks open with a
small gap that grows larger, just so soon there becomes visible from
the other side of the abyss the actual moment *in the past*. It has
once more become desirable. It is no longer a part of the present.
It is a part of existence. It is no longer attached to the immediate
being that we are. It is joined to the totality of what has already
been lived. It no longer belongs to us. It belongs to our life.

Thence if this schism is as prompt as it is irreparable there is
at the same stroke revealed to our eyes the concluded moment, in
all its strength and verity. We begin to comprehend the place it
really held in our life, the place it is now beginning to occupy in
our thought. We suddenly understand, at the moment we lose it,
the meaning of the moment.

For the true meaning of the moment can never be discovered
until it is fastened to the track of time, which unfolds backwards.
We comprehend what it is only when we see it join what has gone
before. Then, instead of perceiving the present as the unique object of our life, we perceive our life as the unique source of our
present. In itself, our present is a strange, insignificant thing; it is
nothing. Attached to what engenders it, it comes to have grandeur
and profundity. All the past is in the present; all that is alive in the
present plunges its roots into the past, and draws therefrom its
strength. But we are not aware of it; or rather, we are aware of it
only when it is no longer present, when it is past. We begin to desire
it again, and the feeling of ties broken causes us deep sorrow.

No one lived as intensely as Benjamin Constant the sorrowful drama of ruptures: a drama doubly sorrowful, since he lived simultaneously the drama of others as well as his own drama. It·is in the awareness of the sorrow he caused that Constant found the illumination necessary to understand his own. In discovering "how many are the deep roots of the affection which one thinks to inspire without sharing it," [54] Adolphe and Constant discovered how equally deep in them were the roots plunged into their existence by each of the moments in which they had continued to live with the being from whom they wished to be separated:

> There is something so profound in prolonged love affairs! Without our knowing it, they become so intimate a part of *our existence!* [55]
> They feel that in their very heart, which they did not think committed, are buried deep the roots of the feeling which they inspired.[56]

To tear loose these roots, therefore, is to cause between oneself and oneself the most grievous of ruptures: "I see that you find me very weak. But is it my fault if a habit of thirteen years has left deep and sorrowful roots?" [57]

Constant's greatness is to have accepted that sorrow and not to have rejected any of the bitterness of it. He did not spare himself. He did not turn away. He accepted the greatest possible grief, because he had lived this grief not only in his sensibility but throughout the whole field of his consciousness; because he infinitely multiplied it in himself by the lucidity with which he explored it. And as a consequence he transformed that grief into thought, into a general thought applicable to all humans. He saw better than anyone in what that grief consists, and what the cause of it is. He saw that habits are not a simple, mechanical repetition of ways of living, but the degree of fidelity we show to our past and to our existence. Their value is moral. "Morality has need of time," said Constant;[58] it has need also of the consciousness of time. The moral significance of a novel like *Adolphe* resides in the progressive development of the consciousness of time within a being who at first is capable only of ardent impressions. Thus in the life of Constant moral progress consists in the more and more profound consciousness of the solidarity that exists between all the moments of life. Not to take them into account is "to strike dead a portion of his mind":

Moral beings cannot be submitted to rules of arithmetic or mechanics. The past sends down into them deep roots which cannot be
broken off without grief: One makes them undergo, in tearing up
those roots, the torment of Polydorus. There is not one of them that
does not resist and that, torn away, does not shed drops of blood.[59]

[The revolutionaries] were astonished that the memory of several
centuries did not disappear at once with the decrees of one day. . . .
The slow and gradual effect of the impressions of childhood, *the
direction the imagination had been given by a long succession of
years,* seemed to them acts of revolt. They gave to habits the name
of malevolence.[60]

Thus, the true present is not an *imposed* present, not an *isolated*
present, but a present in which the mind freely agrees to follow a
direction given by a long succession of years; to follow it, and to
prolong it into the future. For habits do not exist unless man has
the feeling of being able to apply them beyond the present: "The
idea of the future is an element of habitude no less necessary than
the past." [61]

The value of the present resides, then, in the fact that the past is
transmitted through it to the future. In itself it is pure nothingness: "As I grow older, I like to consider the present as nothing,
and men as simple repositories of a heavenly flame which they
transmit from generation to generation . . . ." [62] And man must
incessantly sacrifice this present which is nothing:

Unless a violent and sudden shock deprives him of the use of all
of his faculties, man always sacrifices present sensation to the
memories of past sensation or to the hope of future sensation.[63]

VI

The advance of the human species being gradual, any innovation
which inflicts a violent shock upon it is dangerous; but this advance
being at the same time progressive, all that is opposed to this
progression is equally dangerous. If the opposition is efficacious,
there is stagnation and ere long degradation in the faculties of man.
If the opposition is impotent, there are strife, discord, convulsions,
and calamities.[64]

In this passage one finds a summary of both the political thought of
Constant and his intimate history. All violent shock is dangerous;
all sudden rupture with the past makes the roots of being bleed,

strikes dead a portion of his mind. But any opposition to his leap toward the future, any obstacle to his sacrificing freely the present in view of the future, no less dangerously paralyzes that delicate adaptation of the past to the future which constitutes the polity of duration. Without freedom, no *human time* is possible. The future is closed, the present vegetates, even the past is vitiated. If *Adolphe* is an infinitely complex novel, that is because one finds in it, besides the discovery of the value of a living past, the discovery of the noxiousness of a dead past. At the very time Adolphe understands, thanks to the "memory of the heart," the worth of a love that has ended, at the same time as, wishing to remain faithful to it, he tries through memory and sacrifice to adapt his present and future life to it, Ellénore demands of him something else than memory and sacrifices; she demands fidelity to a stationary, petrified love, which no longer belongs to a living past, but is a present made of a dead past:

> Thus it is that we want to make the present bow down, not before a past with which it is identified, but before a past which no longer exists for it, as innovators want to make it bow down before a future that does not exist.[65]

But every form has a tendency to become petrified. Every past has a tendency to impose its form forever upon the present. If on the one hand, fundamentally, the past keeps the visible image of the free transport by which thought is lifted up to a purified consciousness of existence, on the other hand, in its formal aspect, the past curbs that transport, constrains that freedom, threatens to obscure that consciousness. Man's present perpetually risks being paralyzed by a dead past, or, by reaction, risks breaking irremediably with a living past.

There is only one means of avoiding these opposite dangers: "It is to yield to the imperceptible changes which take place in the moral nature as well as in the physical nature." [66]

Let us be obedient, then, to time.[67]

This is the last word of a man who began by *being obedient to the moment* and whose whole experience of life consisted in feeling himself *wrought by time*. His is a counsel of continual abnegation, since it is a question of unceasing renunciation of living the moment for itself; a counsel also of the supple and incessant accomodation of the moment to the lessons of the past and the hopes of the future. Resignation and mobility, these are indeed the essential marks of the Constantian duration:

I think that with the resignation which is the habit of my mind, and the mobility which is at the same time both the defect and the resource of my character, I shall always manage, after a fashion what is personal to me.[68]

NOTES

[1] Rudler, *Jeunesse de Benjamin Constant*, p. 337.
[2] *Journal*, ed. du Rocher (Monaco), p. 220.
[3] *Adolphe*, chap. i.
[4] *A Barante*, November 11, 1811, *Revue des Deux Mondes*, XXXIV (1906), 547.
[5] *Polythéisme*, II, 83.
[6] *Journal*, p. 226.
[7] *A Mme de Nassau, Lettres*, ed. Mélégari (Paris, Albin Michel), p. 288.
[8] *A Barante*, August 22, 1809, *Revue des Deux Mondes*, XXXIV (1906), 530.
[9] *A Mme de Nassau*, ed. Ménos (Paris, Stock), p. 508.
[10] *A Mme de Nassau*, Nov. 1, 1802, ed. Mélégari, p. 358.
[11] *Esprit de conquête*, ed. Laboulaye, p. 149.
[12] *De la religion*, I, 60.
[13] *Esprit de conquête*, p. 237.
[14] *Adolphe*, ed. Rudler, p. xi.
[15] *Lettres à Mrs. Lindsay*, p. 9.
[16] *De la religion*, I, xxviii.
[17] *Cahier rouge*.
[18] *Adolphe*, chap. vii.
[19] *A Mme de Nassau*, Feb. 1, 1805, ed. Mélégari, p. 285.
[20] *A Mme de Charrière*, May 21, 1791; Rudler, *Jeunesse*, p. 385.
[21] *A Hochet, La Revue*, 1904, p. 152.

[22] *A Barante*, Sept. 25, 1810, *Revue des Deux Mondes*, XXXIV (1906), 538.
[23] *A Mme de Charrière*, Dec. 3, 1794, ed. Mélégari, p. 486.
[24] *A Barante*, July 27, 1808, *Revue des Deux Mondes*, XXXIV (1906), 262.
[25] *Ibid*.
[26] *Ibid*.
[27] *Ibid*., p. 538.
[28] *Ibid*., January 30, 1812, *Revue des Deux Mondes*, XXXIV (1906), 551.
[29] *Ibid*., p. 562.
[30] *A Mme Récamier*, p. 298.
[31] *Adolphe*, chap. vii.
[32] *De la religion*, I, 46.
[33] *Esprit de conquête*, p. 173.
[34] *Adolphe*, chap. iii.
[35] *Adolphe*, preface to the second edition.
[36] *A Mme de Krudner*, quoted by M. Levaillant, *Revue de Paris*, July, 1945, p. 30.
[37] *Adolphe*, chap. iii.
[38] *Polythéisme*, II, 311.
[39] *Adolphe*, chap. iii.
[40] *Ibid*., chap. iv.
[41] *Ibid*., chap. vi.
[42] *Ibid*., chap. vii.
[43] *A Mme de Nassau*, April 24, 1808, *Adolphe*, ed. Rudler, p. 132n.
[44] *A Mme de Nassau*, May 26, 1811, ed. Mélégari, p. 435.
[45] *Ibid*., July 19, 1808, ed. Ménos, p. 254.

[46] *Journal*, p. 274.
[47] *Ibid*., p. 173.
[48] *Ibid*., p. 175.
[49] *Ibid*., p. 192.
[50] *Ibid*., p. 263.
[51] *A Barante*, January 30, 1812, *Revue des Deux Mondes*, XXXIV (1906), 551.
[52] *A Mme de Nassau*, April 24, 1808.
[53] *A Barante*, April 22, 1808, *Revue des Deux Mondes*, XXXIV (1906), 255.
[54] *Adolphe*, preface to the 3rd edition.
[55] *Ibid*., chap. v.
[56] *Ibid*., preface to the 2d edition.
[57] *A Rosalie de Constant*, July 7, 1807, ed. Ménos, p. 221.
[58] *Esprit de conquête*, p. 149.
[59] *Ibid*., p. 271.
[60] *Ibid*., p. 211.
[61] *Eloge de Sir Samuel Romilly*, coll. Plancher, IV, 67.
[62] *A Mme de Nassau*, Dec. 10, 1811.
[63] *Mélanges*, p. 393.
[64] *Esprit de conquête*, p. 272.
[65] *Réflexions sur les constitutions*, p. x.
[66] *Esprit de conquête*, p. 273.
[67] Coll. Plancher, IV, 19; *Esprit de conquête*, p. 273.
[68] *A Mme de Nassau*, Dec. 15, 1808, ed. Ménos, p. 289.

✳
✳
✳ VIGNY

I

✳   Emotion was born so deep and intimate a thing with him that
it plunged him from childhood into involuntary ecstasies, into
interminable reveries, into infinite inventions.[1]

How is one to describe the starting point of Vigny's thought? Emotion, ecstasy, revery, invention—no one term can precisely express
what is simply a movement of both heart and mind, but a movement without a precise aim, without a distinct cause, without other
awareness than that of something deep and intimate that is born
and bursts forth. What one notices first with Vigny is that, against
a background of emptiness, there stands out a spontaneity so absolute that it seems to him to be detached from everything, even
himself:

My imagination is like Phaeton, it dies if it is not free.[2]

The imagination lives only by the spontaneous emotions that are
particular to the organization and inclinations of each person. . . .[3]

But our swift mind abounds in motion. . . .[4]

Movements of poetry that dart forth despite me.—O my Muse!
my Muse! I am separated from thee. . . .[5]

Before taking shape, before becoming thought, Vigny's "muse"
already exists, then, in his consciousness; an existence that is distinguished only by virtue of the very impulse that detaches it. It is
first of all that which is not present, that which abandons the present in order to realize itself and, in a fashion, to invent itself in
another world:

The imagination possesses him over and above all. . . . It carries
his faculties toward the sky as irresistibly as a balloon lifts its car. At
the slightest impact it takes off; at the tiniest breath of wind it flies

away, never to cease wandering through the space uncharted by human paths. Sublime flight toward unknown worlds, you become the invincible habit of his mind! [6]

Thus the start is a movement of flight. The limits of the present would paralyze pure freedom. The only positions in time which might be tolerable are the hours when time least affirms its presence, the hours of the night,

> hours of the Spirits, the airy Spirits that buoy up our ideas on their transparent wings and make them sparkle with a more fiery splendor. I feel that I carry my life lightly in the span of time which is measured by them.[7]

For this nocturnal "span of time" is precisely that in which there is no indication of measure, in which thought is buoyant simply because it exists by its own effort alone and feels itself free just because it escapes actuality: "My mind is never freer than when the work I do has no connection with my present situation." [8]

And so Vigny's activity of mind will detach itself so completely from immediate reality that the latter will always appear to it to be a place in which it cannot take any delight, in which it cannot even breathe or live, and from which it must escape at any price:

> . . . I have always had such a dread of the present and of the real in my life that I have never represented in art a painful or delightful emotion while I was experiencing it, but have attempted instead to flee to the sky of poetry from that land whose brambles have, at every step, lacerated feet too fragile and perhaps too ready to bleed.[9]

A movement of flight from the present, the thought of Vigny can only be described at first by this negation of all form or limit. But immediately this spontaneity imparts to it something positive, that is to say, a direction:

> Each day, on awakening, man's mind darts and glides like the swallow, turning, soaring, descending, hurling itself down, then suddenly springing up to highest heaven.[10]

This "sky of poetry," this "space uncharted by human paths," lacking, as it still does, any configuration, is nevertheless that *toward which* the "sublime flight" is directed. It is not situated in the here and now but in the further fields of space and time; and if the poet projects beyond the present the emotion that makes him tremble, it is to give it the import of a summons from the future: "I have faith in myself, for there is no beauty, no grandeur, no harmony in nature that does not cause a prophetic thrill in me . . . ." [11]

Thus the first positive manifestation of Vigny's genius is the "genius of presentiment." [12]

II

Let us try to imagine what first concrete form that genius will take, in what future all this power of "involuntary ecstasies," of "interminable reveries," of "infinite inventions" will be molded: "I do no more, as you know, than to dream of certain projects in the future . . . ." [13]

Is there any other future of which Vigny's adolescence could dream than the future of glory? The whole epoch resounded with the reverberation of a single name; all the youth of the time was the passionate witness of an adventure that appeared lofty and fascinating precisely because it promised to be everyone's future:

> We felt ourselves matured all at once by the rays of an unforeseen star: that star was glory. The dream of the glory of arms lasted thirty years for me. . . . Do you realize to what heights the temper of the time carried our minds? [14]

The future, in the presentiment of which the young Vigny "matures" and finds his mind exalted, is a future of glory: "Glory, sparkling-eyed, attended me from the first/Casting before my footsteps its pure and aerial flares . . . ." [15]

A radiant future, toward which a mind "matured all at once" hurls itself with so great an impatience that the present has no ties for it—a future which no longer is simply the undefined place where the mind both finds and loses itself in the play of its spontaneity, but that which is situated in the direct line of time, in the immediate prolongation of the moment in which one is. To seize and possess it, one must be at the prow; one must participate in the very act by which the present advances and becomes the future. For the glory is in the action by which man contributes to the advancement of duration, and it is not enough to live the duration;

one must think it, make it, anticipate its changes, and determine its course:

In this rapid and continuous voyage toward the infinite, to travel out ahead of the crowd is sheer glory, to keep abreast is life; to fall behind is very death.[16]

In this attitude which allows of no hesitation and tolerates no slackening, no other choice is possible: "He who is not ahead is behind." [17] "Woe to laggards! To fall behind is to die." [18] Now this participation in time is a participation in its rhythm and in its rapidity. It is with an imperious speed that the young Vigny sets out upon the pursuit of glory. If for the crowd the march of time is similar to the imperceptible progression of the hour hand of a watch, for him it will be like

. . . the seconds hand, that darts so alive, so unquiet, so bold and at the same time so tremulous, that hurls itself ahead and shivers with the feeling of its audacity or the pleasure of its conquest over time; I have never considered it without thinking that the poet has always had and must have this hurried pace toward the centuries to come, and beyond the general state of mind of his nation. . . .[19]

So much haste, however, to meet the future, involves singular consequences. First of all, time never seems short enough, the future never comes soon enough. Besides the hours of inspiration favored by the "Buoyant Spirits," there are the "ill-omened" hours brought by "Time as invisible as the air, and weighed and measured like it." During such hours as these, one feels "all the inordinate length of the entire day." [20] Then it is no longer with the marvelous speed of the second hand that one seems to travel through duration. On the contrary, "the hand is slow";[21] each grain of the hourglass "is of a great heaviness." [22]

Besides, during the inauspicious hours, there seems to be added to the shrinking of the future the acceleration and the lengthening of the past. By a surprising but logical phenomenon, those winged moments when the imagination was hardly any longer aware of the yoke of duration and, multiplying its points of view, filled up the space of one second with as much as might have been furnished by a whole day—those moments, now that they are accomplished, seem to appear not only as if having lasted an infinitely shorter

time than the second but also of *being extended* over a period of
time infinitely longer than that of a day. Simultaneously, it seems
that the time before had passed in a flash and that, nevertheless,
one had lived an inordinate number of years. The faster the course
toward the centuries to come, the more it seems to have been only
the fugitive passage of an infinite duration:

> My brain, always mobile, toils and whirls with frightening speed
> under an immobile brow. Between the word someone says to me and
> the word with which I reply, whole worlds pass before my listless
> eyes.[23]

These worlds that pass always leave behind them shadows which
grow always longer. Vigny's imagination becomes feverish. A "stub-
born perpetual working" goes on, a labor "whose great wheel turns
day and night in his brain," setting in motion "a thousand other
accessory wheels that whirl and gear in its cogs";[24] but this labor
and the multiplicity of its effects have for their sole result the replacing of the consciousness of the "conquest of time," by the
consciousness of an ever-turning wheel of a time ceaselessly conquered and ceaselessly conquering.

                    III

> Time has flown in this century. The experience of old age has come
> to visit our astonished, saddened youth. . . .[25]

The reversed perspective of a "time that has flown" awakens in
Vigny the feeling of precocious senility. His gaze is turned, "astonished, saddened," toward horizons which now are no longer before
but behind. And all the imaginary existences previously lived in
fever and haste make their weight felt upon his mind more heavily
than if they had been real.

> My life is two hundred years old.—Imagination ages us, and it
> often seems that one has lived through more time in dreaming than
> in his life.[26]

Then, little by little, the past is discovered in the mind; a past
fuller of images and forms than ever the future had been:

> Empires destroyed, women desired, loved, passions worn out,
> talents acquired and lost, families forgotten, ah! how much I have

lived! Has it not been like this for two hundred years? Survey of my whole life.[27]

But multifarious as this past of his reveals itself to him, there is very soon added to it a past which is not his own, but out of which he will make, as it were, a retrospective protraction of his existence. Throughout his youth, Vigny continually lived among persons like that parent of whom he says that he "never saw anyone dwell so completely in the past." [28] From childhood, the stories of his father taught Vigny to relate himself to a world that has ended, of which he is the heir, and which is continued within himself. Ancestors are "still present." [29] He pictures them to himself not only according to that oral tradition transmitted to him and in itself hardly more lively than the historical memory, but with all the creative intensity which his naturally prospective genius, reversing its flow, now throws into its retrospections:

> While the night was bringing to me the hour of my thoughts,
> Alone, but surrounded by the images of the past,
> I loved to adorn them with the graces of their time,
> And restore the fatherland to its old inhabitants.
> There, just as they lived, I saw them reappear,
> Recovering their sorrows at the same time as their being,
> Like the garments of all men born
> That are the only signs by which history knows them.[30]

Thus, little by little, Vigny came to endow creatures of the past with feelings which were his own and, simultaneously, to receive from these beings the antique garments with which he could adorn the nakedness of his emotions. Added to that is the intense feeling of solidarity with the time of his ancestors, for which everyone in his set had a deep religious respect; and then one understands how, with a person as preoccupied as Vigny was with imagining the future, there was added and mingled with that an inverse sort of imagining, but of the same nature, which gave him as it were presentiments of persons and things of the past:

> The eyes that had seen them stamped their image upon my own eyes as well as that of many famous personages that were dead long before I was born. Family stories have the advantage of engraving themselves more deeply upon memory than written narratives; they, like the venerated narrator, are alive, and they protract our life behind us, just as the divining imagination can extend it on into the future; [31]

an enlargement, moreover, not only of the length of duration but also of the particular images that fill it. For if ancestors were always present, and the personages of former times are always alive in "family stories," they appear there at the most moving moments of their lives, involved in the actions which illustrate their virtues and make them larger than life. It is thus that the concrete image of glory, so longed for by the adolescent in dreams of the future, is seen outlined, specified, in paintings of a past transfigured and ennobled. The glory ". . . enlivens the effaced traces of days/For the mind enlarges images of the past . . ." [32] and so engraves upon Vigny "the burning mark of the Roman Eagle." [33]

It is thus—"so profound are the impressions of childhood" [34]—that Vigny comes little by little to *turn into the past tense* everything prospective and spontaneous in his thought. By listening so often and so attentively to the tales of his elders, he ends by himself acquiring their taste for going backward and for retrospection. A taste that is never to leave him. As he says of his *Servitude,* he will give his books *white hairs.* And whenever he goes back in thought to times well before those whose successors have "stamped the image upon his eyes," it is invariably because he is impelled by the same need of filling his imagination with great images:

> There is a great charm in going back in the mind to former times: it is perhaps the same as that which prompts an old man to recall his earliest years first, and then the entire course of his life.[35]

IV

> Thus I always carried within me the memory of times that I had not seen, and the discontented experience of old age entered into my child's mind and filled it with mistrust and a precocious misanthropy.[36]

A singular combination this, that of a virgin imagination and a senile lucidity! At first it seems as if it ought to have for its effect in Vigny some tragic interior conflict, as with so many other romantics. But the "precocious misanthropy" of Vigny happened to be contained within precise bounds by the voluntary ignorance he maintained toward the realities of the present. Enveloping it with a disdain accentuated by "mistrust," he found himself only the freer to search in the depths of the past for the images of that glory of which he had dreamed on the summits of the future. "Counting for the experience of the glory of arms neither upon the present, nor upon the future, I sought it in the memories of my companions." [37]

"Nor upon the future . . .": we must not imagine, however, that this condemnation of the future was as definitive as that of the present. In the very need which impelled Vigny to revive the memories of his parents or companions there was, intact and as pure as ever, that extraordinary faculty of prospective imagination that hurled him "toward the centuries to come." The reminiscences of his elders were illumined for him by rays of glory. A glory whose essence is surely in the motion by which genius detaches itself from the crowd and strikes out ahead of the present into the fulness of the future; but whose greatness is clearly appreciated only if one holds in view the whole length of a line of duration and the fast gait by which the crowd is left behind and time is conquered. The spectacle of the past apprises us of how the future is to be made, of what nature it can be. Understood in this way by the poet, the feeling of glory leads him to a knowledge of duration. From the viewpoint of the present, it shows him the future into which it projects the poeticized past: "Before eternity creates a future for him,/ Shows it to him on a level with the grandest memory . . . ." [38]

Finally, experience, fretful as it may be, has always the value of experience. It is made of things lived through, of concrete forms, of palpable materials with which it becomes possible to *imagine images,* to construct a new world visible to the eyes of the imagination. "The march of the Mind is not direct. If its flight were in a straight line, without turnings, it would be lost in the infinite . . . ." [39]

The creative flight in a straight line had preceded everything with Vigny, even his ability to invent the future toward which his genius took flight. Thus he was reduced to "wandering in the space that has no human paths." But from the moment in which to his brief personal experience he was able to add "the memory of times he had not seen," he found himself in possession of the whole of a past apt to be converted into future—and into poetry.

The *conversion of past into future* is the operation which will become for Vigny one of the very most important in his spiritual activity. He writes, on one occasion, of his state of mind when working on one of his books: "I was like the Jesus of Manzoni: *remember-*

ing the future." [40] This conversion of past into the future has for him not only the purely poetic value of the initial élan; it is not any longer a simple presentiment that produces the mysterious "prophetic thrill"; it is a factor of knowledge, a science: *foresight.*

> Prophecy is the poetry of foresight. Isaiah foresees, warns the name of Heaven. [41]

> The Poet reads in the stars the path that the finger of the Lord points out to us. [42]

This stellar reading (in *Stello,* Vigny had first written: "The poet *searches among* the stars"; the correction is significant) is an art which is acquired only by the continual calculations of the mind. The early inspiration is doubtless not forsaken; it has never been so much alive; but Vigny knows now that to the *prophetic thrill* must be joined the *prophetic thought.* On the one hand he can, like Stello in his profession of faith, affirm the primary divining faculty which renders the poet spontaneously conscious of the two depths of duration:

> I believe in myself, because I feel in the depths of my heart a secret power, invisible and indefinable, entirely similar to a presentiment of the future and to a revelation of the mysterious causes of present time. [43]

But on the other hand he can distinctly affirm the lucid and rational character of poetic thought, in which past and future are measured according to observations, meditations, comparisons incessantly repeated, and for which the march of time is determined according to the judgments of the reason and the acts of the will:

> The Neutrality of the solitary thinker is an armed neutrality which springs up in case of need.
> He puts a finger on the scales and tips them. Sometimes he weighs upon, sometimes arrests the mind of nations; he inspires public actions or protests against them, accordingly as it is revealed to him to do so by the consciousness he has of the future. What does it matter to him if he risks his neck in hurling himself ahead or behind? [44]

No, what matters to him is simply that this movement ahead or behind be a deliberate act, no longer determined only by the attraction but by the consciousness of the future. A delicate exercise it is, for the forces of preservation and rupture are weighed in the balance; a dangerous exercise, for the return to the past and the flight toward the future detach the thinker from the crowd and put him in a perilous position, ahead of it or against it; "men crush without pity the man who outstrips them and the man who fights against the current of their own course." [45]

Outstripping or opposing, opposing to outdistance, transferring from the future to the past and from the past to the future the perpetual attention of the reflective consciousness, making no use of the present except as the point from which one can "See those who have passed and those who shall pass"—this is to be for Vigny the policy of mind, the policy of "see-saw" that he will apply throughout his whole life.

v

To accomplish this policy three things were necessary: a powerful faculty of preserving the past; a no-less-powerful faculty of anticipating the future; and finally a profound sense of the order in which the elements of duration are distributed.

Now, as to the first two faculties, Vigny was confident of possessing them to the highest degree.

First memory:

> I was born with such a memory that I have forgotten nothing of what I have seen or of what has been told me since I came into the world.[46]
>
> I have an almost infallible memory. . . .[47]
>
> I have the gift, often painful, of a memory that time never alters; my entire life, throughout all its days, is present before me like an ineffaceable painting. . . .[48]

With regard to foresight, Vigny's declarations are just as positive:

> I have never once, at first sight, been mistaken as to what an event, a conversation, a word, was going to be. All my life I have exercised this faculty on the future, and never up until this very moment have I been mistaken in foreseeing what a man would become—what he would do in such and such circumstances; [49]

a statement that Vigny was pleased to make André Chénier repeat, in almost identical terms: "It is rare that my first impression, my first glance, my first presentiment is ever mistaken." [50]

Finally in Vigny's correspondence there is a particularly illuminating passage in which this double anticipative and preservative faculty of the poet appears in all the plethoric abundance it stores up in the consciousness:

> You know with how many things, sensate or insensate, my head is filled and tormented; how strongly the pains and real felicities of life are graven there and multiply to infinity, because of that folly of mine of claiming never to lose any of the memories of the past, and simultaneously to foresee and arrange everything to my will, in the future.[51]

Under this double aspect the Vignian consciousness appears as a field of vast extent, which, on its two panels, grants to the pictures painted there an extraordinary clarity. In the present moment the poet is capable not only of recapitulating each of the episodes of his past life, each of the stages he has discerned in his future life, but also of drawing a comprehensive image of the whole existential field, forward as well as behind. Hence we have those "surveys of his whole life," which for him constitute an exercise, a discipline, and, more than that, a means of knowledge:

> . . . my entire life, throughout all its days, is present before me like an ineffaceable painting.[52]
> All the pictures from my tiniest infancy are before my view. . . .[53]

Hence again that capacity of embracing the entirety of the *picture* at a single glance, and that so astonishing faculty of Vigny's of perceiving his life as a temporal panorama which, completely unrolled, static and as if fixed in its frame, thus exhibits to his eyes its permanent face. The interior regard, from a unique point of view, seizes all the expanse of life, which in the vastness of space finds a stirring correspondence. And it is not only for their spatial beauty that Vigny loves above all in nature the depths of perspective, the vast horizons; but for the temporal significance they symbolically present:

> You have before your eyes, and under your melancholy gaze, great horizons and a verdure that gives them a rest from a life in candlelight. You have about you that silence and that calm of the fields which lets us hear our soul speak to itself for hours on end, which allows it to collect itself in infinite meditations, to return again to its feelings and thoughts, to purify them, to give them a pur-

pose, to enjoy in advance what the future has in store, and to have a foretaste of recompense for tasks accomplished; [54]

and in the magnificent lines of the *Maison du berger:*

> All human pictures that a pure Spirit brings me,
> Shall come alive for thee when, before our door,
> The great silent lands shall spread afar out.

At its apogee this almost infinite extension of the consciousness spread out over two slopes of duration almost ends in the illusion of having attained the divine eternity which, in the terms of Saint Augustine admired by Vigny, is a "perpetual now":[55] a present eternally identical to itself and comparable to a simultaneous contemplation of all the points of duration:

> The Lord holds everything in his two great arms.

Could not human thought, like God, thanks to "all the arsenal of its powerful energies," become all-containing? It is this ambition that Vigny expresses in the two following passages:

> . . . It behooves only Religion, Philosophy, Pure Poetry, to go farther than life goes, beyond all time, as far as eternity.[56]

> . . . When the indefinable force that sustains my life, Love . . . circulates within me, all my mind is illumined by it; I think that I understand, all together, Eternity, Space, Creation, creatures, and Destiny; it is then that Illusion, phoenix with gilded plumage, comes to rest upon my lips, and sings.[57]

The same illusion, if we can believe one of his "Elevations," carried him one day

> Up to the sill of the door
> That eternity holds ajar,

and let him live for an instant in the perpetual now, composed of an infinite knowledge:

> Today, I know all, I see thee, and I embrace
> The future that is not yet, the past which is no more,
> The times to be born, and the times that are ended.[58]

But, different as he was from the other Romantics, if Vigny often has the presentiment and sometimes the illusion of attaining the

infinite, he never is lost in the inconceivable idea of God or His
divine attributes. What he finds there is, like the immensity of nature, a symbol of the extent of the field of human consciousness.
Nevertheless, the particular clarity with which images are preserved and ideas conceived in him makes it repugnant to him to
abandon himself to an ecstasy in which everything is confounded
in one vast emotion, unified but indistinct—as much so as to allow
himself to live within the narrow bounds of the present emotion, intense as it might be. As a consequence there was his project of a
Fourth Consultation of the Somber Doctor, which would have
dwelt "on the idea of the love that exhausts itself in searching for the
eternity of voluptuousness and emotion." [59]

From here on, Vigny's innate aversion for a life reduced to the
present is to take the form of a deliberate condemnation. Those
who live only in the present instant not only stupidly limit the field
of their consciousness, but in the very interior of those limits the
consciousness thus limited loses its sense of direction and its sense
of values. It is a degradation of the soul and a paralysis of the consciousness. It is necessary to cite all of the passage in the *Journal*
where, in an analysis of a sad lucidity, Vigny paints the unforgetta-
ble moral portrait of her in whom he found—to his sorrow—the
very type of person in whose eyes "all is in the present moment": [60]

> There are two sorts of minds among us; one sort enjoy the present
> moment and forget, at the instant they are possessed of this intoxi-
> cating emotion, both what has preceded and the preoccupation with
> what is going to follow.
> They can arrive at the point of a complete drying up of the heart.
> Owing to their perpetual dizziness, any impression becomes for them
> as good and as lively as any other; they give themselves up to it
> entirely and without reserve. A mind of this sort, since it sees com-
> ing the moment when it is going to feel remorse and fright at the
> emptiness of its life and heart, is eager to divert its thoughts and
> throw itself into the exaggerated acting out of whatever is presented
> to it, or looks for an occupation that will impassion it. It quickly
> takes on the tone, allure, and movement of this passion and suc-
> ceeds in killing its own memory and feelings. Now and then it
> awakens, appalled, and asks itself if it is true that it loves or might
> be loved; then as the moment seizes it again, it weeps abundantly
> over the destruction of its being which it does not understand and of
> which it has not the strength to take account. But let a gay troop of
> women and men come before it, and the impression it had is past; it
> now remembers only just enough of it to ask itself if it was not

ridiculous; it will turn itself immediately to delicate or gross gaiety (as one wishes) and finally it will sink back again, overwhelmed and besotted. Perpetual chameleon, it ends by being neither happy nor unhappy, it is only a flame that takes fire from the motion of others, and by itself, no longer having any life of its own, remains incapable of *being,* no longer deserving to have any one count on it as anything more than a soap bubble, forever carried about by the wind and colored by the objects it encounters.[61]

A striking passage, not only for its verbal beauty and the tone of its feeling, but for what it reveals of the basic thought of Vigny. If these minds of which he speaks are condemnable, it is for Vigny, in the last analysis, because they are *incapable of being,* and that the aptitude to be, consequently, resides in the strength with which one can hold under his gaze, independently of all help or of all external cause, the diverse points that one has occupied and that one will occupy in duration.

A knowledge of the whole graphic curve of his duration is the central point in Vigny's philosophy of consciousness. It is what he superbly explains in the same passage:

The contemplative mind, on the contrary, is attentive at one and the same time to the three points of existence, the past, the present, and the future, never ceasing to re-examine what *has been,* and to evoke it by memory, to consider what *is* in contemplating it with judgment, to conjecture about the probabilities of what *will be* by an imagination submissive to the calculations of reason and to the laws of the will. It knows, it sees, and it feels profoundly. It refers to the heart the emotions its triple view gives it, and at this center of love and of goodness, the greatness and power of its being are incessantly perfected and enlarged.

The highest conception that Vigny forms of the human consciousness, thus, has for its necessary condition the triple knowledge of the distinct elements of duration. Attention to these three points consists in keeping them at once separate and present; the *totum simul* of Vigny does not aim at the unity of the object, but only at the simultaneity of presence. Such indeed is the role of the "contemplative" mind, which is content to represent ideas, not to blend them. As in Platonic thought, there is in Vigny the notion of the plurality of ideas and, as with Kant, that of a world numbered and ordered by the mind. But it is a question here, however, neither of idea-types nor of categories. The triple duration of which Vigny speaks is that of existence. Nothing is further removed from his thought than a philosophy which "cancels being in eternity." [62] By dialectical reflection, but still more by the lived experience of anticipation and retrospection, Vigny arrives at a conception of "being." Being is first of all consciousness—and consciousness *is* in the measure that it is consciousness of the triple internal experience that constitutes duration for it.

VI

But the being thus obtained is pure consciousness: a consciousness as acute as can be of human existence distributed over the three points of existence. And consequently, by very reason of the clarity with which the mind is perceived to be situated in the temporal order, an essential problem dramatically appears in thought. Is it necessary to situate oneself "at the general point of view of the immensity in which the universe swims," [63] and from this nontemporal place to contemplate the series of causes and effects by seeing there only the *"inflexible law of progress* whose movement ceaselessly carries with it the three degrees of the human mind which are indifferent to it"? [64] Or is it necessary, on the contrary, renouncing the knowledge of what will be "the future of our existence in eternity," [65] to apply ourselves to knowing what the past, present, and future of our existence are in this life?

> . . . all my ideas about life. They are consoling by their very despair.
> It is good and salutary to have no hope.[66]

Vigny's despair is a choice. Renouncing the eternal order, he chooses human duration. If he is opposed to Stoic thought as well as to Christian philosophy, it is because both of them imply a renunciation of what for Vigny is essential and profess a despair of life and time that for him is worse than a despair of eternity.

> The finest effort of optimism toward the future was the Christianity that said, seeing how evil the world is: "Give up this unhappy world, and your soul shall find sweet repose.
> But it is also the last cry of despair.[67]

> All the books which attest to Christianity have only one idea, the nothingness of everything human, and a scorn for life and time in

view of the cross and eternity. . . . It is a complete renunciation of the earth.

On the other hand, the ancient wisdom of the Stoics reduces the art of living to that of suffering without complaint, and in holding fast one's mind in a perpetual interior peace, in always maintaining it in a forced contemplation which renders it insensible to life. . . .[68]

In other words, if Christianity "despairs of life and places its hope only in eternity," Stoicism, while placing no hope in eternity, does not despair any the less of life. The inverse despair of Vigny rises up against these other two despairs.

But this reversal of choice implies tragic consequences. First a sad ignorance of the first and last end of man:

The resignation most difficult for us is that of our ignorance. Why do we resign ourselves to everything, except to being ignorant of the mysteries of eternity? [69]

Condemned to . . . ignorance of the future and the past of humanity and of divinity, and to thinking of them always.[70]

Moreover there comes the consciousness of the perpetual conflict between the inexorable forces which thrust man along the length of an anonymous duration and the human effort which attempts to construct a human time. Here again it is in terms of duration that the problem was posed for Vigny. If consciousness renounces all participation in the universal order and feels it exists only in its creation of an order of its own, the universal order has to appear to it as emanating from outside and, in consequence, as a determination which—imposed from the world outside—weighs down, hems in, and forces man along; a determination that is always urgent, always oppressive, always ready to impose upon the moment its ever-lasting ends. To yield to it would be to let oneself be carried along by the current of an inhuman duration, in which neither past nor future exists, but only the obscure flux of its presence. The human being has the choice between two different durations: one is that of destiny, formed of the immense and anonymous motion that "carries man along like the sea"; the other is that of man, "great because he outstrips destiny or because he resists it." [71]

If Vigny chooses human duration, it is because the latter *outstrips* or *resists;* it is because, in the present, it resides by turn in the future and the past.

The Vignian consciousness, anchored as it is to the three points of duration, thus is no longer revealed as simply an agent of knowledge but as a factor of action. If it rejects the "optimism over the future" of religious faith, it is because that optimism, based on an ignorance of the future, reduces everything, in the last analysis, to the play of a fatality or of a Providence that exerts itself in a brute present in which the mind is rendered useless. Exactly the opposite is the faith of Vigny, the faith of the pessimist, of the hopeless one. Recalling the mind to what it knows, without hope but not without will, purely human faith rests upon a consciousness of the continuity which the mind can impress upon its thought when it wishes to. To have faith, in Vigny's sense of the word, is not only to aspire limitlessly to future glory; it is not to "allow his imagination to wander over the fields of theology and superstitition"; it is to "struggle in time present without wishing to prejudge of eternity."

In other words, Vigny's faith is faith in the possibility of constructing his existence, his thought, and his work on the plan of time and life: foresight is more than knowledge; it is an act.

No doubt,

> Man will always be an uncertain swimmer
> In the waves of measurable flowing time,[72]

always uncertain, but capable of willing: "The will is the faith of the human being. Know how to will to create your ideas and you will create them";[73] to will in the present, that is to say, to act: "Act in the present with vigor without dreaming too much of the future . . . ." [74] Act without dreaming too much of the future, but act in order to create the future—or, like the captain of a foundering ship throwing a bottle into the sea—to preserve the past for the future.

With Vigny, the dialectic of the knowledge of time and the experience of the triple duration lived and thought end in a moral and voluntary construction of life, in action:

> Perform energetically thy long and heavy task . . .

VII

Long and heavy task, accomplished in time by time. The whole work of Vigny will simply be an immense labor by which thought is preserved, purified, and crystallized. An infinitely slow effort, interrupted by rests, by silences, made of renewals and returns, which has significance only for a mind that can keep faith in duration and gradually enlarge its aspirations, not in dependence upon the chances of moments of genius, but upon the length of an existence devoted to its object.

To appreciate such a work it is not enough to examine the outcome of it. One must reinvest in their duration the forces that have presided over its elaboration and reinstall them not in a unilinear duration—which would suggest to us the false notion of a continuous and regular progression in a single sense—but in the tridimensional duration in which the Vignian consciousness endlessly makes succeed each other the regressive and progressive waves within the actuality of its thought.

From the moment the work begins to be formed in Vigny, one can glimpse the play of these complex forces. Earlier, with respect to one of his first productions, Vigny described thus his mental attitude toward its creation: "I take a singular pleasure in forgetting what I have done. I shall return to it afterward in order to perfect it, but I like new pastures";[75] and a little later, speaking of a tragedy he planned to write:

> I believe I shall make a passable thing of it with time, but it is still very necessary to perfect the plan, and I am trying now to forget it completely in order to meet it again as the work of a stranger.[76]

Thus, in the maturing of the work, the primary operative force is that of forgetting it: that is to say, the possibility, thanks to forgetting, of establishing a certain temporal distance between the thought and its object. *In the future* the work will be found to be still more beautiful, retrogressively:

> . . . I don't know how it happens that an event so little noticed at first becomes dear to me in proportion as I draw away from it; as if time were a magic crystal that adorned, preserved, and embellished it with its indefinable brightness and with its glowing colors.[77]

We shall examine below this "crystallizing" role of Vigny's duration. Let us note for the moment only this idea of an almost invisible labor by which it seems that time, of itself, modifies the first conception and changes its value: "I do not make a book, it makes itself. It ripens and grows in my head like a fruit." [78]

Thus, by the "forgetting" and the "returning," the work of Vigny is built little by little. Vigny informs us of this in the greatest detail with regard to *Cinq-Mars* and *La colère de Samson:*

> There is no book [says Vigny of *Cinq-Mars*] that I had for a longer time and more seriously contemplated. I did not write it, but I continually composed it and compressed the plan of it in my head. It is very good, as I see it, thus to let a new conception ripen, like a fine fruit that one must not hasten to pick too soon;[79]

and apropos of *La Colère de Samson:*

> For a long time I had the feeling of the conception of that poem in my head, but the design did not satisfy me. Stopping on a journey at Tours, I wrote at an inn, in the month of December, a rough prose draft in which the movement was well cast. I had pencilled it and I had forgotten it in my portfolio. One day in London I looked at it as a painter looks at the sketch of another painter, and, judging it as a work of art, I approved of it and gave myself the authorization to paint the picture. Yesterday, here, I took the canvas and painted it in two days. It is a good way of doing.[80]

These texts show us with great clarity Vigny's process of maturation: the primary invention under the form of design or plan, then a detachment, like a distance voluntarily established by the mind between its thought and the nascent work, then a series of alternate rests and returns, of deliberate meditations and sudden glances thrown anew at the ripening idea; finally the latter seized at the point of perfect maturity, achieved at a stroke, as one picks a piece of fruit:

> Suddenly I conceive a plan, I am a long time perfecting the mould of the statue, I forget it and when I come back to the work after a long respite, I do not let the lava cool for a moment. I write after long intervals, and for several months afterward I occupy myself with my life without either reading or writing.[81]

Slowly matured in this way by its passage through diverse moments, subjected to various operations of the mind, the work will be of a complex nature. First it will be "an anticipatory view of the accomplished form and beauty of a superlatively fine work";[82] that is to say, the idea of the work before the work itself, the prevision of it. But then, "discontented with everything that does not fit into the pure order he has conceived," the thinker separates himself from his work, turns away his eyes, forgets it for a long time so that he may come back to it.[83] It is a forgetting, however, of only that in the work which "does not fit into the pure order," not the part of it which is perceived intact on each return and more distinct proportionately as the eliminations of forgetfulness are operative. Thus, the "pure order" appears in the final analysis as none other than the very continuity of the thinking activity and the permanence of the idea thought in time. To foresee and to review are joined in the spiritual fixity of the pure order conceived by the mind.

To that degree of lucidity, the consciousness thus becomes the "entire possession of thought." [84] But it remains at the same time "an interior exercise of ideas," [85] an exercise which consists precisely in the fortuitous combination of the ideas among themselves or with feelings. But now this play takes place in successive moments, each of which has its own nuance. It is thus, for example, as Vigny remarks in a completely Proustian phrase, that "suffering is not *one*. It is composed of a great number of ideas which besiege us and which are brought to bear upon us by feeling or by memory." [86]

Suffering that lasts is made up of a thousand distinct sufferings, each one of which in its own right donates its own unique and changing character to thought. And this goes for all human feelings. But if by the operations of forgetfulness only the permanence of the pure order of the work subsists, is that to say that these momentary nuances (truer, nevertheless, than the continuous tonality which finally one sees in them) will be abolished forever? This is what Vigny cannot resign himself to. For him it is necessary that in some way what is most fugitive and unique in each successive moment of the felt and thought duration be saved, in the work and by the work, from total oblivion. It is necessary to make the very substance and reflection of the long cortege of distinct experiences, which precisely constitute maturation, pass into it—in such a way that each episode or stage of maturation brings to the work in its turn and forever, its particular hue:

> Each wave of the sea adds a whitish veil to the beauties of a pearl, each billow works slowly to make it more perfect, each flake of foam that wavers over it bequeaths it a mysterious tint, half-golden, half-transparent, in which one cannot but divine an interior ray diffused by its heart.[87]

Mysterious hue bestowed by each flake of foam, by each present moment, and caught, eternally to dwell there, in the luster of the pearl! With Vigny the maturation of the idea does not imply only the conservation of the idea; it does not tend solely to make of it something hard and luminous like a diamond, which owes its permanence only to the purity of its intellectual substance; but also, and on the contrary, it makes of it the infinitely delicate depository of particular emotions, experienced at such and such a point in duration—emotions which, being of an essentially ephemeral nature, nevertheless give to the luster of the permanent thought the whole gamut of affective colors and thus heighten its spiritual beauty with an undefinable grace, in which the transitory and the eternal are found to be enfolded.

VIII

But how is this alloy to be obtained? If, for Vigny, pure thought tends of itself toward permanence, emotion lives only in the instant. The life of the heart is *actual;* only the life of the mind is truly *temporal,* in the same way as a song that is continued in the attentive silence of consciousness, at the listening post:

> Silence is the true poetry for me.[88]

Emotions exist only at the very instant they are produced. They are like skyrockets which, their moment of splendor over, are extinguished in the night; or like those soap bubbles to which Vigny compares minds that live only in the present moment, "carried about by the wind and colored by the objects they encounter."

Thus for Vigny there is no memory of the heart. Nor is there any affective foresight. This is what explains the apparent contradiction between despair and the Vignian prevision. They do not bear upon things of the same nature. Knowledge of the future is for Vigny only confidence in the permanence of thought alone. What he claims to foresee is the future of the idea, not at all the affective contingency which will be able to envelop it. The despair that comes from the certitude of never knowing of the final destinies of man is paired with that of not knowing what sorrowful or charming emotions tomorrow's fate has in reserve; it has only the compensation of receiving with surprise or recognition the always unexpected moments of happiness:

If happiness were only for an hour? If it were given us only by instants? [89]

Hope is the greatest of our follies. With that well understood, anything that happens will surprise us.[90]

Consequently I accept with gratitude all the days of pleasure, all the days even that do not bring me unhappiness or grief.[91]

And so, therefore, without foresight or memory, the happy moment seems reduced to its brief explosion in the immediate. But for Vigny, as for Maine de Biran before him and for Henri Delacroix today, both ordinary memory and the exercise of thought are capable of reproducing in us states of mind which although not those we have experienced are nonetheless similar to them:

The heart exists truly, in the moral sense. One feels its motions of joy and sorrow; but it is a dark chamber whose light is the head. Memory and thought illuminate it and make feelings apparent there. Without the head they are extinguished.[92]

Memory and thought procure for us, then, the new skyrockets whose bursts reproduce the fires of those that had been irrevocably consumed.

As a consequence of this, one perceives all the affective value of the symbol of the pearl in Vigny. It represents not only the act by which thought preserves its integrity but also that act by which it provokes, at no matter what moment of our thought, the simultaneous apparition in the consciousness of all the past states of mind, each of which in its turn is found along the road of that thought. The most different emotive aspects which, one after another, an idea long cherished had been able to assume seem disposed in its substance, as if in layers, and are visible as if transparent. The idea becomes in some way prismatic, charged with all sorts of instantaneous colorations and yet of different periods which summon to the present life the emotions of the past and which, without impairing or veiling the intellectual purity of the idea, maintain it in the concrete and human, bathe it even in an essence of general affectivity that is slowly distilled.

Moreover, this general affectivity does not subsist in the idea in the same fashion as the idea itself. The permanence of the idea is

in its nature, or more exactly, it is of the nature of the consciousness, which, by its unceasing activity, holds it unfailingly under its
regard. Affectivity—even when general—can survive only by coming back after having been forgotten. However, at a certain degree
of maturation this return happens of itself; but, for that, it is necessary for the idea to have become pearl, diamond, or crystal, to have
taken, because of the coloration it has received, a *form:* a form
which can only be symbolic. When this point is attained, the continuous duration of the pure idea and that—discontinuous, intermittent, incessantly actual—of the emotion are blended together in
the quasi-eternity of the idea-symbol and attain a communal permanence, in which the ephemeral and the durable are found magically united.

Thus,

> . . . not one of the treasures of Isis and Osiris, no azure-colored
> sphinx was lost, not a letter of papyrus was effaced, thanks to that
> enormous crystal that covers the mummy in its whole extent. This
> crystal is transparent, and through the reddish, silvery, violet-colored
> glimmerings that the torches and stars cast upon it, and which give
> it the aspect of a marvelous lake or of an unknown sky discovered
> in the shadows, one never ceases to perceive the immobile visage of
> the mummy.[93]

Thus, again, "the profound thoughts" reassemble their fires "in thy
pure diamond"; thus, "on each of the roads of his life the thinker
gathers up the treasures of his experience" [94] and "amasses the
colors which must *form* the pearl";[95] thus all the pictures remain "as
alive and as colored";[96] thus, in the diamond-set symbol of the poet
are distinguished

> . . . the two equal gleams
> Of thoughts the most fair, of love the most pure;

thus, finally poetry becomes

> . . . a voluptuousness enveloping thought and rendering it luminous
> by the refulgence of its protecting crystal.[97]

At this height, all of human life is confounded with the work of
which it is the substance; and the work itself tends to be no more
than an interpretation, at once most lucid and most moving, of the
life of the consciousness; of a transparency so *crystalline* and of a
coloration so *prismatic* that, in the same reflection, there can be

distinguished all the unique moments which existence brings and all that it is in its totality. One sees there

All the human pictures that a pure mind brings me . . .

but also, forever:

What one shall never see twice.

NOTES

1 *Théâtre* (*Oeuvres*, ed. Conard), II, 234.
2 *Correspondance*, I, 13.
3 *Stello*, p. 264.
4 *Maison du berger.*
5 *Journal*, p. 241.
6 *Théâtre*, II, 235.
7 *Stello*, p. 96.
8 *Journal*, p. 86.
9 *Ibid.*
10 *Journal*, quoted by Bonnefoy, *La Pensée religieuse et morale de Vigny*, p. 381.
11 *Stello*, p. 23.
12 *Journal*, p. 8.
13 *Correspondance*, I, 13.
14 *Journal*, p. 49.
15 *Poèmes*, p. 324.
16 *Ibid.*, p. 396.
17 *Journal*, p. 57.
18 *Ibid.*, p. 72.
19 *Théâtre*, I, xl.
20 *Stello*, p. 96.
21 *Journal*, p. 571.
22 *Ibid.*, p. 430.
23 *Ibid.*, p. 419.
24 *Ibid.*, quoted by La Salle, *Vigny*, p. 380.
25 *Ibid.*, p. 49.
26 *Ibid.*, p. 24.
27 *Ibid.*
28 *Ibid.*, p. 11.
29 *Ibid.*, p. 616.
30 *Poèmes*, p. 329.
31 *Servitude*, p. 9.
32 *Poèmes*, p. 324.
33 *Servitude*, p. 10.
34 *Ibid.*
35 *Poèmes*, p. 386.

36 *Journal*, ed. Ratisbonne, p. 226.
37 *Servitude*, p. 11.
38 *Poèmes*, p. 324.
39 *Journal*, quoted by Bonnefoy, *La Pensée religieuse et morale de Vigny*, p. 381.
40 *Correspondance*, I, 286.
41 *Journal*, p. 313.
42 *Théâtre*, 2, 331.
43 *Stello*, p. 23.
44 *Ibid.*, p. 266.
45 *Daphné*, p. 277.
46 *Journal*, ed. Ratisbonne, p. 226.
47 *Lettre à Mme Lachaud*, 1862.
48 *Servitude*, p. 20.
49 *Journal*, ed. Conard, p. 79.
50 *Stello*, p. 159.
51 *A Alexandrine du Plessis*, July 29, 1848.
52 *Servitude*, p. 20.
53 *Journal*, ed. Ratisbonne, p. 216.
54 *A Mme Lachaud*, 1848.
55 *Journal*, ed. Conard, p. 195.
56 *Cinq-Mars*, p. v.
57 *Stello*, p. 24.
58 *Journal*, pp. 33–34.
59 *Ibid.*, p. 312.
60 *Ibid.*, p. 376.
61 *Ibid.*, pp. 358–59.
62 *Ibid.*, p. 76.
63 *Journal*, ed. Ratisbonne, p. 164.
64 *Théâtre*, I, xl.
65 *Journal*, p. 164.

66 *Ibid.*, ed. Conard, p. 171.
67 *Ibid.*, p. 291.
68 *Ibid.*, p. 315.
69 *Ibid.*, p. 215.
70 *Ibid.*, p. 238.
71 *Ibid.*, p. 54.
72 *Destinées.*
73 *Journal*, p. 263.
74 *Ibid.*, p. 286.
75 *Correspondance*, I, 13.
76 *Ibid.*, I, 18.
77 *Servitude*, p. 262.
78 *Journal*, p. 377.
79 *Journal*, ed. Ratisbonne, p. 231.
80 *Journal*, ed. Conard, p. 522.
81 *Ibid.*, p. 343.
82 *Journal*, quoted by Bonnefoy, *La Pensée religieuse et morale de Vigny*, p. 399.
83 *Discours de réception.*
84 *Journal*, quoted by Bonnefoy, *loc. cit.*
85 *Ibid.*
86 *Ibid.*, p. 469.
87 *Servitude*, p. 231.
88 *Journal*, p. 162.
89 *Ibid.*, p. 296.
90 *Ibid.*, p. 171.
91 *Ibid.*, p. 181.
92 *Ibid.*, p. 540.
93 *Daphné*, p. 349.
94 *Discours de réception.*
95 *Maison du berger.*
96 *Journal*, p. 216.
97 Quoted by La Salle, *Vigny*, p. 311.

*

*

* FLAUBERT

I

* Sometimes (during my grand days in the sun) when I was lit
up by an illumination that made my skin tingle from my toes
to the roots of my hair, I had an inkling of a state of mind so superior to life that compared to it glory would be nothing, and happiness vain.[1]

Those grand days in the sun, those "happy days when the mind is as
open to the sun as the countryside," [2] form in the life of Flaubert a
series of radiant peaks about which works, thought, existence, all
cluster. He is, primordially, a romantic: a romantic not so much
for his love of the picturesque, as for the consciousness of an exceptional interior experience. But unlike that of the Romantics, the
consciousness of this interior experience does not turn Flaubert in
upon himself; it opens his mind to the sun; it turns him outward.
Like Diderot, like Gautier, from the moment he makes use of his
faculties for literary ends, those faculties which he exercises the
most and which dominate all the others are precisely those which
direct the mind not toward a knowledge of the self but toward a
grasp of the non-self and a representation of the world:

I have an extraordinary faculty of *perception* . . . .[3]

I have almost voluptuous sensations simply from seeing things,
so long as I see them well.[4]

Only rapports are true, that is to say, the manner in which we
perceive objects.[5]

The starting point with Flaubert is thus not Flaubert himself; it is
the rapport between the perceiving self and the object perceived:

Often, a propos of no matter what, a drop of water, a shell, a
hair, you stopped and stayed motionless, eyes fixed, heart open.
The object you contemplated seemed to encroach upon you, by

as much as you inclined yourself toward it, and bonds were established . . . .[6]

Sometimes by dint of gazing at a pebble, an animal, a picture, I
felt myself enter into them. Communications between human beings
are not more intense.[7]

Certainly these are capital passages; they reveal to us the fundamental orientation of Flaubert's mind. Self-awareness is fully experienced by him in the moment when he emerges from himself
to become identified—by the simplest but most intense of the acts
of the mental life, perception—with the object, whatever it may be,
of this perception. Thus objectivity, far from being an acquired discipline with Flaubert, is a natural state, the only truly natural state
of his thought. If it is realized fully only in exceptional instances,
that is because ". . . man is so made that each day he can savor
only a little of nourishment, colors, sounds, feelings, ideas";[8] but
this nourishment, made up in the first place of colors and sounds
and secondarily of feelings and ideas, is the sole possible food. It is
to it that one must turn for support and subsistence. Life exists,
but only where there are colors, sounds, the outdoors, the sun. One
must incline toward it, penetrate into it or be penetrated by it, and
become what one feels by the very act of feeling.

An act of identification by which there are abolished not only the
interval between subject and object, but their existence as distinct
beings:

Then, by dint of looking, you no longer saw; listening, you heard
nothing, and your mind itself ended by losing the notion of that
particularity which kept it on the alert.[9]

The particularity of the object exists only for him who maintains
in his consciousness a gap between the thing perceived and the perceiving mind; it no longer exists for him who, effacing within him
any idea of a representing self and a thing represented, limits his
present consciousness to the representation itself. In his moments
of "contemplative effusion," [10] in his "grand days in the sun," Flaubert arrived at an integral phenomenalism. The mind being what it
represents, and the object existing only in its representation in the
mind, what remains is simply a unique being that can be called indifferently mind or nature:

The interval between yourself and the object, like an abyss whose two sides come closer and closer together, was getting increasingly narrower, so much so that this difference disappeared. . . . One degree more and you became nature, or nature became you.[11]

This "one degree more" by which one becomes nature is reached elsewhere:

By dint of being penetrated by it, of entering into it, we also *became nature*, feeling that it was overpowering us, and taking a measureless joy in that process.[12]

It is a joy that becomes measureless from the moment one is identified with the whole extent of nature and of the activity which animates it:

Everything in you palpitates with joy and beats its wings with the elements, you are bound to them, breathe with them, the essence of animate nature seems to have passed into you . . . .[13]

At this degree of pantheistic ecstasy, the conception of a mere spatial and logical order proves to be transcended. It would be inexact, therefore, to see in Flaubert only a poetic transcription of Spinozism. What man attains in the Flaubertian experience is less the sense of an *ordo et connexio idearum* than the intuition of life in its cosmic expansion. Life is diffusion, a tireless projection of forms in a space that is the divine immensity:

There is no nothingness! There is no emptiness! Everywhere there are bodies that move in the immutable depths of Vastness.[14]

To be identified with cosmic life is to be diffused over a divine vastness which can be considered indifferently as holding the variety of things and that of the representations which one makes of them. Thought and the world are an identical extent: "I was, in the variety of my being, like an immense forest of India, where life palpitates in each atom . . . ."[15]

But precisely because it is sheer variety, life cannot be apprehended except through the motion by which it varies. It is not enough to reach some point from which the sentient mind can spread its thoughts over the whole representative field. It is also necessary that, from this point, and without leaving this point— which is the durationless point of the present—the mind should "live within all that life in order to array all its forms, *to endure to-*

gether with them, and forever varying, to extend forth its metamorphoses under the sun of eternity." [16] Since life is duration, the moment that absolutely expresses it must be a moment in which the very working of duration is visible. Sometimes this presence of duration in the moment is found by Flaubert in a direct intuition of the genesis of things: "O happy am I! I have seen life born, I have seen motion begin";[17] but more often it seems occasioned in his work by a sensory event. There are the moments when sensation is so perfectly yoked with the general life of things that one becomes, so to speak, the metaphorical expression of the other. Then to feel oneself live is to feel oneself live life, to feel the pulse of duration beat. For instance, we have the scene of carnal love in *Madame Bovary:*

> The silence was everywhere; a sweetness seemed to emanate from the trees; she felt her heart begin beating again, and the blood circulate in her body like a stream of milk. Then she heard afar off, beyond the woods, over the hills, a faint and prolonged cry, a protracted voice, and she listened silently to its mingling, like a strain of music, with the last vibrations of her stirred nerves.

In this passage Flaubert succeeds in giving the moment a spatial and temporal density so particular that one could say (and it is undoubtedly the effect Flaubert wished to produce) that this moment belongs to a different duration from that of ordinary days, a duration whose *tempo* of things is made sweeter, slower, and therefore more perceptible; a duration that spreads out. It is as if time, like a passing breeze, could be felt in the renewed beatings of the heart, in the blood that flows like a stream of milk. It is no longer the bitter consciousness of an interval, there is no more interval; there is only a gliding motion which carries away simultaneously the things and the sentient mind with the sense of an absolute homogeneity between the different elements that compose the moment. The mind, the body, nature, and life, all participate in the same moment of the same becoming.

II

The state of mind glimpsed by Flaubert in his grand days in the sun is thus not different from that experienced by all the great pantheist mystics: a moment of ecstasy when, in the union of the sentient mind and pure sensation, the self is identified with the universe and has for a moment the experience of eternity.

But with Flaubert, even in his grand days in the sun, that state is only *glimpsed*. Thought can neither be established nor isolated within it. The point at which it happens is not a state but a boundary point; a point that is the extremity of a temporal line, a boundary that is that of a movement of thought. Without an antecedent line and movement, it is as inconceivable as a beach without a tide to flow toward it and mark its delimitation.

It is the same with Flaubert when the substance of the lived present is this time constituted not by sense experiences but by memories. There are, for Flaubert, other grand days in the sun when the mind is not open to the present sun, but to the "golden haze" still emanating from suns which have set long ago. There is for him a present that is the terminal place of recollected images as well as a present that is the terminal place of sensorial images.

For the predilection that Flaubert always had for memory, even at the expense of actual sensation, is not due to a particular preference of his for what belongs to the past as such. What does he look for in sensation except a total intimacy with the object of sensation? Now this feeling of total intimacy is rare by reason of the inflexibility of a self that "will not let itself go," the mind naturally here and the object there. But when the sensation is reborn under the form of memory, it reappears not as a thing outside but as something inside. It is regained within. All distance is now abolished, as in the rarest and most perfect sensuous union. The reviviscence is, like pantheistic ecstasy, a pure viviscence. It has the same intensity, the same richness, it ends in the same synthesis of the object and the self.

And to begin with, it has the same starting point. Just as with Flaubert, sensory activity takes its origin from an object encountered ("Often, a propos of no matter what, a drop of water, a sea-shell . . ."), so it is also through the fortuitous encounter with an object that the retrospective imagination takes birth: "anything, the slightest circumstance, a rainy day, a hot sun, a flower, an old piece of furniture, recalls to me a series of memories . . . ." [18] Sometimes it happens at the sight of a garment worn in days gone by, of an engraving hand-colored a long time ago, at the smell of an odor long ago familiar; it reoccurs oftenest upon revisits to past places.

The object, whatever it may be, lets loose a series of memories. A *series:* the most striking characteristic indeed of the phenomenon of memory in Flaubert is seriality. One memory calls up another, then still another, and so on; and each rises into view under the form of an image which is covered and replaced by the following slide, as in the projections of a magic lantern:

> . . . He saw again, like ghosts conjured up, the different days of his past, some gay, others sad; *and first* those when he played, a child laughing at life, without dream or desire; *and the one* on which he entered high school, *and that other* on which he left, *the one* when he arrived at M. Renaud's, *the one* on which she came into his room . . . .[19]

These images are all distinct. Each of them presents a definite picture but brings also with it other images, trains of feelings, the very emotions of the past surging up from the depths. Now all this awakening of the affective memory takes place, as it were, in the environs and in the gaps in the series of perceptible images; it connects them, suffuses them, and ends by mingling them: "My travels, my memories of childhood, all are colored by one another, fall into line, dance with wonderful gleamings and mount in a spiral." [20] A spiral, enveloping a thousand diverse images and traversing different zones of the past—such is the recreative synthesis which crowns the operation of memory in Flaubert. It does not consist in drawing upon a repository, in combining elements of different periods, but rather in allowing layers of images to rise in tiers in the mind, each of which keeps the particular form it occupied in time, but, on the other hand, takes color from the reflection of the others. Thus, the consciousness that evokes them appears to itself like a painting in perspective, in the depths of which there appear at unequal intervals with their particular hues—but in a unique ambience (which is the true self)—the phantoms of the past:

> I passed along the Rue des Orties which opens on the court of the college. . . . I saw the chestnut trees under which we played. . . . I saw myself there once more, on the first day, entering, unknown, amongst all of you, and you who first came and spoke to me; *and then all the rest slowly unrolled in my memory,* the cries when we were at play, and the racket of our balls against the wire lattices of the windows, and the hot, humid and stifling air of the classrooms . . . .[21]

In the same manner, Emma, noticing on a letter from her father a little of the ashes with which he had the habit of drying wet ink, sees her father once more, "bending over the hearth to pick up the tongs"; then, this first image leading to others, she recalls "summer afternoons full of sunlight"; and step by step, from memory to memory, she follows the course of her life down to the present moment:

> What happiness then . . . what abundance of illusions . . . Nothing remained of them now. She had used them up in the surprising experiences of her mind, through all its successive conditions . . . losing them continually in this way *her whole life long,* like a traveler who leaves something of his wealth at every inn along the way . . . .[22]

One feels that the whole force of this passage (leaving aside the feeling of the attrition of experience, of which more later) relates to the *depth of duration* which it suggests—a depth that is glimpsed through a descending perspective, in which the images are spaced out like milestones, along *the whole length of life.* The first memory is like the top of a slope; from that point there is nothing to do but descend again; and to redescend the slope is to retraverse the whole life, to render visible the very pathway of lived time: "Then, swept along on her memories as if upon a foaming torrent, she soon came to recall yesterday . . . ." [23]

More rarely (for Flaubert's prospective imagination is poor), the same phenomenon is discovered with regard to time to come:

> And immediately pictures unrolled endlessly. He saw himself with her, at night in a post-chaise, then on the bank of a stream on a summer evening, and then under the reflection of a lamp at home together.[24]

But the moment when the "contemplative effusion" is most completely realized is the one when the *pictures without end* instead of seeming to approach or withdraw from the present appear to unroll within its span: "Then all of his past life appeared to Smarh, swiftly, in one stroke, like a flash of lightning." [25]

It is as if suddenly the whole field of existence, without losing anything of its intrinsic multiplicity, were contemplated by the interior gaze in the interior of the moment. For example, when Félicité sees the lights of Honfleur:

A feeling of faintness seized her; and the misery of her childhood, the deception of first love, the departure of her nephew, the death of Virginie, like the waves of a rising tide, returned all at once, and rising in her throat, suffocated her.[26]

In this simultaneity on which all existence is brought to bear, the retrospective movement attains its perfection and its terminal point: a revelation of a temporal expanse filled up by the mind just as in the sensuous ecstasy the mind fills up exterior space.

III

What is there beyond this *eternal moment?* All the internal activity is engaged. The mind perceives with an hallucinatory clearness a series of images whose motion is accelerated. They multiply, they surround it, they besiege it. Exaltation is followed by disquietude, then by anguish. The images that the mind watched appearing within itself it now sees disappearing outside itself. It is like "a kind of hemorrhage of innervation," [27] as if existence drained away through a bleeding wound:

My thoughts, which I would like to clasp together . . . slide away one after another and *escape me,* like a sheaf of arrows from the hand of a child who cannot hang on to them, they fall to the ground hurting his knees . . . .[28]

The same thing goes for the moment of union with the past as for the moment of union with the present and with nature. In each case, without any transition, fissure succeeds fusion. The abolished distance is suddenly rediscovered, gaping in the mind:

One says to oneself: "Ten years ago I was there," and one is there and one thinks the same things and the whole interval is forgotten. *Then it appears to you, that interval,* like an immense precipice in which nothingness whirls round.[29]

It is exactly the inverse motion of that by which the subject had been absorbed in the object of its sensation or of its memory. Then it was a question of an "interval like an abyss whose sides come closer and closer together . . . so much so that the difference disappeared." Now it is a question of the same interval reappearing and affirming the same difference.

A difference which reveals a double change in the nature of

space and time. Space is no longer the field of expansion, from the center of which the mind diffuses itself and radiates outward; time is no longer that extent of the past which the mind—starting out from some given memory—fills and overflows with the flux of its reminiscences; on the contrary, extension has become an empty void separating the self from the object, and time another kind of empty extension which no less irremediably separates the present self from its past:

> How far away all that is! Did I not live then? Was that indeed I? Is it myself now? Every minute of my life seems cut off at a stroke from every other by an abyss; between yesterday and today there is an eternity that appals me.[30]

This eternity is properly called an abyss; it is abysmal because it is the negation of the eternity of plenitude to which it succeeds. It is the infinite absence of things of which one experienced the presence, a sort of atrociously neuter time, since nothing fills or traverses it, whose extent, indifferently comparable to both eternity and a minute, expresses simply an absolute gap. Sometimes this gap is depicted under the aspect of a general petrification of things: "It seems, at certain moments, that the universe is immobilized, that everything has become a statue and that we alone are alive." [31] At other times it takes the form of a perpetual repetition of the same action: "From then on he continually climbed that stairway . . . . He continued to ascend with the strange facility one experiences in dreams." [32] But repetition and immobilization are the unconscious metaphors by which the human mind both expresses and conceals the nakedness of a void, the horror of which he is the only one to perceive. There is no possibility here of that intermediary time which we place mechanically between ourselves and a period of the past which we recall: a consciousness of a duration that is more or less continuous, which joins this moment and that one together. The abysmal time is the time that creates and asserts the abyss, which sees to it that moments do not rejoin each other. The human being is no longer supported from behind by his past. He leans back against nothingness:

> Despite the hubbub in his head, he perceives an enormous silence that separates him from the world. He tries to speak; impossible! It is as if the general bond of his existence were dissolved . . . .[33]

Something undefined separates you from your own person and rivets you to nonbeing.[34]

In a flash our past self is carried to the other side of an abyss, to a side that is directly opposite to us. We see it from afar, and it appears to us as a stranger:

Startled by the fidelity of his memories, rendered still vivid by the presence of those places where they occurred in the form of events and feelings, he asked himself if all of them belonged to the same man, if a single life could have sufficed for them, and he tried to connect them with some other lost existence, so far away was his past from him![35]

Existence is divided in two. Actual life now seems only a feeble reflection of another life already lived, one which must have been the only true life: "There are days when one has lived two existences, the second is already a mere memory of the first . . . ."[36]

Then one turns toward that past with an ambiguous nostalgia. One half-fancies having already lived in some far-off epoch of history. One experiences what Flaubert calls "the thrill of history." [37] It is an inordinate sadness over the idea that those ages have passed with no possibility of returning. "What would I not give to see a triumph, what would I not sell to enter Suburre one evening at the time when the torches were burning at the doors of the brothels . . . ?" [38] One sets oneself to the endless pursuit of retrospective myths; one ruminates upon past existences lived or dreamed. But the more one's thought is absorbed in them, the more the present appears as an illusion. The past "devours it" and "devours us": "I roam in memories and am lost in them." [39]

It is then that the actual moment reveals all its narrowness and dearth: "I do not experience, as you do, that feeling of a life that is beginning, the wonder of a newly-hatched existence." [40] "The world is not big enough for the mind: it suffocates in the present hour." [41]

To the "interminable series of the passions that have faded away," [42] to the lassitude and to the distaste for the ephemeral, it is vain to try to oppose an activity directed toward the future. The imagination, so intense under its retrospective form, sees nothing ahead of it. Since it is entirely representative and cannot picture perceptible objects in the future, it sees nothing at all there:

And from the past, I go dreaming of the future, and there I see nothing, absolutely nothing. I am without plan, without idea, without project, and what is worse, without ambition.[43]

Deprived of a future, devoured by the past, crushed by the weight of the present, the mind cannot any more experience time except as a motion that slows down, as a *tempo* that is slackening. One feels oneself old from having lived through so many of the "minutes that are as years." [44] The sense of existence becomes that of a continuous addition to this length of duration. Life is reduced to being a repetition: "Must you not awake every morning, eat, drink, go, come, repeat that series of acts which are always the same?" [45]

At this point one would say that the course of duration stops. It is no longer a stream, but still water, "a sleeping fen, so quiet that the slightest event that falls into it makes innumerable circles . . . ." [46] An agitation on the surface, and a general feeling of illusion and of wearing away: with Flaubert it is in these things that the feeling of human time is in grave danger of getting lost.

IV

There is in the *Première Éducation sentimentale* a passage that is particularly important because it seems to give us the profound reason for the difference, so visible in Flaubert, between the works of his youth and those of his maturity. This passage begins with a long, morose meditation that one of the characters pursues on the formlessness and dejection of his existence. Then gradually, the thought is transformed into images, and once again the past is put to unrolling a series of memory-pictures. But this time the dominating factor in this succession of images is neither the kind of spontaneous homogeneity which is given to the most disparate things by the current of emotions that carries them along nor, on the reverse side, the feeling of radical heterogeneity which reveals itself in them and between them when the current fails to link them together. This time, on the contrary, it is possible to find there a certain coherence. For the first time one can distinguish not only sensory and imaginative events but also events penetrable by the mind:

Nevertheless from all that there resulted his present state, and this state was the sum of all those antecedents, one which permitted him to review them; each event had of itself produced a second, every feeling had been fused into an idea. . . . Thus there was a sequence and a continuity to this series of diverse perceptions.[47]

It would be hard to imagine a reflection more ordinary or more commonplace. Nevertheless, it is around this reflection that Flaubert tried to reform a life and a work abandoned of themselves to the power of images. The solution he accepts is the middle solution, it is an option in favor of order—an order, moreover, which is perceived and which perhaps exists only when it is discovered as the order of accomplished facts. For it is discovered only in things that are completed and in the postulate that they are completed by reason of other things which have determined their completion: "The thought that comes to you now has been brought to you . . . by successions, gradations, transformations and rebirths." [48] Thus, the order does not depend on the assumption of any transcendence. It is an adequate relationship between what exists in this moment and what existed in all preceding moments. It is an *a posteriori* construction that the mind imposes upon the universe to make it hold together. Thanks to this formula, there are no more *gaps,* no more intervals between things, nor an abyss between the present and the past. We are in the kingdom of immanence, and of so integral an immanence that everything is representable and implied there. Beyond the chain of causes and effects as they are represented in the mind, there is the supposition that the same chain and the same interactivity of causes and effects persist indefinitely; there is nothing else; no mystery; nothing veiled or inexpressible. What the imagination cannot revive the mind can represent to itself.

Representative thought, therefore, chooses a particular moment of life. It perceives this moment and all the sense-data it contains as a relationship between the human being and its immediate environment. Then it proceeds to discern how those sensations are modified by the action of other images coming from the past. From this stage backward, reconstructive thought will begin an ascending movement. It will see how in their turn those images of the past were linked to objects of the past. Behind the environment in which the present self lives, it will discover the milieu in which it has lived and felt; and behind this double past, which is that of being and milieu, it will discover another, and then still another, always making sure of its discoveries and in this way creating a proportionate density of duration in which there is neither hiatus or rupture; a movement which, by its direction as well as by its very nature, is the exact reverse of the "flight of memories," that is to say, the sudden jump by which the mind discovered itself, in the works of Flaubert's youth, thrown away, so to speak, into any moment of the past.

For it is no longer now a question of a sudden plunge into the depths of a former time, from whence one is allowed to descend haphazardly the course of existence. The design of Flaubert is no longer a lyrical but a methodical design. He sketched it in a passage in the *Première Tentation;* there he makes Science speak in the following terms:

> If I could penetrate matter, grasp idea, follow life through its metamorphoses, understand being in its modes, and thus from one to the other, reascending the ladder of causes like a series of steps, reunite in myself those scattered phenomena and put them back into motion in the synthesis from which my scalpel detached them.[49]

Thus, the first movement of the Flaubertian reconstruction is the ascending movement by which thought climbs, in a series of inferences, the stairway of causes, and so progressively withdraws from the domain of sensation or of actual images, in order to pass into that of the order of things, into the domain of law. It is a method strictly opposed to that of Balzac, who, starting with an *a priori* creature, posits at the outset the existence of a law-force, of which there remains simply to express next, in terms more and more concrete, the descending curve into real life. Balzac, novelist of the *determining;* Flaubert, novelist of the *determined.*

But precisely by reason of the fact that in Flaubert that which is first given is this *determined* actual, indubitable, and resisting object upon which the representative faculty can rest all its weight, the Flaubertian construction, as high as it may rise, never risks becoming abstract. The law is not a non-temporal thing. It does not exist in itself but in the action by which it is exercised. In proportion as one ascends to it, one gathers up, at each step, the perceptible matter with which the human being has remodified itself in each of the antecedent moments of its duration. Thus the human being is some-how found to exist in two ways: by its sensations, whether immedi-ate or remembered, which form its variable, contingent reality, though in intimate contact with the reality of things; and on the other hand, by the synthetic order that the concatenating series of causes imposes upon its existence.

A double synthesis, or rather a recapture, in the framework of an objective synthesis, of what had always—but in a subjective, frag-mentary, and fugitive fashion—been synthetically expressed in the works of Flaubert's youth.

This is what he himself seems to indicate in a note written in 1859:

> The artist not only carries humanity within him, but he repro-duces its history in the creation of his work: first confusion, a gen-eral view, aspirations, bedazzlement, everything is mixed up [the barbarous epoch]; then analysis, doubt, method, the disposition of parts [the scientific era]; finally, he comes back to the first synthesis, made wider in the execution.

Having arrived at this peak of synthesis, thought turns itself about to begin its downward movement. If it raised itself up into the regions of causes and antecedents, that was in order to prepare itself to understand and show how, starting out from this region and from the past, the actual is organized. So then the descending move-ment of Flaubert's thought takes on the aspect of a prospective rep-resentation of life which, through a series of states, is brought out of the past up to the present and ends there by giving it the significance of being an effect that is the consequence of all the vast perceptible genetic travail in space and duration—a perspective similar to that which one has when, on the shore, one lifts his eyes slowly to the open sea in order to follow from out there the course of a wave that draws nearer and nearer, and finally perishes at one's feet—an experience that one also has when in writing, say, a periodic sen-tence (the periodic sentence of Flaubert) one finds that from the protasis to the apodosis the different elements are composed in a rising and falling synthesis which, in coming to its completion, af-fords the discovery in the written sentence of an indissoluble unity in which everything becomes present. From that point on, the prob-lem of time is simply a problem of style.

NOTES

[1] *Correspondance (Ouevres,* ed. Conard), II, 395.
[2] *Voyage en Pyrénées et en Corse,* p. 425.
[3] *Correspondance,* III, 270.
[4] *Ibid.,* I, 178.
[5] *Ibid.,* VIII, 135.
[6] *Tentation* of 1849, p. 417.
[7] *Correspondance,* III, 210.
[8] *Par les champs et par les grèves,* p. 131.
[9] *Tentation* of 1849, p. 417.
[10] *Par les champs et par les grèves,* p. 131.
[11] *Tentation* of 1849, p. 417.
[12] *Par les champs et par les grèves,* p. 130.
[13] *Voyage en Pyrénées et en Corse,* p. 425.
[14] *Tentation* of 1874, p. 173.

[15] *Novembre,* p. 180.
[16] *Par les champs et par les grèves,* p. 131.
[17] *Tentation* of 1874, p. 200.
[18] *Mémoires d'un fou,* p. 500.
[19] *Première education,* p. 84.
[20] *Correspondance,* II, 371.
[21] *Première education,* p. 36.
[22] *Madame Bovary,* p. 239.
[23] *Ibid.,* p. 424.
[24] *L'Education sentimentale,* p. 453.
[25] *Smarh,* p. 106.
[26] *Trois contes,* p. 51.
[27] *Correspondance,* III, 270.
[28] *Tentation* of 1849, p. 236.
[29] *Correspondance,* III, 331.
[30] *Novembre,* p. 178.
[31] *Correspondance,* III, 317.

[32] *Salammbô,* p. 102.
[33] *Tentation* of 1874, p. 15.
[34] *Correspondance,* III, 332.
[35] *Première education,* p. 242.
[36] *Novembre,* p. 192.
[37] *Correspondance,* III, 19.
[38] *Ibid.,* II, 6.
[39] *Ibid.,* VI, 377.
[40] *Ibid.,* V, 240.
[41] *Ibid.,* I, 253.
[42] *Ibid.,* III, 308 .
[43] *Ibid.,* II, 201.
[44] *Ibid.,* I, 368.
[45] *Tentation* of 1849, p. 434.
[46] *Correspondance,* III, 289.
[47] *Première education,* p. 244.
[48] *Tentation* of 1849, p. 418.
[49] Page 349.

＊

＊

＊ BAUDELAIRE

I

＊ At the origin there is original sin. Before memory, before
childhood, before all ecstasy and all disgust, for Baudelaire
there are "two simultaneous postulations, the one toward God, the
other toward Satan." [1] This contradiction is repeated in every
man every hour; it is found in him from the first moment of his existence, and is most clearly indicated in the first period of his life;
for "the child, in general, is compared to the man, in general, very
much closer to original sin." [2]

Thus, from the first moment, there are two opposite tendencies
in the child: one which, carrying him toward the infinite reality of
God, makes him feel at one and the same time the infinite imperfection of sensible and actual reality; the other which, carrying him toward Satan, urges him to adhere to the actual, to lose himself in
things, to elicit from them animal pleasure: "When a child, I felt
in my heart two contradictory feelings: the horror of life and the
ecstasy of life." [3]

If the ecstasy of life is the ecstatic acceptance of the present moment, the horror of life is, on the contrary, the movement by which,
in rejecting the present, the human being from his very origin begets a sort of future time. The creature simultaneously throws himself upon the present and rejects it. The present is a prey on which
he gorges himself and a misery which fills him with horror.

In the child, however, these two opposite tendencies, which later
will tear the adult apart in the suffering of a time that is tragic, are
as yet hardly distinguished, by reason of the strength of his faculties
and the swiftness of his reactions. In the instant in which things reveal their insufficiency, the child (like the savage) finds within
himself the necessary resources to make up for it:

The savage and the baby bear witness, by their naïve aspiration
for the bright and glittering, for many-colored feathers and glistening

cloths, for the superlative majesty of artificial forms, bear witness to their disgust for the real, and in this way prove unknowingly the immateriality of their mind.[4]

Here is a distaste for the real, which, however, is immediately transformed into a possessive motion. Hardly, in his distaste, has the child had the time to aspire toward color than he becomes drunk with it, absorbs it into his imagination, and forms of it a more sparkling reality, a more iridescent moment:

> The child sees everything *in its newness;* he is always *drunk.* Nothing resembles more what is called inspiration than the joy with which the child absorbs form and color. . . . It is to this profound and joyous curiosity that must be attributed the fixed and animally ecstatic eye of children before the *new,* whatever it be . . . .[5]

Thus the ecstatic drunkenness of the child is that of a void which is filled up, of a poverty made rich and full. He does not have the time to perceive the imperfection or the materiality of the perceptible life, because he redeems it, reinvents and spiritualizes it, in the same instant and by the same movement that he perceives it. Out of a repugnant or horrible world, instantaneously, unknown to himself, in play, he makes a magic world, a plaything. Instinctively, even in and of evil, he finds and remakes a paradisaical state:

> Yet, under the invisible tutelage of an Angel,
> The disinherited Child is made drunk with the sun,
> And in all that he drinks and in all that he eats
> Recovers the ambrosia and the rose-red nectar.[6]

From that moment there is discovered the ambiguity hidden in our incessant nostalgia for childhood. It appears to us in memory as an authentically paradisaical state, a state in which, *naturally,* action was the sister of dream. We dream of it as Adam dreamed of the lost Eden: as a state of perfection which has been ours, and which we would have enjoyed *in time,* on the earth; a continuous state of ecstatic happiness, in which our aspirations have been satisfied and our nature completed, in which duration was constant, in which the same moment was continued, always new, always like unto itself, in the same wonder. The magic memory of childhood masks us and makes us forget original sin. We forget that there never was a time when we were neither fallen nor disinherited. We dream of regaining a state and a time in which, like the child, we would be *always drunk,* without thinking that with the child this drunkenness was only a momentary precarious victory, which it was unceasingly necessary to obtain anew, over the dread of things, over the failures and perversions of the creature, by the magic of the imagination.

II

There are moments of existence when time and extent are more profound and the feeling of existence immensely enlarged.[7]

There are days when man awakens with a young and vigorous spirit. His eyelids hardly released from the sleep that sealed them, the external world offers itself to him set off in strong relief, with admirable clarity of contours and richness of colors. The moral world displays its vast perspectives, filled with new splendors. . . . Exceptional state of the mind and the senses, that I can without exaggeration call paradisaical, if I compare it to the thick gloom of common and daily existence . . . .[8]

In these happy hours which are illumined by "the latent poetry of childhood," the mind regains its freshness, and the adult becomes *child-man,* ". . . possessing in each moment the spirit of childhood, that is to say, a spirit for which no aspect of life is *blunted.*" [9]

Thanks to the intensity of this perception that has become childlike once more, nature resumes its radiant aspect of former times. It again becomes spiritualized, even supernatural. All its secondary qualities, tonality, sonority, limpidity, vibrancy, take on a sharper and deeper import. The hyperacuity of the senses "gives all tints a magic sense, and makes all sounds vibrate with a more significant resonance." [10] Each sensation in the field of consciousness appears stronger, more alive, more distinct, as if a greater margin bordered it and detached it from other sensations. Each sensation illimitably follows its trajectory and seems by concentric waves to invade a more and more vast expanse, like the circles created in a pond by a stone one has thrown into it. On the other hand, all sensations seem multiplied: they become an infinite number, deployed and projected in musical space. The enormously enlarged horizon discloses an immensity throughout which there vibrates, fragrant and resonant, an iridescent spray, a substance inexhaustibly formed of vapor of water.

To this indefinite amplification of space there corresponds an indefinite deepening of time. It seems as if sensations could never cease to move the affected nerves, sensations interminably prolonging their particular note through all duration. Simultaneous or successive, they meet, they touch, they respond, they form of their harmonies and analogies temporal echoes which reverberate them in transposing them:

> Like long echoes that mingle from afar
> In a dark and profound unity,
> *Vast* as the night and the brightness,
> The perfumes, the colors and the sounds respond to each other.

In this "state of poetic health" time appears under the form of a multiplication of ideas and images; but a multiplication in the interior of a framework, within its limits: a profusion of temporal riches in a cornucopia whose sides are indefinitely extendable. Certain intervals, in which we resume consciousness, allow us to measure them:

> This imagination lasts an eternity. An interval of lucidity with a great effort permits you to watch the clock. The eternity has lasted one minute. Another current of ideas carries you away; it will sweep you around one minute in its living whirlpool, and that minute will be another eternity. The proportions of time and of being are disturbed by the innumerable multitude and intensity of sensations and ideas. One lives several lives in the space of an hour.[11]

But, to examine the matter more closely, if the temporal proportions are disturbed, it is, strangely enough, in two contrary fashions. Insofar as images multiply, they seem to multiply time with them, to accelerate its course, so much so that one thinks that he lives with a prodigious rapidity, that he lives several lifetimes in the space of an hour. But, on the other hand, at each moment one becomes conscious of the real time that elapses during that interval, it seems that time must have prolonged itself in order to contain so great a substance of duration, extended its limits and slackened its pace. Observed *in its depths,* what passes away seems to be disposed over an infinitely greater *space* of duration, seems to have lasted for almost an eternal minute, a *vast* minute. It is, at the extreme, the conception of an eternity that is confounded with immensity, of a temporal depth that is analogous or identical to the spatial depth: "Depth of space, allegory of the depth of time."[12]

Space is made deeper by opium; opium gives a magic tint to all colors, and makes all sounds vibrate with a more meaningful sonorousness. Sometimes magnificent vistas, filled with light and with colors, open out suddenly in these landscapes, and one watches appear *in the depth of their horizons* oriental cities and architectures, vaporized *by distance,* on which the sun throws showers of gold.[13]

It is striking that in these paradisaical states (artificial or not, it makes no difference) objects at one and the same time appear very distinct and yet situated in the very depths of the horizon, in a far distance that idealizes them. It is the same with the images of the past which, awakened in their turn by the evocative magic of the images of the present, appear one after another, or all together, with the same clarity as they once did, the same charm, the same affective power, the same actuality; but situated, nevertheless, at the far depths of an immense temporal horizon, infinitely withdrawn to the end of an expanse of years that seem centuries old, and that are nevertheless effortlessly traversed by the powerful flight of memory.

To the magic of the present is thus added the magic of the past:

> Deep, magical charm, with which we are made drunk
> In the present by the restored past.[14]

If in these moments of "poetic health" the one who lives them is a child-man, that is not only because he has mysteriously "regained the spirit of childhood"; it is not solely because he feels and imagines anew as a child does; it is also because, beyond the *deep years,* he is reunited with the life of his own childhood, finds along its road all perceptible memories, all affective memories, and literally becomes once more the very child he had been:

> Many an old man, bent over a pot-house table, sees himself living again in a circle of people and places that have disappeared; he is drunk with his vanished youth.[15]

It is not simply that the interval of years is abolished, nor even that the mind suppresses distances in order to reach such a point of its former existence. It seems rather that what happens here is an extraordinary intercommunication in the mind of all parts of lived time. As one's gaze freely moves over the whole spatial mass that is offered to it, so the spiritual gaze sees spread out all around it the vast regions of completed existence. The various epochs respond to each other, touch each other, adhere to each other, and prolong in each other their evocative echoes. Whereas in normal thought, the evocation of one epoch excludes the simultaneous evocation of another, and whereas it is impossible for it to contemplate its life except by a successive unfolding of images, in these paradisaical states in which the profundity of life appears, existence is seen, on the contrary, to be deployed over a duration that has become pure extent. In this new direction the joys or the sorrows of different periods do not exclude each other any more; within it, upon the same plane, are found adult and child, voyager and poet, memory and sensation. As in a landscape painting all the forms of nature, the farthest off and the nearest, the richest and the dullest, are found reclothed in an identical charm, which is that of the whole picture, so all the years of existence, different as they may be, distinct as may be their peculiar tints, are not thereby found to benefit any the less from the same *general color,* from a harmony that is formed on the one hand by the infinite network of affinities from epoch to epoch and, on the other hand, by the emotive hue, by the *personal accent,* which, ineluctably, whatever the special nuances of the moments of his life, the same human being indistinguishably gives to all moments.

Thus ecstatic time, by reason of its spatial nature, preserves no trace of what is characteristic of ordinary duration. It is a time-painting that differs from a pictorial painting by the sole virtue of its being projected upon a space that is extended *backward,* a space previously traversed. But this last comparison is really not exact, for if it is fair to say that existence appears as already *traversed,* it nevertheless also appears as being always *traversable;* an open space in which it is always permitted to roam, to feel, and to live; a space which seems the very continuation of the present *backward;* a retrospective expanse which is what the future would be for us if we were able, in the full force of the term, to *foresee* it, *fore-feel* it, before engaging in it.

Thus, there is no longer a question of an irreversible time. One does not feel cut off from his past any more than one feels cut off from space by the consciousness of the point where one is. There is no longer that vertical or transcendent dimension which the law of irreversibility introduces between each lived instant. In this state one is on equal footing with his whole life. There is no longer a contradiction between all the points of nature, between nature and ourselves. For the whole length of its course, and whatever the thoughts that succeed each other, time is always of the same tonality, at once general and individual: the time of youth; the time of paradise.

Lengthening of hours by the multiplication of sensations,[16] by the reverberation of memories, by the discovery of the depth of existence; unification of moments, hours, and epochs by the profound experience of the harmony that exists between all the states of the *self*. At its farthest limit there is no longer either past or present, "nor hours, nor minutes, nor seconds." The *self* mingles sensations and memories in the same unity of feeling. The infinity of sensations, in manifold reflected brilliancy of detail, lengthens, spreads out, abates, and finally puts a stop to duration. The idea of time disappears:

> . . . the hours, slowed down, contain more thoughts . . . the clocks are striking happiness with a deeper and more meaningful solemnity . . . .[17]

> . . . in the depths of her adorable eyes I always see the hour distinctly, always the same, a vast, solemn hour, great *like space,* without divisions of minutes or of seconds—an immobile hour which is not marked by the clocks, and yet light as a sigh, swift as a glance.[18]

III

No! There are no more minutes, there are no more seconds! Time has disappeared; it is Eternity that reigns, an eternity of delights!

But a terrible, heavy knock sounded at the door, and, as in hellish dreams, it seemed to me that I received the blow of a pickaxe in the stomach.

And then a Spectre entered. . . . Time reappeared; Time reigns supreme now, and along with the hideous old man has come back his whole demoniacal train of Memories, Regrets, Spasms, Fears, Agonies, Nightmares, Rages and Neuroses.[19]

There is nothing more sudden than the fall into time. And nothing more tragic. For the time that then appears to the awakened ecstatic is a time turned upside down, a time out of joint, in which all the characteristics of paradisaical time are found once more, but the wrong way around, reversed and as if monstrously perverted by the fall into matter and into evil; a time of dream still, but of a dream that has become a nightmare. The temporal universe in which the dreamer finds himself is no less magic than that from which he has slipped, but of a demoniacal magic whose domain lodges below the normality of things, as the domain of the supernatural dwells above.

If, therefore, the paradisaical duration finds its exact analogy in spatial extent, the internal time finds its correspondence in the absence of space, in the void. Its symbol is the abyss. And as the time of ecstasy is achieved in eternity, so inverted time finds its end in death. Death and the abyss enclose all things and all thoughts:

> Morally and physically, I have always had the sensation of the abyss, not only of the abyss of sleep, but of the abyss of action, of dream, of memory, of desire, of regret, of remorse, of the beautiful, of number, etc.[20]

In place of a plurality which was founded upon a unity and a harmony, there is nothing more now than a chaos of numbers. Isolated, separated, hideously contrasting forms repeat indefinitely the grotesque echo of the original duality. Each moment reaffirms in its turn the infinite difference between the two natures in man. Every instant attests the infinite difference between the actual and the eternal. Instead of a time immanent in the divine, we have now a time that is entirely covered over, as with a lid, by the inexorable transcendence of eternity:

> . . . Styx miry and leaden
> Where no look from Heaven penetrates.[21]

But also at the same time, each minute isolatedly becomes of mortal importance. No longer supported by anything, nor linked to anything, it finds itself possessing no other existence than its own. Reduced to itself, it has no meaning or value except the ultimate and definitive meaning and value which the judgment of the infinite transcendence forever confers upon it, and in the very moment. Thus, if the seconds are now "strongly and solemnly accentuated," [22] it is because each becomes infinitely significant. Each instant, well or badly lived, continues to have been well or badly lived forever.

A new, anguished thought is thereby insinuated into tragic time. At the very instant when the instant *is,* it becomes detached, it falls, and in its fall a second existence begins, an existence in which instants do not cease—never cease—*to have been.* In this enormous lengthening of their spectral duration, they seem to extend eccentric circles into the gulf of the future, just as in paradisaical time each moment of beauty filled up with its growing undulations an extent of harmony:

> Who can think, without shuddering, of the infinite enlarging of circles in the spiritual waves set in motion by a chance stone? [23]

Then appears the thought of the irreparable:

> . . . If in this belief there is something infinitely consoling, in the case where our mind is turned toward that part of ourselves which we can consider with complacence, is there not also something infinitely terrible, in the future case, inevitable, when our mind shall turn toward that part of ourselves which we can confront only with horror? In the spiritual no less than in the material world, nothing is lost. In the same way that any action cast into the vortex of universal action is in itself irrevocable and irreparable . . . in the same way any thought is ineffaceable: [24]

> > The Irreparable gnaws with his cursed fang
> > On our mind, pitiable monument . . . .[25]

The irreparability of things is the indestructibility of the past. The Baudelairean remorse is nothing other than the consciousness of the irremediable character, given, once and for all, to a past that will never cease to be the past that has been lived. Whatever the future life may be, nothing, it seems, will be able to wash away these stains. We are far away now from the tranquil possession, in the present, of a past perceived in the depths of the memory like the natural prolongation, backward, of a magic present. Here is a past which, without ever ceasing to be present to the mind, also will never again cease to be separated from each moment in which it is present, by the irremediable and vertical incision of the law of irreversibility. In the time of evil and of remorse, of sin and of sorrow, the irreversibility appears under its most implacable form. There is absolute discontinuity between our present self and all the rest of our life. The latter appears to us a contradictory thing; that which is ours and that which is not ours; the only thing that might be authentically ourself, and the only thing that our self can neither relive nor efface.

We are now only the witnesses of ourselves. We recognize ourselves in our own memory, but it is with a most secret horror, with disgust.

Like Coleridge's Mariner, we carry a cadaver around our neck: it is our past. Our punishment is that of enduring ourselves. It is the punishment of the damned:

> O Lord, give me the strength and the courage
> To contemplate my heart and my body without disgust.

Meanwhile infernal time follows in us and about us a course which appears both the slowest and the most rapid. Taken between these extremities, at each moment when we perceive its flow, it seems to have passed away at a stroke, to have been hurled into nothingness. We feel it race on and carry us toward the tomb. We feel ourselves gnawed and eaten by it. We multiply our deaths; we live our own decomposition. But, on the other hand, irreversible time seems to become impoverished, to grow sterile, to rarefy. Its slowness becomes an intolerable oppression: a laborious succession of ideas more and more rare, more and more monotonous, which is finally leveled down and unified by the hateful hand of boredom.

> Nothing equals in length the limping days,
> When under the heavy flakes of snowy years
> Boredom, fruit of dull incuriousness,
> Assumes the proportions of immortality.[26]

It is as if, in and out of the mind, everything universally tended to be immobilized, or petrified:

> Henceforth you are no more, O living matter!
> Than a granite encompassed by a vague affright,
> Made drowsy in the depths of a misty Sahara.[27]

The Piranesian image of a staircase of infinite spirals which a damned person interminably descends into the darkness, or that finally of a vessel caught in an ice field and frozen forever to the same spot, such are the emblems of the eternity in reverse into which infernal time issues; hideous travesty of the eternity in which flowed effortlessly and radiantly the happy hours of the paradisaical time:

> Descend, descend, lamentable victims,
> Descend the path to eternal hell . . . .

IV

One must always be drunk. That says it all. There is no other point. In order not to feel the horrible burden of Time that bruises your shoulders and bends you to the ground, you must get drunk incessantly.[28]

"Slaves martyred by Time," men with glittering eyes, with hearts divided between "the horror of boredom and the *immortal desire to feel alive,*" contrive to escape from their human condition and to "possess immediately, on this very earth, a Paradise that had been revealed to them":

> Those unfortunates who have neither fasted nor prayed, and who have refused redemption by work, demand of black magic the means of lifting themselves at one stroke to supernatural existence.[29]

Wine, opium, hashish compose their dark paradise of artificial ecstasies:

> There one breathes a somber beatitude analogous to that which the lotus eaters must have experienced when, disembarking upon an enchanted island, lighted by the gleamings of an eternal afternoon, they felt born within them, to the drowsy sounds of melodious waterfalls, the desire never to see again their household gods, their wives, their children, and never again to climb the high sea billows.[30]

Thus the immortal desire to feel oneself alive is transformed into the mortal desire of nevermore having to will or to do. In claiming to "subdue to their will the fugitive demon of happy minutes," men finally arrive only at subjecting their will to the obstinate demon of unhappy minutes. In vain they tell themselves: "What does the eternity of damnation matter to him who has found within one second the infinity of delight?" [31] The abdication of their will which the instantaneous infinity of their joy involves finally delivers them up defenseless, "incapable of labor and of energetic action," to all the tortures the demon of time inflicts upon them:

> It is not to be forgotten that drunkenness is the negation of time, like every violent state of mind, and that consequently the results of the loss of time must unfold before the eyes of the drunkard, without destroying in him the habit of putting off his conversion till tomorrow, up to the point of the complete perversion of all feelings, and final catastrophe.[32]

From then on, the drama of time becomes the drama of the will: of a will still powerful enough to desire, regret, and to feel fear, horror or shame, but never strong enough to will; strong enough to transform the present moment into deficiency and suffering, but never strong enough to determine the present or decide the future.

Hence the desperate desire of escaping, if not from time, at least from the consciousness of time; the desire to have no more desires. To be able to stifle, deep within oneself, that last vestige of will by which one distinguishes himself from his own destiny, and by which he recognizes in himself the presence of misery. It is the temptation of sleep, the longing of the vanquished for all the brute resignations:

> I envy the lot of the vilest animals
> Who can plunge themselves into stupid sleep,
> So slowly the skein of time winds off.[33]

> Resign thyself, my heart; sleep thy sleep of the brute.[34]

> To know nothing, to teach nothing, to will nothing, to sleep, and still to sleep, that today is my only vow. An infamous and disgusting vow, but sincere.[35]

The immortal desire to feel alive ends in the desire not to feel alive, in the *wish for nothingness,* for continuous night: a fall into the void, a total abandon to the time-abyss:

> Avalanche, wilt thou carry me down in thy fall? [36]

V

> As long as I have not *the proof* that, in the real battle, that of time, I shall be beaten, I will not agree to say that I have made a failure of my life . . . .[37]
> All is reparable. There is still time. Who knows even if perhaps certain new pleasures . . . .[38]

In spite of himself the human creature continues to hope. For him there can never be absolute nothingness, nor total despair. There is never a postulation toward Satan without there being a simultaneous postulation toward God. To the feeling of the irreparable there is contradictorily joined the feeling that *all is reparable.* With the conception of a time that imposes a fate upon us, there is mingled the conception of a time that proposes to us a task;

> We are crushed each minute by the idea and the sensation of time. There are only two ways to escape this nightmare, to forget it: pleasure and labor. Pleasure consumes us. Labor strengthens us. Let us choose.[39]

Let us choose. There is still time—time to perform one's task. And the task to perform is first of all this: to learn to will; to come to have, or to come once more to have, a will. But in order to will once more, it is necessary to be a double person: the one who wills; and the one whom one wills to be. Such is the Stoic hero, such the Cornelian hero. Baudelaire conceives a religion that would have for a God the type of man one would wish to be, and for worship the worship of himself, the constancy and concentration of the effort by which one is maintained at the height of what one wishes to be. The dandy must be "sublime without interruption." Thus there would be formed a purely volitional time, made of a continuous effort.

But in so deifying his own self, the dandy, or the Stoic, does not neglect any less than does the Epicurean, or the drunkard, the ineluctable reality of original sin. The ideal he gives himself is not a true transcendence. The human frailty he ignores is the authentic misery of sin and of evil. The drunkard gave himself the illusion of an *artificial eternity;* the dandy gives himself the illusion of an *artificial duration.* The former in pretending to halt time, and the latter in pretending to impose upon time a forced continuity, take account, neither the one nor the other, of the true temporal conditions of existence. They forget that time is a contradiction.

There remains, then, to make use of time, such as it is. There remains to utilize the small bit of will that one has, to try to conduct one's daily business well. There remains to avail oneself of all his experiences, of all his miseries, but also of all his greatnesses, in order to give himself the courage to live and to act from day to day. Like the music of Wagner, every true work of art, every action by which man has been able to obtain a provisory but notable victory over the forces of dissolution and dispersion, admits of a series of elements or stages, discernible to analysis, which constitute a *suggestive* method and a *mnemo-technic.* These elements are: *will; desire; concentration; nervous intensity; explosion.*[40] These terms are not synonymous. They express a spiritual progress, a determined end. When assiduous exercise of the will in prayer, in conduct, in labor, brings to birth or revives a *desire* which is no longer instantaneously vaporized in dreams, but which is concentrated upon a transcendent object; when thus, instead of "throwing one's personality to the four winds," one gathers his actual resources about a "fixed idea" that is magically evocative, then there is re-discovered in the being and in the mind something of the genius of childhood, a *"nervous intensity"* which, in an *explosion*—analo-gous but not identical to the paradisaical ecstasy—permits the attainment if not of happiness at least of beauty: "Art is a mnemo-technic of the beautiful." [41]

But beauty is not happiness. Following the approximative defini-tion of Stendhal, it is only the promise. It is the acute experience of a reality *promised* but not yet *given*. It is at once what separates and what joins present and future: the present in which we are not happy; and the future in which we shall be. Beauty is the knowl-edge of what would be necessary and what we lack to give the moment its fullness. It is the consciousness of eternity which the moment is not:

> The beautiful is always, inevitably, of a double composition, al-though the impression it produces is one . . . . The beautiful is made of an eternal, invariable element . . . and of a relative, cir-cumstantial element . . . . The duality of art is one fatal conse-quence of the duality of man.[42]

From the double and contradictory character of human nature there emerges in the thought of Baudelaire the conception of a beauty which itself also has a double nature and a double visage: a permanent nature and a transitory nature; a face of grandeur and a face of misery. And, by the same token, there is discovered the possibility of living in a time which is neither the eternal time of the paradisaical states nor the miserable time of the infernal states; but a double time which, amid misery, contains the promise of hap-piness, which makes beauty rise up out of ugliness; a time which is simultaneously *lacking eternity* and *tending toward eternity*.

Human beauty, therefore, is not an abstract ideal. It is the real-ity of a concrete, matter-of-fact experience, of a *terrestrial* experi-ence, by which thought makes to appear in things and in itself the double, transcendent relationship of the temporal to the non-temporal.

VI

But, first, what are things? "Incoherent pile of materials that the artist is called upon to put in order," [43] "suggestive mass scattered about in space," [44] things exist in nature only with a literally *in-significant* existence—like the words in a dictionary. They are, but they express nothing. They are scattered about in space, but they do not constitute a space. They succeed each other in duration, but they do not form a duration. Perceived by the senses, they are heaped up in the memory and form again there another pile of debris.

The imagination makes itself master of this meaningless pile of things. It detaches and reunites, discomposes and recomposes, "creates a new world, produces the sensation of newness." But this newness is not just another incoherence. This new world is a *significant* world. Colors and shapes, sounds and odors have become signs. They have taken on a moral sense. They express the *human*.

In this new kind of evocative sorcery, Baudelaire no longer attempts to attain directly, by a sort of black magic, to a super-human order which, beyond good and evil, would dispose its eternal enchantments. The problem he sets about is both incomparably simpler and incomparably more difficult: simpler because it is a question of expressing, by *natural* symbols, a *human* reality, and infinitely more difficult because this human reality is that of a being whose true significance consists in not being what he would be, and in straining to be what he is not.

From that moment the evocative magic becomes entirely different. It no longer expresses *states* of mind; it indicates and effects metamorphoses. It lays hold of the mind "in the number, the undulant, the motion, the fugitive and infinite." Far from attaining a moment where all the richness of times and spaces simultaneously develop their harmonies, it discovers or follows, in the depths of the years, a moment always different and always similar, which, conscious of its poverty, avid of the riches it lacks, constantly searches, outside and beyond what is, for what is not. There is no longer a question of embracing duration, but of pursuing in its totality the thrill that pervades and animates it, and never leaves off:

> The sea is thy mirror; thou surveyest thy mind
> In the infinite unrolling of its wave.

In the infinite unrolling of existence, nothing is distinguished except the provisory. Just as the discovery of Copernicus changed the aspect of the cosmic universe, so the final thought of Baudelaire reversed the aspect of the interior world. The latter becomes a world without fixed relationships: a world essentially transitory; a world of contingencies in which the creature watches himself pass from the grotesque to the sublime, from ecstasy to debauchery, from fatigue to drunkenness, from corruption to salvation. All his faces and all his fates, all his actions and all his emotions, all his *selves,* contemporary or remote, present themselves to him in order to establish inter-relationships that are always ceaselessly changing. Under the urging of memory and under that of the present, exchanges are made between present and past:

> By thee is gold changed into iron
> And heaven into hell;

also by thee ecstasy is changed into disgust, despair into hope, contrition into expiation. Time becomes reversible, the past redeemable:

> Affected by these pleasures that resembled memories, touched by the thought of a past unfulfilled, so many faults, so many quarrels, so many things reciprocally to be hidden, he started to weep; and in the darkness his hot tears fell upon the naked shoulder of his dear and always alluring mistress. She shuddered, she herself also felt touched and moved. . . . These two fallen beings, but still suffering from what remained to them of nobility, spontaneously clasped themselves in each other's arms, mingling in the rain of their tears and their kisses, the sorrows of their past with their very uncertain hopes of the future . . . pleasure saturated with grief and remorse.
> Through the darkness of the night he had gazed behind him into the depths of the years, then he had thrown himself into the arms of his guilty lover, to find there the pardon that he accorded her.[45]

In such a conception of the activities of the mind, it is no longer a question of *possessing* one's existence. Existence is not possessed. It is no longer a question of seeing in it an ensemble of relationships out of which "the fatality of temperament necessarily makes a harmony," since the fatality of temperament can—even back through the depths of the past—be transfigured and redeemed. Over the whole course of existence, any moment, at any moment, can be "saved."

In this faith, grief loses its sharpness, evil its irreparability, death its sting:

> My humiliations have been graces from God.[46]

Thus Baudelairean thought comes to express simply the grievous consciousness of the human condition. At this point the depth of existence ceases to be an individual depth. It is no longer simply in the temporal spaces of its own life that the soul hears the echo of its plaints and its joys resound:

It is a cry repeated by a thousand sentinels,

sentinels who, since the beginning of time, have exchanged the same cry with each other, a cry that is no longer that of a particular human being, but of a general being in whom human anguish resounds. And as a consequence, the immense reverberatory field of duration appears in its veritable unity, joining to all the past ages through which the same sob has rolled, the prospective depth of the whole distance it leaps over in order to bring each age and each instant to the very borders of the eternal:

For it is truly, O Lord, the best witness
That we could give of our dignity,
This burning cry that rolls from age to age
And comes to die at the edge of your eternity!

NOTES

[1] *Oeuvres*, La Pléiade, II, 647.
[2] *Ibid.*, p. 320.
[3] *Ibid.*, p. 663.
[4] *Ibid.*, p. 355.
[5] *Ibid.*, p. 331.
[6] *Ibid.*, I, 20.
[7] *Ibid.*, II, 633.
[8] *Ibid.*, I, 273.
[9] *Ibid.*, II, 332.
[10] *Edgar Poe, sa vie et ses oeuvres.*
[11] *Oeuvres*, I, 262.
[12] *Ibid.*, p. 306.
[13] *Edgar Poe, sa vie et ses oeuvres.*
[14] *Oeuvres*, I, 52.

[15] *Ibid.*, p. 322.
[16] *Ibid.*, p. 432.
[17] *Ibid.*
[18] *Ibid.*, p. 429.
[19] *Ibid.*, pp. 410–11.
[20] *Ibid.*, II, 668.
[21] *Ibid.*, I, 92.
[22] *Ibid.*, p. 411.
[23] *Ibid.*, p. 355.
[24] *Ibid.*, p. 390.
[25] *Ibid.*, p. 69.
[26] *Ibid.*, p. 86.
[27] *Ibid.*
[28] *Ibid.*, p. 468.
[29] *Ibid.*, p. 318.
[30] *Ibid.*, p. 456.

[31] *Ibid.*, p. 416.
[32] *Ibid.*, II, 691.
[33] *Ibid.*, I, 45.
[34] *Ibid.*, p. 89.
[35] *Ibid.*, p. 582.
[36] *Ibid.*, p. 89.
[37] *Ibid.*, II, 707.
[38] *Ibid.*, p. 670.
[39] *Ibid.*, p. 668.
[40] *Ibid.*, p. 509.
[41] *Ibid.*, p. 99.
[42] *Ibid.*, pp. 326–27.
[43] *Ibid.*, p. 305.
[44] *Ibid.*, p. 265.
[45] *Ibid.*, pp. 638–39.
[46] *Ibid.*, p. 670.

✳

✳

✳ VALERY

✳ In the beginning, according to Faust, was activity. Bolder, above all more rigorous than the Goethean hero, the Valerian hero—M. Teste without a doubt—goes back beyond all activity and puts the beginning of things at the place where the human being can hardly distinguish himself from the nothingness which he was and which he shall become again: "In the beginning will be sleep." [1] At this moment—if it is a moment?—the being is still only silence and absence, absence of himself from himself, silence of the consciousness, which shows him that death is situated not only at the end but at the beginning and in all the interstices of his existence:

> Man imagines he "exists." He thinks, therefore he is—and that naive idea of taking himself for a world subsisting of and by itself, is possible only through negligence.
> I neglect my hours of sleep, my absences, my deep, long, insensible variations.
> I forget that I possess in my own life a thousand models of death, of daily nothingnesses, an astonishing quantity of lacunae, of things suspended, of intervals unknowing and unknown.[2]

At the beginning, therefore, let us postulate nonbeing—that nonbeing in the purity of which the universe and myself are only a flaw—a nonbeing, however, which in a certain manner and by virtue of its very perfection, exists, and exists more than I. For I live only in what I was or what I shall be, that is to say, in a successive time in which the present escapes me: "We see only the future or the past, but not the patches of the pure instant." [3] Only that being who is entombed in his own sleep and in his own absence, really belongs to his present and possesses it: "He is as if eternal, ignorant of himself." [4] He alone is. That is why I cannot say: I am. But "I was, you are, I shall be." [5]

The time of sleep, therefore, primitive and primordial, is the earliest of those "durations independent of each other," whose "contradictory coexistence" constitutes "the strangest problem one can ever propose to oneself . . . ." [6] It is a time without past or future, above all without change, and it does not differ from that hypothetical thing called eternity except in this, that it is bounded on all sides by zones of consciousness. It is like an *island* of eternity, inserted into the intervals of pure time:

> Sleep . . . mild and tranquil mass mysteriously isolated, sealed ark of life that transportest towards day my history, my hazards, thou ignorest me, thou preservest me, thou art my inexpressible permanence; thy treasure is my secret. . . . Thou hast made for thyself an island of time, thou art a time that is detached from the huge Time in which thy duration indefinitely subsists and is perpetuated like a ring of smoke.[7]

Meanwhile if this island of time shelters my sleeping presence, I know nothing of it; but I do know that when I emerge from it to pass into another time, I undoubtedly experience the feeling of leaving an environment of vacancy and beginning to be myself, but not the feeling of an absolute beginning suddenly taking form in a void. The mysterious nonbeing, from which the awakening snatches me, is composed of a certain spiritual matter. "Atoms of silence," [8] "atoms of time" [9]—these constitute it and preserve me in it. I leave it restored—restored in the full sense of the word —given back to the completeness of the possible. It is a state very close to that state of sleep Valéry alludes to in the following passage, in which he deplores the disappearance of *spare* time:

> We lose that essential peace of the depths of being, that priceless absence during which the most delicate elements of life are refreshed and fortified, during which the being, in some way *is washed clean of the past and the future,* of present consciousness, of suspended obligations and ambushed expectations. . . . No interior pressure, but a kind of repose in absence, a beneficent vacancy which restores the mind to its proper freedom.[10]

"In the beginning will be sleep" is equivalent, therefore, to saying: In the beginning there will be a time that is free—time of pure virtuality in which the mind is withdrawn from all the obligations of wakefulness in order once more to become ready to seize new chances, for "each atom of silence is the chance of a ripe piece of fruit." And suddenly we understand why Valéry, in contrast to Goethe, did not speak of the *beginning* in the past tense, as of something which had taken place, but used the future tense, as of something that is still becoming, something that is going to happen: In the beginning *will be* and not *was*. The possible is not the being but prepares it, is simply its future. It is from the possible that one must seize hold of being, when it is becoming actual, in a sleep that becomes an awakening, in a future that is made present:

> Chaos . . . primary disorder, in the ineffable contradictions of which space, time, light, possibilities, virtualities were still in latency.[11]

II

In the beginning will be sleep. But sleep is not consciousness. "It is shifting, irresolute, still at the mercy of a moment, that the operations of the mind are going to be able to serve us." [12] "The idea, the principle, the lightning flash, the first moment of the first state, the leap, the bound out of sequence . . . . Throw the line there. That is the spot in the sea where you will get a catch." [13] But what is there to catch except that lightning flash, that leap, that stunning presence of the moment of which consciousness is the prey? "Disorder is therefore my first point. . . . It animates us." [14] "I consider the state close to stupor, the singular and initial point of knowledge." [15] The first stage of Valerian consciousness is therefore consciousness of the moment at whose mercy it is; consciousness of a successive, discontinuous, disordered, anonymous plurality: "Every instant the mind of the instant comes to us from the exterior." [16]

The exterior is what extends about us; it is space. It is made up of an assemblage of patches incessantly changing. As far as the gaze may travel, as intense as may be the attention, they never meet anything outside except "a chaos of lights and shadows . . . a group of luminous inequalities." [17] "So, in the enlargement of what is given, expires the intoxication with particular things." [18] It expires in the consciousness of "an inexpressible disorder of the dimensions of knowledge." [19] There are nothing but "ephemeral figures," "enterprises interrupted . . . that are transformed one into the other"; the mind expresses them by means of "an interior word, without person and without origin." [20]

But if that exterior world made up of instantaneous spaces is only a chaos of particular things, what is the interior universe of him who reflects and observes it?

> The observer is held in a sphere that is never broken. . . . The observer is first of all only the necessary condition of that finite space. . . . Neither memory nor any other force disturbs him as long as he identifies himself with what he beholds. And if ever I conceive him as lasting thus, I shall conceive that his impressions will never differ in the slightest from those he would receive in a dream.[21]

Thus, *identifying himself with what he beholds,* with an uninterrupted train of enterprises, thought is the prey of a Bergsonian universe whose reverse side is here found to be cruelly unveiled. To be abandoned to the transitory present and to the single flux of duration is to be abandoned to a double nothingness: a nothingness of the object which is never what it is; and a nothingness of thought which by its very spontaneity is made each instant into what it thinks, and thus becomes the object and sharer of its ephemeralness: "Instantaneous nullity";[22] "instantaneous and undivided state that smothers this chaos in nullity." [23]

III

Nevertheless, from this chaos which is instantaneously annulled, it happens that a kind of unity emerges which will assemble things into more or less distinct structures:

> That unity, which necessarily results from what I can see in an instant, that ensemble of reciprocal relations of figures or of patches . . . communicates to me the primary idea, the model and, as it were, the germ of the total universe that I believe to exist around my sensation, masked and revealed by it. I imagine invincibly that a vast hidden system supports, penetrates, nourishes, and reabsorbs each actual and sensuous element of my duration, impels it into being and into taking shape; and that therefore each moment is the knot of an infinity of roots that plunge to an unknown depth in an implicit extent—in the past—in the secret structure of our perceiving and calculating machine, which incessantly feeds back into the present.[24]

The first independent operation of the mind, the first gesture by which it frees itself from sensation, from space and from the immediate, is not a gesture of freedom but of bondage. King of the possible, the mind hastens to give itself masters and bounds. He who can invent all, invents the concept that he cannot produce his self-invention. Outside the present, he imagines the series of causes and determinations of that present:

> In the mythical void of a time pure and bereft of whatever element may be similar to those that border us, the mind—assured only that there had been something, constrained by an essential necessity to suppose antecedents, "causes," supports of what is, of what it is— gives birth to epochs, states, events, beings, principles, images, or histories . . . .
> That is why it came to me one day to write: In the beginning was the Fable! [25]

It is a strange transformation that the mind now inflicts on the moment, and by which it radically changes the nature of it. In place of being, things now demand to have been. They wish themselves surrounded not simply by patches and places but by causes and time. They claim the right to be annexed to a duration. They entreat the mind to set them against the background of a past, one single past, of all possible pasts. Among all the floating images of what one could have been, one makes the choice of a certain image, one decides to think that this really represents what one has been:

> The past is a thing entirely mental. It is only images and belief.[26]

> The past is only a belief. A belief is an abnegation of the powers of our mind, which feels repugnance at forming for itself all the convenient hypotheses about absent things, and giving them all the same force of evidence.[27]

"Naïve and bizarre structure," [28] the belief in the past is nonetheless a structure. It supports its fables; it also supports the present. For that reason the present no longer appears to be suspended above nonbeing. Sustained from underneath and from behind, confirmed by analogies, strong in its ability to represent in the right place a continuing identity, the present makes every effort in order not to be different from what the past was and to present itself as a simple repetition. In this effort it finds itself aided, moreover, by the very coarseness of our perceptions:

> Not subtle enough, my senses, to undo that work so ingenious or so profound that the past is, not subtle enough for me to discern that this place or that wall are perhaps not identical to what they were the other day.[29]

Thanks to this simplification, the originality of each moment no longer risks confronting us without respite with a nature in which there is not one "trace of past, repetition, similarity," [30] a nature, therefore, always instantaneous. By an audacious falsification of the latter, in giving ourselves a past, in giving ourselves similarities, we also give ourselves at the same time the chance and the means of finding constants, of constructing laws, of imagining the universal.

But if things are consolidated in this manner in a mental structure, they are found to lose, on the other hand, in variety and in authenticity. Instead of appearing as they are, they tend to resemble what they have been. They become impoverished; they become involved; they are reduced to signifying: "Memory drives away the present." [31] "Each instant falls down instantly into the imaginary." [32]

Thus the past is simply "the place of forms without forces." [33] It "represents itself, but it has lost its energy." [34]

Doubtless "it is up to us to furnish it with life and necessity," and for that purpose "to endow it with our passions and our values." [35] Let us then recognize in this, not the presence of the "past" but the presence of some "present" in the past. Let us notice the *originality* of memory, "that in which memory is not the past, but the act of the present": [36]

> There is thus engendered a state of mind that is curiously anti-historical, that is to say, a vivid perception of the completely actual substance of our images of the "past" and of our inalienable liberty to alter them as easily as we are able to conceive them . . . .[37]

But in this way the temporal point of view changes once more. Instead of imagining ourselves determined by what was, we now carry our indetermination backwards in order to make of the past a sort of anterior future. From this point of view "to see again and to foresee, to recollect and to forebode, strongly resemble each other." [38] But that is true only because it is possible to "foresee" over all the points of time and in all the positions of the mind. What matters therefore above all is to understand what appears more and more as the "time" of the mind, that is to say the future:

> The idea of the past takes on a meaning and constitutes a value only for the man who finds in himself *a passion for the future*.[39]

For Valéry, as for Vigny, the spiritual activity of man is fundamentally this passionate sense of the future.

IV

What is the future? To understand it, we must bring our attention to bear upon "our most central sense, that intimate sense of the distance between desire and the possession of its object, which is nothing else than the sense of duration . . . ." [40] This sense of duration is the future. It is something that splits and yawns within ourselves, within the moment when we are ourselves; it is the feeling of a void, of a lack, of a gap, with the need of filling it up. The future is first of all dissatisfaction and desire. If, on the one hand, we exist only in the present, if "there is nothing of ourselves outside the instant," [41] on the other hand "we consist precisely in the regret or in the refusal of *what is,* in a certain distance which separates us and distinguishes us from the instant." [42] It is a distance that places before us a being that is still ourself and which seems to us to be more desirably ourself than ourself—the myth of Narcissus: "Man is not all in one piece. One part of him precedes the other." [43]

But this part of himself that precedes him does so only by an infinitesimal fraction of time: "I feel the imminence." [44] "I love nothing so much as that which is going to happen." [45] At this moment the being in whom the imminent future takes form—in whom "the future is the most perceptible portion of the instant" [46] —discovers and experiences himself in his virtualities, in his expectations: "Sweetness of being and not yet being." [47] He is less what he is than what he is on the point of becoming. He is in an exquisitely non-temporal position, where nevertheless all temporality takes refuge, "between the void and the pure event." Thought "beats between the times and the instants." [48] It desires, attracts, brings the possible to existence, and that almost by its ardor alone: "I immolate myself interiorly to what I would wish to be." [49]

Now in this function that is "the simplest, the deepest, the most general of our being, which is to form the future," [50] in this state of presentiment in which the difference that separates and distinguishes us from the instant is a difference of pure thought—it is here precisely that thought becomes visible to itself; and, in creating time, the human being at the same stroke gives himself a consciousness of his consciousness. Thought of thought, the consciousness resides in that temporal distance that makes resound in the mind a depth that is always future. It is "the distance between being and knowing," [51] the property of deviating from the instant, and even "from one's own personality." [52] It is the exact antitype of the figure of Narcissus. There issues from myself and from all the instants when I am myself, another self, a different self, a general and impersonal entity that contemplates me. He is, like M. Teste, "the being absorbed in his variation"; he is the *measure of things:*

> To say that man is the measure of things . . . is to oppose to the diversity of our moments, to the mobility of our impressions, and even to the particularity of our individualism, of our person . . . a Self that recapitulates it, dominates it, comprises it, as the law comprises particular cases, as the feeling of our strength contains all the acts that are possible for us . . . .
> We feel ourselves to be this universal self . . . .[53]

Priceless creation, which is no longer that of an object engaged in time, but of that of a subject disengaged from time. Thanks to it,

> . . . each life, particular as it is, possesses . . . deep within it a treasure, the fundamental permanence of a consciousness which nothing supports; and just as the ear discovers and loses again, throughout the vicissitudes of the symphony, a grave and continuous sound to be perceived—so the pure *self,* the unique and monotonous tone of the human being in the world, discovered by itself and then once again lost, eternally inhabits our senses; this profound *note* of existence dominates, as soon as one listens to it, the whole complication of the conditions and varieties of existence.[54]

But if the permanent consciousness is distinguished from the variable, if it is situated outside of duration, that is in order to give it its laws. The being who is lifted up to the thought of thought can then act on the thought as upon a moldable material. "Everything yields to this generality." [55] "The mind has the power to impart to an actual circumstance the resources of the past and the energies of the future." [56] By pressures or relaxations it can slacken or accelerate the pace of the approach and the flight of whatever travels its roads. It knows what it must do for thought to come to light. It knows also, what is worth more, how it must be cultivated in order that it may not come too quickly to fruit. For the essential factor of this polity of the mind is less a presence among all the other presences than it is the power of keeping thought fixed for a long time, suspended before its attention, just as Joshua kept the sun motionless in the sky. From all sides ideas offer themselves to the mind, waiting on every hand for the chance of being plucked. But what matters is to profit to the maximum by this chance and, with that in view, to delay as long as possible the inevitable moment when all thought returns to chaos and the instantaneous state. It is a question of slipping into the break of continuity of the lode of time, between the moment of imminence and that of accomplishment, a whole new duration, in which the mind takes the time to foresee, to compose, to moderate, or to suppress,[57] that is to say, to make its work durable, as architect and engineer do. These thoughts that come to me, "it is necessary that I stop them . . . that I interrupt the very birth of ideas. . . . It matters to me above all things that I obtain what will satisfy, with all the vigor of its novelty, the reasonable exigencies of what has been." [58] It is necessary, therefore, "to stay in a compulsory attitude." [59]

In this duration which is compelled into being by the mind, and which the mind adorns by its operations, there is discovered a temporal frame of a nature precisely contrary to that of the duration-flux upon which the person leaving the state of sleep emerged in order to surrender himself to it—duration this time is no longer spontaneous but voluntary, no longer natural but artificial; "delicate art of duration," [60] in which there is no longer an *infinity of interrupted enterprises,* but one sole enterprise having a beginning and an end, an orientation towards his proper achievement, the presence and the consciousness of a faith. That enterprise is the poem:

> Even in the lightest pieces, it is necessary to think of duration— that is to say of *memory,* that is to say of form.[61]

One hundred divine instants do not construct a poem, which is a time of growth, and like a figure in time.[62]

A poem is a duration, during which, reader, I breathe a law that had been made ready.[63]

Duration is construction . . . .[64]

It follows then that, for Valéry, the true duration—contrary to the "insupportable flight" and the "happy surprise"—is a work of art, a creation of the mind which, in order to be formed, needs all its resources and all its vigilance; a creation, moreover, which has validity and reality only for the mind, and relatively to the object that it frames and forms—provisorily. There is no duration in itself, and there is no duration without work and object. And again, there is no infinite duration because there is no infinite work, because a work can begin to be only when anticipatively it has already been completed by the mind.

All true duration is, thus, like a grain of duration: something hard, closed in, a "closed cycle," [65] that opposes its wall to emptiness, to chaos, to the formlessness of perceptible events, and within which there is found enclosed a life that is quivering and governed —governed toward its end.

Hardly has it ended when its creator abandons it—it and its duration. He rediscovers himself in his own duration, in a moment that is again an initial moment, *washed clean of the past and the future,* washed clean even of his own work, free, equal to the chances of the moment:

O moment, diamond of Time! [66]

Here am I, the very present.[67]

NOTES

[1] *A.B.C., Commerce* [ca. 1930].
[2] *Tel quel,* ii, p. 238.
[3] *Pièces sur l'art,* p. 146.
[4] *Variété III,* p. 104.
[5] *A.B.C., Commerce.*
[6] *Variété I,* p. 205.
[7] *A.B.C., Commerce.*
[8] *Poésies,* p. 201.
[9] *Variété II,* p. 195.

[10] *Variété III,* p. 284.
[11] *Mon Faust,* p. 55.
[12] *Variété I,* p. 220.
[13] *Monsieur Teste,* p. 125.
[14] *Variété III,* p. 205.
[15] *Tel quel,* ii, p. 243.
[16] *Ibid.,* i, p. 39.
[17] *Regards sur le monde actuel,* p. 22.
[18] *Variété I,* p. 234.

[19] *Ibid.,* p. 193.
[20] *Poésies,* p. 61.
[21] *Variété I,* p. 231.
[22] *Poésies,* p. 61.
[23] *Variété I,* p. 193.
[24] *Ibid.,* p. 134.
[25] *Variété II,* p. 254.
[26] *Variété IV,* p. 134.
[27] *Mon Faust,* p. 25.
[28] *Variété V,* p. 85.

29 *Monsieur Teste*, p. 129.
30 *Mélange*, p. 69.
31 *Pièces sur l'art*, p. 146.
32 *Variété II*, p. 253.
33 *Variété III*, p. 61.
34 *Mélange*, p. 84.
35 *Variété III*, p. 61.
36 *Mélange*, p. 69.
37 *Variété V*, p. 91.
38 *Variété IV*, p. 136.
39 *Regards sur le monde actuel*, p. 16.
40 *Variété III*, p. 283.
41 *Idée fixe*, p. 145.

42 *Mélange*, p. 80; *Tel quel*, i, p. 89.
43 *Idée fixe*, p. 100.
44 *Mélange*, p. 96.
45 *Eupalinos*, p. 35.
46 *Mélange*, p. 37.
47 *Poésies*, p. 128.
48 *Eupalinos*, p. 61.
49 *Monsieur Teste*, p. 124.
50 *Variété IV*, p. 191.
51 *Variété III*, p. 72.
52 *Ibid.*, p. 221.
53 *Ibid.*, p. 257.
54 *Variété I*, p. 204.

55 *Ibid.*, p. 192.
56 *Mélange*, p. 27.
57 *Variété I*, p. 176.
58 *Eupalinos*, pp. 114–15.
59 *Idée fixe*, p. 174.
60 *Monsieur Teste*, p. 28.
61 *Pièces sur l'art*, p. 91.
62 *Variété III*, p. 15.
63 *Poésies*, p. 62.
64 *Tel quel*, ii, p. 334.
65 *Variété V*, p. 135.
66 *Mélange*, p. 96.
67 *Mon Faust*, p. 95.

PROUST

I

And when I awoke in the middle of the night, not knowing where I was, I did not even know at first who I was; I had only in its primal simplicity a sense of existing, such as may flicker in the depths of an animal's consciousness; I was more destitute than the cave-dweller.[1]

At the beginning of the Proustian novel there is, then, an instant which is not preceded by any other, just as with Descartes or Condillac, just as with Valéry. But if this instant is of a "primal simplicity," that is because it is about to become the starting point of the immense development that follows it; but it is oriented not toward this "becoming" but toward the nothingness which precedes it. Here, this first moment is neither a moment of fullness nor of birth. It is pregnant neither with its future possibilities nor with its present realities. And if it reveals a fundamental emptiness, that is not because it needs anything from "ahead" but because it lacks something from "behind": something which *is no longer;* not something which *is not yet.* One might call it the first moment of a being that has lost everything, that has lost itself, because it is dead: "We have slept too long, we no longer exist. Our waking is barely felt, mechanically and without consciousness . . . ."[2]

The sleeper awakes from sleep more naked than a cave man. His nakedness is the nakedness of a lack of knowledge. If he is reduced to the state in which he is, that is because he does not know who he is. And he does not know who he is because he does not know who he has been. He knows *no longer.* He is a being who has lost his being because memory and the past have been lost:

Then from those profound slumbers we awake in a dawn, not knowing who we are, being nobody, newly born, ready for anything, our brain being emptied of that past which was previously our life. And perhaps it is more wonderful still when our landing at the waking-point is abrupt and the thoughts of our sleep, hidden by a cloak of oblivion, have no time to return to us progressively, before sleep ceases. Then, from the black tempest through which we seem to have passed (but we do not even say *we*) we emerge, prostrate, without a thought, a "we" that is without content. What hammer-blow has the being or the thing that is lying there received to make it unconscious of anything . . . ?[3]

He who surges now into existence seems less a being than one emptied of his being. He is a being *in vacuo,* in emptiness; a being "without consciousness," since consciousness can only be consciousness of something. He is "without content," "more lifeless than a jelly-fish," returned to "the most elementary kingdoms of nature"; a being that cannot be described otherwise than by calling it "the being or the thing that is there."

But how is this thing which is there, in a moment "outside of time and all measures," how is it going to be able to leave this moment which isolates it before and behind? How shall it repair its monstrous ignorance of time, place, and its own person? Doubtless, to the animal feeling of its own existence there corresponds the feeling of the existence of a world in which it seems confusedly immersed. Awakened, and at the very instant when it awakes, this sleeper discovers himself and discovers at the same time that he *is there*—there, that is to say somewhere: at a certain time; in a place; among things. But suppose he awakens in the middle of the night, in darkness: in what room is he? in what place? in what time? Certain images of places and times come and go, excluding each other and superimposing themselves upon him:

> Perhaps the immobility of the things that surround us is forced upon them by our conviction that they are themselves, and not anything else, and by the immobility of our conceptions of them. For it always happened that when I awoke like this, and my mind struggled in an unsuccessful attempt to discover where I was, everything would be moving round me through the darkness: things, places, years.[4]

Vertigo of images. The world, as the awakened sleeper discovers it, is indeed a world of things, but of interchangeable things, in which nothing is attached to one particular point of space or duration; a world of things doubtful rather than certain; possible rather than necessary; a world similar to the legendary images of Golo and of Geneviève de Brabant which the play of the magic lantern substituted for the walls of the room of the child Proust, to make "a stained glass window, flickering and momentary."

The being that is uncertain of himself wants to lean upon the stability of things. But what stability can be offered by things which are "even more unreal than the projections of the magic lantern"? Unreal as the forms he has just encountered in the world of sleep:

> . . . deep slumber in which are opened to us a return to childhood, the recapture of past years, of lost feelings, the disincarnation, the transmigration of the soul, the evoking of the dead, the illusions of madness, retrogression towards the most elementary of the natural kingdoms (for we say that we often see animals in our dreams, but we forget almost always that we are ourself then an animal deprived of that reasoning power which projects upon things the light of certainty; we present on the contrary to the spectacle of life only a *dubious vision, destroyed afresh every moment by oblivion,* the former reality fading before that which follows it as one projection of a magic lantern fades before the next as we change the slide).[5]

The awakened sleeper, Proust, is never entirely able to detach himself from this first figuration of the world. One would say that, if Goethe taught himself to represent the universe as a theater of marionettes, Proust learned to represent existence as the "flickering and momentary" play of the light of a magic lantern. The Proustian world is always to be an intermittent world. A world in which things project themselves before the eyes in instantaneous images which in turn are replaced by other images belonging to other moments and other places; a world in which the apparition of any one image does not necessarily entail the apparition of the one following; where one may find oneself going backward as well as forward; where "the magic chair may carry us at all speed in time and space"; a world of "doubtful visions," whose lacunae the mind will have to fill up by its conjectures, whose vacillations it will have to remedy by its beliefs. The Proustian world is a world anachronistic in itself, without a home, wandering in duration as well as in extent, a world to which the mind must precisely assign a certain place in duration and space, by imposing its own certitude upon it, by realizing oneself in the face of it.

But in order to impose our certainties upon the world, we must first find them in ourselves. Now what certainties can a consciousness without content find in itself? What can it offer, denuded of

all, beggar that it is? The human being on the threshold of awakening, the child at the onset of the night, finds itself face to face with
"doubtful visions destroyed every minute," and confronted by
things of which it is impossible to know "whether they are themselves and not others." Thus the child Proust, in the room that
the projection of the magic lantern metamorphosized: "The mere
change of lighting destroyed the customary impression I had
formed of my room, thanks to which the room itself, but for the
torture of having to go to bed in it, had become quite endurable.
For now I no longer recognized it, and I became uneasy, as though
I were in a room in some hotel or "chalet," in a place where I had
just arrived for the first time. . . ." [6] It is a place one no longer
recognizes, which therefore can be any other place, a place which
has become doubtful, strange, anonymous; a place disconnected
from its occupant, because nothing in it responds to the demand
of his thought. Then, in the consciousness of the hostile refusal of
things to put themselves in touch with the mind, the child Proust
takes account of the depth of his solitude, and the anguish begins:

> Having no world, no room, no body now that was not menaced by
> the enemies thronging round, invaded to the very bones by fever, I
> was alone, I wanted to die.[7]

For the anguish of solitude is not only that of being detached
from things and beings; it is being detached from fixity, from the
permanence one would like to have beings and things possess and
give us by return; it is to feel oneself betrayed, without any help
from them, to the indeterminate power of thought, which ceaselessly imposes upon us metamorphoses, which perpetually changes
us into another "self," and which every instant makes of us, and for
us, a stranger.

Thence proceed those contractions and rebellions of the threat-
ened parts of our whole selves "which we must recognize to be a
secret, partial, tangible and true aspect of our resistance to death,
of the long resistance, desperate and daily renewed, to a fragmentary and reiterated death such as interpolates itself through the
whole course of our life . . ." [8] successive deaths, more imminent,
more reiterated, more total in proportion as a thought without content finds in itself no resource for establishing fixity and consistence.

The human being, for Proust, therefore, is a being who tries to find justification for his existence. Not knowing who he is, either he is like someone stricken with amnesia who goes from door to door asking people to tell him his name, or he feels himself to be what things indifferently become in him: a bundle of anonymous images that obliterate themselves and reform, like the iridescent spray from fountains of water. He is nothing or anything by turns, anything which is still nothing. Now this being who is nothing finds himself thrown into a moment lost in the midst of others, that is to say, a moment which resembles nothing and rests on nothing. And since this instant is inevitably going to be annihilated by another, he sees in this instant his own death, and he does not know whether he will be born again, or into what sort of being he will be reborn.

I think each day is the last day of my existence.[9]

All my effort has tended in the opposite way [from Maeterlinck's], not to consider death as a negation, for this is meaningless and contrary to all death makes us feel. It manifests itself in a terribly positive way.[10]

For to be dead, for Proust, is not simply to be no more; it is to be *another being*. Such is a man who after an illness is shocked to see that his hair has turned white.

And when I realized that I felt no joy at the thought of her being alive, that I no longer loved her, I ought to have been more astounded than a person who, looking at his reflexion in the glass, after months of travel, or of sickness discovers that he has white hair and a different face, that of a middle aged or an old man. This appalls us because its message is: "the man that I was, the fair young man, no longer exists, I am another person." And yet, was not the impression that I now felt, the proof of as profound a change, as total a death of my former self and of the no less complete substitution of a new self for that former self, as is proved by the sight of a wrinkled face capped with a snowy poll instead of the face of long ago? [11]

What is death but to be different from oneself? The fear of death is not so much the fear of no longer feeling and no longer being conscious; it is the fear of no longer feeling that which one feels, and of no longer being conscious of that of which one is conscious. Yet such a death seems an ineluctable reality, not only at the end of total existence, but at the end of each of these tiny closed existences, of these "drops of time" which are each one of the moments of our life:

> . . . truly a death of ourselves, a death followed, it is true, by resurrection, but in a different ego, the life, the love of which are beyond the reach of those elements of the existing ego that are doomed to die.[12]

Condemned, then, to a fragmentary and successive death, not knowing whether he will come to life again or in whom he will come to life, the human being such as Proust depicts is haunted by the anguish of this substitution of self for self which for him is death. Against this anguish he has only one recourse: to give himself the assurance of this survival; to believe that, beyond all this, one will be able to find *oneself again*. But it is impossible for this faith to assure him as to the future, since one cannot find there anything imaginable; since this future is the present of the monstrously inconceivable being into which death will have changed us. From this side, *from the side of the death to come,* the grave is insuperable. The future is closed by death; confronting the closed future, we are in anguish.

Free-floating anguish, indeterminate, "at the service one day of one feeling, the next day of another." But whether it presents itself under the form of the indefinable dejection into which the spectacle of a strange room throws us, or under the form of the anxiety of the child who waits in vain for the kiss of his mother before going to sleep, fundamentally this anguish is of a being who, finding himself in an existence which nothing, it seems, can justify, incapable of discovering for himself a reason for being, incapable at the same time of finding anything which guarantees the continuation of his being, experiences simultaneously horror of a future which changes him, contempt for a present which seems powerless to establish him, and the exclusive need of saving himself, come what may, from his cruel contingency by discovering in the past the basis of this being that he is, and yet that *he no longer is*.

For if it is impossible beforehand to burst open the precincts of death, is it not possible to do so, one might say, behindhand? If we are always *on this side* of our death to come, are we not always *on that side* of a death *already come,* a death beyond which lies our past life? Is there not then an act by which one might be able to rediscover himself and the basis of his existence?

This question is answered in the strange beginning of Proust's novel, where, with hardly an initial moment admitted, the thought gets underway and begins to march, but in reverse. A journey backwards, as if at the very moment the being discovers his existence, he experiences as well the need of sustaining rather than fulfilling it, of giving himself reasons for being rather than reasons for acting.

Proust's novel is the history of a search: that is to say a series of efforts to *find again* something that one has lost. It is the novel of an existence in search of its essence.

> One is no longer a person. How then, seeking for one's mind, one's personality, as one seeks for a thing that is lost, does one recover one's own self rather than any other? . . . What is it that guides us, when there has been an actual interruption . . . ? There has indeed been death, as when the heart has ceased to beat and a rhythmical friction of the tongue revives us. . . . The resurrection at our awakening—after that healing attack of mental alienation which is sleep—must after all be similar to what occurs when we recapture a name, a line, a refrain that we had forgotten. And perhaps the resurrection of the soul after death is to be conceived as a phenomenon of memory.[13]

II

In Proustian thought memory plays the same supernatural role as grace in Christian thought. It is this inexplicable phenomenon that comes to apply itself to a fallen nature, irremediably separated from its origins, not to restore it integrally and at once to its first condition, but to give it the efficacy to find the highway of its salvation. Remembrance is a "succour from on high" which comes to the being in order "to draw him from the nothingness out of which, by himself, he would not have been able to emerge." Also it appears continually in the work of Proust under a form at once human and superhuman. It is at one and the same time an unforeseeable, "involuntary" thing that is added to the being, and the very act of this being, the most personal act because constitutive of the person. And, as there are some graces which fall on rich soil, and others on barren ground, some graces to which one responds and others which one ignores, so it is with memories. There are numerous examples in the work of Proust of these mysterious solicitations which a spirit distraught by its own ends fails to heed. More numerous still are those in which a debased memory finds itself reduced to being only a vassal of the intelligence or a sort of habit: grace corrupted, which then loses its efficacy and becomes a "frozen memory," a "memory of facts":

> . . . the memory of facts, which tells us: "You were such," without allowing us to become such again, which avers the reality of a lost paradise, instead of giving it back to us through remembrance.[14]

A memory no longer supernatural, a fallen memory by the will of which it is vain to hope to "re-establish ourselves in that state we were in," for we can do nothing by our own strength and our own will, and all depends from the first on supernatural chance.

But if it all depends from the first on this miraculous contingency, if it is this originally which is the first cause, it is not a unique cause; it calls for our collaboration; it exacts the maximum effort from us. The Proustian memory has often been identified with the affective memory of the psychologists. And—psychologically speaking—it is that without doubt: that is to say, a revival in us of a forgotten state of mind. Furthermore the very term *involuntary,* by which Proust qualifies it, seems to confirm this identification, since for the psychologist the affective memory is in the final analysis spontaneous and unforeseeable, the simple raising of old emotions up into the mind; a raising up in which the mind assists less as an actor than as a patient. But for Proust profound remembrance is not only that, something involuntarily undergone, but at its point of arrival in us something which is or which ought to be the point of departure for our spiritual action. It is an invitation, an appeal, which is addressed to all our being, and to which all our being ought to respond. It opens to us a road through the depths, but it is up to us to advance on that road. Paradise lost is returned to us if we wish it, but only if we wish it.

It is for that reason that there are in the Proustian novel so many examples of abortive memories and portions of the past ultimately lost. For that reason also there are many more memories which, brought to light, leave only, after the spectacle of their brief resurrection, the regret for a "paradise lost," lost for the second time. Just as for the Scholastics there was an infinity of degrees in the "perfection" of grace, so for Proust there is an infinity of degrees in the "perfection" of memory. But in his case each of these degrees is like that of one descending scale, and sometimes the being seems stopped at one level, sometimes a little lower, when what he seeks is away below. But most of the time "we lack the strength to penetrate to the very depths where truth lies, the real universe, our authentic impression."

Nothing could be more false than to consider Proust's novel a simple novel of the affective memory. That would be to confound it with the novels of Loti, each one of which—and from beginning to end—is a journal of such emotional encounters, mysterious wells, by which the soul should be able to penetrate to the depths of itself, but into which it is more often content simply to peer. And nothing could be more inexact than to make Proust the author of a purely psychological novel, in which everything is explained in the final analysis, as with Taine or Ribot, by the law of association of ideas. This would be to confound him with a writer of fiction like Bourget, who, moreover, wrote novels whose entire plots are articulated about a central phenomenon of affective memory.

From this point of view the most famous of all the passages of Proust, the episode of the madeleine, ought not at all to seem to us to have exhausted the meaning of the novel. It contains it without doubt, but it does not reveal it. Or rather, if it reveals something of it, it is precisely that the whole mystery lies beyond the psychological explanation of it: "I still did not know and must long postpone the discovery of *why* the memory made me happy."

The real significance of the episode of the madeleine resides entirely in precisely this: that it gives us a moment of happiness. To the unhappy instant with which the book began there now succeeds a happy instant, as if the grace of memory consisted in exchanging the one for the other. In the moment of awakening one sees the hero discover a nocturnal world, anguished, in which he knows neither who he is nor whether things are as they seem; in the moment of remembrance we watch him find himself in diurnal life, in the broad daylight of a Sunday morning of his childhood, surrounded by customary things, in a familiar time and place: "Everything that took *form and solidity* had sprung, town and gardens, from my cup of tea."

Form and solidity. If it is true then that remembrance is an exchange, it is also true that the moment exchanged has no longer the tragic inconsistency of what it replaces. It is a moment in which things have a form, in which they are solid, in which one knows what they are as well as one knows who one is. And it is such a moment because it represents this daily face of the life of child-hood, this *face of the sun,* in which things in full light offer their form and solidity to a being who addresses toward them his desire and his faith. Deep remembrance is only the return of a deep impression. Now if it appears to us so beautiful, if its return makes us so happy, that is because it expresses between the being who feels and the object felt a spontaneous accord in which the desire of the one meets with the solidity of the other; as if the external world were now precisely what we would desire it to be:

> For a desire seems to us more beautiful, we repose on it with more confidence, when we know that outside ourselves there is a reality which conforms to it, even if, for us, it is not to be realized.[15]

If reality conforms to it, then and only then, we can *believe in it* and not simply feel it. Thus the deep impressions are not merely impressions we are content to submit to, even in a repetitive fashion, but experiences in which we add something to what they bring us, namely the adherence of our *complete being,* that is to say, our love. Such a desire is experienced by Marcel for the milk-seller who passes along the length of the train:

> She passed down the line of windows, offering coffee and milk to a few awakened passengers. Reddened with the glow of morning, her face was rosier than the sky. I felt in her presence that desire to live which is reborn in us whenever we become conscious anew of beauty and happiness. . . . Alien to the models of beauty which my fancy was wont to sketch when I was by myself, this strapping girl gave me at once the sensation of a certain happiness (the sole form, al-ways individual, in which we may learn the sensation of happiness), of a happiness that would be realized by my staying by her side. . . . I was giving the milk-girl the benefit of what was really my own entire being, ready to taste the keenest joys . . . .[16]

> When we are young, at the age I had reached at the period of my walks along the Méséglise way, our desires, our faith bestow on a woman's clothing an individual personality, an irreducible essence.[17]

Desire and belief: terms almost interchangeable which express the two aspects of the same activity, an activity of all one's being. For just as the perfection of memory demands the conjunction of a given object and an effort of the mind, so that which is discovered deeper than memory, the primitive impression, contains for us a given object and a movement on our part to seize it. A movement which, insofar as it issues from the being, is called *desire,* and which insofar as it applies itself to and rests in the object is called *faith.*

In the depths of being, then, what comes to light is a moment of the past which is exactly the inverse of the present moment of awakening: a moment when, instead of being separated from things, and of not being sure whether they are themselves or other things, one is sure they are different from all others; and that because one now has the power to bind oneself to them, to confer upon them an individual particularity, an irreducible essence:

> Moreover—just as in moments of musing contemplation of nature, the normal actions of the mind being suspended, and our abstract ideas of things set on one side, we believe with profound faith in the originality, in the individual existence of the place in which we may happen to be—the passing figure which my desire evoked seemed to be not any one example of the general type of "woman," but a necessary and natural product of the soil. For at that time everything which was not myself, the earth and the creatures upon it, seemed to me more precious, more important, endowed with a more real existence than they appear to full-grown men. And between the earth and its creatures I made no distinction.[18]

If the primitive impression, then, is worthy of *faith,* that is because it involves a *moment* and a *place;* and not, as with the being of awakening, a moment which can be any moment, a place that can be any place; but a moment so well defined in time and space that it cannot be confounded with any other, and of so great an authenticity that we cannot doubt it. Extreme depth where truth lies, little universe having its own particular time and place in which our *authentic impression* rediscovers itself in its lost reality, thanks to memory:

> What I had long lost, the feeling which makes us not merely regard a thing as a spectacle, but believe in it as in a creature without parallel . . . .[19]

What was lost and what is found is not just time, but a fragment of time to which clings a fragment of space; and in the interior of this small universe, the self, the individual is indivisibly bound by its faith and its desire to this moment of time and to this point in space. From a feeling of existence detached from times and places, the being finds himself brought back by deep remembrance to a first feeling, truly original, constituent of himself and of the world, the act of faith by which the sentient being adheres instantaneously, locally, to sensible reality.

In bringing us back thus, across the past, to a primitive impression, Proust reminds us of Condillac: "The only means of acquiring knowledge," Condillac says, "is to go back to the origin of our ideas, to follow the generation of them, and to compare them . . . ." But if Proust goes back to the origin, it is not by analysis and a taking of things apart, but by a synthetic intuition—remembrance—because it is not for him a question of arriving at a simple entity, but at a primitive complex which analysis would irremediably lose.

It is rather to Rousseau that he must be compared. For the one, as for the other, at bottom, at the origin, there is a natural identity between the feeling self and the thing felt. But with Rousseau identity is posed simply as such; with Proust, on the contrary, it appears as proposed rather than given; it must be achieved in a movement of the self toward the object and culminate in belief:

> For this is the point to which we must always return, to these beliefs with which most of the time we are quite unconsciously filled, but which for all that are of more importance to our happiness than is the average person whom we see, for it is through them that we see him, it is they that impart his transitory grandeur to the person seen.[20]

Only a transitory grandeur, to be sure, as happens with all correspondences between him who regards and that which is regarded; but an imperishable grandeur as well, because the object thus transfigured by belief, detached by the very fact of the general motion of things and the flux of duration, leaves upon the mind of him who *believed in it* an indelible image. The image *will be found again*. In the midst of a magic-lantern world, a vacillating unreal world made of "doubtful visions" in which one cannot believe, the awakened sleeper, if he remembers, will find once more in the depths of his memory, in his first impressions, this *passing grandeur* which an act of childlike faith has fixed in him forever.

III

The scent of hawthorn which strays plundering along the hedge from which, in a little while, the dog-roses will have banished it, a sound of footsteps followed by no echo, upon the gravel path, a bubble formed at the side of a waterplant by the current, and formed only to burst—my exaltation of mind has borne them with it, and has succeeded in making them traverse all these successive years, while all around them the once-trodden ways have vanished, while those who trod them, and even the memory of those who trod them, are dead. Sometimes the fragment of landscape thus transported into the present will detach itself in such isolation from all associations that it floats uncertainly upon my mind, like a flowering isle of Delos, and I am unable to say from what place, from what time— perhaps, quite simply, from which of my dreams—it comes. But it is pre-eminently as the deepest layer of my mental soil, as firm sites on which I still may build, that I regard the Méséglise and Guermantes "ways." It is because I used to think of certain things, of certain people, while I was roaming along them, that the things, the people which they taught me to know, and these alone, I still take seriously, still give me joy. Whether it be that the faith which creates has ceased to exist in me, or that reality will take shape in memory alone, the flowers that people show nowadays for the first time never seem to me to be true flowers.[21]

In this sort of nothingness or of night, which extends behind him, deep down within him, and which is called the past, the being in search of himself has now discovered certain luminous points isolated; pieces of landscape, fragments of his former life which survive the destruction of all the rest. Behind him is no longer total nothingness but a star-lighted nothingness. Doubtless because of their isolation, their remoteness, these vestiges of the past appear today to be without force. Nevertheless, as in the astrology of the Middle Ages, it is owing to them alone and to their influence that the living being can hope for the support of his own personality and for the power to confer some reality upon the world which offers itself to his eyes today. For he no longer possesses the efficacy of belief and desire to adhere strongly to things. He has "ceased to believe in the truth of the desires directed outside of himself" which he continues to form.

Without renouncing these desires, he has ceased to think them realizable. He has no more hope in the future, and he no longer enjoys the present. From the time of his youth, Proust verified this detachment from desire and this drying up of faith:

> Even the disinterested joys of hope are not left any more to us. Hope is an act of faith. We have undeceived its credulousness; it is dead. After having renounced enjoyment, we cannot any more be enchanted with hope. To hope without hope, which would be wise, is impossible.[22]

And later, in a letter to Princess Bibesco:

> Alexander is right when he says that to cease hoping is despair itself. But though I never cease to desire, I never hope. Perhaps also the great austerity of my life, without journeys, without walks, without company, without sunlight, is a contingency which renews in me the perenniality of desire.[23]

Perennial desire, but without hope in the future as without faith in the present. Proustian desire, then, can *hope,* hope to find an object of faith, only in looking backwards. He comes to "hope without hope," wisdom of the impossible. As in the Kierkegaardian repetition, Proust ends by no longer placing hope in anything except the past. And what can he hope from the past except to be re-established in his faith?

This restoration of faith is memory—ephemeral faith, doubtless, and one which lasts for him only for the instant in which he remembers; *but* for as long as it does last, the being who remembers finds he has become once more a being who once had faith. The immense force, the living force of these small luminous fires he has rediscovered, rises from the depths of an obscure firmament where their rays reside and lengthen, extending their splendor and warmth into the present moment. It is in them alone that he can hope for a reality and a resting place. The being is sustained, from underneath, by a faith he no longer possesses. There is a sort of continued creation of himself, of the being one is by the being one has been, of the moment in which one recollects by the moment that one recollects; the Proustian existence is an existence which always risks destruction or decay, unless it be supported and ravished by the grace of memory.

> . . . We do not believe in the beauty of life because we do not remember it, but if perchance we smell an old fragrance, we feel elated; likewise we think we no longer love the dead, but this is be-

cause we do not remember them; if once again we see an old glove, we dissolve in tears, upheld by a grace or a flower stalk of remembrance.[24]

Like Christian grace, Proustian reminiscence is truly represented under the form of a *flower stalk,* but the essential point is that here the action of this support is exerted not from top to bottom but from bottom to top. That is the reason Proust employs the expression *basement* (*soubassement*) and *deep layer* (*gisement profond*), and also *supporting terrains on which one has to lean* (*terrains résistants sur lesquels on s'appuie*). In the Proustian world, it is not God, it is simply the past which confers on the present its authentic existence. It is *the already lived* that saves *the living;* otherwise it would fall into the insignificance of oblivion, even before being *lived.*

But in order for this past to be indeed the continuer of the self and the founder of an authentic present, in order for it to be the source of our restored faith, will it not seem necessary that *in its time* it had been invested by us with the power which it now exerts over us? It seems that only the memory of a moment of faith can create a new moment of faith. Or should, then, the being who remembers find himself forced to go back from memory to memory in search of a creative moment, as philosophy strove to proceed from cause to cause until it reached a creative cause?

Let us recall, however, the alternative formulated by Proust in the citation which opens this chapter: "Whether it be that the faith which creates dries up in me, or whether it be that reality forms itself only in memory . . . ." Alongside the moment of primal faith there would be then another source of present reality, a source that cannot be assigned either to the single original moment or to the single actual moment, but that would be found *between the two,* in the memory:

> We make little use of our experience, we leave unachieved in the summer dusk or the precocious nights of winter the hours in which it had seemed to us that there might nevertheless be contained some element of tranquillity or pleasure. But those hours are not altogether lost. When, in their turn, come and sing to us fresh moments of pleasure which by themselves would pass by equally slender and linear, the others bring to them the groundwork, the solid consistency of a rich orchestration.[25]

Moments unachieved in their time, slender and linear, which seemed, however, to give the present a consistence, a reality that they themselves did not possess.

But if this is so—and it is so throughout the Proustian novel—the preceding theory becomes, if not false, at least insufficient. It is not necessarily in a moment of early faith that the being finds his creative foundation, since memory can join to a slender present an unachieved past, and their conjunction can bring to birth something that is achieved and that is consistent.

On the other hand, there would no longer be only certain privileged moments of the past which could have the chance of being saved from oblivion. Any moment could be regained, or better, brought to significance. There is no sensation, puny as it may be, which has not a chance to see the light again and find its completion in the present; as if, the interval of years being nothing, or equal simply to a brief distraction of the mind, this could, almost without solution of continuity, reassume the impression it had formerly left and bring to it now the complement it lacked.

But what is the nature of the complement? Assuredly it is not at all a question here of affective memory, but of an act authentically new by which the mind operates upon remembrance, as earlier, in infancy, it operated upon the first impression. One might call it an act of faith indefinitely retarded, then tardily accomplished; as if the reality regained in memory appeared richer in import, worthier of faith than it was lately in sensation. This is the invariable experience the Proustian novel gives us. For the adult being, there is something incurably imperfect in the present, something impure in exterior perception, which leaves the perceiver indifferent and incapable of believing in it; but let this present become past, let this perception become memory, and immediately, with the same energy as the child in its act of faith, the adult adheres to this memory.

Faith centers in an impression that is immediate, or regained, or completed. Proustian thought always inevitably returns to the mystery of the relation between an object and a consciousness. It all comes finally to this question: how can an exterior object be transmuted into this interior and immaterial thing, as intimate to us as ourselves, in which the mind freely plunges, moves, takes delight and life?

But in immediate impression we know how rare and difficult this
spiritualization of the object can be. The object is the thing which
is there. Flower, tree, or church, steeples of Martinville or bushes
of hawthorn, the thing is there, outside, in its existence as thing. To
look at it is to feel oneself joined to it only by a sensation which
attests less its reality than its absolute otherness. How shall we
penetrate it or draw it into ourselves when we have no affinity
with it other than a sensation which we are well enough able to
intensify and to repeat but not to transcend? And yet already this
very sensation invites us to do so. It gives us the further presentiment of something it does not communicate to us, but of which it
makes us divine the existence. It prompts our desire. We feel confusedly called to discover in a prolongation of sensation we know
not what secret:

> . . . Suddenly a roof, a gleam of sunlight reflected from a stone,
> the smell of a road would make me stop still, to enjoy the special
> pleasure that each of them gave me, and also because they appeared
> to be concealing, beneath what my eyes could see, something which
> they invited me to approach and seize from them, but which, de-
> spite all my efforts, I never managed to discover.[26]

It is the same in one of the most famous passages of the novel, the
episode of the hawthorns. Before the flowering hawthorns the child
on his walk experiences in the contact of the sensation the same
feeling of pleasure and expectation. But this time, twice over, and
in two quite distinct fashions, the sentient being leaps over the frontier of what is felt, and, going on beyond the sensation, penetrates
into the mysterious intimacy of the object. The first occasion is
when, in the exaltation into which the beauty of the flowering bush
throws him, he is no longer content to feel this beauty; he tries unconsciously to reproduce it in himself:

> Higher up their corollas were opening, keeping around them so
> negligently, like a last vaporous garment, the nosegay of stamens
> which so entirely enveloped them with the mist, that when I tried to
> mime in the depths of my mind the gesture of their efflorescence, I
> fancied it, without being aware of the process, the flighty motions
> of a thoughtless and vivacious young girl.[27]

Marvelous image, and so significant that Proust takes and uses it
for the title of one part of his novel: *A l'ombre des jeunes filles en
fleur*. For the meaning of this image does not consist simply in its

exactitude, in the felicity with which it translates what it describes; but also in the visible motion of the mind which brings it to its existence and its perfection of image. It seems here that one comes upon the spiritual operation ordinarily the most hidden, even from the eyes of him who performs it: the operation by which, *in miming within his own depths the exterior gesture of the sensible object,* one *imagines,* one creates something which is still the object of sense, but this time no longer outside: rather, it is on the inside, no longer strange and impenetrable, but recognizable, identifiable: for this thing comes of us; it is us.

It seems that here we are assisting at the very genesis of an image: an image so perfect that surely the mind has, in this moment, accomplished the task incumbent upon it, even without clearly perceiving its nature. It has accomplished it, not without effort, but without realization, almost inadvertently; and not having recognized that it has found what it sought, it continues to search.

It is then that the second spiritual operation is accomplished. While the child remains in contemplation before the flowers, someone calls him and shows him a little farther on some other hawthorns, but this time of a different color, no longer white but pink:

> Then, inspiring me with that rapture which we feel on seeing a work by our favourite painter quite different from those that we already know, or, better still, when someone has taken us and set us down in front of a picture of which we have hitherto seen no more than a pencilled sketch, or when a piece of music which we have heard played over on the piano bursts out again in our ears with all the splendour and fullness of an orchestra, my grandfather called me to him, and, pointing to the hedge of Tansonville, said: "You are fond of hawthorns; just look at this pink one; isn't it pretty!" And it was indeed a hawthorn, but one whose flowers were pink, and lovelier even than the white.[28]

Between the instant in which the child sees the white flowers and the one in which he catches sight of the pink, there is, so to speak, no transition; nevertheless, the first is the moment of a past sensation, and the other of a present sensation. The one achieves and crowns the other; it is not the repetition but the transfiguration of it. Hence the child's joy, a joy of a very particular kind, and one which the Proustian character experiences continually in the course of the novel. It is the joy of Swann, finding again in the visage of a

servant the traits of a person contemplated some time before; that
of Marcel in discovering in the Septuor of Vinteuil the little phrase
of the Sonata. It is the joy that one always feels when one perceives under the variations of a "common type" a "same palpable
quality," when one *recognizes* in what he feels something he recalls
having felt before. To recognize is to identify; and to identify is to
find an equivalent between what is there, outside, and on the
other hand what is here, inside, within ourselves, since it is *our*
memory.

In the passage on the hawthorns Proust indicated the two ways
of going beyond the external object: sometimes by a direct effort
which in making us mime interiorly the motion of the object gives
us the "spiritual equivalent" of it—and it is an act of pure imagination; and sometimes by finding and recognizing this same equivalence in the depths of ourselves—and this is the peculiar act of
memory.

"All impression," says Proust, "is double: half enveloped in the
object, and half produced in ourself . . . ." But usually we pay
attention only to the exterior part of the impression, which teaches
us nothing of its nature or of ourselves. But when by an act of the
imagination or of memory we extricate this interior part which is
truly ours, then this "pure and disincarnate" essence withdraws
from the exterior object, and also then from the ensemble of temporal contingencies in which its place is assigned as in a series;
it no longer appears a determination of things, but as a free pro-
duction of our mind. For the act of imagination or of memory is
nothing other than that: to oppose to the exterior perception an
image which might be our own creation; to raise up the impression
into an expression; to find the *metaphor*. Such is the spiritual effort
every tangible object demands of us.

We hear this immediate and urgent demand every moment of
our lives, but nearly always we prefer easier tasks. It now and
then happens, however, that in renouncing for some banal occupation this duty which present sensation incessantly proposes to us,
we experience a kind of remorse, the remorse of having at the
same time renounced ourselves, of having failed to bring to the
light of day this being which is us, and which only exists and is
recognized in the creative act of the making of images. Thus, when,
on a road near Balbec, Proust withdraws from the three trees that

have addressed him in vain with one of those mysterious solicitations, he seems to hear them say:

> "If you allow us to drop back into the hollow of this road from which we sought to raise ourselves up to you, a whole part of yourself which we were bringing to you, will fall forever into the abyss." [29]

Again, when in *Les plaisirs et les jours* a poet who was giving a banquet refuses to extend hospitality to a stranger passing by because this wayfarer enjoined the dismissal of all the other guests, he sees the stranger withdraw saying:

> "You will see me no more. Yet you owed me more than you owed to the others who presently will desert you. I am in you, yet forever I am far from you, I am almost no more. I am your soul, I am you." [30]

Thus, almost always we allow a part of ourselves to be removed or to fall into nothingness: precisely that part of us which should have been created or recreated in the present moment. It is *given* us that we may make of it our substance. But we almost never do so, and for not having done so we lose our present existence.

On the other hand, we may also happen to lose it for the contrary reason: not because we have neglected sensation, but because we have allowed ourselves to be absorbed by it. So it is in the state of drunkenness:

> . . . The alcohol that I had drunk, by unduly straining my nerves, gave to the minutes as they came a quality, a charm which did not have the result of leaving me more ready, or indeed more resolute to defend them; for while it made me prefer them a thousand times to anything else in my life, my exaltation made me isolate them from everything else; I was confined to the present, as heroes are, or drunkards; eclipsed for the moment, my past no longer projected before me that shadow of itself which we call our future; placing the goal of my life no longer in the realization of the dreams of that past, but in the felicity of the present moment, I could see nothing now of what lay beyond it. . . . I was glued to my immediate sensation . . . .[31]

Glued, that is to say, making a lump with the thing felt. Then it alone exists without possibility of equivalence. Its presence abolishes all the rest. There is no longer any past, no longer any future, no longer even that sort of distance which in the interior of the moment the mind tries to establish between the sensation it experiences and the act by which it is conscious. The sentient subject has become what he feels. He has excluded himself from himself. Outward, in the object, he lives an intense, euphoric, but entirely passive life. Instead of transcending the object, he is engulfed in it.

State of pure passion, of brute sensation, which is the very opposite of the creative activity by which the imagination re-invents the object in the self.

Whether it adheres too closely to the tangible object, or whether on the contrary it neglects it, Proustian thought succeeds very rarely in finding at once the metaphoric equivalent. In contrast to Hugo or Rimbaud, Proust hardly ever finds, on the spot, a corresponding image. Or, let us say, the image does not seem chosen by him with this characteristic of sovereign liberty which is precisely the property of invention. It sometimes happens, however, that, in a certain state of mind, confronted by such and such a sensation, the Proustian being somehow spontaneously forms the equivalent image. Thus Swann, amorous of Odette, hears the Little Phrase of Vinteuil's sonata, and as this little phrase has the effect of effacing his anxiety over material interests and so of creating in his soul a sort of margin, he finds himself *free* to inscribe upon it the name of his love.

Now this margin is precisely what time and forgetfulness produce in us. Between the reborn memory and the being we now are, before recognition, before the identification of the one by the other which memory achieves, there is this: the consciousness of a margin, a distance; and this margin appears in the interior region where one has ordinarily the feeling of being determined by causes or series of causes, of being the prisoner of time:

> . . . Between our present state and the memory that suddenly comes back to us . . . there is such a wide distance that that fact alone, regardless even of any specific individuality, would suffice to make comparison between them impossible. Yet, if, thanks to our ability to forget, a past recollection has been able to avoid any tie, any link with the present moment, if it has kept its distance, its isolation in the depths of a valley or on the tip of a mountain peak, it suddenly brings us a breath of fresh air—refreshing just because we have breathed it once before—of that purer air . . . which could not convey that profound sensation of renewal if it had not already been

breathed; for the only true paradise is always the paradise we have lost.[32]

A single minute released from the chronological order of time has recreated in us the human being similarly released, in order that he may sense that minute.[33]

Because the sensation which comes back to us, and from so great a distance, is not bound to the temporal motion which actually sweeps us along, we find ourselves for an instant detached from this current. We cease "to feel mediocre, contingent, mortal"; we feel *free:* free to determine ourselves; free to recognize ourselves in what we were; free to establish the metaphoric relationship between our past and our present.

Sometimes, however, this relationship remains merely an outline within us. Memory, then, appears to be no more than a kind of negative; beyond the feeling of this margin which is created within us, we simply know that there is something we are unable to read. Of past and present only the latter shows itself clearly upon the field of consciousness, and yet between the two one still feels there is already an invisible affinity formed which one would like to be able to identify. Such is the phenomenon of the *already seen* that one finds in every degree in the work of Proust. Sometimes the mind experiences it in the vaguest degree, and then it wonders and worries, searching vainly within itself for a corresponding image.

Sometimes the mind, in approaching from a new angle a world once upon a time familiar, discovers the known in the unknown, and, after a moment of hesitation, sees surge unexpected and assuaging from the depths of memory the sensory equivalent. And then sometimes at the call of the present object it seems to spring complete, without effort, as if the silent work of memory had been precisely to prepare for this meeting, and then the sole duty of the mind is to *recognize* this identity of the past and the actual, and to recognize itself within it:

The concert began. I did not know what they were playing, I found myself in a strange land. Where was I to locate it? Into what composer's country had I come? I should have been glad to know, and seeing nobody near me whom I might question, I should have liked to be a character in those *Arabian Nights* which I never tired of reading and in which, in moments of uncertainty, there arose a genie or a maiden of ravishing beauty, invisible to every one else but not to the embarrassed hero to whom she reveals exactly what he wishes to learn. Well, at this very moment, I was favoured with precisely such a magical apparition. As, in a stretch of country which we suppose to be strange to us and which as a matter of fact we have approached from a new angle, when after turning out of one road we find ourselves emerging suddenly upon another every inch of which is familiar . . . so, all of a sudden, I found myself in the midst of this music that was novel to me, right in the heart of Vinteuil's sonata.[34]

Now to recognize oneself in a place, in a piece of music, in a sensation, is more than to regain this sensation; it is to rediscover there one's own being. A passive memory has no more meaning than a brute sensation for Proust. Neither the one nor the other has anything to communicate except its obscure sensible reality. Neither the one nor the other by itself can raise the being to the expression of what it really is. The thought in search of itself glides over the sensation as over a smooth and impenetrable surface. It cannot rest there any more than it can found itself on an abstract memory of what it once was. For what has one been except what one has felt, and how shall there be any recognition unless one feels it anew? Perhaps the greatest difficulty of the Proustian enterprise consists in the fact that for him knowledge can never cease to remain impression. It is possible to know only that which can once more become immediately contemporaneous to the heart. Now "knowledge in these matters being intermittent and incapable of surviving the effective presence of feeling," the result is that for Proustian thought the *knowing* as well as the *being* finds itself bound to a world essentially ephemeral and intermittent, the very affective or emotional world in which Maine de Biran had given up trying to find permanence and identities. It seems that the mind is caught in a dilemma: either of knowing nothing but what it feels, or of recalling it has felt without recalling how it has felt. In both cases it is condemned never to attain its being.

The only cognition of self that is possible, then, is re-cognition. When at the call of present sensation past sensation resurges, the relationship established lays the foundation of the self because it lays the foundation of its own cognition. The being one recognizes as having lived becomes the basis of the being one feels to be alive. The veritable being, the essential being, is he whom one recognizes, not in the past, nor in the present, but in the rapport which binds past and present together, that is to say *between the two:*

> . . . The person within me who was at that moment enjoying this impression enjoyed in it the qualities it possessed which were common to both an earlier day and the present moment, qualities which were independent of all considerations of time; and this person came into play only when, by this process of identifying the past with the present, he could find himself in the only environment in which he could live and enjoy the essence of things, that is to say, outside time.[35]

At this point the dialectic of being ends in Proust. One sees the whole length of the road it has traveled. Emerging from sleep, the awakened sleeper was first discovered empty of his past, without content, without connection with vacillating sensations, himself metamorphosable, unknowable, plaything of time and death. Then, by the grace of profound remembrance, certain impressions of a totally different species surged up within him. These seemed to affirm the existence of a world of specific things, and to each of these things there was attached the action of a being who put his faith in them, and who found his reality in this act. But this being was infinitely remote; he re-found himself only after an intermittent and fortuitous fashion. His strength of faith, the source of his true existence, was exhausted. He was the being that had been; he was also the being that was no longer.

Now besides these rare reviviscences of a being forever vanished, others are discovered, less total but more numerous, more frequent, each one bringing to light a former sensation. Between this regained sensation and the present sensation there is established a relationship of the same nature as that between the faith of the child and the object of his belief; and from this metaphoric relationship between two impressions there has finally surged up the self; not a present self, without content, at the disposal of time and death; and not a past self, lost, and hardly retrievable; but an essential self, liberated from time and contingency, a primal and perpetual being, the creator of itself, the author of an "eternal song immediately recognized":

> . . . that peculiar strain, the monotony of which—for whatever its subject it remains identical in itself—proves the permanence of the elements that compose his soul.[36]

It is thus that, leaving the moment and having made an immense voyage across lost time, the existence traveling in search of its essence finds it in timelessness.

IV

The Proustian novel began with a moment *empty of all content.* It completes itself in a series of other moments as different from the first as can be, since they contain "certain impressions veritably *full,* those which are outside of time." Nevertheless the quest of the novel is still not entirely accomplished. Embarked upon the search for lost time, the Proustian being has found two things: certain moments; and a kind of eternity. But he has not regained time itself. Doubtless in a certain measure he has conquered time:

> . . . A profound idea which succeeded in enclosing within itself space and time, is not any more submitted to their tyranny and cannot perish.[37]

But if, thanks to the metaphoric operation of memory, the mind has escaped the tyranny of time as well as of space, the time and space that it has enclosed in this profound idea are only the time and space of a moment recaptured. A moment, it is true, of an extraordinary profusion and one which, as in Baudelaire, seems to be due to a power of infinite expansion: "An hour is not merely an hour. It is a vase filled with perfumes, sounds, plans and climates." [38] But this vase is similar to those spoken of in the *Thousand and One Nights,* which Proust made one of his favorite readings: when one uncorks them, a genie floats out capable of condensing or dilating itself indefinitely. Each moment is one of these vases, and each moment has its distinct genie:

> . . . The most insignificant gesture, the simplest act remains enclosed, as it were, in a thousand sealed jars, each filled with things of an absolutely different colour, odour and temperature. Furthermore, these jars, ranged along all levels of our bygone years—years during which we have been constantly changing, if only in our dreams and thoughts—stand at different altitudes and give us the impression of strangely varied atmospheres.[39]

Closed vases, walling in their particular and mutually exclusive qualities, the diverse moments of time are like places in space which cannot be simultaneously traveled:

. . . The habit we had of never going both ways on the same day, or in the course of the same walk, but the "Méséglise way" one time and the "Guermantes way" another, shut them up, so to speak, far apart and unaware of each other's existence, in the sealed vessels— between which there could be no communication—of separate afternoons.[40]

"Imprisoned in the cell of distinct days," regained moments are then not a true duration but, so to speak, atoms of full time, swimming far from each other in a sort of open, empty time, a nothingness of oblivion. From there, intermittently, their fires flash upon us.

Thus nothing is more false than to compare Proustian duration to Bergsonian duration. The latter is full, the former empty; the latter is a continuity, the former a discontinuity:

. . . We live over our past years not in their continuous sequence, day by day, but in a memory that fastens upon the coolness or sun-parched heat of some morning or afternoon, receiving the shadow of some solitary place, enclosed, immovable, arrested, lost, remote from all others . . . .[41]

What we suppose to be our love, our jealousy, are, neither of them, single, continuous and individual passions. They are composed of an infinity of successive loves, of different jealousies, each of which is ephemeral, although by their uninterrupted multitude they give us the impression of continuity, the illusion of unity.[42]

Nothing could be less Bergsonian than these passages. Far from being as Bergson wished it, a *"continuité mélodique,"* human duration in Proust's eyes is a simple plurality of isolated moments, remote from each other. But, as Proust himself remarked, the difference in nature between these two durations necessarily entails an equal difference in the ways by which the mind must proceed to explore them. It is as an easy and gentle gliding backwards that Bergson conceives the search for lost time. Loosening itself in the course of a reverie, the mind allows itself insensibly to be merged into a past whose liquid and dense substance never stops pressing in gently from all sides. For Proust, on the contrary, the exploration of the past seems at the outset so tremendously difficult of achievement that it requires nothing less than the intervention of a special grace and the maximum effort on the part of him who is the subject. Thus aided, thought must first pierce or dissipate that

whole zone of deceitful appearances which is the time of the intelligence and of the habits, chronological time, in which conventional memory disposes all that it thinks to conserve, in a rectilinear
order that masks in each case its nonentity; then, having dispersed
these phantoms, it must face the true nothingness, that of oblivion:

> Memory . . . nothingness out of which, from time to time, a
> similitude lets us draw, resuscitated, dead remembrances.

"Immense patches of oblivion," negative time, pure absence,
place of nonbeing, whose sight brings vertigo, and across whose
emptiness, in order to land upon some lost island, one must leap.

Time vertiginously traveled, time of a fall. With no intermediary
stage, the being fallen from the present moment is in time past.
Nevertheless, the being that has traveled these spaces with such
lightning speed has felt the depths of them:

> I can measure the resistance, I can hear the echo of great spaces
> traversed . . . .[43]

> . . . resisting softness of this interposed atmosphere which has the
> same expanse as our life and which is the whole poetry of memory.[44]

In discovering the strange time-mutation which in a flash it has
achieved, the mind measures "the abyss of the difference in alti-
tude." And the consciousness of this temporal distance, the contrast
of epochs at once linked and separated from each other by all this
emptiness, finally and especially the feeling that between them
there is established something analogous to spatial perspective,
all that ends by transforming this negative time, this pure nonbeing, into a palpable appearance, and into a dimension:

> This dimension of Time . . . I would try to make continually
> perceptible in a transcription of human life necessarily very different
> from that conveyed by our deceptive senses.[45]

Thus, little by little, Proustian time is constructed into an entity
at once spiritual and tangible, made of relations of moments which
are infinitely remote from each other but which, nevertheless, in
spite of their isolation and their fragmentary character, stud with
their presences the depth of temporal space and render it visible
by their shining multiplicity.

Already more concrete than vacant time, another form of time
now appears which is constituted by the incoherent and diverse

ensemble of all the moments the mind remembers. For the being who recollects himself does not discover his life in the form of a continuous thread along which one passes insensibly from the similar to the dissimilar; but on the contrary one discovers it under the aspect of a perpetual and radical dissimilarity of all the elements composing it. Life which is not a life, time which is hardly a time: "simple collection of moments," each of which occupies a particular and variable position with respect to all the others, in such a way that in this time of plurality the problem consists in constantly trying to reunite these universes, these modes of feeling, and of living so mutually exclusive. Moreover, like the stars in the sky, these universes do not remain immobile, fixed in a static order, by aid of which one could construct a chronology. They disappear and reappear. Sometimes they seem monstrously remote, sometimes miraculously near. A vast, essentially erratic motion, the activity of memory, guides them along paths it is impossible for the mind to determine.

Thus time appears to the eyes of Proust as a thing of exclusions and resurrections, of fragments and spaces between fragments, of eclipses and anachronisms; a time fundamentally anarchic and, since to regain it at one point is not to regain it at another, a time *unregainable,* perhaps permanently lost to the mind.

As early as the period of *Les plaisirs et les jours* Proust had already given an expression to this feeling of spiritual powerlessness which among all our thoughts that of time makes us most painfully experience:

> His only sorrow was not to be able to reach immediately all the sites which were disposed here and there, far from him, in the infinity of his own perspective.[46]

And yet is it not with concrete time as with concrete places? If space also, at first—just as erroneously as time—is taken for a continuum whose simultaneous spread seems to be easily understandable, does it not reveal itself later on as a plurality of *aspects* which are mutually exclusive? Space then would be really only an ensemble of points of view each of which could be discovered only in its turn amidst successive perspectives. And yet does not its real signification consist in the totality of these perspectives, as in those cubist paintings in which the painter tries to give at one and the same time all those aspects of an object which one could ordinarily discover in it only by viewing it turn by turn from different angles? And is it not properly the role of time to surmount this reciprocal exclusiveness of points of view which is the property of space? The spires of Martinville, for example, appearing first in front of an immobile spectator, in the depth of an immutable perspective, grant an aspect only "episodic and momentary"; but when they find themselves engaged by the displacement of the spectator in an inverse motion, they enter, by the simple, successive changing of their lines, into an entirely different universe; a universe that is no longer one in which the three dimensions of space compose an episodic and momentary totality, but a universe in which the fourth dimension, that of time, divests the object of all that is episodic and momentary in order to bestow *all* of its aspects upon a spectator moving at once in space and in time. Thus this sunrise perceived through the windows of a moving train:

> . . . I was lamenting the loss of my strip of pink sky when I caught sight of it afresh, but red this time, in the opposite window which it left at a second bend in the line, so that I spent my time running from one window to the other to reassemble, to collect on a single canvas the intermittent antipodean fragments of my fine scarlet, ever-changing morning, and to obtain a comprehensive view of it and a continuous picture.[47]

Time, then, is like a fourth dimension which in combining with the other three perfects space, assembling together and providing a new canvas for those opposed fragments, enclosing in a veritable continuity a totality which otherwise would remain irremediably dispersed. Seen through the perspective of time, space is set free, transcended.

But can anything do for time what time can do for space? Is time in itself a place of nonsimultaneities, of reciprocal exclusions, incapable of unification by a supra-temporal action which would allow us to possess all its successive aspects simultaneously? Are the Méséglise Way and the Guermantes Way consigned irremediably to be forever sealed in the closed vases of different afternoons?

But, as we have seen, there is such a supra-temporal action: it is the metaphoric action of memory. Between times, between "intermittent and opposite qualities," the mind is found capable of establishing those rapports which are now no longer negative rap-

ports. Between the regained moments of its existence the mind discovers identities; it finds in each of them a common root, its own
essence. Applying this timeless presence, by means of art, to the
entirety of existence, it is transported to a high place where all the
temporal horizon is seen to rise tier on tier. Thus at the beginning
of the novel, when the Méséglise Way and the Guermantes Way
seem entirely and forever separated, a phrase of the parish priest
of Combray gives presage of a day when they will be united. For
from the top of the steeple, he says, "one encompasses at once
things he can habitually see only one by one." This is the characteristic of metaphoric memory. It is the steeple which surmounts
temporal extension, but which, in dominating it, far from abolishing
it, gives it its completion. Time is truly achieved only if it is
crowned by eternity. This human eternity, seized by the being in
the possession of his essence, permits him retrospectively to contemplate beneath him that very time, his temporal being, formed of
different levels of which each constitutes a stratum. A time which
now seems to him singularly positive, an architecture. This musical
architecture brings him sounds emanating from different parts of
the edifice. As in the thought of Joubert, Proustian time expresses
a music made of a spray of themes, each one of which remains distinct and constitutes a being, the ensemble of which is a *sum total:*
"a plenitude of music, made complete, in effect, by so many various
musics, each one a being."

Time regained is time transcended.

On the one hand, then, the Proustian novel seems to be a novel
without duration. A being awakens in a moment of dearth which is
replaced by a moment of plenitude—such plenitude that an immense meditation cannot suffice to exhaust its meaning. But within
it, in the instant when it is accomplished, as in the *Cogito* of
Descartes, everything is contained. Everything proceeds from one
instant, from one cup of tea.

On the other hand, the novel of Proust seems, in the manner of
other novels, to embrace the duration of an existence. But this
existence is a retrospective existence. It is not a unity advancing into
the future. It is an "ulterior unity found between fragments which
are simply to be joined." It is from a preliminary plurality that it
gently disengages itself and always under the form of a retrograde

perspective which is found behind one, when one advances in the work, so to speak, backwards. For there is not a line in the book which does not purposely "provide the reader with an improvised memory" and produce in him the repeated and tardily meaningful memory of what he has already read. Everything is disposed under the form of recalls, so that the entire book is one immense "resonance box."

Resonance box in which are perceived not only the *times* of an individual existence and the *timeless* traits of a particular spirit; but where retrospectively are found also all the *times* of French thought, to its origins. For this being which awakens in a naked moment, like the being in Valéry, is going to immerse itself in the past, in the temporal depth of which Baudelaire sang, and for which Romanticism has had such a deep longing. If in the depths it regains the primitive impression, it is, like eighteenth-century thought, in order to grasp hold of itself in sensation and in the instantaneous. But it cannot equate itself with sensation, and, in spite of all, its being affirms itself essentially, not as an impression, but as a consciousness perpetually creating its moments of thought. A being always recreated, always re-found and always re-lost, as the human being is in all thought since Descartes, depending also on a precarious grace, as does the human being in all religious thought whether of the Reformation or of the Counter-Reformation, the Proustian being in the final count attains to this total structure of itself which human existence had lost after the Middle Ages. Like the vast *Summae* which were erected then, all is simultaneously discovered here on the different levels which are the tiers of time. And so the work of Proust appears as a retrospective view of all French thought on time, unfolding in time, like the church of Combray, its nave.

NOTES

[1] I, 5. The translated passages from *À la recherche du temps perdu* are those of C. K. Scott-Moncrieff, *Remembrance of Things Past* (2 vols.; New York: Random House, 1927–32), with a few changes. Permission to use these passages has been granted by Random House, for which we would like to express our appreciation.

[2] *Ibid.*, II, 464.

[3] *Ibid.*, p. 271.

[4] *Ibid.*, I, 5.

[5] *Ibid.*, p. 617.

[6] *Ibid.*, p. 8.

[7] *Ibid.*, p. 506.

[8] *Ibid.*, p. 510.

[9] *Lettre à Nathalie Clifford Barney*, N. C. Barney, *Adventures de l'esprit*, p. 65.

[10] *Lettre à G. de Lauris*, *Revue de Paris*, June 15, 1938.

[11] *Remembrance of Things Past*, II, 833.

[12] *Ibid.,* I, 510.
[13] *Ibid.,* p. 776.
[14] *Pastiches et mélanges,* p. 197.
[15] *Remembrance of Things Past,* I, 539.
[16] *Ibid.,* p. 498.
[17] *Ibid.,* p. 994.
[18] *Ibid.,* p. 146.
[19] *Ibid.,* p. 50.
[20] *Ibid.,* p. 708.
[21] *Ibid.,* p. 141.
[22] *Les plaisirs et les jours,* p. 232.
[23] *Cahiers Marcel Proust,* No. 4, p. 119.
[24] *Lettres à René Blum,* Bernard Grasset, Louis Brun, p. 61.
[25] *Remembrance of Things Past,* I, 1002.
[26] *Ibid.,* p. 137.
[27] *Chroniques,* p. 93.
[28] *Remembrance of Things Past,* I, 107.
[29] *Ibid.,* p. 545.
[30] *Les plaisirs et les jours,* p. 210.
[31] *Remembrance of Things Past,* I, 614.
[32] *Ibid.,* II, 994.
[33] *Ibid.,* p. 996.
[34] *Ibid.,* p. 553.
[35] *Ibid.,* p. 995.
[36] *Ibid.,* II, 559.
[37] *Chroniques,* p. 186.
[38] *Remembrance of Things Past,* II, 1108.
[39] *Ibid.,* p. 994.
[40] *Ibid.,* I, 104.
[41] *Ibid.,* p. 1003.
[42] *Ibid.,* p. 285.
[43] *Ibid.,* p. 35.
[44] *Pastiches et mélanges,* p. 108.
[45] *Remembrance of Things Past,* II, 1121.
[46] *Les plaisirs et les jours,* p. 171.
[47] *Remembrance of Things Past,* I, 497.

APPENDIX: *Time and American Writers*

 Emerson

The work of Emerson pursues in time a reflection on experience that only takes place outside of time, contrary to time, in
the moment.

That work has first, therefore, a negative function. It applies
itself to destroying time, before summoning up in the void of time
the positive reality of the moment.

To destroy time, says Emerson, is to destroy what does not exist,
to destroy a dream. Time has no spiritual reality. It and space are
simply "relations of matter." [1] They are phenomena of sensibility,
veils that are drawn between us and a presence which is forever
absolute and forever instantaneous: "The influence of the senses
has, in most men, overpowered the mind to that degree, that the
walls of time and space have come to look real and insurmounta-
ble." [2] Time is "optical";[3] it is, so to speak, a visual illusion, "which
lends all its force to hide the values of the present time. . . . Ah!
poor dupe, will you never slip out of the web of the master jug-
gler . . . ?" [4] "In stripping time of its illusions, in seeking to find
out what is the heart of the day, we come to the quality of the moment and drop the duration altogether." [5]

But how are we to attain the heart of the instant, how discover its
secret quality? Let us resume our critical assessment of duration.
When we have destroyed the false continuity of time, we have still
not attained the instant; we only distinguish the true discontinuity
of the temporal life. Time is not one, it is a "succession of thought,"
a "distribution of wholes into causal series." [6] Passing from Kant
to Locke and perhaps to Hume, Emerson sets out to *disaggregate*
time, to make clear its psychological plurality: "The world lacks
unity . . . . It lies broken and in heaps . . . ." [7] "We live in

succession, in division, in parts, in particles." [8] In a word, when our analysis of time is complete, we find a time that is reduced to the multiplicity of the particles that compose it. Time decomposes, but not infinitely. For its apparent unity there is substituted that of its parts, which is to say its lived moments.

If in the apparent and phenomenal world it is the totality of time that seems one, and the moments a simply fragmentary reality, in the spiritual world on the contrary, it is time that is fragmentary and plural, and the moment that possesses unity and even totality.

In fact, each moment is a representative totality. In each present moment everything is present: "Nature keeps herself whole, and her representation complete in the experience of each mind." [9] "The least forms exist so perfectly and universally as to involve an idea representative of their entire universe." [10] Spiritual unity is not in the least temporal. It is a relationship between the lived moment and the universal totality. It is an immediate and total representation of the universe that is formed in the mind every moment. Omnipresence is present in the present.

Thus Emerson arrives at a strictly atomistic conception of duration. It does not differ from that of Leibnitz. In each moment the Emersonian monad has a representative perception of the universe. Time is only an apparent order, a simple aggregate. The instant alone is true. But despite the mind's effort, that verity and universality of the instant most often remains hidden from it. How, once more, are we to attain to that "heart of the day," that "quality of the moment," concealed by the habits and weaknesses of the mind?

Yet there are sometimes moments that, without any effort on our part, seem to unfold themselves to thought. Such moments are those in which are revealed the mysterious phenomena of animal magnetism, prayer, poetry, and the wisdom of children:

> These are examples of Reason's momentary grasp of the sceptre; the exertions of a power which exists not in time or space, but an instantaneous in-streaming causing power . . . . [11]

> In nature every moment is new; the past is always swallowed and forgotten; the coming only is sacred. Nothing is secure but life, transition, the energizing power. [12]

Thus what dissipates within us the deceptive marvels of duration, what brings us back to the instant and its magic, is the consciousness of the force that constitutes us, and in constituting us, constitutes the world also and our action upon it. As soon as our thought becomes active, it disengages itself from time and becomes instantaneous: "Time and space are but inverse measures of the force of the soul." [13] "The least activity of the intellectual powers redeems in a degree from the condition of time." [14]

At the height of this activity we gain full consciousness of ourselves: "In short, all our intellectual action does not promise but bestows a feeling of absolute existence. We are taken out of time . . . ." [15] "We apprehend the absolute. As it were, for the first time, *we exist.*" [16]

In identifying ourselves with the instant, we thereby at the same time become capable of apprehending the absolute and of apprehending ourselves. The Emersonian *Cogito* is curiously close to that of Descartes. It is by a destruction of space and time similar to hyperbolical doubt that we arrive at a certain intuitive verity, by the very act, the instantaneous act, by which we apprehend our active thought. We perceive our substance, we know who we are. And the act by which we perceive who we are leads us to discover also Him by Whom we are. In the present moment of thought what is discovered is not only the present of that thought but the non-temporal presence of the Creator of that thought. A creation which, like that of Cartesian thought, is ceaselessly continued, since in that non-temporal but perpetually instantaneous reality each new moment requires, as much for its existence as for its substance, the reiterated act of the Creator:

> . . . it is wrong to regard ourselves so much in a *historical* light as we do, putting time between God and us; and it is fitter to take account every moment of the existence of the Universe as a new Creation, and all as a revelation proceeding each moment from the Divinity to the mind of the observer.[17]

Not only our existence, therefore, but also that of nature, or at least the representative image that we make for ourselves of it, depends on an act of God, which is found in all instants, since it constitutes all instants. Each moment we think is one in which there begins again to exist in our mind the correspondence between the divine omnipotence and the omnipresence of things. An all-powerful God reveals Himself everywhere and always in the repre-

sentation we make for ourselves of universal nature. The immanence of the moment is unceasingly animated by the transcendence. Thus, each moment in which we exist is also the moment in
which, beyond the intuition of our existence and that of nature, we
have the intuition of the divine immensity: "If you are sure of your
truth, if you are sure of yourself, you ascend now into eternity." [18]
"We pierce to eternity, of which time is the flitting surface." [19]

In abolishing time as well as space, in reducing existence to the
moment, Emerson thereby aims to make of it a deified moment, a
human eternity. As is the case with Carlyle, the Emersonian critique of the time-illusion ends in the conception of an "everlasting
Now." [20] Time is no more. "A miniature Eternity" [21] remains. An
eternity which, like God's, contains in itself the totality of the past:
"In the present moment all the past is represented." [22] The instantaneous thought envelops the temporal totality—or rather it holds it
as a kind of central point in which all that is enclosed within the circumference has its origin and its constant relatedness. Around the
center all is disposed in circles. Circles which, like those set in motion by a stone falling into a body of water, ceaselessly widen, in
every direction, to the infinite. The illuminating grace of God, by
descending to thought, sets in motion there a representative act that
universally expands. And in falling into that thought, it also reveals
itself to that thought. Thus we become "borrowers of eternity . . . . Life culminates and concentrates." [23]

✱ Hawthorne

The present moment in Hawthorne is meager and quickly
dismantled. "It is but for a moment, comparatively, that anything
looks strange or startling." [24] Each instant in turn "fades into
the dark grey tissue common to the grave or glad events of many
years ago." [25] Thus, existence is formed of the perpetual swal-
lowing up of what has just been lived. The being we were disappears, not by extinction or evaporation but by a slow submersion
into regions where the light of day loses all its illuminating force.
Like a flotilla of small sailing vessels that founder, our moments

sink in gray water. It closes over our secrets. It conceals the bed where our treasures and our shames have come to lie. It draws between them and us the curtain of oblivion.

And yet this lusterless cover is now and then broken asunder by the floating up again of what had lain buried beneath it. The perfume of flowers is often the talisman thanks to which, from the somber depths where they lay asleep, the reawakened emotions rise once more to the surface:

> There as he lay more than half lifeless on the strand, the fragrance of an earthly rose-bud had come to his nostrils, and as odours will, had summoned up reminiscences of visions of all the living and breathing beauty amid which he should have had his home.[26]

In this manner "the spell peculiar to remembered odours," [27] occasionally also to sounds, to tastes, less often to sight, produce with Hawthorne, as with Baudelaire, Flaubert, or Proust, the phenomenon of the affective memory. By association there is unloosed a recollecting motion which gradually brings closer and closer to consciousness the emotions or sensations experienced over a long period of the past. The present no longer covers over the latter with a gloomy veil. Forgetfulness gives place to a memory that is living, fresh, and various. In reascending to the daylight the past is illuminated, and in the charming body of this Ophelia that floats lightly on the surface we recognize our former existence, which had been mysteriously preserved in us, but remote from us.

Sometimes that recognition takes place outside all association, in a supreme moment in which one sees the panorama of one's entire life unroll itself. This is true of Hester Prynne on the scaffold:

> Reminiscences, the most trifling and immaterial, passages of infancy and school-days, sports, childish quarrels, and the little domestic traits of her maiden years, came swarming back upon her, intermingled with recollections of whatever was gravest in her subsequent life. . . . The scaffold of the pillory was a point of view that revealed to Hester Prynne the entire track along which she had been treading, since her happy infancy.[28]

But what is brought to light here is not only the more or less vast field of lived existence; it is also the moral significance of that existence, which enables the mind to understand and judge itself as it

really is. In peering into the mirror in which the revivified past completely unveils itself to the consciousness, the being who re-
examines his life once more sees not only deeds, gestures, actions
and emotions that are over. He discovers that in withdrawing themselves from the present where each in turn had a fleeting life, these
actions and emotions wound themselves together in the darkness to
compose a continuous thread, a homogeneous picture. The past is
the place where little by little there is secretly formed the indelible
portrait of a person of whom we were ignorant, whom we had
never seen, and in whom, nevertheless, when he confronts us, we
are constrained to recognize ourselves. Suddenly we see identify
themselves with us the whole procession of beings we thought we
had laid aside forever. They hold fast to each other and to us. We
are only the utmost point of a line, the last link of a chain that is
ever longer and ever stronger, which holds us in servitude to the
past. For the past imparts to us its seeds, and transmits to us its influences: " 'How much of old material goes to make up the freshest
novelty of human life.' " [29] We never cease to be shaped by our previous actions and passions. The past is not only the source of our
reminiscences. It is an "inextinguishable flame." [30] It is the hoarder
of our faults, the preparer of our shames, the alchemist that com-
pounds the bitter drink of the present moment.

Of all those memories that combine to condemn us, there is none
more cruel than that of our youth: unalterable image of a purity
which we have corrupted; grievous presence, at a distance, of a
young, accusing ghost.

In the face, then, of this consciousness of self that reverberates
throughout the whole field of duration, the only wish one can still
make is to escape that spectacle at any price, to turn away one's
eyes from a past which shows us what we are in showing us, step
by step, how we have become what we are: "Shall we never, never
get rid of this Past? . . . It lies upon the Present like a giant's dead
body!" [31]

Such a desire ceaselessly manifests itself in Hawthorne. It is that
of the husband who wants to remove the birthmark from his wife's
cheek. To create a face on which there no longer remains the slightest vestige of any defilement, a smooth spotless countenance, a
present free of sin and the past! Or again, it is the wistful and sud-

den appearance of gracious creatures who, like the Marble Faun or Hester's daughter, "have no conscience, no remorse, no burden on the heart, no troublesome recollection of any sort; no dark future either." [32] These creatures "have nothing to do with time, but have a look of eternal youth on their face." [33] But precisely because they are free of the tragic temporality of the Puritan conscience, they have no more existence than they have remorse or memories. They do not live. Ephemeral, they are born and die within the fleeting circumference of the present moment.

Exactly like Poe, Hawthorne dreams of an intermediate state between the dream and the awakening, between the past and the future: "What a singular moment is the first one, when you have hardly begun to recollect yourself, after starting from midnight slumber . . . ." There, between the darkness of sleep and the raw light of consciousness, one is able to experience "that strangest of enjoyments, the forgetfulness alike of joy and woe. . . . Yesterday has already vanished among the shadows of the past; tomorrow has not yet emerged from the future. You have found an intermediary space, where the business of life does not intrude; where the passing moment lingers, and becomes truly the present; a spot where Father Time, when he thinks nobody is watching him, sits down by the wayside to take breath. O that he would fall asleep and let mortals live on without growing older!" [34]

But for Hawthorne, even more than for Poe, it is impossible to linger in the pure present. The latter is only an illusion of pause, of calm and of youth in a continuity whose essence consists not in the present but in the determining of the future by the past. Hardly has the haunted mind begun to enjoy a moment relieved of the burden of existence, when that existence falls back on its shoulders and forces it once more to transport to the future the weight of the past:

> Pray that your griefs may slumber, and the brotherhood of remorse not break their chain. It is too late.[35]

Or if it is not too late, that is only because in another duration, "beyond the shadowy scope of time," a predestinating God, yet still of aid in their distress, will permit his elect "in eternity, to find the perfect future in the present." [36]

* *Poe*

> Inspired by an ecstatic prescience of the glories beyond the grave, we struggle by multiform combinations among things and thoughts of Time to attain a portion of that Loveliness whose very elements perhaps appertain to Eternity alone.[37]

The whole dialectic of time in Poe is involved in this passage. To create a beauty that cannot exist in time, the poet is obliged to recompose the elements of that time and to invent with the help of their multiple combinations a new, imaginary duration, analogous to the divine eternity.

This imaginary duration is that of dream. Cut off from communication with the exterior world, the dream has its own interior place, circumscribed, independent of all other places. It is the "land of dream." In like manner, possessing neither past nor future, existing within itself, unattached to any antecedent or subsequent life, dream has its own time. It is a perpetual present.

Its symbol is the sunken city:

> No rays from the holy heaven come down
> On the long night-time of that town;
> But light from out the lurid sea
> Streams up the turrets silently . . . .[38]

If time is nocturnal, it is because it does not depend on solar time. The light that streams up the towers comes from the encircling sea, as if the place produced its own illumination. On the other hand if the nocturnal time is long, it is because the hours that comprise it are not differentiated one from another like the hours of solar time. They indefinitely protract themselves into each other, without showing any evidence of a real succession in their passage. Actually they do not pass. They remain. They form an hour that is always the same, a time that is *sheltered* from diurnal duration. This time is effortlessly engendered by an interior diffusion similar to that of light.

But this world is a submarine world. If it exists, it exists beneath the surface. Like the city, the deep time that we have here is a sunken time. Sleep covers it. Between it and waking time a veil is drawn, now half transparent, now opaque. If consciousness perceives it, it is entirely within the depths of itself, not as a part of the present, but as a region infinitely withdrawn from duration. The dreamer who would isolate himself in the exclusive contemplation of his dream is condemned either to bury himself with it in sleep and silence, or to awaken, that is to say to find his way into a present that is entirely different, a momentary present that can only consign to the past this imaginary time that is eternal. Indeed, the poetical work of Poe is less the *presentation* of a dream-universe than the *reminiscence* of it, such as is realized through thicker and thicker layers of distance and oblivion. Thus the work shows itself to be profoundly different from the surrealistic oneirism which, far from recollecting the dream, claims to embody it in an actual world that has become magical. Now the dreams of Poe are never magical. Though once they were, they are so no longer. Thence their unreal, vaporous character, like a thought which in losing its actuality has also lost its consistency. But there is more. Incapable of finding a place in the present, these dreams are no less incapable of finding a place in the recognizable past. For dreams have only been dreams. They cannot range themselves, like events of the real past, in chronology or history. Excluded from the known past, they try to locate themselves in the unknown past. They present themselves as the memories of a prenatal epoch. Being of no time, they seem to belong to an epoch that transcends times. Here for example:

> There will occasionally flash across my mind a sensation of familiar things, and there is always mixed up with such indistinct shadows of recollections, an unaccountable memory of old foreign chronicles and ages long ago.[39]

Floating without any anchor in duration, the memories of dreams become more and more fleeting and indistinguishable. They are "a memory like a shadow—vague, variable, indefinite, unsteady . . . ."

Finally there is no memory at all. Everything becomes immemorial. By dint of immersing itself in the depths, of withdrawing into the distance, of dissolving itself in the space of thought, the eternal present is metamorphized into an eternal past. This transformation is impressive, not by reason of its beauty, but, on the contrary, its ugliness. Different from the "fabulous past" of Melville, which energetically unfolds its myths only to collapse all at once through a

caprice of the author or of destiny. Poe's oneirous past dies a slow
and even nauseated death. A kind of gangrene corrupts it, disinte-
grates it, transforms it into mental rot. It is nevertheless the greatness of Poe to have fastened his gaze on this spectacle. He wanted
to live his dream to the last moment, if not of its eternity, at least
of its temporal existence—and, further still, through the charnel
house.

Thus, Poe's dream ends in death but not in total extinction. The
consciousness of the dreamer survives the death of the dream, a
witness of its disappearance. In the *Colloquy of Monos and Una,*
Poe describes this posthumous consciousness. In experiencing the
death of all his thoughts, the dead-alive person attains to the pure
perception of a time without thought:

> Let me term it a mental pendulous pulsation. It was the moral
> embodiment of man's abstract idea of Time . . . existing independ-
> ently of any succession of events . . . .[40]

Thus, at the extremity of dream there is death. And yet at the
extremity of the dream there is also the awakening, that is to say
life.

Sudden passage from death to life, or from the consciousness of
death to the consciousness of life.

If the time of dream is an eternal present which degenerates into
the past and finally into death or the void, the time of life is first of
all a simple moment of life. It is the moment when one awakens and
there is still no duration, but rather the simple and immediate feeling of physical existence: "Very suddenly there came back to my
soul motion and sound—the tumultuous motion of the heart, and,
in my ears, the sound of its beating." [41] All the attention is directed
to what is happening, at the instant it happens. It would be difficult
to conceive anything that less resembles the dream. Life is absorbed
with an incomparable intensity in the mysterious phenomenon of
its rising up into the instant.

But this awakening is not concluded, and as first it places consciousness in a *true* moment, so thereafter it brings it into a true
time. In other words, having recalled a person to the consciousness
of his actual existence, it then recalls him to the consciousness of his
nonactual life, that is to say his past and his future. Now aroused,
he can escape neither the past nor the future. Hence the invariable

fright into which, at the end of a former moment, the awakened sleeper finds himself thrown:

> Then the mere consciousness of existence without thought—a condition which lasted long. Then, very suddenly, thought, and shuddering terror, and earnest endeavor to comprehend my true state.[42]

Now, to comprehend his true state is to comprehend that state as it presents itself, not only in the moment but in duration. There is a knowledge that bears upon the whole ensemble of facts which, constituting our past and determining our future, determines as well the precise position in which we find ourselves situated in that ensemble. Almost invariably Poe places his awakened dreamer in such a situation; a situation so tragic that it requires his complete attention to comprehend it. The more threatening the situation, the more the person is forced to manifest that vigilance of the alerted consciousness which is the very contrary of the consciousness of dream. In opposition to the duration of the dream, which is composed of the undefined continuity of long hours, there now appears a mental duration defined with such precision that knowledge of the future is as plain to it as knowledge of the past. Everything constitutes a rigorously comprehensible fatality. By knowing who one has been, one knows who one will be, and when and how one will die. Like the hero of *The Fall of the House of Usher:* "I shall perish," said he, "I *must* perish in this deplorable folly. Thus, thus, and not otherwise, shall I be lost . . . ."[43]

The final knowledge, therefore, is a knowledge of the linkage of the causes which constitute duration and destiny. This linkage necessarily exists in a closed cycle. There can be certain knowledge of our temporal destiny only if that particular time is situated off by itself from the ordinary duration, so that it realizes itself independently of chance. For chance is incalculable. Poe eliminates interventions of chance as much as he can in his stories. It is not only the location of the House of Usher, which is situated apart from all others; it is also the time of Roderick Usher. If the atmosphere of the house has no "affinity with the air of heaven," its inhabitants, on the other hand, descend from a race that has been perpetuated only in a direct line. This particular time, therefore, is a time that cannot be confused with exterior duration. It is an internal fatality, conceived in isolation, and accomplished in isolation. A sort of temporal circle surrounds Poe's characters. A whirlpool envelops them, which, like that of the Maelstrom, disposes its funnel by degrees from the past in which one has been caught, to the future in which one will be dead. Whether it moves in the limitless eternity of dream or in the limited temporality of awakening, the work of Poe thus always presents a time that is *closed*.

*   *Thoreau*

In contrast to Hawthorne, Thoreau does not see the moment as something that passes and disappears. For him it is something that *appears,* "an incessant influx of novelty into the world." [44] Hence of all the points of time the one that matters most to him is the moment when this novelty is immediately perceptible, that is to say the present moment: "I am simply what I am. . . . I live in the present." [45] "We cannot afford not to live in the present." [46] The present is the moment in which one exists. It is also —what is even better—the moment in which the world exists. Infinitely narrow in the order of duration, it is infinitely vast in the order of extent. It is the place in which all places are together present, the hour in which our being coincides with nature:

> Let us preserve religiously, secure, protect the coincidence of our life with the life of nature. . . . My life as essentially belongs to the present as that of a willow tree in the spring. Now, now, its catkins expand, its yellow bark shines, its sap flows, now or never you must make whistles of it. Get the day to back you. Let it back you, and the night." [47]

To the incessant flow of novelty into the world, then, there must correspond in me an equivalent perception of that novelty. In order to achieve this I must "transcend my daily routine . . . have my immortality now, in the *quality* of my daily life." [48] To perceive with fresh senses is to be inspired. But what would one become if he were no longer inspired? "I am stranded at each reflux of the tide, and I, who sailed as buoyantly on the middle deep as a ship, am as helpless as a mussel on the rock . . . ." [49] What can one do when he has appended his whole spiritual life to the hour and to nature, and when nature stops speaking and the hour becomes neutral and mute? The moment of union is inevitably followed by a moment of dryness and disunion. Then the present is "without halo," [50] the hour owns its insufficiency.

Thus it is with all Quietist thought. Passive, it depends upon a grace which, given for the moment, will perhaps not be given in the moment following. Spiritless moments often replace moments of communication and grace. It seems then as if everything were already over and the universe congealed. The eye now discerns only conventional forms. It is not only the actual world, that is to say nature, that appears to us thus, when we regard it with the eyes of common sense and the rational intelligence, but also the corresponding extent of the past, when we wish to understand it in its historical significance:

> There seem to be two sides of this world presented to us at different times. . . . For seen with the eye of a poet, as God sees them, all things are alive and beautiful, but seen with the *historical eye,* or the eye of memory, they are dead and offensive. If we see nature as pausing, immediately all mortifies and decays; but seen as progressing she is beautiful.[51]

The repulsion of Thoreau for history is thus of the same nature as that of Bergson or Péguy. History is a fixation, an arbitrary intellectualization of life. Life, on the contrary, exists only in fluctuation. It is a sudden fire, a ceaseless emergence, a coloration always new:

> We should read history as little critically as we consider the landscape, and be more interested by the atmospheric tints and various lights and shades which the intervening spaces create than by its groundwork and composition. . . . In reality, history fluctuates as the face of the landscape from morning to evening. What is of moment is its hue and color. Time hides no treasures; we want not its *then,* but its *now*.[52]

Under the antihistorical eye of Thoreau, history decomposes. It is dissolved in the multiplicity of its parts. Contrary to what Hawthorne maintains, the past, as past, has neither secret nor treasure. It hides nothing besides moments which, each in its time, have been present moments.

Thus, history is not time, it is not even simply time past. For time past existed before being transformed into history; it had its peculiar tints, a future, a motion of its own, a novelty. Long before

Bergson, Thoreau insists on the anterior *actuality* of the past. But has this past which was then living now lost its life? Are we forever condemned to seeing what no longer is as no longer being? Should we reject all our memories as turning us away from the only thing that counts, the present and living hour? That is the conclusion of the Gide of the *Nourritures* and the *Immoraliste*. It is, so it seems, sometimes that of Thoreau too: "He is blessed over all mortals who loses no moment of the passing life in remembering the past." [53] But Thoreau also knows—better than most—that memory is not necessarily historical. Memory is not content simply to put us in rapport with the past; it restores it to us, it brings it alive once more in the actuality of our thought. Let us not renounce memory, therefore. Like nature it makes up an integral part of the present moment. Let us not even renounce regret. On the contrary, let us intensify it: "To regret deeply is to live afresh. By so doing you will find yourself restored to all your emoluments." [54]

From the time of our earliest infancy, each of our lived moments can thus be replaced in its own actuality: "My imagination, my love and reverence and admiration, my sense of the miraculous, is not so excited by any event as by the remembrance of my youth." [55] "As I come over the hill, I hear a woodthrush singing his evening lay . . . . It reinstates me in my dominion . . . ." [56] "The summer's eternity is reestablished by this note." [57] Here memory is no longer the retrograde motion by which thought quits the present and plunges itself into anterior regions; it is, on the contrary, the prospective motion which, leaving the past, goes toward the present in order to transmit an eternal richness to it. Like Kierkegaardian repetition, Thoreau's reinstitution is not directed backwards but ahead. It makes the present the future of the past. If the past has accumulated in the depths of the mind, it is not in order to constitute history or predetermine the future, but to transmit to the present an impulse which is that of life itself: "All the past plays into this moment." [58]

But this *play* of the past into the present is that of streaming waters that never stop and which, of themselves, perpetually flow from the present to the future as well. Of the three dimensions of duration, the one that is finally established for Thoreau as the most important is that of the future: "My future deeds bestir themselves within me and move grandly towards a consummation, as ships go

down the Thames. A steady onward motion I feel in me . . . ." [59]
"We anticipate the future with transcendental senses." [60]

Now these senses, transcendental as they may be, remain senses nevertheless. Recovering the past, disclosing the future, they continue to be nonetheless attached to the eternally perceptible actuality of nature. What the mind foreshadows in its future is the perpetually renewed play of a nature that is refreshed simply by beginning the round of its seasons again:

> Some flitting perspectives and demi-experiences of the life that is in nature are in time veritably future, or rather outside time, perennial, young, divine, in the wind and rain which never die.[61]

But this perennial life, as we have seen, is as much that of past nature as of future nature. Thus in situating ourselves upon the present, we situate ourselves "on the meeting of two eternities, the past and the future, which is precisely the present moment." [62] In this present moment God culminates. He culminates by the motion of the seasons. Each "gives a tone and hue to my thought." [63] All together, at one and the same time recollected, prefigured, and lived, they form "an annual phenomenon which is a reminiscence and a prompting." [64] Time itself is "a shallow stream," [65] "cheap and rather insignificant." [66] But the seasons are not in time; they are in eternity; they are eternity. An eternity of changing colors, a perpetual cycle. He who apprehends it lives in another time, a time that has nothing to do with chronology or clocks; he lives in a *seasonal* time, where, to the phases of nature, the phases of human life exactly correspond: "The seasons and all their changes are in me . . . . My moods are thus periodical." [67]

✱ *Melville*

> O my God! What is this that shoots through me, and leaves me so deadly calm, yet expectant,—fixed at the top of a shudder! Future things swim before me . . . .[68]

Such is the moment in which the Melvillian personage finally takes full stock of himself; he sees himself immobile at the top of a shudder. This immobility is that of a destiny that is fixed; or, rather, one which reveals its eternal fixity. Just as for Poe, consciousness for Melville is never so complete as when it is consciousness not only of existence, but also of the ineluctable end of existence. The human being recognizes himself in the foreknowledge of a future catastrophe which has nevertheless been resolved upon for a long time. He recognizes himself to be predestined; "seeing reflected to him, by visible and uncontradictable symbols, the tyranny of Time and Fate." [69]

A tyranny that is simultaneously divine and infernal. A God who, in the terms of the Puritan canon, predestines some to life, and others to eternal death, and decides outside of times what times will be:

> But God His former mind retains
>   Confirms his old decree;
> The generations are inured to pains,
>   And strong Necessity
> Surges, and heaps Time's strand with wrecks.[70]

Times of happiness and unhappiness, of damnation and sublimation, all times are equally necessitated: "In time past, the future must have been foreordained. . . . Out of all the events destined to befall any one man, it is not impossible that previous knowledge of some of these events might supernaturally come to him." [71]

Supernatural foreknowledge of the future, therefore, is supernatural foreknowledge of the past in which that future was contained. All times are linked together in the same chain: "All the ages of the world pass as in a manacled procession." [72] Absolute predestinationism has for its consequence the enslaving of all the points of duration and their reduction to a nonvariant which has the same unchangeability as the past. Nothing is and nothing shall be that has not been fixed by a divine antecedent will.

Now it is the greatness of Melville not to have been willing to accept this situation. He protests, he appeals a decision that he nevertheless knows to be irrevocable. Like Kierkegaard, he is the Job of temporality.

It is true, he recognizes, that "the Past is, in many things, the foe of mankind. . . . In the Past is no hope. . . . Those who are solely governed by the Past stand still like Lot's wife, crystallised in

the act of looking backward, and forever incapable of looking before." [73]

Thus, it is necessary to look before, into the Future: "The Future
is the Bible of the Free." [74]

To look into the future is to look into space. The motion by which
Melville tries to escape the crystallizing predestination is a motion
which urges him ahead, abroad, over the ocean, in search of the
Isles. *Typee, Omoo,* and the first pages of *Mardi,* as well as the
descriptions of the sea in the *White Jacket* or *Redburn,* are the
traces of a material adventure, in which one surrenders to the hazards of the waves and the land, to the elements, and to men, in order to elude through these adventitious fatalities an omnipresent
and essential destiny. If the rigorous continuity of fortune can be
broken by the irruption of hazard and chance, in that case human
liberty will perhaps be able to wedge itself into this fault and,
changing the universal order of events, give itself *another* future.
Such is the occasion Melville seeks. The slightest chance, if it is indeed a chance, should alter the course of time and bring about a
saving mutation. That is why the Melvillian being is going to seek
frantically for adventure beyond the seas. Not for the sake of the
new, or a nostalgia for happiness, but because of a nostalgia for
freedom itself, the desire for the appearance of an event that God
himself would not have foreseen. For if that event should happen,
anything can happen. Not only love but life, the universe, are rein-
ventable. That is what the hero of *Pierre* understands at the moment when the discovery which forces him to change the image he
had of his father, calls upon him to change also his entire existence:
"Every other image in his mind attested the universality of that
electral light which had darted into his soul." [75]

That universal and universally transforming light, which had
darted through because of a fortituous discovery, is the same experience that comes from an act of the will: "I like all men who
dive. Any fish can swim near the surface, but it takes a great whale
to go down five miles or more." [76]

In those submarine depths in which the diver is engaged, there is
discovered a free universe, a world removed from the power of fate,
and given over to dream and to chance. One can make a periplus
of it, invent countries within it, adorn its spaces with all the caprices

of an imaginary geography. This world has also its fabulous duration. The future now becomes a phantom future:

> This new world . . . is the world of the mind; wherein the
> wanderer may gaze round, with more of wonder than Balboa's band
> roving through the golden Aztec glades. But fiery yearnings their
> own *phantom-future* make, and deem it present.[77]

More astonishing still, a metamorphosis of the past exists in this
world of the mind. For of all times the past is ordinarily the one
that most visibly submits to the law of destiny. But here there appears, unexpected, free as the future, a past without constraint,
one that is purely legendary. It is the disturbing and delicious past
of Isabelle, upon which her brother and lover in *Pierre* fastens an
inexhaustible curiosity. It is also, in *Mardi,* the past of Yillah: "So
etherealized had she become from the wild conceits she nourished,
that she verily believed herself a being of the land of dreams. Her
fabulous past was her present." [78]

Thus the past and the future are now confounded with the present. They indescribably form, all together, one and the same mythical time. It is the time of mind, the time of fable, a time without
determination or succession, in which all the hours in their variety
resemble and equal each other. For the relative horological time,
there is thus found substituted a time that is absolute, a human eternity, which at all latitudes, like the Greenwich chronometer, marks
the same minute. "Finding in himself a chronometrical soul," the
Melvillian being "seeks practically to force that heavenly time
upon the earth." [79]

But Melville at once adds: "In such an attempt he can never succeed, with an absolute and essential success." [80]

The sudden disappearance of Yillah and all happy dreams, the
catastrophe of Pierre, who wanted to impose his heavenly time
upon earth—the work of Melville everywhere confesses the insol-
vency of fabulous time, which is invariably followed, in him as in
Baudelaire, by a time of collapse and breaking apart: "I feel that
the Godhead is broken up like the bread at the Supper, and that we
are the pieces." [81] "What avails it now that Solomon my father was
wise? Rehoboam succeeds. Such oscillations are not of a day." [82]
Melvillian time is now going to become a time of oscillations and

fractures: "There is no steady unretracing progress in this life; we do not advance through fixed gradations."[83] The way behind will suddenly take the place of the way ahead. Melville's stories, as he himself says, "go forward and go backward, as occasions call."[84] They go by leaps and bounds and exist only in fragments, like the poem he planned to write about the officer on the verge of dying, who in his delirium "sings *by snatches* his good-bye and last injunctions to two messmates."[85]

But this movement of oscillation is itself, in the final analysis, caught up in a movement more vast: "In the minutest moment momentous things are irrevocably done."[86] Chance happenings, free acts of will, thus like all the rest, re-enter the frame of necessity: "Ay, chance, free will and necessity—no wise incompatible —all interweavingly work together."[87] To the double discontinuity of chance and human freedom there is joined and superimposed anew, finally, the loathsome, re-enjoined continuity of destiny. A destiny which is no longer either divine or infernal, which is the reality of a circular time, eternally captive in its revolutions: "Thus deeper and deeper into Time's endless tunnel, does the winged soul, like a night-hawk, wend her wild way; and finds eternities before and behind; and her last limit is her everlasting beginning."[88] All becomes cycle and circle; not the serene cycle of the seasons that Thoreau contemplates, but an eternal and mortal cycle in which the Melvillian character, like Poe's hero, finds himself enclosed and absorbed: "Sucked within the Maelstrom, man must go round."[89] The horror of Ahab's destiny consists not in his being lost with all his crew, but in his having to begin the pursuit all over again after his death, only to find a new engulfment awaiting him at the end of this new quest. Time turns, and all the events of all lives turn on the same wheel; in such a way that in this circular course which is at once horrible and dull, it is possible to see "the parts of the past as parts of the future reversed."[90]

> The grass it dies, but in vernal rain
> Up it springs and it lives again;
> Over and over, again and again
> It lives, it dies and it lives again.[91]

The universe again before us; our quest, as wide.[92]

✱ *Whitman*

> There is a dream, a picture, that for years at intervals (some-
> times quite long ones, but surely again, in time), has come noiselessly
> up before me. . . . It is nothing more or less than a stretch of in-
> terminable white-brown sand, hard and smooth and broad, with the
> ocean perpetually, grandly, rolling in upon it. . . .[93]

This expanse is the very expanse of Whitman's thought: an open,
naked smooth stretch, without obstacle and without any characteristic; a sort of anonymous field that is overlapped by a vast reality
rolling in from outside. One could say that Whitman's thought does
not exist in itself. It is nothing, except that infinite receptivity which
is the quality proper to shores; it depends entirely on an exterior
universal phenomenon which, by overrunning it, gives it animation and existence. This phenomenon is time. Whitman's present is
essentially the collecting place of that movement which is duration.
A movement that can be conceived either as the one by which
things, in passing from virtuality to actuality, become present, or as
that by which in passing from the past to the future, they are made
actual: "The poet places himself where the future becomes present":[94] a present which is also, Whitman says, "the passage from
what was to what shall be." [95] The movement of duration is an in-
vading force, that carries all times to the edge of the present or
that traverses it. Or more exactly, duration being a double movement that comes simultaneously from the future and from the past
—as do two waves running from opposite directions—the present is
their meeting place: that place of confluence where past and future
are joined to make of the present an extent that is filled with all
times, an eternity formed of the union of the three elements of duration:

> I know that the past was great and the future will be great,
> And I know that both curiously conjoint in the present time . . .
> And that where I am, or you are this present day, there is the
>   centre of all days, all races. . . .[96]

In receiving all times, the present becomes the meeting place of
times. A multitude crowds into its emptiness. Thought is miraculously filled up to the brim:

I dote on myself, there is that lot of me and all so luscious,
Each moment and whatever happens thrills me with joy. . . .[97]
. . . .
To me every hour of the light and dark is a miracle. . . .[98]

But it would be wrong to imagine that this present is purely receptive and static. In contrast to Thoreau, Whitman is not content
to await passively the gifts of duration. The Whitmanian present
easily unites all temporal movements because it is itself intensely
dynamic. If the past and future converge toward it, it diverges toward them. It is not satisfied to await their arrival, but, like a host
impatient to see his invited guests, it goes out to meet them: "Locations and times, what is it in me that meets them all, whenever and
wherever, and makes me at home?" [99] Thus the mind is stretched,
the present is distended. Times are not only eagerly received, they
are invaded. The dilated moment takes possession of time itself. It
becomes time. It is made equal by expansion to the extent of duration and of space:

> But that I, turning, call to thee, O soul, thou actual Me,
> And lo, thou gently masterest the orbs,
> Thou matest Time, smilest content at Death,
> And fillest, swellest full the vastness of Space.[100]

But what is this spatial and temporal extent? First of all, it is "a
vast and multiform show." [101] No more than the extent of places,
the extent of time is not an empty space. It is a world that is full—
full of things, of men, of cities, of countries, of roads and of rivers
—a swarming of beings that are living simultaneously, but each of
which is also living in his own time. As in Hugo's universe, everything is present at once, and every little bit helps to fill it up. But
how then is one to find a homogeneity in this anachronistic plurality? One might imagine the world of Whitman to be a world of
anomalous realities in which nothing is linked together and there
exists only a throng of mutually exclusive entities. All the times
could exist simultaneously but independently of each other, as it is
with places in space, since Vancouver is not Vladivostok, nor Paris
San Francisco. But the opposite happens:

> A vast similitude interlocks all,
> All spheres grown, ungrown, small, large, suns, moons, planets,

All distances of place however wide,
All distances of time. . . .[102]

Eternity gives similitude to all periods and locations and processes, and animates and inanimates forms, and . . . is the bond of time.[103]

Thus Whitman conceives eternity as an equalizing medium that unites and reconciles the most disparate epochs. Heterogeneous in their form, they are homogeneous in their general duration and their total place. Like objects stacked one upon another in a room, the epochs hold together. The distances that separate them are also the spaces that join them. Time is not made up of independent elements, "past and present and future are not disjoin'd but join'd." [104] The very same pulsation is communicated from one to the other, "throbbing forever—the eternal beats, eternal systole and diastole of life in things." [105]

Shaken from one end to the other by the same rhythmic pulsation, the universe of Whitman is thus not a simple, static coherence. It is a universe traversed by movements, but one in which forces and masses, without ceasing to act, are mutually counterpoised. The intuition of Whitman is that "of absolute balance, in time and space, of the whole." [106] A universe that is full, but with a shifting fullness, where times unroll upon space, and space swells thanks to the movement of times. A universe, finally, which overflows with things and which, more than that of plenitude, is the universe of plenteousness and consistency.

To express this world, it is sufficient, therefore, to enumerate its details. For it is the ensemble of its details, the number of its numbers. The Whitmanian enumeration is already the enumeration of Péguy. It is an enunciation, at once successive and cumulative, of all that has been, and of all that will be. Thus, time defiles with its epochs, in an order that is not chronological but rightly poetic and cosmic. Epochs are like stars, they are perceived all at once, but are enumerated one by one. Together they form a sidereal procession: "The universe is a procession with measured and perfect motion." [107] Nevertheless this processional universe is not oriented towards a transcendent reality. With Péguy, the procession has a termination; it traverses the plain, because the cathedral stands at the end of it. But Whitman's procession has nothing terminal or sacramental about it. It simply advances, and in advancing unfolds itself; it occupies the worlds and the times; but never, in contrast with Emerson, does it transcend worlds and times.

For it is in the world and in time that the pulse of life beats:

> Pressing the pulse of the life that has seldom exhibited itself . . .
> Chanter of Personality, outlining what is yet to be,
> I project the history of the future.[108]

The future has therefore *already* a history; as the past *still* has a life. Everything is linked together and everything is historically and poetically expressible. To the total universe corresponds a total word. The "ensembles of time and space" [109] become the ensemble of time-space: "The past, the future, dwelling there, like space, inseparable together." [110] Everything is expressible because everything is acceptable. From the totality of duration the poet substracts nothing, just as he adds nothing: "I accept time absolutely." [111] This accepted time, contained as it is in the present of the word, does not cease to enlarge and to produce "poems of the present, ever solidifying and expanding into the future," [112] but always expressing the same totality. "The cosmic spirit" [113] is the spirit that makes up the sum of the cosmos and absorbs it. If Whitman finds the universe so acceptable, that is because it is "equal to his vast appetite." An appetite that is exactly satisfied, because it is exactly the measure of the totality of things. This hunger does not go any further. It is not greater than its belly. It is content to absorb all times and all places.

✳ *Emily Dickinson*

> 'Tis an instant's play.
> 'Tis a fond Ambush
> Just to make Bliss
> Earn her own surprise! [114]

The first moment of the real life of Emily Dickinson has nothing to do with her earlier life as a young girl. It is a moment of absolute surprise that lifts her out of her life, removes her from parents and friends, from customary shores, to fling her out upon the open sea:

> Exultation is the going
> Of an inland soul to sea,
> Past the houses—past the headlands—
> Into deep Eternity.[115]

But this moment without past is also without future. Or rather it has for the future its immediate recession, its loss:

> Just lost, when I was saved!
> Just felt the world go by! [116]
> . . . .
> More distant in an instant
> Than Dawn in Timbuctoo.[117]

At once for the instant of ecstasy, there is substituted another instant which is that of the disappearance of ecstasy. Nothing is graver in Emily's life than the apparition, in the closest succession, of these two moments, in one of which everything is given, and in the other everything taken away. It matters little that this double experience may be repeated afterwards. What matters is that each time Emily reflects on her existence, she sees it begin with a grand victory immediately followed by a bitter defeat. All her spiritual life and all her poetry are comprehended only in the determination given them by two initial moments, one of which is contradicted by the other, a moment in which one possesses eternity and a moment when one loses it:

> The Moments of Dominion
> That happen on the Soul
> And leave it with a Discontent
> Too exquisite—to tell. . . .[118]

In the existence that begins with this loss, what strikes one at first is the persistence of regret, the constant rawness of the wound. It seems that time is composed of a repeated pain and that in each of its moments one is stricken as if for the first time:

> It struck me—every Day—
> The Lightning was as new
> As if the Cloud that instant slit
> And let the Fire through.[119]

"Time never did assuage," [120] on the contrary it constantly reinforced regret. And sometimes the pain spreads, and in spreading expands time itself, in such a manner that it seems that "ages coil within the minute Circumference of a single brain";[121] sometimes, on the contrary, it seems that eternities are suddenly condensed into a single moment of pain:

> Pain expands the Time . . .
> Pain contracts the Time
> Occupied with Shot
> Gamuts of Eternities
> Are as they were not.[122]

The more one suffers, the more cruel becomes the contrast between past ecstasy and the present, which is precisely the deprivation of that ecstasy:

> Paradise is that old mansion
> Many owned before—
> Occupied by each an instant
> Then reversed the Door. . . .[123]

All duration is made to be the eternal exclusion of an instantaneous eternity. Then one understands how the fullness and intensity of the pains of which existence is composed are exactly the ransom of the lost, unique joy. Time is a pain lived piecemeal, and the sum of the pieces equals a moment of joy:

> For each ecstatic instant
> We must an anguish pay
> In keen and quivering ratio
> To the ecstasy.[124]

> I took one Draught of Life—
> I'll tell you what I paid—
> Precisely an existence—
> The market price, they said.[125]

Such is Emily's lot: Condemned all her life to unhappiness in order to pay the price of a single instant of happiness. But what is striking is not that she is rebellious and finds her lot unjust. On the contrary, always suffering, she will the sooner repent of remembering too often the single moment which was free of suffering. In her long defeat she will reproach herself for dreaming of her brief triumph. That is what she calls remorse:

> Remorse—is Memory—awake—
> Her Parties all astir—

> A Presence of Departed Acts—
> At window—and at Door.[126]

If Emily rejects "remorse," it is because the "presence of Departed Acts" in the mind that contemplates them prevents it from being resigned to their absence. The last sacrifice that seems to be exacted of her is the sacrifice of even the memory of joy. No one is less abandoned than she to the nostalgia for lost happiness and to all the delightful, melancholy, or exasperated feelings that flow from it. A past image should not mask the bitterness of the present nor falsify its meaning and value. It is not enough that happiness is lost; the mind must recognize its loss, loosen its last grip, and explicitly renounce what it no longer possesses. To regret, to remorse, Emily opposes the inverse virtue of renunciation:

> Renunciation—is a piercing Virtue—
> The letting go
> A Presence. . . .[127]

There is no longer a presence, no longer even the feeble link which the mind kept with this presence by memory. To have been once and forever saved would have been too easy. An instantaneous eternity does not suit the human condition. The latter must accommodate itself to time, that is to say to renunciation, to the consciousness of absence and distance, to the patient continuity of pain.

A pain that now is without regret, without past, but also without hope, without temporal future. For it would be as culpable in hoping for a return of ecstasy as it would be in lamenting the ecstasy. The joy had no other reason for being than to make us see that of which we are unworthy. Without once having known happiness, we could not know how ill it suits us, and how well suffering agrees with us. Defeat is our part. Let us be content with defeat. Let us consummate our resignation in despair.

A despair that one must not confuse with the feeling of revolt that often bears the same name. True despair is exactly the lack of hope; or, as Emily herself puts it, "the slow exchange of Hope for something passiver":[128]

> The Service without Hope—
> Is tenderest, I think. . . .[129]

Without hope, without regret, contracting in both directions, breaking all links with past happiness as with possible happiness,

thought no longer has any anteriority or future. It is entirely identified with present grief:

> Pain—has an element of Blank—
> It cannot recollect
> When it began—or if there were
> A time when it was not—
>
> It has no Future—but itself—
> Its Infinite realms contain
> Its Past—enlightened to perceive
> New Periods—of Pain.[130]

Thus suffering in Emily Dickinson comes in the end to the same
result as the feeling of nothingness in Mallarmé; it unifies the times,
it confounds them in the same monotonous continuity, outside of
which, it seems, there is nothing that one can see:

> The Mind is smooth—no Motion—
> Contented as the Eye
> Upon the Forehead of a Bust—
> That knows—it cannot see. . . .[131]

There is no longer any difference between moments. Everything
is made equal by the same pain. And this extent that is perpetually
identical to itself, that is found again in every moment and in all
moments, is the symbol of an invisible eternity:

> Forever—is composed of Nows—
> 'Tis not a different time. . . .[132]

A time never any different from itself and also equal to space,
since in its continuous development it never ceases to be the consciousness of the distance to which the lost object is withdrawn. And
this consciousness would continue indefinitely to prolong its monotonous contemplation over this extent, if finally at the end of it, at
the extremity of the future, there were not, as at the extremity of
the past, a supreme instant which forms the transcendent termination of the level plain. That termination is death.

On the face of someone dying, Emily catches the arrival of that
instant which ends and begins all:

> 'Twas Crisis—All the length had passed
> That dull—benumbing time. . . .
> . . . .

The Second poised—debated—shot—
Another had begun—
And simultaneously, a Soul
Escaped the House unseen.[133]

✳ *Henry James*

"Consciousness is an illimitable power. . . ." [134] As soon
as Jamesian thought achieves consciousness of itself and of others
it achieves at the same time a consciousness of the infinite character of its task. Whether it will or no, it has to reflect all that
happens outside or within it. In the first place, the consciousness
of the external world is that of a life inextricably proliferating,
which is multiplied over all its surface: "Life is, immensely, a matter of surface . . . ." [135] Yet the interior world reveals the same
immensity and complexity. From the very first, James felt the extreme danger of "the terrible fluidity of self-revelation";[136] a fluidity
which was so dangerous for him because it was fed by an inexhaustible reservoir of memories. James' family were astonished at his
"reach of reminiscence." [137] They well might have been astonished
still more at its fertility. Far from being, as with Proust, a past that
was rarely and fortuitously recaptured by the operation of the
involuntary memory, the past for James is always present, always
spreading out like a drop of oil upon consciousness; so much so
that, in the final analysis, the great problem for James is not remembering but, on the contrary, disencumbering his thought by
forgetting. For it is in swarms that images of the past, exactly like
representations of the present, spread over consciousness:

> Aspects began to multiply and images to swarm. . . . To knock at
> the door of the past was in a word to see it open to me quite
> wide. . . .[138]

> I lost myself, of a truth, under the whole pressure of the spring
> of memory proceeding from recent revisitings and recognitions. . . .
> These things, at the pressure, flush together again, interweave their
> pattern and quite thrust it at me. . . .[139]

There is nothing more striking in James than this *loss* of the self
in the multiplicity of its memories. If thought is lost, it is not lost by

contraction but through superabundance. The mass of remembered images threatens to stifle it. And the mind is already overrun by the richness of actual perceptions: "Therefore . . . experience has to organize, for convenience and cheer, some system of observation —for fear, in the admirable immensity, of losing its way." [140] Instead of allowing memory constantly to enlarge and deepen the field of consciousness, James acts to restrain it, to give it limits. These limits are those of the present. Life is a surface affair. Let us leave memory to the clothes closet: "The ragbag of memory hung on its nail in my closet . . . . I learnt with time to control the habit of bringing it forth." [141]

The Jamesian novel, therefore, will most often be divested of the past. Its characters undergo an infinity of experiences and incessantly discover themselves in new relationships with each other, but these experiences and relationships are oftenest the direct effect of present junctures; they are a new disposition of beings that corresponds to their displacement. An affair of the surface, and not one of depth; a movement in space, and not one in time. Ordinarily the Jamesian character has little duration; or rather his duration is not composed, like that of the Flaubertian or Tolstoian character, of a temporal density; between his immediate existence and the depths of his mind stretch no thick layers of memories. The duration of his characters is similar to the duration of celestial bodies; not that it is particularly long—rather the contrary—but it consists in the successive localization of a selfsame entity in different points of space. In one minute or in one year it is here; in another minute or year it is there. Its nature does not change; what changes is the relationship all the other points of space have with it. That presents a complex calculus in which time is of great importance, yet still less so than space. To go from Europe to America or from America to Europe implies in this regard a more significant mutation than to pass from adolescence to manhood. In any case it is more calculable. It is also more easily contained within the voluntary limits the mind sets to itself.

It is thus that James manifests "the little taste in general he has for the past as a part of his own history," [142] even of the history of others. What interests him is "the planned rotation of aspects." [143] He invents a new kind of time, what one might call aesthetic time. It consists in establishing about a center a moving circle of points of view, from one to the other of which the novelist proceeds. There is no change except in point of view. Thus time is constituted by passage, not from one moment to another, but from one point of perspective to another. This process is demonstrated to perfection when there is found situated at the center an entity, an object or an ensemble of objects, as in *The Spoils of Poynton*. For these objects have no past, they are not situated in time but in space. The only time one finds here is that which would be employed in contemplating a statue from all angles, in the course of discussing it with other connoisseurs. This is "the law of successive aspects," [144] by which James carefully reduces time to a local duration, and by which he saves himself from being lost in the "admirable immensity."

But there is still another way for James to keep from going astray. It is to give himself or his character a duration that is not deep, a duration that is least removed from the world of the surface:

> I delight in a palpable imaginable *visitable* past—in nearer distance and the clearer mysteries, the marks and signs of a world we may reach over to as by making a long arm we grasp an object at the other end of our own table.[145]

The near past is thus neither dangerous nor prolix. By reason of its shallowness it is almost flush with the present; it is without distance and without depth. Therefore it is not a true past. It is made one with places.

But then what is to be done with the true past? Are we to ignore it? That is what James is oftenest content to do. But sometimes the demon of curiosity and that other demon, more perverse still, which incites a novelist to choose for a subject precisely what he fears most and least desires, draw him down into the depths. It is what happens in *The Turn of the Screw*. But the occasional visitation of an impalpable, unimaginable, unvisitable past, such as one finds there, is at bottom less perilous for James than the journey into the farthest past, "the desire to remount the stream of time, really to bathe in its upper and more natural waters . . . ." [146] That is nevertheless what he tried to do in *The Sense of the Past*, in giving his hero a disposition exactly opposite to his own, one which renders the mind "oddly indifferent to the actual and the possible." [147]

But this past, far away as may be situated its upper range, does not in fact differ basically from the close past; for it is also a distanceless past enclosed within precise limits: "It was when life was framed in death that the picture was really hung up." [148] It is in the same fashion that the central character of *The Altar of the Dead* retrospectively pays his respects to his departed friends. They constitute for him a numerable total of household gods. It is because they are dead that one can add up the sum of them. There is no depth to the past. Itself bordered by death, it forms the vacant under-margin of the present, and thus a delimitation.

But if the past is a limitation it is so insofar as it has become a past. When it was not yet a past, it was a future in the making. Like his brother William, Henry James has to the highest degree the sense of the "saddle-back" present, the feeling of riding upon a palpable and appreciable present whose span comprises a bit of the past and a bit of the future. And by a finally triumphant return of the repressed memory, what once more enters the mind of the aging James is a past that is now without limit, a past profound and remote, which still holds all its associative power, all its admirable immensity, and, above all, its old ardor and its youthful leap toward the future: "That, with so many of the conditions repeated, is the charm—to feel afresh the beginning of so much that was to be." [149] Thus James finally abandons himself to the charm of the bygone future. And as he does not cease to remain a novelist, that is to say, to be less preoccupied by the reconstruction of accomplished facts than by the possibility of imaginatively developing the germs that were contained in them, James plunges himself with delight into the memories of his former life only to discover in them the possibilities of other lives; and if he chooses to journey by memory to such and such a place in the past, it is often because from that point of departure he can imagine a different sort of existence for himself. Thus the past becomes the place where one can not only recapture oneself but where one can also recapture "the possible development of one's own nature one mayn't have missed." "That mystical other world that might have flourished," [150] though it did not do so at the time, could still perhaps find the chance of opening up and expanding, if the seeds of it, long ignored and sleeping, were to be transplanted in new soil. This is the adventure which happens to Strether when, in transporting himself from one continent to another, he unconsciously at the same time transports with him the possibility of another Strether "buried for long years in dark corners" which is going to "sprout again under forty-eight hours of Paris." [151] It is thus that James discovers and finally develops a virtual past.

✳ T. S. Eliot

Like a wayfarer robbed, stripped, and thrown at night into a river, whose chill water brings him back to consciousness, the thought of Eliot finds itself plunged into duration. A swift current carries along and stupefies the mind. If only it were possible to cling to the present moment as to a fixed point! But there is no fixed point. The moments pass. They pass so swiftly, so completely, that the sole image which survives them is that of "flickering intervals of light and darkness." [152] Far from having the slightest continuity, duration is entirely composed of the multiplicity of intervals and the successive disappearance of the images they separate. A time comparable to a woof perpetually torn to pieces, or to "a heap of broken images," [153] whose pieces fall over backwards. The sole concern is with the incessant and, so to speak, frantic passage from *before* to *after:*

> Only a flicker
> Over the strained time-ridden faces
> Distracted from distraction by distraction
> Filled with fancies and empty of meaning
> Tumid apathy with no concentration
> Men and bits of paper, whirled by the cold wind
> That blows before and after time. . . .[154]

A blinking, a distracting, a whirling time is an insensate motion that carries people no matter where, anywhere except where they find themselves, and which, being aimless, returns in the end to its beginning: "In and out, in an endless drift of shrieking forms in a circular desert." [155]

There is nothing to hope, it seems, from this time or this world. But now and again the song of a bird arrests the step of the hurried traveler; or it may be "the leap of one fish, at a particular place and time, the scent of one flower, an old woman on a German mountain path, six ruffians seen through an open window playing cards at night at a small French railway junction where there was a water-mill . . . ." [156] These images mysteriously affix the mind to their momentary reality. They are profoundly different from the time just described. They subsist in themselves. They are outside of motion, outside of time perhaps. Each one constitutes a "sudden illumination." [157] Non-temporal and yet situated in a moment and in a place, these visions possess a sort of peculiar plenitude. Like certain Proustian images, they seem to be set down at the point of intersection of duration with a non-temporal reality.

Driven by forces of which he has a horror, jostled by the crowd, delivered over to the violent mobility of the epoch, Eliot occasionally finds the means of halting, at countercurrent, at countertime, and listening, as to the song of a bird, to the prelude of another time: "There is a first, or an early moment which is unique, of shock and surprise, even of terror (*Ego dominus tuus*); a moment which can never be forgotten . . . ." [158] In this "partial ecstasy" [159] it seems that one has a presentiment, not of the secret of one instant, but of all instants; for "the pattern is new each moment." [160]

But the ecstasy is only a partial ecstasy. "The glory of the positive hour" is "infirm." [161] The sense of it escapes us. The moments fly, and their meaning with them. Later, a long time after, one will be able to fathom their message: "Only in time can the moment in the rose-garden . . . be remembered." [162] Never will the moments be repeated; they will be content to "survive in a larger whole of experience." [163] Far from us, far from the present, in our memory, having become past, they will become attached to all the traditions which constitute that past.

From the fugitive seizure of the present, thought thus passes to the permanent seizure of the past. That cannot happen without a primary and grievous sacrifice. To renounce the present in order to contemplate the past is not only to renounce joy, since that exists only in the actual, but also to renounce the direct apprehension of truth by "sudden illumination": "What happens is a continual surrender of the poet as he is at the moment to something which is more valuable." [164] Everything will depend now on a precarious contact with a precious and remote truth which memory badly preserves, and which is corroded by the brutal indifference of present time toward all traditions. And yet, says Eliot, it is necessary to accustom oneself to "depend upon tradition and the accumulated wisdom of time." [165] This dependence, or this "historical sense," implies a "perception, not only of the pastness of the past, but of its presence." [166] It is necessary to consider the past as a "simultaneous order," to live "in what is not merely the present, but the present moment of the past." [167]

The search for lost time in Eliot is therefore totally different from what one finds in Proust, but no less important. It depends on a voluntary memory, on a continuous abnegation, on a patient effort to recover, to reassemble, to readapt under new conditions, what was lost. Far from being restored at one stroke by the affective memory, the past is regained only by the exercise of all the mental and physical powers. It is less a memory than a reacquired habit, the effect of a vow of fealty. A new time is revealed which is no longer the furious movement by which, in order more easily to possess the future, the present disencumbered itself of the past, but the reflective motion by which, resigning itself to not existing by itself, the present concentrates upon the actions necessary to assure the preservation and the transmission of the past:

> Not the intense moment
> Isolated, with no before and after,
> But a lifetime burning in every moment. . . .[168]

But from this fact a new character of the past is also revealed. It is its integrality. To decide to transmit the past to the future is to decide to transmit to the future *all* of the past. For a long time Eliot thought that present duty consisted simply in choosing what was best in the past. But he had to recognize that he could not be dispensed from accepting the worst also. Acceptance of the past does not solely imply the acceptance of its virtues, but also its sins. There is no discrimination, no prescription, no liberation by rejecting or forgetting. "Time is no healer." [169] To accept the past is to accept the burden of its sins and the necessity for their expiation. It is to accept time with all its consequences.

Thus the new time takes on a significance no less tragic than the former time. For the tragedy of discontinuous moments there is substituted the tragedy of a time that is ineluctably continuous. In the former view, nothing seemed linked to anything; everything appeared to escape and elude itself. Now all seems linked together in so dense a fashion that no moment can escape any other, and each appears to have to assume the responsibility for the whole duration: "How can we be concerned with the past and not with the future? Or with the future and not with the past?" [170] All our past actions and thoughts look to all our future actions and thoughts as to acts of justification or expiation. From the beginning to the end of time, our actions depend one upon another. They adhere to each other, and so very closely that between the beginning and the end of the series which they constitute, there is no break and, it would seem, very little difference. Like a reverberating echo whose sound returns to the same place, all the beings we have been and shall be, form one uninterrupted being that unceasingly receives its heritage from its own hands: "In my beginning is my end, and in my end is my beginning." When we accept the burden of our past, we also accept our future. They have the same face, the same being, the same time. This time of absolute responsibility, like that of radical irresponsibility, is circular.

In neither case can one escape the motion of the wheel. There is not a moment of our existence, nor of the history of the world, which does not turn with all the other moments around the same pivot.

But epochs and moments do not exist simply in the process of their circular mutation. And if they follow one another in an order which is that of the rotation of duration, each one of them, fixed to the circumference, remains in constant relationship with the pivot which precisely determines that constancy. At the center of general mobility there always appears, and always at a distance, an immobile reality that continuously keeps the mobility from losing itself in the unlimited and the moments from falling into the most indescribable incoherence. It is because this point never ceases to exist and to act, that all the other points are alligned in a circle, and that by reason of the rigorous solidarity which is imposed on them, there is not a simple anarchy of moments but a duration. And it is also because this point continues to exist and to act that the circular continuity of the moments does not become a meaningless and fatal concatenation of causes and consequences. Each moment is in relation with all other moments; but each moment is also in relation with a moment that is outside of all the others, because, contrary to what they are, it itself is fixed and eternal. As the fleeting experience of "partial ecstasies" had indicated, each circumferential moment of duration is immediately traversed by a ray that issues from that transcendence. Each moment is, therefore, in time, and yet outside of time, animated as it is by a non-temporal power. Horizontally, so to speak, it receives from the past an impulsion which it will transmit to the future; but vertically, shall we say, it still receives its own peculiar efficacy. Along the length of a supernatural road there travels to it a force that permits it not, to be sure, to escape from time, but to give it a supra-temporal significance and value: "It is out of time that my decision is taken." [171] Thus, each decision we take, each action we begin, each sacrifice we make, is not necessarily the exclusive effect of antecedent causes and the cause of subsequent effects. At every moment it is possible for us to give time a new and permanent inflection. It is in our power to "redeem the time," [172] but not to annihilate it.

But we can accomplish this redemption of time, in and through time, only by resigning ourselves to time, that is to say to our human condition: "Only through time is time conquered." [173] Christian time is the time of sacrifice. The sacrifice that we make of our passions, our joys, our own person, in order to accept, first, the order of the past, next the duties imposed by the future, and finally the total submission to the central authority of The Being; "still point of the turning world," that point which we left in order to undertake our peripheral and dolorous Odyssey in duration,

> And the end of our exploring
> Will be to arrive where we started
> And know the place for the first time.[174]

Thus, the thought of Eliot rediscovers and relives all the stages of the experience of time, as it is revealed in, among others, American literature. Like Melville and like Poe he undergoes the terrors of gyratory time. Like Emerson and like Thoreau he perceives the importance of the isolated moments that are the revealers of transcendence. Like Hawthorne he comprehends the profound solidarity of the present and the past. But this retrospective solidarity leads him to discover, like Whitman, a solidarity more vast, which links to past and present the prospective reality of the future, and makes him understand finally, with James, that if all times adhere to one another, each moment contains also an infinite virtuality. It is in the power of man, not to change time, but to change the meaning of time. And of all the ways in which this power is exercised, there is none more efficacious, as Emily Dickinson understood, than abnegation. Thus Eliot remains faithful to tradition in expressing his own thought, which is precisely a reflection upon fidelity and tradition. In expressing himself he preserves a heritage. All the times of his predecessors are found once again in *his* time.

NOTES

1 *Prose Works* (3 vols.; Boston: Riverside Press, 1879), I, 32.
2 *Ibid.*, p. 359.
3 *Journals*, June 13, 1838.
4 *Prose Works*, III, 99.
5 *Ibid.*, p. 104.
6 *Ibid.*, II, 488.
7 *Ibid.*, I, 40.
8 *Ibid.*, p. 358.
9 *Ibid.*, p. 543.
10 *Ibid.*, II, 61.
11 *Ibid.*, I, 40.
12 *Ibid.*, p. 384.
13 *Ibid.*, p. 359.
14 *Ibid.*, p. 360.
15 *Ibid.*, III, 381.
16 *Ibid.*, I, 32.
17 *To Mary M. Emerson*, September 23, 1826.
18 *Journals*, October 30, 1841.
19 *Prose Works*, III, 104.
20 *Ibid.*, p. 99.
21 *Journals*, March 17, 1836.
22 *Ibid.*, October 16, 1837.
23 *Prose Works*, III, 101.
24 *The House of the Seven Gables, Works* (15 vols.; Boston: Riverside Press, 1882–98), III, 286.
25 *Ibid.*
26 *Ibid.*, p. 173.
27 *Ibid.*, p. 137.
28 *The Scarlet Letter, Works*, V, 79.
29 *The House of the Seven Gables, Works*, III, 18.
30 *The Dolliver Romance, Works*, II, 31.
31 *The House of the Seven Gables, Works*, III, 219.

32 *The Marble Faun, Works*, VI, 28.
33 *Ibid.*, p. 29.
34 *The Haunted Mind, Works*, I, 343.
35 *Ibid.*
36 *The Birthmark, Works*, II, 69.
37 *The Poetic Principle, Works*, ed. J. A. Harrison (17 vols.; New York: Thomas Y. Crowell, 1902), vol. XIV.
38 *The City in the Sea.*
39 *Ms. Found in a Bottle, Works*, II, 10.
40 *Colloquy of Monos and Una, Works*, IV, 209.
41 *The Pit and the Pendulum, Works*, V, 70.
42 *Ibid.*
43 *The Fall of the House of Usher, Works*, III, 280.
44 *Walden, Writings* (11 vols.; Boston: Riverside Press, 1884–94), II, 512.
45 *To Harrison Blake*, March 27, 1848.
46 *Walking, Writings*, IX, 301.
47 *Journal*, January 26, 1852.
48 *Ibid.*, March 15, 1852.
49 *Ibid.*, January 17, 1841.
50 *Ibid.*, December 8, 1859.
51 *Ibid.*, March 13, 1842.
52 *A Week on the Concord and Merrimack Rivers, Writings*, I, 201.
53 *Walking*, p. 301.
54 *Journal*, November 13, 1839.

55 *Ibid.*, June 14, 1850.
56 *Ibid.*, June 22, 1853.
57 *Ibid.*, April 3, 1842.
58 *Ibid.*, February 3, 1841.
59 *Ibid.*, February 27, 1841.
60 *Ibid.*, June 7, 1851.
61 *A Week on the Concord and Merrimack Rivers*, p. 8.
62 *Walden*, p. 29.
63 *Journal*, June 6, 1857.
64 *Ibid.*
65 *Walden*, p. 155.
66 *Journal*, March 24, 1855.
67 *Ibid.*, October 26, 1857.
68 *Moby Dick*, chap. 135.
69 *Pierre*, Book 12, 3.
70 *Collected Poems*, ed. H. P. Vincent (Chicago, 1947), p. 5.
71 *Mardi*, chap. 135.
72 *Pierre*, Book 6, 1.
73 *White Jacket*, chap. 36.
74 *Ibid.*
75 *Pierre*, Book 5, 1.
76 *To Duyckinck*, March 3, 1849.
77 *Mardi*, chap. 169.
78 *Ibid.*, chap. 51.
79 *Pierre*, Book 14, 3.
80 *Ibid.*
81 *To Hawthorne*, November, 1851.
82 *Collected Poems*, p. 414.
83 *Moby Dick*, chap. 114.
84 *Pierre*, Book 3, 3.
85 *Collected Poems*, p. 183.
86 *Pierre*, Book 4, 5.
87 *Moby Dick*, chap. 47.
88 *Mardi*, chap. 75.
89 *Pierre*, Book 2, 1.
90 *Mardi*, chap. 161.
91 *Collected Poems*, p. 397.

[92] *Mardi*, chap. 168.
[93] *The Complete Poetry and Prose*, ed. M. Cowley (2 vols.; New York: Pellegrini, 1948), II, 92.
[94] *Ibid.*, p. 273.
[95] *Ibid.*, p. 279.
[96] *Ibid.*, I, 234.
[97] *Ibid.*, p. 83.
[98] *Ibid.*, p. 346.
[99] *Ibid.*, p. 260.
[100] *Ibid.*, p. 368.
[101] *Ibid.*, II, 255.
[102] *Ibid.*, I, 249.
[103] *Ibid.*, II, 279.
[104] *Ibid.*, p. 273.
[105] *Ibid.*, p. 259.
[106] *Ibid.*, p. 173.
[107] *Ibid.*, I, 120.
[108] *Ibid.*, p. 43.
[109] *Ibid.*, II, 255.
[110] *Ibid.*, I, 349.
[111] *Ibid.*, p. 81.
[112] *Ibid.*, II, 289.
[113] *Ibid.*
[114] *The Poems*, ed. T. H. Johnson (3 vols.; Cambridge: Harvard University Press, 1955), No. 338.
[115] No. 76.
[116] No. 160.
[117] No. 981.
[118] No. 627.
[119] No. 362.
[120] No. 687.
[121] No. 967.
[122] *Ibid.*
[123] No. 1119.
[124] No. 125.
[125] No. 1725.
[126] No. 744.

[127] No. 745.
[128] No. 652.
[129] No. 779.
[130] No. 650.
[131] No. 305.
[132] No. 624.
[133] No. 948.
[134] *To Grace Norton*, July 28, 1883.
[135] *Partial Portraits* (London: Macmillan, 1888), p. 207.
[136] *The Ambassadors*, Preface, *Works* (New York: Charles Scribner's Sons, 1922), XXI, xix.
[137] *A Small Boy and Others* (London: Macmillan, 1913), p. 73.
[138] *Ibid.*, pp. 2–3.
[139] *Ibid.*, p. 242.
[140] *Roderick Hudson*, Preface, *Works*, I, v.
[141] *A Small Boy and Others*, p. 73.
[142] *The Altar of the Dead, The Short Stories*, ed. C. Fadiman (New York, 1945), p. 329.
[143] *The Reverberator*, Preface, *Works*, XIII, vii.
[144] *The Ivory Tower, Works*, XXV, 276.
[145] *The Aspern Papers*, Preface.
[146] *The Sense of the Past* (New York: Charles Scribner's Sons, 1917), p. 48.
[147] *Ibid.*
[148] *Ibid.*
[149] *A Small Boy and Others*, p. 366.

[150] *The Jolly Corner, The Short Stories*, pp. 614 and 618.
[151] *The Ambassadors*, p. 86.
[152] *The Complete Poems and Plays* (New York: Harcourt Brace, 1952), p. 250.
[153] *Ibid.*, p. 38.
[154] *Ibid.*, p. 120.
[155] *Ibid.*, p. 277.
[156] *The Use of Poetry and the Use of Criticism* (London: Faber, 1933), p. 148.
[157] *The Complete Poems and Plays*, p. 133.
[158] *Dante* (London: Faber, 1929), p. 33.
[159] *The Complete Poems and Plays*, p. 119.
[160] *Ibid.*, p. 125.
[161] *Ibid.*, p. 60.
[162] *Ibid.*, p. 119.
[163] *Dante*, p. 33.
[164] *The Sacred Wood* (London: Faber, 1920), p. 52.
[165] *Selected Essays* (London: Faber, 1932), p. 29.
[166] *The Sacred Wood*, p. 49.
[167] *Ibid.*, p. 59.
[168] *The Complete Poems and Plays*, p. 129.
[169] *Ibid.*, p. 134.
[170] *Ibid.*, p. 259.
[171] *Ibid.*, p. 212.
[172] *Ibid.*, p. 64.
[173] *Ibid.*, p. 119.
[174] *Ibid.*, p. 145.

DATE DUE

MAY 25 '98			
GAYLORD			PRINTED IN U.S.A.